SEVENOAKS

1790–1914

Map 1 West Kent and the County boundaries, 1885,
showing the major place names mentioned in this book.

SEVENOAKS

1790–1914

Risk and choice in West Kent

Iain Taylor and David Killingray

UNIVERSITY OF HERTFORDSHIRE PRESS

First published in Great Britain in 2022 by
University of Hertfordshire Press
College Lane
Hatfield
Hertfordshire
AL10 9AB

British Library Cataloguing in Publication Data

A catalogue record for this book is available from the British Library

ISBN 978-1-912260-61-4

Design by Arthouse Publishing Solutions
Printed in Great Britain by Charlesworth Press, Wakefield

Contents

Illustrations

Maps

Acknowledgements

Thanks go to the Sevenoaks Historical Society and to the Kent Victoria County History Trust for financial support. We wish to thank a number of people who have helped with research and access to private papers: Gwen Bowen, the Bowen papers, Halstead; Fiona Knight, the diaries of William Knight; Dieter Friedrich for providing the portrait of Edward Kraftmeier; Adriene Rogers, for access to the archives of the Sevenoaks Methodist Church; and Knole Estate, for the Brigden portrait, courtesy of Lord Robert Sackville-West. Dr R. Logan, of the Foresters Heritage Trust, carried out research on our behalf. For images included in the book we thank the Sevenoaks Society; Tonbridge History Society; Kent History and Library Centre, at Maidstone; and the Sevenoaks Library. Roger Quick supplied other images, as did Richard Clout, of the Sevenoaks Vine Cricket Club, and the Sevenoaks Community Facebook page. Andrew Coates provided advice on the theory of risk.

We also wish to thank Professor John Becket, Peter Tann, and Ian Walker, all of whom took the time to read and comment on an earlier, and longer, draft text, giving us the benefit of their professional and local knowledge.

We are also grateful for the patient and thoughtful advice, skilled and critical editing by Jane Housham, and the work on the maps and layout by Sarah Elvins, of University of Hertfordshire Press.

Iain Taylor, Billingshurst, West Sussex
David Killingray, Sevenoaks, Kent

Abbreviations

ACLL	Anti-Corn Law League
ASHDP	Amalgamated Society of House Decorators and Painters
BL	British Library
CPS	Commons Preservation Society
HMPS	Holmesdale Medical Provident Society
ILP	Independent Labour Party
JP	justice of the peace
KG	*Kentish Gazette*
KHLC	Kent History and Library Centre
KSC	*Kent and Sussex Courier*
KSLU	Kent Sussex Labourers' Union
KT	*Kent Times*
KWP	*Kent Weekly Post*
LB	Local Board
LC	*Leicester Chronicle*
LCS	London Corresponding Society
LPL	Lambeth Palace Library
MC	*Maidstone Chronicle*
MJ	*Maidstone journal*
MP	*Morning Post*
MT	*Maidstone Telegraph*
n.d.	no date
NALU	National Agricultural Labourers' Union
NDL	National Democratic League
NFLS	National Freehold Land Society
NPG	National Portrait Gallery
NS	*Northern Star*
NUAL	National Union of Agricultural Labourers
NUWSS	National Union of Women's Suffrage Societies
PSA	Pleasant Sunday Afternoon
SBBS	Sevenoaks Benefit Building Society
SC	*Sevenoaks Chronicle*
SCA	Sevenoaks Commercial Association
SDF	Social Democratic Federation
SEG	*South Eastern Gazette*

SPA	Sevenoaks Progressive Association
SPU	Sevenoaks Political Union
SRA	Sevenoaks Ratepayer's Association
SRDC	Sevenoaks Rural District Council
SUDC	Sevenoaks Urban District Council
SWBS	Sevenoaks Wesleyan Benefit Society
TNA	The National Archives, Kew
B	Bankruptcy
FS	Friendly Societies
HO	Home Office
IR	Inland Revenue
MH	Ministry of Health
T	Treasury
UKPP	United Kingdom Parliamentary Papers
WKG	*West Kent Guardian*
WKPU	West Kent Political Union
WSPU	Women's Social and Political Union

Chapter 1

Risk and choice

This is a story about Sevenoaks, a market town in west Kent, and the villages within a ten-mile radius of it, from roughly 1790 to 1914. This area of over 300 square miles, which constituted the greater part of the 'mental maps' referred to by many of its residents, is examined during a time of increasingly dramatic social, economic, political and cultural changes. Many stemmed from the town being 25 miles south-east of the burgeoning London metropolis, the population of which expanded rapidly from one million in 1800 to nearly seven million a century later.

There are many histories of English market towns and rural areas for this period, but many are very limited, failing to address the various complex interactions taking place in these societies. Almost all suffer, in one form or another, from what John Marshall calls the 'tyranny of the discrete', with an over-narrow focus, while generally ignoring the important national and regional factors that undoubtedly influenced those localities to a very significant degree.[1] We seek to avoid falling into this trap by concentrating on how extra-local issues impacted on the broader Sevenoaks area, to give a more complete picture of events. Most importantly, we wish to introduce an entirely new approach to studying local history, for the main thread running through this book is the twin ideas of risk and choice.

Our basic argument is that, particularly for poorer people in early nineteenth-century west Kent, their lives revolved around overcoming the everyday risks that could and often did impact their very survival, especially the struggle to obtain the four bare necessities: food, clothing, housing and fuel. Those efforts are placed within their contemporary contexts, examining what types of risk mitigation strategy were available to the disadvantaged in relation to employment opportunities and family support. We then analyse other areas of risk, including those arising from poor health and substandard sanitary conditions, and the ways that these too might be mitigated. Our contention is that focusing on the risks people had to bear, how they coped with them, what impact that might have had

---

1 John Marshall, *The tyranny of the discrete: a discussion of the problems of local history in England* (Aldershot, 1997).

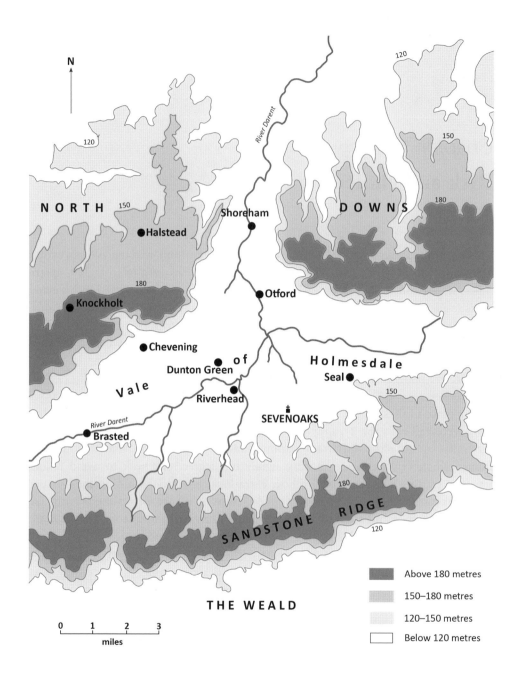

Map 2 Physical map of the Sevenoaks district.

on other social groups (with the potential for political conflicts) and how those risks were eventually removed or reduced, provides a fruitful new way of looking at the history of the Sevenoaks area in this period. And there is no reason why it might not be applied to others, too.

The small market town of Sevenoaks

Here are some very neat houses, inhabited by independent persons, which renders the place highly respectable. The principal ornament of the town is the park and mansion of the Dorset family. This august and venerable pile stands in the centre of the celebrated Knole Park which is considered one of the finest in England: the walks, the fine and diversified scenery ... form a rare concentration of beauty and advantage ... The church ... is an handsome and interesting fabric. Here is also an Hospital for yielding comfort and maintenance to 32 aged decayed trades people, which is laudably conducted. A school for educating poor children by Sir William Sevenoak. Lady Boswell's school is another excellent charity. The market is large and well supplied and is on Saturdays.

Source: Pigot's directory of Kent, 1824, pp. 412–13.

Since risk bore disproportionately heavily on the poor, the primary emphasis will be on history 'from below'. Thus our concern is the mass of the population, most of whom were poor; despite the recent labours of many historians, 'there are still few histories of the working poor and they have names and faces, and stories to tell'.[2] This means we need 'so far as possible, to see things their way', which requires digging deep in the available sources to uncover what the lower social orders were thinking, doing and feeling.[3] This does not mean ignoring the well to do and the 'middling sort', whose lives and fortunes also changed in this period. Our starting point is therefore those things central in the lives of labouring people in west Kent. One flipside of risk is choice; others might include trust and hope. Risk diminished as economic improvements from *c*.1850 put more money in people's pockets, including some of the poorest in society. Choice was not merely expressed in terms of greater disposable incomes and a growing ability to choose a wider range of consumer goods. For choice or, perhaps better, pluralism made accessible to a larger number of people many more opportunities and rights: the entitlement to vote; alternate places in which to worship (or not); access to knowledge and education; more spare

---

2   Alison Light, *Common people: the history of an English family* (London, 2014), p. xxii.
3   Quentin Skinner, *Visions of politics*, vol. 1, *regarding method* (Cambridge, 2002), pp. 1–8.

time and a wider choice of leisure activities. How and why people (especially the poor) clamoured for more choice, and how and why they expressed those choices when they had the opportunity to do so, we believe drove the historical process in, broadly, the second half of the nineteenth century in much the same way as risk did the first. Pressure from below to reduce risk or enhance choice was not necessarily welcomed by all, giving rise to political factions and class conflict. Steering a way through life's difficulties was a complex and multi-influenced process, so we believe describing it in terms of risk and choice is an entirely valid approach.

These emphases feature in few other local histories. Politics in its broadest sense is often ignored. Religious belief and activity tends to concentrate on buildings and the clergy, while ignoring how faith impacted on the lives of ordinary people. Politics and religion were so interwoven in people's minds and responses in the long nineteenth century that they deserve to be considered together. After a chapter examining west Kent society and the power and authority structures that governed it, we combine politics and religion in two chapters under the broad heading of 'Ideas, Beliefs and Values'. These deal with adherence to and expressions of both religious and political ideas and opinions. This means seeing 'parish pump' politics as important to communities and assessing religious (and non-religious) beliefs as powerful and dynamic influences that helped shape the ideas and actions of individuals, in both local affairs and national issues. This, in turn, requires historians seriously to understand the moral imperatives of religious belief and practice as they were played out locally in relation to the national political stage.

In addition, a risk- and choice-centred framework enables us to examine more fully during the long nineteenth century the impact on west Kent of important socio-economic developments: Britain's rapid increase in population; Sevenoaks' close proximity to rapidly expanding London; the growth and change in agricultural output; industrialisation and urbanisation; the growth of steam and steel; changes in working practices; the national railway network; the growth in the power and influence of the state both locally and nationally; radical changes in labour relations; changing religious affiliations and the decline in religious belief; advances in the medical sciences; an increase in ideas of individualism and personal leisure time; and ideas of progress. By the early twentieth century parts of west Kent could boast a distinctive working class, whereas a hundred years earlier there were only incipient signs of that major reordering of society and attitude.

Risk in west Kent

Life for the poor was a constant struggle to make ends meet. In 1838, Sevenoaks rector Thomas Curteis wrote an open letter to prime minister Robert Peel. It included the weekly budget of local agricultural labourer 'G.B.' and his wife and five children. His living expenses were about 11s and his wages averaged 12s a week in summer and 10s in winter as he, not the farmer, bore the risk of not being able to work through bad weather or from some other cause. Curteis concluded that

Figure 1.1 Tubs Hill, London Road, Sevenoaks, drawing by William Knight, 1864. A wagon descending the turnpike road to London; to the right of the image is one of the public pumps providing water for the town; in the right foreground a culvert of an open drain, indicating the primitive sanitary state of the town.
Source: Sevenoaks Society, folder 3.

G.B. 'can just support his family whilst he has health and employment. If either fail, instant starvation is before him.'[4]

Low wages were the root cause of the many problems faced by labourers in Sevenoaks, since their poverty made affording even the bare necessities problematic. One necessity, water, was freely available but had to be carried from pumps in the High Street or wells such as those at Tubs Hill and St John's Hill, a laborious and time-consuming process. As late as 1887, poorer inhabitants of Old Greatness relied on water drawn from a ditch, which was 'dirty and unwholesome'.[5]

Other risks abounded. Public health services in Sevenoaks were rudimentary for most of the nineteenth century, and one contemporary author drew attention to the abysmal sanitary conditions endured by the poor, nationally, as just one of 'the risks

---

4   Thomas Curteis, *A letter to Robert Peel on the principle and operation of the New Poor Law* (London, 1842), p. 46. We have not been able to identify 'G.B.'; his initials may imply he stood for an entire class of British people.

5   *Sevenoaks Chronicle* (henceforth *SC*), 5 Aug. 1887, p. 8.

that people run everyday'.[6] Industrial injuries, disproportionately affecting working men, were common in both town and country as people suffered accidents involving farm or other machinery and on building sites. Being a victim of crime was another distressingly common risk for west Kent residents, of all social classes, as indicated by the weekly indictments dealt with by local magistrates.

When things did go wrong, invariably the poor 'were thrown back on their own resources'.[7] They had to devise their own, often co-operative, risk-reduction strategies, both licit and illicit; these actions have been termed the multifaceted 'makeshift economy' or 'the patchy, desperate and sometimes failing strategies of the poor for material survival'.[8] Illegal solutions included taking fuel or game, which carried with them the possibility of incarceration in gaol or workhouse. But poaching, often done with 'passionate determination and courage', was rarely very lucrative in the Sevenoaks area, although it was a criminal activity that was quite obviously 'a matter of profit and risk'.[9] Smuggling, with its concomitant violence, had a long history in Sundridge, a village near the main road to the coast.[10] The contemporary agriculturalist Arthur Young thought a single night running contraband might bring in 10s 6d, or more than four times a labourer's average daily wage.[11]

Lawful strategies might involve begging, borrowing, moral or in-kind kinship support, private or church-derived charity and poor relief. The only effective insurance against accidents or ill health came in the form of friendly societies, such as the Sevenoaks Amicable, from 1767 to 1844. However, many of its 64 members were from the commercial elite of the town, no fewer than 12 of whom (19 per cent) were either professionals or tradesmen, such as an attorney and a wine merchant.[12] Of the 30 others whose occupations are known, all except one were shopkeepers or skilled artisans. That comes as no surprise, since most labourers, especially in hard times, would have found it difficult to pay the contributions of a shilling a month or so. Curteis' solution was Parochial Benefit Societies, managed by parish officers and with funds guaranteed from parish rates, to overcome the present feeling of the poor 'that a man is not at all better off in consequence of his economy'.[13] An

---

6   George Godwin, *Another blow for life* (London, 1864), p. 23.

7   Eric Hopkins, *Working class self-help in nineteenth century England* (London, 1995), p. 2.

8   Alannah Tomkins and Steven King (eds), *The poor in England 1700–1850: an economy of makeshifts* (Oxford, 2010), p. 1.

9   D. Hay, 'Poaching and the game laws on Cannock Chase' in D. Hay *et al.*, *Albion's fatal tree: crime and society in eighteenth century England* (New York, 1975), pp. 191, 207.

10   Carl Winslow, 'Sussex smugglers' in D. Hay *et al.*, *Albion's fatal tree: crime and society in eighteenth century England* (New York, 1975), p. 120.

11   Arthur Young, quoted in *ibid.*, pp. 151–2.

12   Kent History and Library Centre (KHLC) U1000/27/O2, occupations gathered from *Bailey's British directory* (1784) and family history websites such as www.familysearch.org.

13   Curteis, *Peel*, p. 30.

Employment or Labour Society was established in Sevenoaks by 1843, and similar organisations existed elsewhere in Kent.[14]

Other collective mitigation strategies carried significant risk factors. One was for workers to combine in trades unions. They risked dismissal from work, but it was an option that became increasingly viable towards the end of the nineteenth century. Although labourers reportedly 'flocked' to join the Grand National Consolidated Trades Union in Brighton as early as 1834, there is limited evidence that trades unionism met with any serious popular response among west Kent agrarian workers before the Revolt of the Field in the 1870s.[15]

Conversely, the gentry and tradesmen of west Kent never went hungry, as the poor regularly did, and they could always afford to buy the bare necessities. Their better living conditions and higher economic and social status also meant that they suffered much less from environmentally based diseases and workplace injuries, although childbirth was 'a hazardous and often life-threatening experience' as much for middle-class mothers as it was for labourers' wives.[16] Invariably, though, their assets, incomes, savings and standards of living were much greater, and other risks such as sickness could be insured against by joining a friendly society.

The significance of 'Swing'

That overwhelming sense of social, economic and political superiority, deeply ingrained into contemporary west Kent society, is what makes the story of Jonathan Thompson, a tenant farmer at Hendon Farm, Sundridge, so unusual and significant. Starting in summer 1830, his workers turned on him in a furious and prolonged bout of incendiarism. By November the County Fire Office reported that Hendon Farm and another of his holdings, at Ide Hill, had been fired ten times in three months.[17] In 1832 all his rebuilt outbuildings (but not his dwelling house) were set alight again and that November he was mugged on the way home from Sevenoaks, four or five men relieving him of the substantial sum of £8, saying as they did so that 'this is better than burning your stacks'.[18] The *coup de grace* came three years later when his 'recently erected' freehold villa residence at Ide Hill was auctioned at Westerham 'By direction of the Assignee under a Fiat in Bankruptcy against Jonathan Thompson'.[19]

---

14 *Sevenoaks Advertiser* (henceforth *SA*), Aug. 1843, p. 167; Sept. 1843, p. 171; KHLC P45/8/3 and P347/25/1.

15 Carl Griffin, *Rural war: Captain Swing and the politics of protest* (Manchester, 2012), p. 312.

16 Joan Lane, *A social history of medicine: health, healing and disease in England, 1750–1950* (London, 2012), p. 120.

17 The National Archives (TNA), HO 64/1/109 ff. 313–16; *The Times*, 8 Sept. 1830, p. 5; 17 Sept. 1830, p. 3; 15 Oct. 1830, p. 3; 23 Oct. 1830, p. 3.

18 *Maidstone Journal* (henceforth *MJ*), 27 Nov. 1832, p. 4.

19 *South Eastern Gazette* (henceforth *SEG*), 20 April 1841, p. 1.

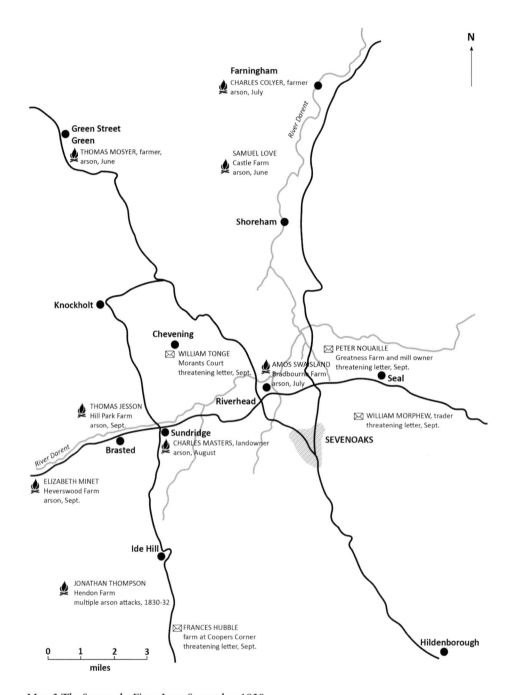

N

Farningham
CHARLES COLYER, farmer
arson, July

Green Street
Green
THOMAS MOSYER, farmer,
arson, June

SAMUEL LOVE
Castle Farm
arson, June

River Darent

Shoreham

Knockholt

Chevening
WILLIAM TONGE
Morants Court
threatening letter, Sept.

PETER NOUAILLE
Greatness Farm and mill owner
threatening letter, Sept.

AMOS SWAISLAND
Bradbourne Farm
arson, July

Seal

Riverhead

THOMAS JESSON
Hill Park Farm
arson, Sept.

WILLIAM MORPHEW, trader
threatening letter, Sept.

Sundridge
CHARLES MASTERS, landowner
arson, August

SEVENOAKS

River Darent

Brasted

ELIZABETH MINET
Heverswood Farm
arson, Sept.

Ide Hill

JONATHAN THOMPSON
Hendon Farm
multiple arson attacks, 1830-32

FRANCES HUBBLE
farm at Coopers Corner
threatening letter, Sept.

Hildenborough

0 1 2 3
miles

Map 3 The Sevenoaks Fires, June–September 1830.
Arson attacks, and letters threatening the same, were frequently visited upon west Kent farmers
during the 'Swing' summer of 1830. It is clear that those responsible generally targeted the
properties of those living near the few good roads of the period, or the river Darent path, to give
themselves the best chance of escaping undetected.

Thompson was a serial early victim of the infamous 'Captain Swing' riots, which broke out in 1830 and swept first from Kent to Sussex, then west to Hampshire and Dorset and north to East Anglia and beyond. In successive waves of action, eventually becoming a highly politicised protest movement that spread across much of England, labourers demanded wage rises and, if they failed to get them, started to destroy threshing machines and to fire hayricks and farm outbuildings, or send bloodcurdling letters to farmers threatening to do so. But, contrary to the view that Swing 'started' with machine breaking in east Kent in August 1830, the attention of government was first drawn to the 'yet more insistent and desperate' plight of the agricultural poor across much of southern England by the spiralling – and almost certainly co-ordinated – protests that centred around Sevenoaks earlier that summer.[20]

Why did this national movement begin in the Sevenoaks area? Contemporary press reports indicate that Thompson's labourers were unhappy about the efficient way that he and his landlord, Charles Masters of Oxted, were squeezing the illicit incomes of the local poor, for '[t]here are many persons in the neighbourhood who follow the joint occupations of smuggling and poaching', but farmer and landowner were 'particularly active in repressing' them.[21] That was precisely when those traditional risk mitigation strategies often 'meant the difference between bare subsistence and worse'.[22] Most Swing victims, such as unpopular Sevenoaks draper and smallholder William Morphew, suffered only one or two attacks. But Thompson's atypical experience illustrates a further important dimension to risk. In those extreme circumstances, those at the bottom of the social ladder might act to remove or diminish calamitous risks by seeking to shift them onto others better able to bear them, which generally meant the higher echelons of society. This 'risk transfer' approach, as it might be termed, is an important extension of the risk/ choice idea because it enables us to uncover much that is currently unknown about both the perpetrators of agrarian unrest and their victims, and what both groups were thinking, doing and feeling at the time. As an undoubted recipe for conflict, it also helps explain several other otherwise puzzling aspects of events in west Kent during the period.

So risk transfer helps us understand the counter-intuitive nature of Swing, or the 'economic "logic"' that lay behind hungry labourers 'firing the means and results of production' that they needed to live on, far beyond simple intimidation in the hope of gaining wage increases.[23] Simultaneously and symbolically, such coercion

---

20 Griffin, *Rural war*, 9; Iain Taylor, 'One for the (farm) workers? Perpetrator risk and victim risk transfer during the "Sevenoaks Fires" of 1830', *Rural History*, 28 (2017), pp. 137–60.

21 *Rochester Gazette*, 11 Sept. 1830, p. 4.

22 Winslow, 'Sussex smugglers', p. 150.

23 Carl Griffin, 'The mystery of the fires: Captain Swing as incendiarist', *Southern History*, 32 (2010), pp. 21–40 (p. 38).

Figure 1.2 Title page of *The Life and History of Swing, the Kent Rick-burner. Written by himself* (London, 1830). This widely reproduced image illustrates the profound power differential between the plump farmer/landowner on the horse and the starving farm labourer and his family below.

sought to bring farmers into a more equal relationship with their labourers by depriving them of some of the most important assets (farm buildings, machinery and crops) that divided rural entrepreneurs from wage earners. Radical journalist and MP William Cobbett understood this 'homely reasoning' (as he called it) of the labourers, one telling him: 'I work twelve hours a day to produce their food; I do all the real labour; and you, who stand by me and look over me, deny me even subsistence out of it: no, if you give me none of it, you shall have none yourself.'[24]

Most of the time, even during bad years, irregular work and the makeshift economy just about ensured survival for the labouring classes, albeit at the cost of

---

24 *Cobbett's Weekly Political Register*, 13 Nov. 1830, p. 713.

severe privation and hunger. By 1830, after consecutive bad harvests and a severe agricultural depression, the labouring poor were stretched to breaking point. Wages were cut and some who could not find work had to endure humiliating forced labour, such as being hitched to the parish cart like animals by order of poor law overseers. West Kent was at the forefront. In March a county meeting petitioned the House of Commons about the 'intolerable distress, which had naturally excited general discontent' in the county.[25] A petition to parliament from Ightham warned that the long-term distress of the poor had reached 'a height beyond control because many contributors to the poor rate are themselves bordering on pauperism'.[26] In Sevenoaks, so severe was the distress that winter that the parish had to supply 400 poor families a week with wood and coal.[27]

With starvation looming for many, and risks catastrophic, it was no surprise that the labourers employed by Thompson responded as they did. But not all resorted to violence, in Sevenoaks and elsewhere. Other solutions were available. One was flight to other parts of Britain in search of higher wages and living conditions, or overseas, either of their own volition or assisted by members of the parish. This was called 'shovelling out paupers' and thousands 'left the country which could not offer them a tolerable maintenance for America [i.e. Canada] and the colonies'.[28] A local example of 'voluntary' emigration is revealing. In April 1832, when the parish vestry considered whether 'some of the poor families' of Sevenoaks were eligible to go to Upper Canada, their 'expenses will be defrayed by private individuals who will be repaid from the parish funds'.[29] The only one deemed suitable was Daniel Epps from Greatness (and his family), who had been employed in the silk mills until they closed in 1827. A total of £45 was subscribed for Epps from 32 local worthies, including Greatness mill owner Peter Nouaille, himself a Swing victim in 1830.[30]

The class conflict so visible in 1830 came as a nasty shock to those who thought their economic, social and political power within the local community unassailable, such that 'It is difficult to convey the mixture of fear and anticipation in the minds of those who lived through 1830.'[31] But how could they control this risk? Unlike the poor, the elite had recourse to the institutions of government and law and order, the

---

25 *MJ*, 2 March 1830, p. 2.

26 John Henry Barrow (ed.), *The mirror of parliament for the … sessions of the … parliament of Great Britain and Ireland*, vol. 1 (London, 1831), 7 Feb. 1831, p. 47.

27 *MJ*, 9 Feb. 1830, p. 4. Shirley Burgoyne-Black, 'Swing: the years 1830–32 as reflected in a West Kent newspaper', *Archæologia Cantiana*, CVII (1989), pp. 89–106 (p. 99).

28 Keith Snell, *Parish and belonging: community, identity and welfare in England and Wales, 1700–1950* (Cambridge, 2006), p. 149; John Burnett, *Plenty and want – a social history of diet in England from 1815 to the present day* (Abingdon, 2005), p. 35.

29 Private archives, William Knight, *Diaries*, vol. 1, 26 and 30 April 1832.

30 KHLC P330/8/5, 2 May 1832.

31 Barry Reay, *The last rising: rural life and protest in nineteenth century England* (Oxford, 1990), p. 74.

magistrates, in whose social circles many belonged. The very wealthy could access those in central government. Former governor of the Bank of England William Manning of Combe Bank, Sundridge, did just that in September 1830, writing to the Home Office about 'fires in the farmyards and offices of the resident gentlemen and farmers of the town'.[32] Given his prominence, he was invited to a meeting there, where an official suggested he call a meeting of local magistrates, which set up an anti-incendiary association in response.[33]

Another aspect of the elite's risk reduction strategy against agrarian unrest was their (and their insurance companies') ability to finance rewards of up to £500 to those who provided information about incendiaries that led to conviction.[34] They could also influence newspaper reports so that they were written to elicit as much sympathy for the middle- or upper-class victims as possible: for example, the so-called 'poor widow' Frances Hubble, who was threatened with a' rap on the head', but who – as a single mother with two young teenagers – farmed 138 acres on her own account at Ide Hill.[35] Or they could combine to create Home Office-inspired mutual defence or prosecution associations. In Sevenoaks, the upper classes pledged in writing to assemble in the market square 'with what assistance we can collect'. Such associations existed in the town from 1830 until at least 1840, and enabled any member 'who was a victim of crime to use [their] pooled resources to hire the mechanisms of restitution'.[36] The maximum sentences for the few found guilty of Swing offences in west Kent in summer 1830 was nine months' imprisonment, which many in government thought unduly lenient. Later, when official Special Commissions tried those accused of Swing crimes – for example, in Winchester that December – many were transported.

West Kent, in line with England in general, had became for most people a much less risky and more comfortable place to inhabit by 1900 than it had been a century earlier. Speaking in Sevenoaks Weald in 1884, Charles Beale, assistant secretary of the Kent & Sussex Labourers' Union, said that 'No one can deny that the condition of the farm labourer is better today than it was sixty years ago; he is better paid, better housed and clothed, and has the advantage of a better education.'[37] And one might imagine that these ideas merely exemplified the growing progress and respectability of the region, in circumstances of reduced risk, coupled with more choices and growing pluralism. But the history of the area in the long nineteenth

---

32 TNA HO 52/8/119 ff. 259–60.

33 TNA HO 52/8/120 ff. 261–2; Griffin, *Rural War*, p. 79.

34 TNA HO 64/1/109 ff. 313–16; HO 52/8/168 f. 374.

35 *The Times*, 17 Sept. 1830, p. 3; KHLC CTR/42B.

36 KHLC U442/O67; U840/O239–41; Francis Dodsworth, 'Risk, prevention and policing, *c.* 1750–1850', in Tom Crook and Mike Esbester (eds), *Governing risks in modern Britain: danger, safety and accidents, c. 1800–2000* (London, 2016), pp. 29–53 (pp. 43–4).

37 *SC*, 26 Sept. 1884, p. 8.

century could never be described as following an upward and uninterrupted trajectory, for less risk and enhanced choice were won only at the cost of significant and growing social and political tensions in and around Sevenoaks.

Sources and contents

The risk-and-choice methodology and the concentration on the constant interplay between politics and religion, we believe, heralds a new way of writing local history. In short, we are asking local historians to read and think more widely on the periods that they are researching, and to dig more deeply with an enhanced, perceptive mind and eye into local and national sources. This, we think, will help them better to explain the complexities of the lives and relationships of people within those communities and to write about them in a more comprehensive way.

Attempting to write any local history, especially one primarily from below, entails the challenge of available sources. Few non-literate people left a personal record of their lives and thoughts, although many are recorded by name and behaviour in a range of records. For west Kent in the long nineteenth century there are several 'ego-documents', such as memoirs, diaries and collections of letters, in existence, mostly by the literate better-off, although many of the diaries cover short periods of time and the memoirs are hardly comprehensive.[38] Perhaps the most significant are the little-known diaries of Sevenoaks landscape painter William Knight (1811–68), for the years 1832 to 1837. To give a single example, he gives the first known personal account of how the town celebrated the Reform Act in 1832. Others are the short memoir of his life written by Charles Bassett (1861–1933) of Seal; the brief manuscript journal kept by Sevenoaks Methodist minister Robert Barratt from 1874 to 1877; the unpublished memoirs of Gilbert Gasson (1893–1986) of Ide Hill, and Jim Johnson (1906–95) of Seal; and the diaries of Halstead timber merchant Percival Bowen, which cover the period from 1864 to 1883. From a very different social station are the letters Robert Herries (1773–1845) wrote to his cousin, John Charles Herries (1778–1855), about St Julian's between 1819 and 1838. Two west Kent women are also represented – Mrs Catherine Martin (1820–61) of Sevenoaks, whose somewhat hagiographical biography was published by her brother Benjamin Field in 1862, and Mrs Frances Allnutt (1796–1865) of The Grove, near Penshurst, whose diaries cover 1831 and 1832.

Thankfully, there are also many useful surviving sources at local and national level that provide insight into the lives of ordinary people. At the parish level there are registers of baptisms, marriages and burials, which enable research on family reconstitution, which can be furthered by using the official records kept from 1837 and the important decennial census data from 1841 onwards. For the nineteenth century, official Parliamentary Papers increasingly contain a wealth of local information, such as on the working conditions of women and children

---

38   Light, *Common people*, p. xxii.

at the silk mill in 1816, recipients of poor relief, agricultural and railway labour, reports on health and sanitation and local social and economic activities. Other central government papers for the modern period report bankruptcies and wills. Parish and church records include vestry minutes, bastardy proceedings and poor law proceedings, which can be used alongside the records of friendly societies, school log books and political organisations. A recent and most valuable resource are digitally indexed newspapers and journals, which may now be cross-searched for the names of individuals, organisations and events.

Chapter 2
Power and authority

After a brief introduction to the geography of the Sevenoaks area, this chapter examines its social structure and assesses how centres of power and authority changed over time in that mainly agrarian society.

At a height of over 150 metres, Sevenoaks stands near the top of the Greensand ridge referred to by the late eighteenth-century historian Edward Hasted as the sand hills, while a few miles north were the chalk hills, or North Downs.[1] A visitor arriving in 1870 at either of the railway stations would soon have become aware that it was a hill town. There was the mile-long walk up roads through fields to reach the town centre, at the junction of the Dartford and London roads, with its market square and nearby parish church (see Plate 1). For much of the nineteenth century Sevenoaks held a weekly market for livestock close to the 'Shambles', the area where for centuries butchers and fishmongers had traded.[2] It was not an especially pleasant place, for this huddle of timber-framed and brick buildings presented several risks to their occupiers: fire, poor sanitation and cold draughts. The courtyard, lit by a gas lamp, would have been the repository for much of the human and animal waste and rubbish generated by its residents.

The ecclesiastical parish of Sevenoaks stretched south from the River Darent in the Vale of Holmesdale up the sandstone ridge and then down into the claylands of the Weald. From the sixteenth to the nineteenth centuries it formed an administrative unit six miles long and two miles wide. It stood on generally poor soils, providing some cultivable land for hops and food crops with a substantial area of rough grazing on the sandy ridge above the Weald. This can be seen on the tithe apportionment survey, with its accompanying map of 1841: most arable land was in the northern part of the parish, while the pasture tended to be on the heavier soils to the south. The first official census in 1801 recorded the small rural town as

---

1   Edward Hasted, *The history and topographical survey of the county of Kent* (Canterbury, 1797), vol. 3, p. 80.

2   Gordon Anckorn, *A Sevenoaks camera – Sevenoaks, Westerham and surrounding villages in old photographs* (Bath, 1987), foreword.

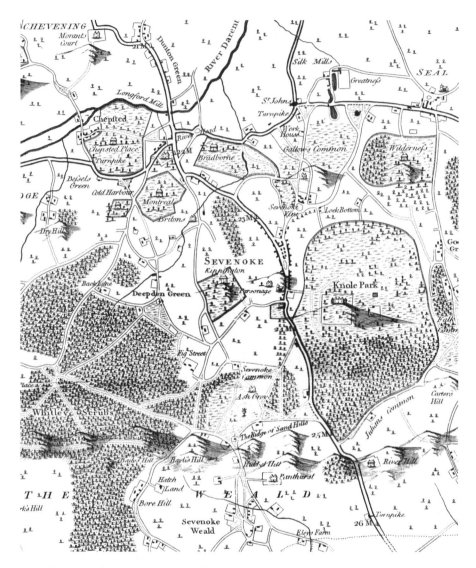

Map 4 The Sevenoaks area, recorded as the 'Hundred of Codsheath' (an ancient division of land), in Edward Hasted, *The history and topographical survey of the county of Kent* (Canterbury, 1797). Large scale and detailed county maps for Kent were produced in the mid-eighteenth century, for example the maps surveyed and published, on a scale of two inches to the mile, by Andrews, Dury and Herbert in 1769. As can be seen from Hasted's map of the Sevenoaks area, the cartographers' prospective market was aristocrats and gentry whose seats and estates are given prominence. But there is other detail, for example north of Sevenoaks town centre: 'the 'Vine', then an established cricket field, further on 'Gallows Common' and the minor road (now Bradbourne Road) running north-north west, and the parish 'Work House' on the hill leading to 'St Johns'. The Work House and Nouaille's 'Silk Mills' at 'Greatness' were places where poor people lived and worked long hours close together.
Source: Edward Hasted, *The history and topographical survey of the county of Kent* (Canterbury, 1797–1801; Wakefield, 1972).

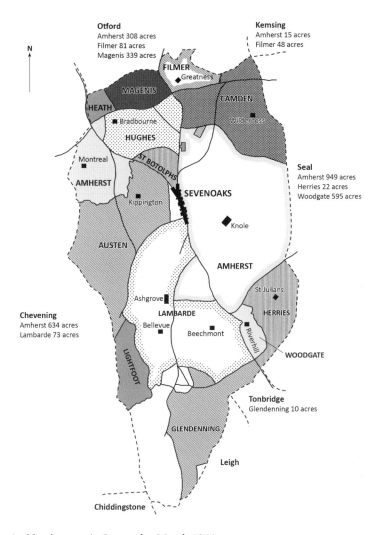

Map 5 Principal landowners in Sevenoaks, March 1841.

This map, based on the Tithe Award Schedules for Sevenoaks, shows much of the parish owned by eight men and their families. Also shown is the acreage of land they, and others, owned in the five adjoining parishes of Otford, Kemsing, Seal, Tonbridge, and Chevening. Land was acquired by purchase, marriage, and inheritance. Some landowners lived outside the area, for example, Richard William Magenis, an army officer, who lived in Bexley and later in Bedford.

		Acreage
Lord Amherst	Knole	1,531
William Lambarde	Beechmont	763
Thomas Austen	Bellevue	400
Alexander Glendenning	Ashgrove	377
John Charles Herries	Rose Bank (St Julian's)	359
Sir Edward Filmer	Greatness	250
Earl of Camden	Wilderness	212
Henry Hughes	Bradbourne	208

containing 2,640 people. By 1841 the population had nearly doubled, remaining about that level until 1881, when, after communications improved, it rose to over 8,000. Thereafter growth was steady until 1911, when the population numbered nearly 11,000.

Sevenoaks town and district populations, 1801–1911

	Sevenoaks	% rise	Sevenoaks Poor Law Union parishes	% rise
1801	2,640		13,415	
1811	3,444	30	15,576	16
1821	3,942	14.4	18,146	16.5
1831	4,709	19.5	20,050	10.5
1841	5,061	7.5	22,209	10.8
1851	4,878	-3.6	22,095	-0.5
1861	4,695	-3.8	22,039	-0.3
1871	5,949	26.7	24,262	10.1
1881	8,305	40	27,190	12
1891	9,341	12.5	29,997	10.3
1901	9,741	4.3	30,790	2.6
1911	10,953	12.4	33,211	7.9

The social structure – and the landscape – of the Sevenoaks area had long been dominated by several large estates. The most extensive was Knole, with its imposing late fifteenth-century house and deer park, the home of the Sackvilles, on the eastern side of the town. Another was the seat of the Amhersts at Montreal Park, who by marriage alliance with the Sackvilles in the 1840s extended their dominance of the area. The Camdens, Lambardes, Austens and Herries also had large landholdings, as shown on the Tithe Award map of 1841. The landed classes continued to exercise power and influence, although the simple adage that land equalled power needed substantial revision by the end of the nineteenth century. Changing economic circumstances, with declining rents from agricultural land, the extension of the franchise and changes in class attitudes steadily eroded patrician power and public deference towards hierarchy and rank.

The area also had an increasingly assertive middle class, including tenant farmers, 60 of whom rented a total of 1,835 acres in Sevenoaks parish in 1841. In 1880 there were several tenants with holdings of 100 acres or more. From the mid-eighteenth century a few professional men practised as lawyers, surveyors,

Figure 2.1 Upper St John's, Sevenoaks. A street very close to Hartslands. By the early twentieth century (when this photo was probably taken) Upper St John's had several shops and a pub. *Source*: Sevenoaks Society, D0660.

dentists, doctors, teachers, musicians and 'engineers'. Landowners, farmers, shopkeepers and small business owners of the 'middling sort' employed the lower orders of society. In the mainly rural environment of the first half of the nineteenth century many of these were agricultural labourers, who either lived in tied cottages or rented accommodation.

A working-class enclave in a middle-class town

Daniel Grover (1794–1880), a local builder, bought Hartslands, a large greenfield site to the north of Sevenoaks, in the late 1830s. There he began to create a working-class 'village' near the recently opened gas works, which was separated, both spatially and socially, from the polite, middle-class centre of the town. Besides the ubiquitous agricultural and general labourers, it also attracted men and women with artisanal skills. Grover obviously tapped into a strong latent demand for rented housing at Hartslands, for its growth was swift.

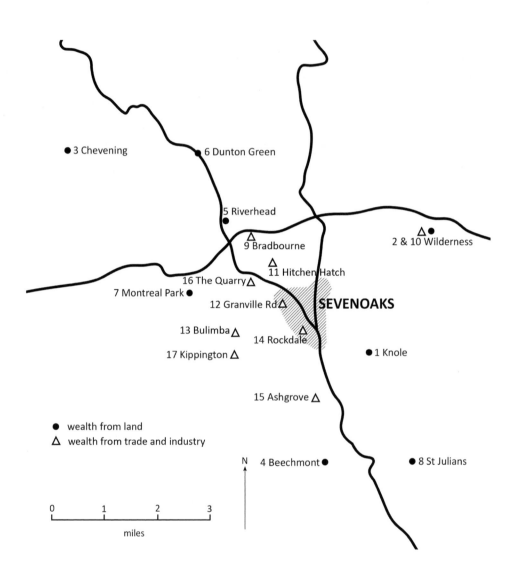

3 Chevening

6 Dunton Green

5 Riverhead

9 Bradbourne

2 & 10 Wilderness

11 Hitchen Hatch

16 The Quarry

7 Montreal Park

12 Granville Rd

SEVENOAKS

13 Bulimba

14 Rockdale

1 Knole

17 Kippington

15 Ashgrove

● wealth from land
△ wealth from trade and industry

N

4 Beechmont

8 St Julians

0   1   2   3

miles

Map 6 (Left) Elite wealth in Sevenoaks, 1880–90s.
The landed elite who owned inherited estates retained much power and patronage, but it was increasingly being challenged by those who had made fortunes by trade and industry. Some wealth, derived from war and speculative dealing in wartime, was invested in land, for example by Jeffrey Amherst and Charles Herries. After the 1870s a growing agricultural depression reduced the attraction of investing in land other than for personal comfort and status. Some who had made fortunes in commerce bought or rented old estates (e.g. Mills at Wilderness, and Kraftmeier at Ashgrove). Others, such as Swaffield and Swanzy, despite their wealth, lived in modest houses within the town.

Wealth in inherited land	acreage	gross ann. value £
1 Lord Sackville, Knole, Sevenoaks	1,960	3,450
2 Marquis Camden, Wilderness, Sevenoaks	7,241	9,836
3 Earl Stanhope, Chevening	4,343	3,891
4 Multon Lambarde, Beechmont, Sevenoaks	3,453	4,485
5 Marquis of Abergavenny, [Eridge], Riverhead	5,854	9,867
6 Sir John Farnaby Lennard [West Wickham], Dunton Green	3,002	4,900
7 Lord Amherst, Montreal Park, Sevenoaks	4,269	5,441
8 Sir Charles Herries MP (1815–83), St Julian's	2,000 (by 1910)	?

Commercial wealth assessed by wills		£
9 Francis Crawshay (1811–78), Bradbourne	Welsh mines and iron work	70,000
10 Charles Henry Mills (1830–98), Wilderness	banking	1,400,000
11 Samuel Bevington (1832–1907), Hitchen Hatch	tanning	116,000
12 Henry Swaffield (1834–1912), Granville Rd	stock market	210,000
13 William Hemmant (1837–1916), Bulimba	Australian wool and railways	92,000
14 John Dawson Laurie (1872–1915), Rockdale	stock market	215,000
15 Edward Kraftmeier (1851–1916), Ashgrove	explosives	285,000
16 Francis Swanzy (1854–1920), The Quarry	West African trade	233,000
17 William Thompson (1820–1904), Kippington	tea merchant	329,680

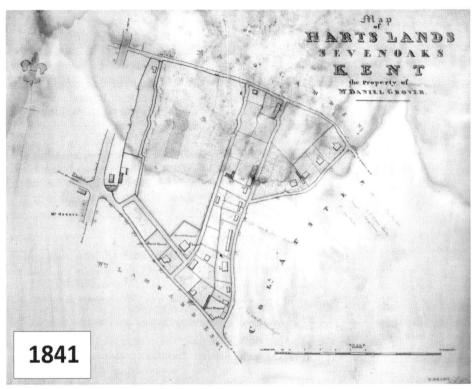

1841

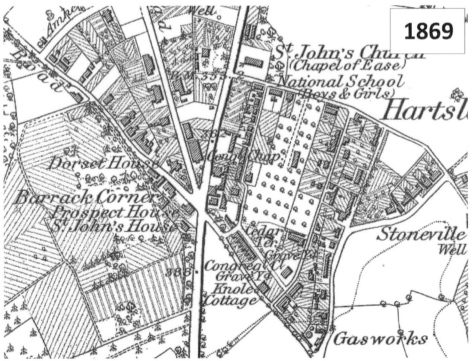

1869

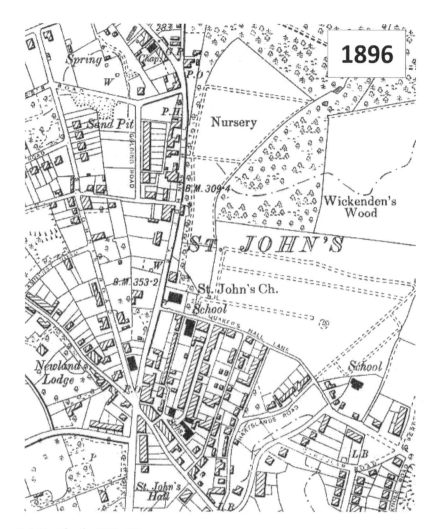

Maps 7–9 Hartslands, 1841–96.
These three maps show the steady growth of Hartslands after 1840. The plan dated 1841 was
drawn up when building work had just begun (*Source*: KLHC. U269/P45); the OS map of 1869
shows the open land faced by rows of houses, and the OS map of 1896 the completed terraced
houses of Cobden Road, the removal of the gas works, and new houses on surrounding former
estates. Initially Hartslands grew as a self-contained working-class community separated from
the town by open country. Revealingly, the 1841 Census enumerated the area separately from
the rest of the town. At the outset the town gas works (1838) was on the south-eastern edge
of Hartslands. The tithe map, surveyed in the late 1830s, identifies the land as 'field: arable';
the census of 1841 describes 56 out of the new 107 male householders, or more than half, as
'agricultural labourers'. Houses were mostly 'two up, two down', in 1841 each occupied by an
average of almost five people. Some dwellings contained more: there were seven households of
eight, three of nine, and one each of ten and eleven. Numbers increased as many families took in
lodgers to help pay the bills (nine per cent of the population in 1841). By the 1880s nearly 900
people lived in Hartslands, over ten percent of the population of Sevenoaks.
Source: 1841–91 census returns, Sevenoaks (Hartslands). [Author's collection]

Property, wealth and privilege

Economic insecurity haunted the lives of the majority of people in west Kent in the early nineteenth century, including those living in Hartslands. Curteis' Sevenoaks agricultural labourer 'G.B.' might serve as an example, although there is no corroborating evidence of his existence and he was probably generic.[3] Assuming he was born in 1810, experienced hunger as a child, witnessed the Swing riots and saw unemployment in the 1840s, by mid-century he would have been eager to be rid of the risks that had plagued his formative years. But how to defend and secure any material gains he had made? Without a vote he was electorally powerless in a society controlled by privileged wealthy property owners, most of whom were intent on upholding the political status quo. Working men and women could raise their weak voices in public protest, associate with a local pressure group or join a national political body, all of which might sometimes challenge the existing structures of power and authority. The Knole Park access dispute of 1884, for example, was a dramatic but short-lived event that turned on a town-wide repudiation of traditionally expressed aristocratic privilege and hegemony.[4]

Power and authority within the town largely promoted the interests of those who ruled, although sensible men supported measures of social amelioration that they hoped would prevent or limit threats to the political and social order. Public health was advanced by the provision of a clean water supply and a comprehensive drainage system, paid for from the rates. Such risk-reduction strategies faced opposition from vested interests in the town and the groups or lobbies they represented shaped contesting political factions. At the same time there were coherent and determined groups that sought to extend the franchise and widen political representation both locally and nationally. In the minds of the upholders of privilege the spectre of Swing, Chartism and unbridled and irresponsible mass politics echoed the regular tumults and revolutions that took place in France from 1789 to 1871 – stark reminders of what hasty reform might bring to Britain.

The standard way of managing or limiting such risks to the *status quo* was to ensure that any political debate took place within suitably devised institutions such as the vestry, 'the open meeting of the people of the parish or village', which occurred roughly every month.[5] But that traditional forum for debate often became antiquated and, in Sevenoaks, was dominated by a small oligarchic clique. More opportunity for debate was offered in new managing institutions such as the Poor Law Guardians (1834), the Local Board (1871) and the School Board (1875). The replacements presented significant political opportunities for some. The great related themes of the shifts in power and authority during our period were, first, that many of the governed achieved greater levels of political choice than ever before

---

3   Curteis, *Peel*, p. 46.

4   David Killingray, 'Rights, "riot" and ritual: the Knole Park access dispute, Sevenoaks, Kent, 1883–5', *Rural History*, 5/1 (1994), pp. 63–79.

5   Bryan Keith-Lucas, *Parish affairs: the government of Kent under George III* (Maidstone, 1986), p. 70.

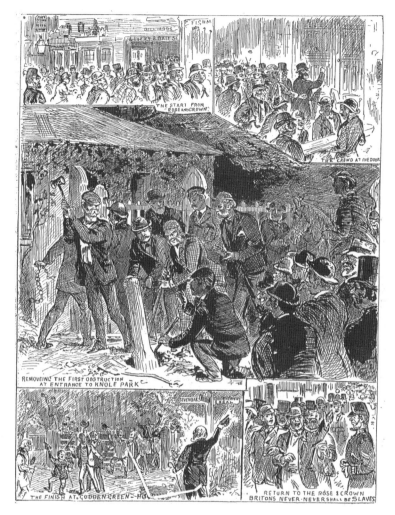

Figure 2.2 The Knole Park access dispute, taken from the *Penny Pictorial News*, 28 June 1884, p. 7. On the evening of 18 June 1884, hundreds of Sevenoaks people marched to the entrance of Knole Park and broke down obstacles that Lord Mortimer Sackville had erected to restrict access. This was a public response to a long dispute that had united local people of all social classes, who by custom used the park as a right of way and a place for leisure. Prominent at a protest meeting earlier that evening was James German J.P., a Deputy Lieutenant of the County, Albert Bath of the Farmers' Alliance, John Bligh, owner of the Holmesdale Brewery, and William Stepney, the Vestry Clerk. The good-natured crowd that invaded the park on two evenings engaged in various ritual acts: a man on a horse riding through the main gates, some men cross-dressed as women, and the singing of 'Rule Britannia' and the National Anthem. Townspeople thought they were acting lawfully to uphold their rights against the high-handed behaviour of a privileged aristocrat. Sackville telegraphed for police reinforcements; by 20 June over 50 policemen patrolled the town. The outcome was a court case which Sackville won, but with derisory damages. Effectively defeated, Sackville went to live in an hotel in Scarborough. Thereafter the Park remained open, free for all the people of Sevenoaks to enjoy. *Source*: Sevenoaks Museum.

and, secondly, that the governors became far more accountable to the governed than previously. But this local trend, significant though it was, merely mirrored the similar contemporary imperative behind the creation of many new national social and economic bodies, from poor law unions to sewerage boards.

But much more was at risk in the political sphere than it was in those counterparts, for, once opened, the Pandora's box of greater involvement by those further down the social scale was not easily slammed shut again. What might the middle – or even the working – classes *do* with power once they got hold of it? How could the political equation be solved, such that the risk of riot and revolution could be minimised by giving the lower orders the prospect of a better stake in society, without compromising political and social stability?

The rest of this chapter examines how and by whom west Kent was governed in the early nineteenth century, and how and why change took place, focusing especially on the new institutions devised to deal with specific issues. Despite such aspirations, until well into the nineteenth century power and authority in most English small towns and villages was wielded by aristocrats and large landowners. Until the 1830s most people's 'only contact with officialdom and their only experience of political authority … was the "parish state"'.[6] The small numbers able to vote in parliamentary elections owed that right to their property and wealth. Local magistrates were almost entirely drawn from the ranks of the wealthy landowners and Anglican clergy, who met at Petty Sessions. More serious crimes were dealt with at Quarter Sessions at Maidstone, and capital offences by the Assizes; the number of the latter on the statute book were steadily reduced as the nineteenth century progressed. Most people had limited local influence; although some might have their say at local vestry meetings, often that counted for little.

Although common people had no effective power they were not entirely without rights, enjoying – in theory – equality under the rule of law and before the courts. In practice the law took a different course, combining more regulation and restraint, which, while continuing to protect individual rights, took more notice of collective interests. Wealth and privilege often prevailed over the interests of the poorer and more vulnerable members of society, but free speech was a strongly guarded liberty used frequently by individuals, lobbies and organisations to express grievances and perceived injustices. Gradually the restraints on personal liberties were removed as legislature and judiciary further recognised the inviolability of persons, property and the press. By the end of the nineteenth century Britain was both a 'national' state and a bureaucratic, quasi-democratic country with a growing concern for public welfare, but the pattern of change was always by 'accommodation and accretion'.[7]

---

6   David Eastwood, *Government and community in the English provinces 1700–1870* (Basingstoke, 1997), p. 47.

7   Prudence Ann Moylan, *The form and reform of county government Kent 1889–1914* (Leicester, 1978), p. 18.

The parish vestry

Before the Local Government Act 1858, local civil administration largely resided in the monthly parish vestry meeting. The vestry was elected by ratepayers, effectively property owners, and consisted of the church minister as chairman, two churchwardens and leading parishioners. Sevenoaks, together with a few other local parishes – Otford, Westerham, Chevening and Edenbridge – were 'select' parishes, having a system of parochial government dominated by 'an inner group of substantial inhabitants', mainly gentry and farmers and numbering perhaps a dozen or so.[8] As elsewhere in England, local labourers 'could probably exercise no influence at all on its management'.[9] The vestry had significant responsibilities: setting church and general rates, including the annual tithe to support the church, and administering poor relief, which was a major and growing expenditure after 1800. The Sevenoaks vestry was unrepresentative of the town's population: few people attended its meetings and its decisions and actions were seldom exposed to the public gaze. A rare exception was in 1833, when a local newspaper not only highlighted how a meeting was delayed for an hour and a half by the (upper-class) trustees but also called on dissenters in the town 'to stir themselves against the crying evil of compulsory payments for the church' – or tithes.[10]

The voice and weight of the established church often explicitly reinforced local power and authority (and vestry government by implication) by instructing lowly parishioners how to behave. The Rev. Thomas Knox at Tonbridge warned that no man should join 'any riot, tumult or public commotion'; almost all clergy, including dissenters, would have agreed.[11]

A more thoughtful long-term response to ameliorate and conciliate rural hardship was the West Kent Labourer's Friend Society, established in 1835. This established a 'system of letting allotments of land to the labourer by which he would be kept from the alehouse ... and be impressed with a feeling that he had something to lose'.[12] Within a few years local societies with allotments were created in Sevenoaks (40 families applied), Ightham, Tonbridge and Plaxtol.[13] The latter society in 1836 acquired nine acres, with 40 holdings 'for which as many industrious labourers drew lots, and were put in possession at a moderate rent'.[14] But by 1837 Plaxtol's acreage had shrunk to just four acres of allotments, which were regarded with 'extreme indifference ... by the

---

8   Bryan Keith-Lucas, *The unreformed local government system* (London, 1980), p. 92. Keith-Lucas, *Parish affairs*, ch. 5, 'Parish Vestry'. Sidney and Beatrice Webb, *English local government from the Revolution to the Municipal Corporations Act, vol. 1, parish and county* (London, 1906).

9   Owen Chadwick, *The Victorian Church – Part 2, 1860–1901* (London, 1997), p. 196.

10 *SEG*, 10 Sept. 1833, p. 4.

11 Thomas Knox, *An exhortation to the poor* (London, 1831), p. 26.

12 *West Kent Guardian* (henceforth *WKG*), 25 July 1835, p. 1. See also Jeremy Burchardt, *The allotment movement in England, 1793–1873* (Woodbridge, 2002).

13 *MJ*, 23 Feb. 1841, p. 3.

14 Letter from Major Wayth, dd. 28 July 1836, reprinted in *The Farmer's Magazine*, 5 (1836), p. 184.

Figure 2.3 A winter agrarian scene. This sketch looks north from Pound Lane, Sevenoaks and dates from 1845. The oast houses indicate nearby hop gardens. The weather is severe with the cartwheel almost up to its axle hub in mud. On the left men are hand-flailing in the barn. *Source*: Sevenoaks Library, SC1025.

public at large', indicating that they were by no means the quick-fix solution to the risks of hungry agrarian workers many large landowners had hoped for.[15]

Some landowners believed that social order rested, in part, on a mythologised idea of sturdy rural 'yeomen' who represented the best of 'Old England', the solid heart of an hierarchical but harmonious society.[16] When that myth was punctured in 1830, they tended to blame outsiders for influencing normally docile and acquiescent farm labourers against their natural rulers. One newspaper correspondent, 'Freeholder', one of many local voices opposing parliamentary reform, wrote 'should this measure be carried to the extent proposed [...] a Yeoman of Kent may hereafter be found in the page of history, but he will be sought in vain upon the surface of the soil'.[17] In other words, his point was that the existing structure of power and authority rested on the maintenance of an enlightened ruling class imbued with a vested interest in property and a strong belief that the 'peasantry' be kept in their place.

15 *MJ*, 9 May 1837, p. 3.

16 Kathryn Beresford, '"Witnesses for the defence": the yeoman of Old England and the land question, *c*.1815–1837', in Matthew Cragoe and Paul Readman (eds), *The land question in Britain, 1750–1950* (Basingstoke, 2010), pp. 37–56.

17 *MJ*, 25 Oct. 1831, p. 3.

National events, such as the coronation of Queen Victoria in 1838, provided opportunities to provide paternalistic largesse. Newspaper reports highlighted the political subtext of the 'Grand Coronation Festival' staged in Sevenoaks that July. Official invitations to a dinner to be laid out on tables in the High Street were sent to 2,400 inhabitants: one newspaper described how 'England's pride, her deserving and industrious peasantry, were summoned … many a brightly beaming eye was cast down on the poorer but sincerely welcomed peasantry.'[18] Thus in a spirit of bounty, firmly marked by social class segregation, the town welcomed the new monarch.

Such ideas held by wealthy aristocrats and gentry may seem to modern readers narrowly conceived, self-interested and cloaked in paternalism. But look beyond that and often there was a deep concern about the welfare of their poorer neighbours. The gravestone of Otford farmer James Selby (1793–1851) described him as 'The Poor Man's Friend', and that he may well have been. It is wrong to think of the wealthy classes being entirely indifferent to the 'earthly necessities' of their less fortunate neighbours. Private charity may seem patronising, but it sought, if only temporarily, to aid the 'deserving poor' with food, clothes and boots, coal for heating and cooking, basic schooling and nursing care by committed and caring women.

Changes in local government after the 1830s

According to Anthony Brundage, 'The Swing riots were seared into the memory of many MPs, who consequently felt the need to restore the social fabric of the countryside.'[19] This hastened reform to the poor laws, the replacements of overseers by elected Guardians and the official registration of all births, marriages and deaths in the 1830s, marking an extension of central government regulation. This increase in state direction, especially when it impinged on local rates, had little to do with ideology and was more a response to the challenges posed by a rapidly growing population, industrial development and urbanisation.

A growing electorate at local and national level also demanded official intervention to promote social welfare and to curb the excesses of a market economy, all of which required increased state spending on, for example, education and vaccination against infectious diseases. The result was significant increases in taxation, such as the reintroduction of income tax in 1842, plus new laws to guard public health and housing, to improve working conditions and labour relations, to provide state-funded education and to regulate professional practice and private service. By the early twentieth century state intervention was providing 'entitlements' such as old age pensions and a system of national unemployment insurance.

---

18 *MJ*, 17 July 1838, p. 3; Sevenoaks Library, Gordon Ward notebooks; 'Coronation. Sevenoaks Festival', 11 July 1838.

19 Anthony Brundage, *The making of the New Poor Law: the politics of inquiry, enactment and implementation, 1832–39* (London, 1978), p. 15.

These developments were mirrored in local administration. In Sevenoaks, using the Poor Law Union parishes as a template, new highways boards were introduced in 1866 and a rural sanitary authority in 1872. The town established an elected 12-member Local Board in 1871 and, in the face of the growing demand for schooling, a local School Board was created in 1875.[20] These reforms offered new opportunities for people further down the social scale to take a more active part in local affairs than existed under the often poorly scrutinised vestry system.

The Local Board 1871–94

The regular meetings of Poor Law Guardians offered a space where elected members might express rival political views as to the relief of the poor within the Union and how rates were to be spent. In Sevenoaks the Guardians were mostly farmers and landowners, intent on reducing the risks to their wallets by keeping the poor rate down, but there were occasional voices of dissent against the harsh treatment that implied. After 1880 women were elected to the Sevenoaks School Board and served as Poor Law Guardians, where they often provided a more sympathetic voice on the condition of the young and the poor.

Sevenoaks dragged its heels in adopting new structures and its Local Board was constituted seven years after its counterpart in Tonbridge, but some local voices still resisted reform. In 1871 ratepayers demanded a Board particularly to address the specific and conspicuous problem of poor drainage and sanitation, which the existing vestry was powerless to solve.[21] The Board was an elected body, initially all male. The first General District Rate levied in March 1872 was 6d in the pound and produced an annual sum of £470.[22]

The Board's responsibilities steadily increased during its 25 years in existence. Initially, most discussions focused on local rate levels, water rates, street lighting, watering dusty roads and the removal of 'nuisances'. New demands resulted in the formation of new committees to deal with highways, building regulations and the enforcement of local bye-laws. Importantly, in 1875 the Public Health Act introduced separate urban and rural sanitary authorities, each with a medical officer of health. This helped concentrate local attention on improving sanitation for the area, although this required higher rates. Reform invariably came with a price tag attached.

The presence of the Local Board increased popular political participation. In contrast to the select vestry of the few, nearly 7,500 votes were cast in the inaugural Board election of 1871 and the social composition of the governors was far broader than the unchallenged gentry and farmer elite of earlier years. Twenty-two candidates stood for 12 places. Lord Buckhurst was elected but he came only tenth

---

20   Sevenoaks Library D67. See also KHLC UD/Se/Am/1/1.

21   *MJ*, 30 April 1870, 6; 10 June 1871, p. 6.

22   *MJ*, 15 April 1872, p. 5.

Figure 2.4 Arthur Hickmott (1862–1933) came to Sevenoaks in 1890, opening a draper's shop in Upper St John's. He was a socialist, poet, and Fabian pamphleteer. He and his wife Ellen campaigned to improve the lot of ordinary people through the Sevenoaks Progressive Association, and the Independent Labour Party (ILP). Arthur was elected on an ILP ticket to the new SUDC in 1894, and thereafter regularly re-elected.
Source: Detail from Figure 5.6. Author's collection.

in the poll, with 353 votes. Comfortably ahead of him were a draper, a plumber and Daniel Grover, builder of Hartslands, earlier a recipient of poor relief from Buckhurst's family in November 1830.[23] Merit may have been the key qualification for the role.

However, for much of its existence the landed or propertied interest chaired almost every meeting of the Board (Buckhurst being unanimously elected Chair at the first) and other members often deferred to those still perceived as their social superiors. Thus, Buckhurst's successor in 1877, Multon Lambarde, received glowing praise for how 'he had conducted the past business of the board in a manner most satisfactory to all parties'.[24] The Local Board was more representative of electors than the vestry, and also more accountable because its decisions were reported at length in the local media. Wisely, perhaps, those in west Kent generally tried hard to court journalists, the Darent Valley Main Sewerage Board deciding from the outset 'that the meetings should be open to the representatives of the Press'.[25]

---

23 *SEG*, 26 Sept 1871, p. 5; KHLC P330/8/5, 16 Nov. 1830.
24 *SEG*, 21 April 1877, p. 3.
25 *SEG*, 9 Dec. 1878, p. 5.

Sevenoaks Local Board election, September 1871

The electoral system for Local Boards was undemocratic and based on that used to elect Guardians of the Poor, a plural system whereby a small ratepayer might have one vote and a large landowner several.

	Elected	
1	Mr John Palmer, gentleman	641
2	Mr E.E. Cronk, auctioneer	580
3	Mr W. Pawley, hotel proprietor	571
4	Mr D. Grover, snr, builder	532
5	Mr S. Bligh, farmer	515
6	Mr M. Lambarde, Esq., magistrate	491
7	Mr T. Hancock, plumber	476
8	Mr G.M. Hooper, wine merchant	397
9	Mr S. Young, draper	369
10	Right Hon. Baron Buckhurst	353
11	Mr H.H. Lindsay, gentleman	353
12	Mr C.M. Thompson, surgeon	309
	Not elected	
13	Mr J.M. Hooker, architect	284
14	Mr W. Loveland, leatherseller	278
15	Major J. German, magistrate	268
16	Mr H.H. Sutton, hotel proprietor	247
17	Mr J. Parker, grocer	237
18	Mr S. Slater, accountant	228
19	Mr J.W. Whibley, farmer	142
20	Mr N. Weston, grocer	79
21	Mr J. Stannard, plumber	64
22	Mr G.D. Thorpe, maltster	40
Total votes cast		7,454

Source: *SEG*, 26 September 1871, p. 5.

Reforms: county, urban district and parish 1889 and 1894

Reform of county administration came in 1889 with the creation of elected county councils. The Kent body comprised 24 alderman and 72 councillors. There was a single alderman from Sevenoaks, Lord Stanhope of Chevening, and three councillors. But, although its members were now voted in, there were surprisingly few changes from the old system of justices of the peace (JP) meeting in Quarter Sessions. The new county council was as dominated by the wealthy as the old regime: 'individual members came and went on the council but the general character of the membership remained the same'.[26] The landed gentry retained effective control of the council through chairmanship of various committees to 1914. Similarly, the membership and issues facing the new Sevenoaks Urban District Council (SUDC) were little different from those of its predecessor. The compass of national government had greatly broadened, so also that of local government. By the end of the century a growing number of people, both locally and nationally, expected the state to act on their behalf to protect their interests and to advance public wellbeing – as seen, for example, in Arthur Hickmott's plea for an Eight Hours Bill in 1890.[27]

A new electorate

Those big issues were argued locally but also fought over in regular parliamentary elections. Polls were often rumbustious affairs. Who voted for whom was public knowledge, listed in printed Poll Books; the secret ballot was not introduced until the Ballot Act of 1872. Throughout our period the franchise was restricted to men aged over 21 and was based on property and income qualifications. However, in local elections unmarried women ratepayers were allowed to vote and, after 1870, they played a more prominent part in local politics, standing for and being elected to public office.[28] Until the Reform Act of 1832 the national franchise was limited to men who paid the land tax, which in west Kent was less than 5 per cent of the adult male population. Economic and social changes, especially after the 1850s, resulted in growing wealth and an expanding electorate, further increased by the Reform Acts of 1867 and 1884.

This irregular expansion of the electorate after 1832 still left most adults in 1914 ineligible to vote. However, they could petition parliament on local political issues, a process that rapidly increased in the first half of the nineteenth century. In addition, there were numerous local grassroots lobbies in west Kent that sought to promote specific interests ranging from tenant farmers to vaccination, often taking as their

26 Moylan, *County government*, p. 70.

27 *Sevenoaks Telegraph and Kent Messenger*, 17 May 1890, p. 3.

28 Miss Ann Nouaille was elected to the School Board, *SC*, 8 April 1881, p. 4; the following were elected members to the Board of Guardians: Miss Escombe and Mrs Rycroft (1895), Mrs Ellen Hickmott (1898), Mrs Pearce Clark (by 1907) and Mrs Hodges and Miss Bartlett (by 1910).

model the skilful methods demonstrated by the anti-slave trade committee from 1787 to 1807.[29]

For much of our period, many of those who had the vote argued that possession of property or a regular good income gave an elector a vested interest in social and economic stability. Those ideas echoed those of 'Freeholder' in 1831 and had at their root the concern that extending the franchise to those deemed socially, morally and intellectually incapable of exercising the vote presented a grave risk to society. The contrary idea that it was an inalienable right of all adult citizens to vote remained a radical and deeply mistrusted concept for many people before 1914.

Number of parliamentary electors in Sevenoaks Poll Books, 1790–1868

1790	70		1847	162
1802	74		1857	142
1832	Reform Act		1859	134
1835	116		1867	Reform Act
1840	140		1868	278

Source: West Kent Poll Books, 1790–1868. See also John Vincent, *Pollbooks: how the Victorians voted* (London, 1967).

The relationship of clergy to power and authority also changed in the long nineteenth century. In 1831 Thomas Knox had beaten the drum for obedience to the law, which at the time was enforced by many established church ministers who served as JPs. By 1900 many fewer clergy served on the bench, and the Rev. Thomas S. Curteis was chairman of the local Conservative party. As the size of the electorate increased, so nonconformist clergy had opportunities to serve in civil elected office. Baptist minister John Jackson (1837–1911) sat first on the Local Board and then on the SUDC, as did his successor Charles Rudge, while the Rev. Percy Thompson, vicar of Kippington, brought another reforming voice to the SUDC when he was elected in 1905.

Policing and punishment
Ultimately, power and authority rested on the application of executive force. Law and order, the business of policing or the executive arm of government, was a parish responsibility in Sevenoaks until 1857, a constable being appointed by the vestry.

---

29 David Killingray, 'Grassroots politics in west Kent since the late eighteenth century', *Archæologia Cantiana*, CIXXX (2009), pp. 33–54.

The town had a lock-up 'cage', or small prison cell, demolished only in 1902. In emergencies JPs could read the Riot Act and call for military aid, as happened in Goudhurst during the Swing riots.[30] Minor offences could also be dealt with by local magistrates; for example, in 1809 Thomas Underhill, who stole 'a clod of beef' in Sevenoaks, was 'publicly whipped' for 50 yards on market day and discharged.[31] More serious crimes, usually dealt with at the Assizes, earned harsher sentences. So William Mitchell, who was found guilty of a violent assault with intent to rob at Riverhead in 1822, was sentenced to transportation for seven years.[32] Between 1829 and 1843, 15 men from the Sevenoaks area were transported to Australia for offences ranging from highway robbery to horse stealing and housebreaking. One local example of someone facing this draconian form of punishment was 33-year-old Henry Butcher. In 1827 he was arrested at his home in Riverhead for the theft of a knife, some books and a 'large quantity of copper coin' from the mill at Greatness. Convicted on the word of several witnesses at the Kent Assizes, he was sentenced to transportation for life to Van Diemen's Land (Tasmania).[33]

Vagrancy, which often involved begging, was also an offence that for much of the nineteenth century could incur a prison sentence. Official policing also encompassed what was known as 'vice and immorality' – prostitution, drunkenness, gambling – in an invasion of what some thought the private sphere of life. The New Poor Law overseers often acted to advance the 'moral condition' of the poor, deciding who was 'deserving' or 'undeserving' of relief, labelling certain women as 'wanton' and men as 'work-shy' – all part of a system of policing behaviour both within and without the workhouse.

Kent was reluctant to accept a county constabulary, which was eventually forced on it by central government. Before 1857 rural areas of the county relied on parish-appointed constables who in Sevenoaks overlapped with the county police until 1872, a most unwieldy system that made catching criminals harder. By 1864, when the local county force numbered a superintendent and six constables, a constabulary and magistrates court had been built.[34] The slowness to embrace a county-wide system of policing sprang from local fears that it would place a further tax burden on ratepayers. At the same time there were increasing demands for better policing, attention being drawn to the growing number of petty crimes and nuisances on weekly market days, during the October Fair and on holidays and 5 November. The presence of many boisterous navvies building the railways in the 1860s added to the local crime statistics. Drunkenness, swearing in public, theft

---

30 *SEG*, 11 Jan. 1831, p. 3.

31 *KG*, 4 April 1809, p. 4.

32 *Kent Weekly Post* (henceforth *KWP*), 3 May 1822, p. 4.

33 TNA HO 11/6, 237 (120); *SEG*, 13 March 1827, p. 4; 27 March 1827, p. 3.

34 David Killingray and Elizabeth Purves (eds), *Sevenoaks: an historical dictionary* (Andover, 2012), p. 133.

and assaults on persons, including constables, were the most common offences brought before the magistrates.

Sentencing could be severe: seven days' hard labour for stealing an orange valued at one penny, and one month's hard labour for stealing a duck egg worth 'three-halfpence'.[35] On the few occasions when riotous behaviour occurred or threatened, constables from other divisions could be brought in, aided by the telegraph and the railway, as happened in 1884 during the Knole access dispute. Kent could also call on the Metropolitan Police for aid, but this was strongly resisted by successive chief constables, conscious of the impact on the reputation of their own force. By 1897 the Sevenoaks sub-division could muster a superintendent and 23 constables, all with truncheons and one armed with a sword.

Men transported for crimes committed in Sevenoaks, 1830–49

Name	Age	Born	Date	Offence	Sentence (years)
William Bennett	30	Unknown	13.3.1843	Stealing	?
George Dott	23	Unknown	16.12.1844	Poaching	10
Thomas Flint	22	Sussex	15.9.1844	Housebreaking	7
Thomas Gilbard	26	Sussex	30.4.1829	Stealing	Life
John Goldsmith	26	Chelmsford	17.10.1843	Stealing	7
John Hoare	27	Stafford	12.3.1830	Housebreaking	7
John Lackhurst	40	Unknown	20.8.1849	Stealing	15
James Lear	22	Unknown	23.11.1843	Stealing	7
Jonathan Lee	22	Kent	8.1.1835	Stealing	7
James Lloyd	31	Hereford	23.3.1837	Stealing	7
George Moore	26	Maidstone	23.7.1849	Highway robbery	7
William Rowles	35	Hereford	14.10.1833	Housebreaking	14
John Ryan	15	Unknown	29.11.1841	Stealing	7
William Spearman	34	Warwick	30.7.1836	Stealing horses	Life
James Wills	50	Surrey	2.7.1839	Housebreaking	10

Where did power and authority reside?

Two major changes occurred during the long nineteenth century with regard to the exercise of power and to popular ideas of hierarchy. Much of it was driven by the desire of many to exercise political choices themselves, but political debate was

---

35 SC, 21 March 1885, p. 3; 2 May 1885, p. 5.

Figure 2.5 Sevenoaks Sub-Division Police, 1897. Centre is 59-year-old William Holman, the superintendent, who had served in the Royal Navy and then joined the recently formed Kent Constabulary in 1863. He served in Sevenoaks 1895–99. Beards and moustaches may have given constables a sense of masculine authority.
Source: Author's collection.

normally conducted within institutional frameworks that helped control the inherent risks involved. As we have already seen, increasingly merit, not birth or property, was considered the most important criterion for election and the governors became far more accountable to the governed than before. By the late nineteenth century there was a growing consensus – among people of all classes – that the state had a greater burden of responsibility to mitigate the results of individual economic misfortune and to give more people access to the means of personal advancement. This was deemed right not only for individuals but also for the public good. Private patronage by the community's elite continued; the Sevenoaks United Relief Committee, for example, was set up by clergy and leading men and women to address the problem of unemployment during the severe economic recession of 1907–09. It co-operated with the local Poor Law Guardians, operated a soup kitchen and a labour exchange in the town and sought work for unemployed men, mainly in neighbouring stone quarries.[36] An increasing number of people believed the state should be responsible for mitigating the risks of economic disorder and to be active in promoting public welfare. It is impossible to overstate how important government-inspired action was

36   *SC*, 10 Jan. 1908, p. 8; 24 Jan. 1908, p. 4; 11 Sept. 1908, p. 4; 13 Nov. 1908, p. 5.

in removing or reducing risks of various kinds from the lives of millions of British people during the second half of the nineteenth century.

An important ingredient for both local society and the nation was a sense of identity: that people accepted that they belonged. Many working-class men and women might have had grievances, but even if they often felt excluded there were means by which their voices could be heard. This vital vent for anger or grievance was an important means of giving strength to social cohesion, as it was another factor helping to lessen the desire shown by some of the poor to transfer their risks onto those who ran local society.

For many, new choices could be made, such as migrating from country to town, or overseas. Expectations of personal improvement and material progress helped dim a sense of despair. On balance, living in west Kent in 1914 was greatly preferable to living there in 1790 because people's lives were much less risky. People lived longer, they were better fed and healthier, many more were literate and, despite large pockets of distress, incomes were higher and allowed for some surplus. And yet, for those enduring the rigours of unemployment, such as the 30 or so men at Ide Hill in the winter of 1908 who were reported to be close to starving, their lot was little better than that of their forebears over a century earlier.[37] Nevertheless, the resources of the state were increasingly being mobilised to meet the needs of the poor and less fortunate.

Choice was also a recipe for conflict, albeit mainly confined within new political institutions. New risks were posed by central government demands and by local responses. How, and when, should changes be implemented? And, perhaps most pertinently of all who, precisely, should pay for them? The next two chapters will detail some of those vitally important political questions, the answers to which were often rooted deep within the ideas, beliefs and values prevailing in contemporary west Kent.

---

37   *SC*, 20 Nov. 1908, p. 8.

Chapter 3

Ideas, beliefs and values: parish and vestry

Everyone has opinions, most of which are rooted in their ideas and values. Some are rarely expressed. Others are publicly proclaimed and demonstrated. Those ideas and values vary greatly, but all exemplify the choices we make, some of which seek to remove or mitigate the risks we face. When people actively start that process by taking political action (often as part of some conscious or unconscious process of risk transfer), sooner or later they collide with structures of power and authority. Those conflicts were numerous in nineteenth-century west Kent, but to properly understand them requires knowing as much as possible about the ideas and beliefs of the people involved. This chapter seeks to do that at parish and vestry level, remembering that politics very often interacted with religion. The key question it seeks to answer is: how did religious belief inform and motivate political action?

Religious belief and influence

Beliefs and values across England in the nineteenth century were thoroughly rooted in Christianity. People in west Kent generally adhered to its Protestant variant, primarily Anglicanism, but the period also witnessed a major expansion in choice of worship, so much so that 'By the 1840s, an extensive religious marketplace was firmly established', as in the rest of England.[1] The background to this is complex and must be explored in some detail, but it was influenced by eighteenth-century Enlightenment ideas that helped shape notions of religious tolerance.

In 1800, the Anglican church of St Nicholas was the largest public building in Sevenoaks, capable of seating over 1,000 people, and central to the parish. Although by then parishioners were not legally required to attend public worship, many could not easily reach the building, especially when the weather was inclement. New 'chapels of ease' were built, often with the support of local landowners, to make church attendance easier. The first was in Weald, completed in 1822; the second was

---

1   Linda Colley, *Britons: forging the nation 1707–1837* (New Haven, CT, 1992); Emma Griffin, *Liberty's dawn – a people's history of the industrial revolution* (London, 2013), p. 200.

at Riverhead, in 1831, on land provided by Lord Amherst of Montreal and Multon Lambarde of Beechmont, in order 'to save their households and the villagers the long uphill walk to St. Nicholas in the town'.[2]

Dissent, or nonconformity, had early seventeenth-century origins in west Kent with small congregations of Baptists, Congregationalists and Quakers meeting privately and cautiously. The Test and Corporation Acts of 1690, which excluded dissenters and Roman Catholics from any public office, were repealed in 1828–9. Similar rights were extended to Jews, but only in 1858, and to atheists as late as 1886.

A growing body of New Dissent was the Wesleyan Methodists, who had their own meeting place in the centre of Sevenoaks and who, by the first decade of the nineteenth century, had partly separated from Anglicanism. While the Church of England was the normal, but not invariable, spiritual home of the establishment, Christians lower down the social scale, such as the respectable How family we will regularly encounter in later chapters and Catherine Martin, were often nonconformists; those two families were strong Methodists. Working-class people in Hartslands had the benefit of a General Baptist chapel (from 1842), which attracted about 150 people a week. Perhaps worried by the competition, the Rev. Thomas Curteis caused another chapel of ease to be built there in 1858, financed by the Marquess of Camden, which became the separate parish of St John's.[3]

Religious revival from the 1740s gave birth to evangelicalism, which pervaded both Anglican and dissenting churches. Little evangelical fervour was apparent in Sevenoaks district churches, the exceptions being Vincent Perronet, vicar of Shoreham from 1728 to 1785 and a close friend of John Wesley, and James Sutcliffe, curate at Knockholt 1837–55.[4] In contrast, many dissenters were evangelicals, their lives often shaped by a personal conversion experience, a firm belief in salvation by Christ's redeeming grace on the cross and devotion to regular Bible reading, all of which promoted personal piety and missionary activity at home and overseas. Increasingly, evangelicals viewed their surrounding society and world events in moral terms.[5] For example, Wesleyan Methodists regularly recorded numbers at church and obituaries praised faithful devotion and acts of charity. For the Anglican clergy at mid-century, charity began at home, and they showed little interest in working among annual hop-pickers or the navvies building the railways. These were evangelistic opportunities for local nonconformists or outside mission agencies.[6]

---

2   David Killingray (ed.), *Sevenoaks people and faith. Two thousand years of religious belief and practice* (Chichester, 2004), pp. 169–72, 75–7.

3   Killingray, *Sevenoaks people and faith*, pp. 89–90, 82.

4   Richard Watson, *The life of the Rev. John Wesley, A.M.* (London, 1831), p. 117.

5   Boyd Hilton, *The age of atonement: the influence of evangelicalism on social and economic thought 1785–1865* (Oxford, 1986).

6   Tessa Leeds, 'The construction of the Sevenoaks railway tunnel, 1863–68', *Archæologia Cantiana*, CXX (2000), pp. 187–204.

The nationwide religious census, 1851

The nationwide official religious census was taken on a wet Sunday in March 1851. Clergy provided figures for adults and children, and the average attendance for the previous 12 months. In Sevenoaks more people attended Anglican churches than dissenting chapels. In the list below the two dissenting chapels in Bessels Green are included, although they were in the parish of Chevening. Some 700 children attended Sunday schools each week. The population for Sevenoaks town in 1851 was 2,187, for Riverhead 1,728 and for Weald 963, totalling 4,878.

Church of England	Morning	Afternoon	Evening
St Nicholas Sevenoaks	200	200	700–1000

The Rev. T. Curteis wrote: 'I would have tried to make it more complete had I had more time, but the dates are uncertain'.

	Morning	Afternoon	Evening
Riverhead Chapel	450	450	250–450
Weald Chapel	185	199	225
Baptists			
Town	231	80	158
'Bethel, Harts Lands'	160	60 'scholars'	125
Bessels Green	110	100	100
Wesleyan Methodists			
Sevenoaks	224		186
Weald			52
Unitarian			
Bessels Green	60		50

Source: Margaret Roake (ed.), *Worship in Kent: the census of 1851* (Maidstone, 1999), pp. 128–31.

Although the nineteenth century is often portrayed as one of religious enthusiasm, which in many ways it was, many people rarely went to church. Beilby Porteus, bishop of London, built a chapel of ease at Ide Hill in 1807, describing the 'poor inhabitants' of this upland area as having 'the most deplorable ignorance of the great truths of revelation'.[7] The sole national census of religious worship, taken in March 1851, caused consternation to many Anglicans, as it revealed sporadic

---

7   Robert Hodgson, *The life of the Right Reverend Beilby Porteus, D.D., late bishop of London* (London, 1811), p. 167.

church attendance and the growing influence of dissenting congregations, more pronounced in urban areas than rural west Kent.[8]

Religious belief was neither uniform nor inclusive, therefore, but for much of our period the Church of England and its clergy invariably saw themselves as an arm of the state. In the troubled 1790s, overshadowed by the French revolution and war with France, when the government sought to curb political dissent, the rector of Sevenoaks exhorted his parishioners to uphold the authorities in a sermon entitled 'Religion and loyalty'.[9]

The Curteis family

The Curteis family owned the advowson of St Nicholas, Sevenoaks, from 1716 to 1907, with six generations of the family serving this benefice. Thomas Sackville Curteis, rector from 1775 to 1831, was described as being 'pastorally lethargic, financially improvident, physically unhealthy and personally quarrelsome'. In accordance with the will of Thomas Curteis, who died in 1861, Henry Sidebottom, a relative, was brought into the parish on the understanding that he would keep the 'seat warm' until the next direct descendant (Curteis' grandson, Thomas Samuel Curteis) was old enough to become rector. This abuse of the system of patronage was widely commented on in the press (e.g. *Kentish Mercury*, 12 October 1861, p. 5, and *London Daily News*, 8 October 1861, p.1, and in 1874 when Sidebottom resigned to make way for the youthful Rev. Thomas Curteis (1848–1913).

Thomas Sackville Curteis	1777–1831 (died aged 78)
Thomas Curteis (nephew)	1831–1861 (died aged 73)
Henry Sidebottom (a relative)	1862–1874 (resigned)
Thomas Samuel Curteis (g'son)	1874–1907 (sold advowson)

Sources: Nigel Yates, 'A Kentish Clerical Dynasty: Curteis of Sevenoaks. Part I', *Archæologia Cantiana*, CVIII (1990), pp. 1–10, and 'Part II', CXVII (1997), pp. 161–72.

Personal belief about religion, and Christianity in particular, varied. Alongside profound and active Christian believers were vague theists, freethinkers and some

---

8   Margaret Roake (ed.), *Worship in Kent: the census of 1851* (Maidstone, 1999), pp. 122–40.
9   'A Sermon, preached before both Companies of the Sevenoaks Volunteers, in the Church of the said Parish, on Sunday, 16 Sept. 1798. By the Rev. T.S. Curteis, Vicar and Chaplain', mentioned in *London Chronicle*, 18–20 Sept. 1800, p. 287.

who exhibited little religious faith, such as High Tory Robert Herries of St Julian's, who nevertheless thought religion vital for social order. He wrote to his cousin in 1837, during a decade punctuated by rural unrest: 'if the church is to be upheld, now is the time to show our adherence to it in every possible way'.[10] For others, their Christian beliefs were shaped by folklore from an earlier age that many in churches and chapels would have been deemed superstition. One example was observing the hardening of candle wax, known as the 'winding-sheet': a belief that the way tallow collected around the wick of a candle foretold the death of someone in the family.[11] Such beliefs, perhaps more prevalent among the poorer classes, helped 'reinforce their view of the external world … which provided a means of dealing with the chance incidences of personal loss, illness, economic hardship and the uncertainties of life'.[12]

Religion and politics

How did religious beliefs impact on local political activities and conflicts? The level of local taxes, or rates, ever contentious, was frequently contested by dissenters, who strongly resented being required by law (until 1868) to pay church rates and to support schools run by the Church of England, to which they did not belong and whose theology they disavowed. For example, they verbally opposed the Sevenoaks vestry imposing an additional statutory church rate to pay for substantial repairs to the church tower in 1811, a debt not paid off for more than fifty years.[13]

Occasionally dissenters complained more loudly. In 1832 in Sevenoaks there was a dispute over 'sacramental gifts' (a church charity), when draper William Morphew, using his office as a churchwarden and in defiance of the law, secured from Curteis, the rector, the exclusive right to provide clothing for the parish poor. Before then the clothing had been bought equally from the four drapers in the town. The fact that both Curteis and Morphew were Tories further increased local annoyance.[14] Normally the vestry passed the rates, including those concerned specifically with Church affairs, with little scrutiny and even less comment. However, in 1854 they were seriously contested, when two dissenters, Joseph Bradly and Thomas Chappell, forced a vote by 'shew of hands' that rejected an amended rate, a victory gained although many of the dissenters present abstained from voting.[15]

---

10   Private archives, Herries papers. Robert Herries to John Charles Herries, dd. Lynmouth, 9 Oct. 1837.

11   *SC*, 9 May 1884, p. 3. Other ideas involved 'birds of bad omen', touching certain objects, and avoiding specific obstacles.

12   Bob Bushaway, '"Tacit, unsuspected but still implicit faith": alternative belief in nineteenth century rural England', in Tim Harris (ed.), *Popular culture in England, c. 1500–1850* (Basingstoke, 1995), p. 192.

13   David Killingray, *St Nicholas Parish Church, Sevenoaks, Kent* (Sevenoaks, 2015), p. 12.

14   *A copy of the correspondence between the Rev. Thomas Curteis, vicar of Seven Oaks … and Francis Barnett, relative to the distribution of sacramental gifts in the said parish* (London, 1833).

15   *SEG*, 13 June 1854, p. 5.

Tithes were another major bone of contention. In 1833 a meeting was held at the Royal Crown hotel in Sevenoaks to petition parliament for their abolition. Among those attending were dissenters and radicals including Bradly, James Parrish (a shoemaker) and Nicholas Chatfield.[16] Another remarkable instance, which made the national press, occurred at Riverhead that year, both illustrating the distance between Anglicans and dissenters on the issue and providing political evidence of how many inhabitants of west Kent desired to make local government more accountable. When some dissenters refused to pay the 'illegal charges' of the annual tithe, Morphew, as churchwarden, summoned Chatfield for non-payment and he was ordered by the magistrates to comply. Chatfield refused and Morphew, accompanied by a constable, attempted to distrain two pigs to be sold by auction in lieu of payment. Seizing the pigs had been difficult, residents disrupting the attempt, and in the ensuing struggle the constable ended up on all fours in the mud, grasping one of the animals, whereupon he and Morphew were hissed by the large crowd. The attempt to auction the pigs also failed. Eventually Chatfield, Richard Parrish and Zechariah Baker were charged with riotous behaviour. At their subsequent trial in August 1833 they were acquitted, and their court fees were defrayed by public subscription.[17]

Local artist William Knight, who voted Liberal when he was enfranchised in 1867, records in his diary the steps he took on Chatfield's behalf. He suggested Baker might lay 'information against Morphew for having served the parish of Sevenoaks with goods while churchwarden', which looks suspiciously like a reference to the sacramental gifts incident and which, when placed in the public domain, might not have redounded to Morphew's credit. Knight's evidence was a bill Morphew had previously submitted to Knight's father, presumably when parish overseer between 1831 and 1833. Knight's diary also shows that Baker and Parrish travelled 'to London to consult a lawyer' to begin an action against Morphew and the constable for having 'overstepped the line of their duty'.[18] This indicates that the defendants had both the confidence and the financial wherewithal to challenge the town's political elite in court. The payment of church rates was a legal obligation but it often ran counter to some dissenters' religious consciences. Knight's actions also illustrate that dissenters had more options to defend their religious integrity, and that establishment elites could be called to account in the newspapers, in law and by a larger number of people in polite society.

This new-found confidence among some of the lower orders of the town, partly one suspects the result of Swing, eventually collided with the greater accountability of the elite and provides an early example of how the determined exercise of choice

---

16   *SEG*, 19 Feb. 1833, p. 4.

17   *Morning Post* (henceforth *MP*), 20 June, p. 4; 19 Oct. 1833, p. 2; *Bells' Life in London*, 16 June 1833, p. 1; *The Spectator*, 15 June 1833, p. 9; *Parish Reformer's Magazine*, 1833, p. 7.

18   Private archives, Knight, *Diaries*, vol. 1, 27 Oct. 1833; *SEG*, 27 Aug. 1833, p. 4.

by even a small group could sour social and – increasingly – political relations within Sevenoaks.

The Poor Law

Although often not apparent, the governing classes of England were never entirely oblivious to the risks run by the poor and the impact on their lives of seasonal or economic misfortune. Relief of the poor took varying forms, including private charitable endeavour, but the main support, or risk-reduction system, came from the various iterations of the Poor Law system in each parish.

Under the Elizabethan poor law and the Resettlement Act of 1662, each parish vestry was responsible for the relief of the poor born within its boundaries: the Anglican parish was the basis of 'a Christian welfare system that was benevolent and encompassing', especially in comparison to those provided abroad.[19] Poor relief, paid from the annual poor rate, was administered by locally appointed or elected Poor Law overseers. It varied in form: 'outdoor relief' provided money and goods such as food and coal, which allowed the poor to remain in their homes; 'indoor relief' was offered mainly to the elderly, widows, orphans and the sick in the workhouse on St John's Hill, which in 1830 purportedly had accommodation for 300 inmates. The building was described by the new Poor Law Commissioners in 1834 as 'old and inconvenient'.[20]

Ratepayers regularly complained about the burden of poor relief. In line with many parishes across the country the cost of poor relief in Sevenoaks rapidly increased in the years after 1790. By the 1820s this parochial system, even when supplemented by informal charity suited to an earlier agrarian age, was falling apart, as the increasing demands made upon it forced the poor rate ever upwards. In Kent its costs rocketed from barely £100,000 in 1790 to £400,000 by 1818.[21] Those longer-term financial risks were bad enough. But, when coupled with the short-term risks to property of rick-burning and riot in 1830–1, the political nation had had enough. Robert Herries provides a good example, writing to his cousin in 1833 that 'They are raising the poor rates upon us at a most fearful rate, and there seems not to be one Gentleman in all the Parish disposed to take the slightest interest in their application, or in short to interfere in Parish affairs in any way.'[22]

Root and branch reform came when the old poor law was unceremoniously swept away and replaced by the Poor Law Amendment Act of 1834. The Act was highly contentious because the new system was directed by central government and reduced

---

19 Snell, *Parish and belonging*, pp. 160–1, and ch. 2, 'The culture of local xenophobia'.

20 Paul Hastings, 'The Old Poor Law 1640–1834', in Nigel Yates, Robert Hume and Paul Hastings, *Religion and society in Kent, 1640–1914* (Woodbridge, 1994), pp. 112–88.

21 D.A. Baugh, 'The cost of poor relief in south-east England, 1790–1834', *Economic History Review*, 28 (1975), pp. 50–68.

22 Private archives, Herries papers, Robert Herries to John Charles Herries, 3 April 1833.

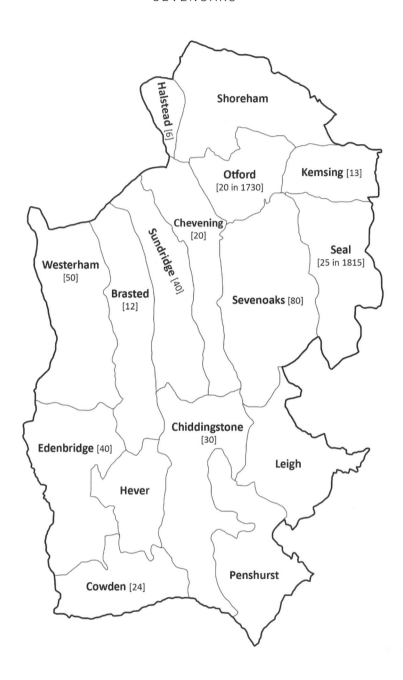

Map 10 The Old Poor Law, 1777.
This map is based on a parliamentary report of 1777, showing parishes with workhouses and the number of inmates in each.
Source: mentioned in Anon [John Toke], *Five letters on the state of the poor in the county of Kent* (London, 1770, amended 1808).

local control over the poor, leading to strong opposition in many English parishes, including Sevenoaks. The famous Poor Law Report that inspired the Act explicitly acknowledged the risks of being poor and the necessity of ameliorating them, admittedly in somewhat pious terms: 'In all extensive communities, circumstances will occur in which an individual, by the failure of his means of subsistence, will be exposed to the danger of perishing. To refuse relief … is repugnant to the common sentiments of mankind.'[23]

In practice, however, overcoming the bare-necessity risks faced by the poor came a distant second behind obviating the financial and political risks to the upper echelons of society, which had loomed (too) large in their minds for centuries. The new Act abolished outdoor relief and introduced a system of parishes grouped into Poor Law Unions, each with its own workhouse. Sir Francis Head, the assistant poor law commissioner charged with establishing the new system in Kent, oversaw the creation of unions for south-west Kent, Sevenoaks and Penshurst, but there was violent opposition in Penshurst to the building of its workhouse. To mitigate such risks Head favoured large unions with large elected boards, which – unlike parish vestries – were far less likely to be influenced by claimants or terrorised by social unrest. He argued: 'Wherever I find the peasantry disposed to act … on the principle of intimidation I strongly recommend a large union.'[24] Head's view prevailed, for Sevenoaks absorbed the short-lived Penshurst Union in September 1836.[25]

Entry to the workhouse under the new Act was dictated by the principle of 'less eligibility', neatly summarised by E.C. Tufnell, who ran the Sevenoaks Union. He wrote: 'the great secret of Poor Law reform … is to place the pauper in a worse condition than the independent labourer'.[26] This sought to impel the poor into gainful employment or, if not, provide them with a guarantee against destitution and starvation. As Sevenoaks Guardian Samuel Bligh wrote to the Poor Law Commissioners in October 1834, if its inmates 'were really necessitous they had no reason to complain, being well fed and clothed'.[27] The system was supposed to work by reducing the risks run by the poor at the lowest possible price to the ratepayers, while simultaneously ensuring that dangerous incidents of violent protest (Swing being the most obvious recent example) against local elites would swiftly become consigned to the history books.

Those on Tufnell's and Bligh's side of the fence deemed it an immediate success, arguing as early as 1835 that 'the introduction of the new poor law in this

---

23   S.G. and E.O.E. Checkland, *The Poor Law Report of 1834* (Harmondsworth, 1974), p. 334.

24   TNA MH 12/5315, Head to Poor Law Commissioners, 29 Nov. 1834.

25   *SEG*, 7 March 1837, p. 4.

26   Quoted by John Bowen, *The union workhouse and board of guardian system* (London, 1842), p. 29.

27   TNA MH 12/5315, 4 Oct. 1834.

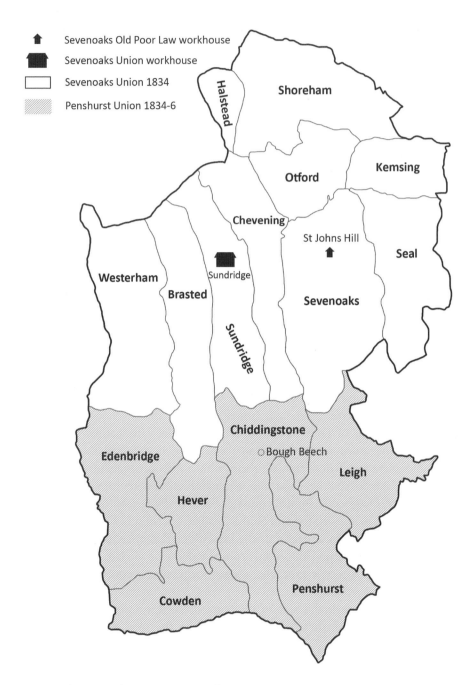

Sevenoaks Old Poor Law workhouse

Sevenoaks Union workhouse

Sevenoaks Union 1834

Penshurst Union 1834-6

Halstead

Shoreham

Otford

Kemsing

Chevening

St Johns Hill

Seal

Westerham

Sundridge

Brasted

Sevenoaks

Sundridge

Chiddingstone

Bough Beech

Edenbridge

Leigh

Hever

Penshurst

Cowden

Map 11 The Sevenoaks Poor Law Union from 1834.
The new Poor Law Union was pieced together from first ten and then 16 parishes in 1835–37. The old Poor Law workhouse, on St John's Hill, remained in use until the New Union workhouse at Sundridge opened in 1846.
Source: *SEG*, 15 March 1835, p. 1, and 7 March 1837, p. 4.

neighbourhood [Sevenoaks] has been productive of a greater degree of moral as well as pecuniary benefit to labourers, than the most sanguine among us anticipated'.[28] Further, it was expected that labourers would join benefit clubs and that the number of beer shops would fall. But that opinion was by no means universal, even within the elite of west Kent, and the Poor Law remained a hot political issue in west Kent for many years, mainly because of fundamentally different conceptions of how the poor should be treated. In Sevenoaks the Rev. Thomas Curteis differed from Bligh and Tufnell; his letter to Peel in 1838 (published 1842) complained that the new Law exacerbated the sufferings of the poor and separated married couples, thus breaking up families, a practice that he had condemned in the old St John's parish workhouse.[29] More broadly he insisted

> if the operation of the present poor-law be continued, much private suffering will be inflicted, ... – your petitioner humbly prays that this law will be repealed, and that a law may be enacted that will secure to the poor their chartered rights to employment; and to the owners of property that power to compel all persons to contribute to maintaining the poor.[30]

Less high-minded objections came from large landowners in west Kent, who saw that the major cash burden of building the new workhouse (which had to be completed within ten years) would fall on them, the principal ratepayers. The West Kent Agricultural Society in Sevenoaks in August 1834 agreed a petition to protest at the expenditure.[31] Nor did the possibility of violent plebeian protest vanish completely. Lord Templemore (1797–1837), the 'local "architect"' of the Sevenoaks Union, who in December 1834 attended 'a very important meeting at Sevenoaks of landed proprietors on the subject of putting this district under the New Poor Law Commissioners', was soon attacked in a manner highly redolent of Swing.[32] As one 'irrevocably associated with the new system', Templemore was just as liable as Jonathan Thompson had been to attack.[33] Thus twice within a year, in September 1835 and 1836, fires blazed at his estate at Combe Bank, Sundridge, the first of which was directly attributed to his 'activity in administering the new Poor Law'. This was confirmed by William Knight, who not only wrote that 'He is very much disliked by the poor' but also delighted in witnessing the great conflagration through an artist's eyes, such that 'the smoke strongly lighted up just where it left

---

28 UKPP *Poor Law Reports* 24 (1835), Appendix B, no. 2 'Report by E.C. Tufnell', p. 195.

29 KHLC P330/8/4, 23 Jan. 1832, Curteis to Sevenoaks Vestry.

30 Curteis, *Peel*, p. 39.

31 *SEG*, 11 Aug. 1835, p. 1.

32 West Sussex Record Office, Goodwood mss. No. 1455, f542, Nov. 1834.

33 Roger Wells, 'Rural rebels in southern England in the 1830s', in Clive Emsley and James Walvin (eds), *Artisans, peasants & proletarians, 1760–1860* (Beckenham, 1985), p. 107.

the blaze – and gradually lost in the darkness – as it rolled off in majestic clouds to the south – had a fine effect'.[34]

Poor Law matters, even under the old regime, also caused heated debate within the vestry. Knight recorded one bad-tempered meeting in 1832, when one Mr Poulter's fitness to run the workhouse was discussed at length: 'After much talking in which unpleasant feelings were evinced on both sides, the meeting came to the conclusion that the charges made by [a] Mr Hooper were unfounded and that Mr Poulter was a proper person to manage the poorhouse.'[35]

When the New Poor Law was imposed on Sevenoaks in April 1835 the Union Board of Guardians had to be formed and the new system introduced. There was considerable local opposition to this attempt at central government control. Local interests hoped that the old workhouse on St John's Hill could be enlarged to serve as the Union building, although by early 1840 it was overcrowded, with 347 inmates. A wooden building was added in August 1841, but conditions remained squalid and insanitary. A shocking story of the dreadful treatment endured by the inmates of the old Sevenoaks workhouse was revealed in the national press in 1841. It concerned 16-year-old Lucy Welch, who died in 'an agony of neglected disease and disappointed hope'. *The Times* rounded on the Sevenoaks Poor Law Guardians, medical practitioners and others responsible. Revealingly, it laid the blame for the 'loathsome inhumanities' she and others endured on the operation of the New Poor Law itself, which had become the 'price the poor pay for the money which the New Poor Law has saved to their betters'.[36] The stinging criticism of *The Times* was that 'In no part of England was the mal-administration of the old poor law greater, or the demoralization of the labouring classes apparently more complete' than in the Sevenoaks area.[37] The 1834 Act was acceptable if – despite its undoubted harshness and the indignity of removing choice of association – it succeeded in removing the risk of starvation to the poor. But if, as in the Sevenoaks case, it merely intensified those risks within a state-administered environment even more damaging to health and welfare than the status quo ante, this was totally unacceptable. The state's job, it was by then widely accepted even at that early date, was to mitigate risk, not grossly exacerbate it. The temperature was cooled only when the St John's Hill workhouse was closed, although building the new one at Sundridge, able to accommodate 500 men, women and children, was a long-drawn-out process not completed until 1845. The regime remained harsh but never again did Guardians have to suffer the opprobrium of 1841.

---

34 *Kentish Gazette* (henceforth *KG*), 15 Sept. 1835, pp. 2, 4; Private archives, Knight, *Diaries*, vol. 2, 5 Sept. 1835. For more on the Templemore incident see Taylor, 'One for the (farm) workers?', pp. 137–60.

35 Private archives, Knight, *Diaries*, vol. 1, 17 May 1832.

36 *The Times*, 10 Nov. 1841, p. 4; 29 Nov. 1841, p. 4; 3 Dec. 1841, p. 4.

37 *The Times*, 12 Jan. 1842, p. 5. Contemporary satirical papers compared the accommodation at the St John's workhouse unfavourably with that provided for Prince Albert's hounds at Windsor: *Punch*, 11 Dec. 1841, p. 256; *Penny Satirist*, 18 Dec. 1841, p. 1; *The Age*, 19 Dec. 1841, p. 404.

Dissent, revival and conflict

Nor were ideas and beliefs, especially those motivated by religious feeling, static in west Kent in the nineteenth century. Many local Anglican clergy viewed dissenters, especially nonconformist clergymen, with hostile eyes, as a divisive influence in the parish. As the rector of Chelsfield wrote, 'the agricultural labourer will prefer any kind of dissenting place of worship to that of the established Church which he associates with the idea of authority and oppression'.[38] But social class and levels of personal wealth also divided Anglican clergy one from another. For example, Curteis of Sevenoaks had a very well-funded living of over £900 a year, while the Rev. J. Hall, a minister for 26 years and incumbent at Knockholt for 15 years, had to manage on a mere £29.[39]

More bitterness came when rifts opened between low Church adherents, often evangelicals, and high Churchmen, many of whom embraced ritualism or the Tractarian ideas of the Oxford Movement of the 1830s. Ritualism sought to restore the Church of England to what its followers believed to be the sacramental glory of pre-Reformation Catholicism, but without the pope. These ideas deeply divided Anglican clergy and placed some extreme ritualists who adorned their churches with furnishings and symbols outside the law. In west Kent the most extreme ritualist church was St Martin's at Brasted, where the Rev. Dr William Hodge Mills, a distinguished Orientalist, introduced ritualistic services during the 1840s, incurring the censure of many parishioners and the archbishop of Canterbury.[40]

At Sevenoaks, the new rector, Thomas Sackville Curteis, set about refurbishing the parish church in the mid-1870s. He also introduced ritualistic forms of service that caused 'great dissatisfaction', so that 'some who attend the ordinary services abstain from partaking of the Holy Communion'.[41] The parish clerk mourned the loss of 'what was' the 'Protestant Church', while evangelical William Thompson, a churchwarden and a wealthy tea-broker, left St Nicholas and successfully petitioned the archbishop for a separate parish and church, which he agreed to finance on his Kippington estate.[42] Kippington became a separate parish in 1878.[43] This all shows that religious choice flourished in the nineteenth century, such that in Sevenoaks in 1900 there were more than a dozen Christian churches, three times the number a century earlier.

---

38 Lambeth Palace Library (LPL) Visitation returns VG3/5a, The Rev. Folliot Baugh to Archibald Tait, Archbishop of Canterbury, 1876, quoted by Geoffrey Copus, *Chelsfield chronicles 1450–1920* (Chelsfield, 2003), p. 93. See also Nigel Yates, Robert Hume and Paul Hastings, *Religion and society in Kent, 1640–1914* (Woodbridge, 1994), pp. 68–80.

39 *KG*, 25 Jan. 1870, p. 4, a report widely published in the national and provincial press.

40 Sevenoaks Library F574. J.W. Faulkner, *Answer to the reply of the Rev. Dr. Mills to the address of the parishioners of Brasted Kent* (1851).

41 *Kent & Sussex Courier* (henceforth *KSC*), 26 March 1876, p. 6; 22 Jan. 1875, p. 7.

42 Sevenoaks Library D1002. 'May 5 1878. The unhappy day. Thoughts on the Services in Sevenoaks dear. What was Protestant Church. By Mr. Chas Winn. Parish Clerk'.

43 H.W. Standen, *Kippington in Kent: its history and its churches* (Sevenoaks, 1958), chs 2 and 3.

Christian church buildings completed in Sevenoaks, 1716–1890

Medieval	St Nicholas parish church (Anglican)
1716	Bessel Green Baptist (became Unitarian 1770)
1760	Bessels Green Baptist
1774	Wesleyan Methodist chapel (later buildings 1854 and 1904)
1776	Particular Baptist High Street (later Vine Baptist 1887)
1822	Chapel of ease [St George] Weald (Anglican)
1825	Chapel of ease [St Mary the Virgin] Riverhead (Anglican)
1842	Bethel Chapel, Hartslands (General Baptist/Congregational)
1858	Chapel of ease [St John the Baptist] St John's Hill (Anglican)
1866	St John's Hill (Congregational)
1878	St Luke's (Anglican)
1880	St Mary, Kippington (Anglican)
1884	St Thomas's (Roman Catholic)
c.1890	Vine chapel (Brethren)

Other religious conflicts

New opportunities for and choices of religious adherence expanded greatly after the 1840s, for reasons including the growing acceptance of dissent, increased literacy and better communications, especially with nascent faith movements in the United States. New religious forms that intruded into west Kent excited support and opposition, for exercising choice often implies conflict, as much in religious as in political discourse. The Latter Day Saints, or Mormons, an American sect, from the 1840s onwards engaged in mission work in rural west Kent, attracting a few converts mainly from among poorer people. Local Christians, particularly nonconformists, rigorously opposed Mormon heretical ideas and interrupted outdoor meetings in Tunbridge Wells, Chelsfield and villages along the Darent Valley. At Eynsford 'some young men of the village put them [the Mormons] to flight by pelting them with rotten eggs, and other similar missiles'.[44] Nevertheless, later a small Mormon meeting was established at Chelsfield and several people from the village migrated to Utah, including 30-year-old James Jackson, a butcher from Pratts Bottom.[45]

A new and unconventional Christian organisation that disturbed the peace and challenged people was the Salvation Army. When the uniformed men and women,

---

44 *SEG*, 31 June 1857, p. 4; for Mormonism in Kent see *Belfast News Letter*, 19 Sept. 1857, p. 6; *MJ*, 21 Aug. 1855, p. 8; *KG*, 22 Sept. 1857, p. 4; *KSC*, 3 July 1908, p. 10.

45 Copus, *Chelsfield chronicles*, chapter 10. Sue Barton, *Pratts Bottom. A journey through life* (Pratts Bottom, 2009), pp. 184–5.

along with their band, came to Sevenoaks in autumn 1887 and marched to the Baptist church in the town centre, the column was pelted with stones by 'the rough element' of the town generally known as the 'Skeleton Army'.[46] In Sevenoaks a handful of Salvationists were convicted of blocking the London Road; they refused to pay fines and were imprisoned. The Skeleton Army in the town remained a persistent nuisance in 1887–8, with assaults on individuals and the disruption of indoor and outdoor services, seemingly without facing prosecution.[47] There is no firm evidence that these bully boys were encouraged by local publicans, brewers and Anglican clergy, as happened elsewhere in southern England, but they did not condemn the violence either.[48]

Another national evangelistic organisation that took root among nonconformists in Sevenoaks was the Pleasant Sunday Afternoon (PSA) movement, founded in 1875, which offered informal 'brief, bright and brotherly' meetings. This became the Brotherhood Movement in the 1890s, a non-uniformed body that also embraced ideas of temperance, pacifism and moral and social self-improvement.[49] There was also the Young Men's Christian Association, and its parallel body for women, and Christian Endeavour. Uniformed organisations for young people included the Boys' Brigades, Church Lads' Brigade and, later, the Boy Scouts. The degree of success that attended these efforts is hard to judge; they probably helped reduce the exit from churches, but not to any great extent.

Mixing religion and politics

Before looking at the complex inter-mix of religion and politics, ideas and beliefs, it is important to reject stereotypical images. Christians may have been sober and often serious-minded women and men. Yet most were not miserable or inhibited. They enjoyed pleasure and relaxation, and were often open-minded in discussion, probably less quick to condemn people than others, and forward in rendering aid to neighbours and the less fortunate. Indeed, much nineteenth-century social work, reform and humanitarian endeavour was initiated by Christians. Some local Christians were very active in promoting political change and did not eschew the company of radically minded and unconventional people. For example, Albert Bath befriended freethinker and atheist William Bradlaugh when he visited Sevenoaks in 1888,[50] while Lilian Gilchrist Thompson (1859–1947), wife of the vicar of Kippington, Percy Thompson, favoured politicians generally unpopular in conservative Sevenoaks. She was active in promoting women's rights, including

---

46   *SC*, 20 April 1888, p. 4.

47   *KSC*, 2 March 1888, p. 8; *SC*, 1 June 1888, p. 4.

48   See *SC*, 18 Nov. 1904, p. 5.

49   Largely neglected by historians, the PSA/Brotherhood Movement flourished from 1875 until the inter-war years.

50   *SEG*, 6 Feb. 1888, p. 3.

suffrage, and provided a radical and a reforming voice on the Sevenoaks Urban District Council demanding improved housing for the poor. Her friend Margaret Bondfield, the first woman member of the cabinet, wrote of her that she often entertained in the vicarage leading Labour politicians such as John Burns and Keir Hardie.[51]

Politics, in its widest sense, involved lobbying, pressure groups, parties and demonstrations about issues of concern to the people of the town as well as national and global matters. But other issues roused great controversy, accompanied by rumbustious meetings. They included such wide-ranging issues as the level of local rates, roads and turnpikes, levies on hops, tithes, the costs of postal and railway services, Sunday observance, the presence of military units in the town and high-handed action by landowners.

Political battles

The Local Board became an early forum for lively political debate, especially about major capital projects such as the new drainage system and its cost to local ratepayers. From the available evidence, however, it is difficult to discern any substantial party political differences among members on the Local Board. One or two members were dominant personalities, but perhaps more significant was their experience in commercial business or public affairs. Certainly, the religious denomination of candidates for office carried some weight with electors, but so did their views on the level of local rates. One obvious and volatile division within the Board was between 'progressives', who were prepared to entertain an increase in local rates for public health improvement, and those 'economists' who opposed such expenditure. Allied, largely to the former, was a willingness to embrace municipalisation – the Board buying the local Water Works Company in 1877, for example.[52] Many Liberals were as eager to limit local rates as were Tories.[53] What appears to have been decisive in Sevenoaks were the political skills and progressive passions of James German. He had been a youthful reforming mayor of Preston, his home town, had gained further skills as a businessman and had made repeated, unsuccessful, attempts to enter parliament as a Liberal. He had political know-how, in public health a moral cause to fight for, and he knew how to gain support, particularly that of the press. It was largely due to German's energies and tenacious skills that Sevenoaks acquired a main drainage system by 1882.[54]

---

51   *The Times*, 9 June 1947, p. 7, Obituary.

52   *KSC*, 5 Dec. 1877, p. 3.

53   An editorial in the *SC*, 16 March 1883, p. 2, said that rates had recently been reduced 'for party purposes out of regard for the exigencies of the approaching election'.

54   Iain Taylor, 'Not going through the motions: Sevenoaks, sewage and selfless ambition, 1871–1882', *International Journal of Regional and Local History*, 9/2 (2014), pp. 123–39.

Sevenoaks local government in the late nineteenth century

The lists below indicate continuity of service by individuals, their occupations, and known or possible political allegiances. It is not possible to see how electors in different parts of Sevenoaks voted for the Local Board and its successor the SUDC, as elections were based on a single list of names for the whole area, which was not divided into local wards until 1948.

Local Board 1871: Baron Buckhurst (chairman), gent; Multon Lambarde, gent; James German, gent; William James Thompson, gent; John Palmer; Samuel Slater; Samuel Bligh, farmer and brewer; E.E. Cronk; T. Hancock; W. Pawley; James W. Whibley; and S. Young.

Local Board 1883: Rev. John Jackson, Baptist minister and schoolmaster (Lib); H. Thompson, surgeon; C. Waterhouse, retired farmer; Thomas Potter, architect (Con); W.H. Stepney, vestry clerk; C.W. Smith, gent; W. F. Morgan, gent; J.B. Nunn, solicitor; J. Moore jnr, gent.

SUDC December 1894 (with known political allegiance and number of votes received) Admiral Henry Miller (chairman), Con, 393; Rev. John Jackson, schoolmaster and Baptist minister, Lib, 354; Thomas Potter, architect and the local Conservative party agent, Con, 418; John F. Carnell, Director Gas and Water Cos, Con, 393; Frederick Wells, 338; Dr Herbert Thompson, medical doctor, 396 (resigned June 1896); Fred Hooker, GPO employee ('Progressive'/Liberal), 421; Arthur Hickmott, draper (Independent Labour Party, 361); George S. Oldfield, Anglican, 432; Henry Swaffield, gent., Wesleyan, Con, 507; Thomas E. Killick, Con, 365; William H. Stepney, vestry clerk and tax collector, Lib, 49.

Sources: *Maidstone Journal*, 27 December 1894, p. 6, and political allegiance taken from other newspapers.

SUDC 1898: Admiral Miller; Colonel Underwood; Rev. John Jackson; Thomas Potter; W.H. Stepney (d. 1906); Alfred A. Clark; John F. Carnell; C.H.B. Ince, editor of *Local Government Journal*; Arthur Hickmott; C.E. Corke; Fred Hooker.

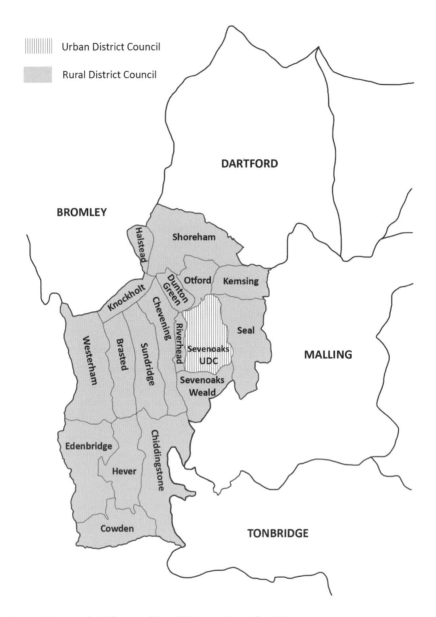

|||||||||| Urban District Council

Rural District Council

DARTFORD

BROMLEY

Halstead

Shoreham

Dunton Green

Otford

Kemsing

Knockholt

Chevening

Riverhead

Seal

Westerham

Brasted

Sundridge

Sevenoaks UDC

MALLING

Sevenoaks Weald

Edenbridge

Chiddingstone

Hever

Cowden

TONBRIDGE

Map 12 Sevenoaks Urban and Rural District Councils, 1894.
Following the reform of County government and the creation of the Kent County Council in 1888, new local government administrative boundaries were agreed in 1894. Sevenoaks town became an Urban District Council with an elected Council of 12 people who served for three years. The villages of Riverhead and Weald were created as new civil parishes and formed part of the new Rural District Council along with parishes that had constituted the Sevenoaks Poor Law Union and the Rural Sanitary Board created in 1872. Local government became more representative than it had ever been. Both the UDC and the RDC had officers who dealt with the collection of local rates, highways, drainage, public health, water supply, parks, and cemeteries. *Source: SC*, 27 November 1894, p. 6.

When did partisan allegiances begin to manifest themselves in the local politics of Sevenoaks? The absence of party spirit on the Local Board at its instigation in 1871 was welcomed: 'we are glad to find that politics are excluded in the selection', upholding the idea that all were working for the public good.[55] But clearly the level of local rates and how they were spent divided members, with certain contestants at most elections claiming support for 'economy with efficiency' or opposing any further 'burden' on local ratepayers. There were also growing contests, which crossed social class boundaries, between the commercial centre of the town and its northern 'suburban periphery'. An Organisation of Ratepayers existed in 1883, presided over by the solicitor John Moxon Clabon. It briefly flourished to oppose additional expenditure and provision of elementary education paid for from local rates.[56]

In October 1880 a Sevenoaks Commercial Association (SCA) was formed, its object being 'the discussion, and advancement of matters of General interest to the town and the Local Board District, and the promotion of … those connected with its commerce'. Commerce, indeed, indicated the membership and primary interest of the SCA – a concern for the prosperity of the town reflected in a proposal to remove the disruptive weekly cattle market from the High Street, shorter days for shop workers – the 'early closing movement' – and, importantly, 'the preservation of their [members'] rights as tradesmen of the town'.[57] A survey of the names of members of the SCA shows that this was largely a 'Conservative' body, many of its members being either active in or signed up to the Conservative cause and the Primrose League. A local response to the SCA saw it as an attempt to dominate the Local Board. A St John's Ratepayers Association, formed in early 1882, feared that in the forthcoming Local Board elections SCA candidates, if elected, 'will have the effect of practically placing the Government of the Town in the hands of the Commercial Association'.[58] In the Local Board elections James German was returned on a St John's 'ticket' and four of the candidates supported by the SCA were defeated.[59] This was localised politics in the town, St John's from the margin versus the centre, another reason perhaps why this northern 'suburb', with its growing working-class population, embraced more 'progressive' views over the next two decades.

A broader-based local body was created in the Residents of Sevenoaks Association, which was formed in 1885 initially in response to the Knole access dispute. Its members, 50 to 60 in number, constituted a watch on local expenditure.[60] The Association appears to have failed as a result of a lack of popular support, its place being taken in March 1892 by the Sevenoaks Ratepayers' Association (SRA). It

---

55 *SEG*, 9 Sept. 1871, p. 3.

56 *SC*, 3 Aug. 1883, p. 4. Clabon (1815–98), a JP, served on the Local Board from 1886 to 1890.

57 *SC*, 2 Dec. 1881, p. 5.

58 *SC*, 31 March 1881, p. 4; 7 April 1882, p. 5.

59 *SC*, 14 April 1882, p. 5. The SCA is not mentioned in the local press after mid-1882.

60 *SC*, 29 May 1885, p. 5, and *SC*, 19 March 1886, p. 4.

was, said W.H. Stepney, 'a body resuscitating from the old association', and perhaps he knew this having been active in the earlier body.[61] In spite of this disclaimer, it did have a moral concern that overrode rates – the welfare of recipients of poor relief. Thus, the SRA supported four candidates for election as Guardians in April 1892, although only one, Albert Bath, was elected. Despite this seeming political intervention, the SRA, stated the Rev. Charles Rudge, 'knew nothing about religion as an association, just as they knew nothing about politics … but [being] a body of men and ratepayers, so that their voices were unanimous in public affairs'.[62]

Left-wing activity flowered in west Kent in the 1890s. Arthur Hickmott, a member of the Independent Labour Party (ILP), helped form the Sevenoaks Progressive Association (SPA) and a branch of the Socialist Labour League.[63] In 1881 the Rev. John Jackson, formerly Baptist minister in Sevenoaks, wrote 'the local government of a town as a rule more directly affects the inhabitants than almost any Parliamentary measure could do'.[64] He was probably correct, and his own interests (as an elected Board member) were in improving the physical environment of the town, but at a price that kept the rates as low as possible. As a dissenter he opposed support of parochial schools from the rates. However, central government was placing increasing demands on local authorities, and Sevenoaks town became an urban district, the old Sevenoaks Sanitary Authority became a rural district council,[65] and parishes, including Riverhead and Sevenoaks Weald, had their own mini 'parliaments' or parish councils.

The idea that the Local Board had not been shaped by politics was probably wishful thinking. In the run-up to the election for the new SUDC in late 1894 ten of the candidates, all members of the Board, publicly stated that they hoped for a continuation of a system that had functioned 'without recognising either sect or party'.[66] Ten of the candidates may have thought they were non-political, but two who were elected did not: Arthur Hickmott, who stood for the Independent Labour Party, and Fred Hooker, who announced that he was a 'Progressive'.[67] Eighteen candidates stood for election to the 12-man SUDC. However, the actual elections showed little evidence of political dissonance, being 'largely influenced as to whether the parochial cemetery [at St Nicholas] should be consecrated or simply

---

61 *SC*, 25 March 1892, p. 8; 3 June 1892, p. 8.

62 *SC*, 1 April 1892, p. 4, 8; 14 April 1892, p. 8.

63 See Julian Wilson, *Revolutionary Tunbridge Wells. The remarkable role of Tunbridge Wells and the development of revolutionary politics in Britain 1884–1919* (Tunbridge Wells, 2018), pp. 116–17.

64 *SC*, 4 March 1881, p. 4.

65 The SRDC, effectively a continuation of the old Board of Guardians, met in the Sundridge Workhouse.

66 *MJ*, 13 Dec. 1894, p. 4. The statement was dated October 1894.

67 *Salisbury Times*, 23 Nov. 1894, p. 7. The Independent Labour Party was founded in 1893; a Sevenoaks branch was formed by early 1894 with Hickmott as secretary: *SC*, 5 May 1894, p. 5. There was a Sevenoaks Fabian Group: see *Dover Express*, 7 July 1893, p. 5.

dedicated'.[68] This issue divided the Church faction from dissenters and was again a live issue when the municipal cemetery was opened 12 years later.

Most of those elected regarded themselves as 'independent', but several carried a party label and party politics gradually intruded; for example, when the chair of the SUDC was contested in 1900, John Jackson deplored that 'there was a considerable amount of talk going on outside the Council and a kind of conspiracy in force to endeavour to give colour to the election of a chairman'. The ensuing vote between Henry Swaffield and C.H.B. Ince was tied and W.H. Stepney was elected as vice-chairman, with Swaffield chairman *pro tem*.[69]

'Progressives' or modernisers continued to battle in the Council with those who advocated 'efficiency with economy'; in 1900 James Outram, a saddle and harness maker, sought to represent the business interests of the town with regard to 'due economy'.[70] 'Progressives' were not alone in suggesting that the SUDC buy the local waterworks, and similar ideas were expressed in Council about public ownership of gas and electricity supply.[71] Their opponents rebutted these claims by talking of 'extravagant municipal trading schemes' and dismissed proposals for 'lighting the Town by electricity'.[72]

Education

The provision of local schools became a contested issue for both political and religious reasons. After the 1860s successive governments tried to develop a nation-wide system of elementary education. Under the Education Act 1870, Gladstone's Liberal government established locally elected school boards empowered to raise rates to build and support new schools in order to 'fill up gaps' in elementary educational provision.[73] Two new Board schools were built in Sevenoaks, which, along with voluntary schools run by the Church of England, provided a basic education for the town's growing number of children.

The religious tensions between 'Churchmen' and dissenters were graphically displayed in the elections for the Sevenoaks School Board in June 1884. Rival committees campaigned for each faction, the wealthier Anglicans arguing for the maintenance of the *status quo* and 'economy' and the nonconformists emphasising religious 'principle' and the need for further elementary school accommodation. Strong support for the three nonconformist candidates who were elected appears to have come mainly from the St John's district. The result was a new Board balanced

---

68 *London Evening Standard*, 18 Dec. 1894, p. 2, *MJ*, 6 Dec. 1894, p. 6.

69 *SC*, 20 April 1900, p. 5.

70 *SC*, 30 March 1900, p. 4.

71 *SC*, 30 March 1900, p. 4; 27 March 1908, p. 4; 3 April 1908, p. 5; 25 March 1910, p. 4.

72 *SC*, 3 April 1903, p. 5; 3 April 1908, p. 5; 23 Feb. 1912, p. 4.

73 'Fill the gaps', the phrase used by W.E. Forster when introducing the Education Act 1870.

in its membership.[74] An additional irritant for both factions was the creation of a Roman Catholic school in Hartslands in 1881.

The 1902 Education Act tried to rectify the shortcomings of earlier legislation, but it unleashed a torrent of fury from nonconformists, who opposed 'Rome on the Rates'. In Sevenoaks opposition to the Act that year coincided with a by-election largely fought on the question of education. Prominent nonconformists, such as Dr John Clifford, stormed the electoral stump and sitting Conservative MP, Henry Forster, saw his previous majority (in 1900) slashed from 4,812 to 891; he had to refight his seat as he had accepted an office of profit under the crown as a lord commissioner of the treasury. Subsequently a Sevenoaks Passive Resistance Committee was created; its manifesto stated that the Act 'is an attack on Evangelical religion' to which 'WE WILL NOT SUBMIT'.[75] Its members were 'Christian men [who] refused voluntarily to pay that portion of the new Educational Rate which is levied for the support of Denominational Schools', which, across the country, were 'entirely in the hands of clerical managers'.[76] Passive resistance continued until 1906, with some defendants (men and women) appearing repeatedly before the bench and their goods being distrained, although on several occasions local auctioneers refused to handle them.[77]

Open spaces and cemeteries

A further public concern for working-class people, who comprised most of Sevenoaks' population but were barely represented on the SUDC, was for recreational space. 'Re-creation' then had a special meaning: relaxation and leisure away from the long hours of work. Providing parks and gardens, and securing access to Knole Park, were aims widely acceptable to most members of the SUDC. A children's recreation ground on the rates was another issue, especially when it was proposed that land should be bought that might otherwise be used for housing, which would in turn boost the number of ratepayers and thus, potentially, reduce the tax burden.

Eventually open spaces also became a hot political issue. Hickmott fought to safeguard common land threatened with enclosure, arguing that open spaces were vital for the community: 'The "lungs" of a district are too valuable an asset to part with lightly', he told his fellow council members.[78] At the election of 1909 the need for a children's recreation ground was mooted by W.H. Counsell, a local

---

74 The rival arguments were paraded in letters and reports in issues of the *Sevenoaks Chronicle* from March to June 1884.

75 'Manifesto of the Sevenoaks Passive Resistance Committee', dd. June 1903; *SC*, 3 July 1903, p. 8.

76 *KSC*, 2 Sept. 1904, p. 5.

77 *SC*, 6 April 1906, p. 5; see also Taylor, 'Pressure groups', p. 342.

78 *SC*, 24 Feb. 1905, p. 4.

schoolteacher, as his main issue.[79] Once elected to the SUDC, Counsell helped push the case for the purchase of the 12.5-acre Holly Bush Lane site as a recreation ground. Francis Swanzy agreed to advance £1,000 for it, which persuaded even a die-hard 'economist' councillor such as Jabez Mann to change his mind and support the scheme. Even so, five councillors remained resolutely opposed to this 'extravagant expenditure', one collecting 303 signatures. They argued for a cheaper site north of the Bat and Ball and pushed for a reduction in the rates.[80] After much debate, and a public enquiry, the site was bought and the town got its recreation ground. In 1914 public baths, paid for by wealthy benefactor Edward Kraftmeier, were opened on land owned by the SUDC adjoining its offices (see Plate 2).

Anxieties about the shortage of space in St Nicholas cemetery were voiced in the 1880s. A few years later fears were raised that the 'New Cemetery' (opened in 1863) was in danger of polluting the nearby town's water supply in Oak Lane.[81] Those fears resurfaced in 1909–10 and led to large-scale protests in the town centre, answered by costly scientific tests on the purity and quality of the local water supply. By then a new municipal cemetery had been opened on the Seal Road in 1906, but even this was dogged by an at times bitter sectarian controversy over whether the land should be consecrated, as required by Anglicans, or dedicated, as demanded by dissenters.[82] The decision, reached with Solomonic wisdom, was to divide the new cemetery equally into two, one part consecrated, the other dedicated.

Housing

The provision of good accommodation for working-class people in Sevenoaks became a major political issue in the later nineteenth century. Daniel Grover's initiative in building Hartslands from the late 1830s had been a straightforward commercial venture. The working-class development at Lime Tree Walk forty years later, however, was both a commercial venture and an overt political statement made by a committed Liberal party supporter, Thomas Graham Jackson, who despised the social engineering that spatially separated poor from rich.[83] Improved housing was closely linked to the need to replace poor-quality private dwellings, such as the slums at the heart of the town and in some rural areas. The Workmen's Dwellings Act 1890 enabled local boards to raise money and build such houses, a measure urged on the Board and the subsequent SUDC by various members, although few in Sevenoaks wanted it done on the rates. Initially such provision was largely left to private individuals and enterprise, such as the artisans' and tenants' organisations.

---

79 *SC*, 2 April 1909, p. 8.

80 *SC*, 28 Jan. 1910, p. 8. Henry Forster, the local MP, supported the Holly Bush proposal.

81 *SC*, 27 May 1892, p. 5.

82 *SC*, 22 June 1906, p. 8.

83 Nicholas Jackson, *Recollections of the life and travels of a Victorian architect: Thomas Graham Jackson, 1835–1924* (London, 2003), p. 130.

The first public activity was in 1896 by the Newington Vestry, in London, which owned a refuse site on the Otford Road. 'Six well-built workmen's dwellings, which are let to the Vestry Workmen' were constructed at a weekly rent of 6s. The interest in similar possible schemes was such that a £5 prize for 'best design and specification of working-class housing at Sevenoaks' brought in 48 entries.[84] The only houses fully funded by west Kent local authorities in this period, the precursors of the council house boom of the 1920s, were the six 'Pioneer Cottages' built in Penshurst in 1900, thanks to the stubborn energy of Jane Escombe. They cost £250 each and were rented at 5s a week. The first land acquired by the SUDC for that purpose was at Greatness in 1914. Even in leafy west Kent by this period 'Socialist ideas had begun to permeate the least likely places.'[85]

Religious decline

Religious belief appears to have declined across every social class in the late nineteenth century. This was visible in falling church attendance by the 1870s, which continued into the early twentieth century. Although there are no figures of regular church attendance in west Kent for this period, a *Daily News* survey in London in 1902–3 showed that regular adult worshippers comprised 11.7 per cent of the population in poor districts, 16.1 per cent in upper-working-class districts, and 36.8 per cent in the wealthy suburbs.[86] A similar pattern probably prevailed then in west Kent. The trend was visible in many contemporary informal comments about non-attendance and assessments of the reasons for it. Thus, in 1883 the vicar of St John's thought it worthwhile to warn his parishioners of 'a large sect of persons who exist in the present day, and call themselves scientific philosophers'.[87] One of Mayhew's interviewees told him 'I never go to church. I used to go when I was a little child in Sevenoaks. … I've forgot what the inside of church is like.'[88] Some people probably attended church out of a sense of respectability, and at the same time fashioned a set of personal religious beliefs with which they felt comfortable.

That said, certain churches had growing congregations. One example was St Nicholas, Sevenoaks, following the change of minister in 1907, when the high church and never very popular T.S. Curteis was succeeded by the evangelical John Rooker. Sunday schools, which also had a semi-secular role as promoters of literacy

---

84   Arthur Hickmott, *Houses for the people* (London, 1897), pp. 8–9, 11.

85   Patricia Hollis, *Ladies elect: women in English local government, 1865–1914* (Oxford, 1987), pp. 367–9. Jane Escombe was elected to Penshurst Parish Council in 1895, for more see her *Five years: fruits of the Parish Council Act* (London, 1901), p. 10; Wilson, *Revolutionary Tunbridge Wells*, p. 94.

86   Richard Mudie-Smith (ed.), *The religious life of London* (London, 1904). See also K. Theodore Hoppen, *The mid-Victorian generation, 1846–86* (Oxford, 1998), chapter 12, 'Godly People'.

87   *SC*, 12 Oct. 1883, p. 6.

88   Henry Mayhew, *London labour and the London poor*, vol. 1 (London, 1851), p. 100.

and numeracy, were first recorded at St Nicholas in the late 1790s.[89] Their presence acknowledged that children needed to be taught separately from adults, and that this encouraged life-long attendance at church. Thereafter they grew in importance as an essential component of nearly all churches, although congregations divided by social class commonly provided separate Sunday schools for working-class children. The Wesleyan chapel in Bank Street, Sevenoaks added a Sunday school room to its church building in 1862, at a cost of £300.[90] By 1911 it is estimated that over six million children nationwide attended Sunday school. Late in the nineteenth century a variety of initiatives were adopted to retain or to regain people for the churches, all of which were tried in Sevenoaks and in neighbouring communities. These ranged widely, often with a social and economic purpose: slate clubs; boot and clothing clubs; choirs and bands; sporting activities; and camping holidays.

In conclusion, in both the political and religious arenas pluralism (or choice) was enhanced as the nineteenth century progressed. Despite later numerical decline, many new churches were built across west Kent by Anglican and dissenting Protestants and Roman Catholics. Non-Christian bodies such as Unitarians, Mormons and Christian Scientists had meeting houses in west Kent, and even unbelief thrived, although the *Chronicle* rejected any 'special privilege in favour of avowed atheism' during the Bradlaugh case.[91] A widening electorate challenged the status quo in demanding a greater say in the exercise of power and authority, but that came at a price, as rates and tithes were a focus for ongoing conflict through the nineteenth century, not least because the wealthy were aware that the less well-off were seeking to transfer the financial risks of social and other improvements from themselves to the ratepayers. Few relished that prospect, although the simultaneous and increasingly widely accepted trend towards greater accountability made it far harder for them to escape such responsibilities in the long term.

New political divisions opened as the electorate increased. New institutions, especially the Local Board, were neither designed nor employed as overt 'party' platforms, but they could be used by canny political operators such as James German to push through major changes in the face of stiff opposition. By the time the Urban and Rural District Councils were in place in the 1890s, although appearing little changed from their predecessors, they offered firmer platforms for alternative political views.

---

89   KHLC P330/8/1, St Nicholas, Sevenoaks, Vestry minutes, 15 Nov. 1798.

90   This was the case for St Nicholas and for the Congregational church on St John's Hill; see Sarah Thorne, 'Protestant ethics and the spirit of imperialism: British Congregationalists and the London Missionary Society 1795–1925', PhD thesis (University of Michigan, 1990), pp. 353–4. The Congregational chapel in Hartslands was not segregated because where it 'is situated is inhabited chiefly by the poor'; see *Maidstone Telegraph* (henceforth *MT*), 15 Aug. 1863, p. 5.

91   *SC*, 10 July 1885, p. 4. Atheist and republican Bradlaugh was elected to the House of Commons in 1880. He achieved notoriety when he was precluded from taking his seat because he refused to subscribe to the oath of allegiance to God and monarch.

To what extent had the lower classes of Sevenoaks succeeded in exercising some say in who exerted power and authority over them by 1914? They still had little or no *direct* influence over the direction of political debate or policymaking. But, *indirectly*, several powerful radical voices were by then speaking up for ordinary people. Different in many ways, men and women such as German, Bath, Hickmott, Hooker, Swanzy, Escombe and the Thompsons all shared a concern for the economic and communal welfare of the working classes and the risks they faced daily, hence their efforts to reduce working hours, provide good housing and advance opportunities for local education and leisure.

That was very different from the top-down paternalistic charity displayed by Sackville, Amherst and Stanhope earlier in the century. They were no doubt sincere in their desire to improve the economic lot of local labourers by giving doles of beef at Christmas or free firewood from Knole Park. But those aristocrats acted to reduce the risks to the lower orders primarily to uphold the political and social status quo, and certainly not to allow them any meaningful choice in how and by whom west Kent, let alone the country, was governed. The provincial voice of progressivism more accurately read contemporary demands for economic and social change and believed that it was vital to gradually extend opportunities for working people to have a permanent stake in the society in which they lived.

That laudable aim implied a constant struggle with those less amenable to social and political progress, especially if it implied a rise in the rates and a move away from ratepayers having exclusive authority, as illustrated in many protracted battles to advance the social welfare of the town. That also meant that social and political relations in the town were rarely as unified or contented as Sevenoaks – especially its more genteel citizens – wished to portray to the outside world. In the late nineteenth century the inhabitants of Hartslands and other working-class districts were engaged in a long-running dispute with the commercial sector as to the social and economic direction of travel of the town, losing when the annual fair closed in 1874, winning when Holly Bush recreation ground opened in 1910. It is no coincidence that winning was much easier and more likely when the working classes had the progressive voice as their proxy, as they did from the 1880s onwards.

But it is important to emphasise that life was not entirely about the local. Only 25 miles from London, west Kent was throughout the long nineteenth century always an interested spectator and often a significant player in many national and international political issues. The following chapter shows how and why many residents expressed choices in those areas – and with what results.

Chapter 4

Ideas, beliefs and values:
locality, nation and the world

Parish pump issues often revolved around individuals or groups seeking to enhance their own choices and/or reduce the risks to their own positions or wallets. National concerns, on the other hand, often turned on humanitarian questions, trying to protect those who were weak and vulnerable, such as American slaves or Greeks suffering Ottoman persecution, and seeking to project that moral imperative further by advancing the rights – and thus the choices – available to such groups. But enhancing the choices available to foreign victims could impact those campaigning on their behalf in perhaps unforeseen ways – for example, giving up sugar for moral reasons to do with slavery meant a deliberate *loss* of choice for those prepared to do so. Heavily involved politically, both at home and abroad, were religious dissenters, who represented what became known as the 'nonconformist conscience', a movement that reached the peak of its influence in the 1870s.

Both local and national were, however, similar, to the extent that they often consumed local political passions and contributed to the wider national canvas of a society in process of undergoing dramatic change. All this was driven, to a great degree, simply by west Kent's location in the south-east of England. Its relationship to London was always highly significant, so much so that the area 'experienced a high degree of political agitation over national issues, partly because of its proximity to the capital' in the early nineteenth century.[1]

National politics in west Kent

On the evening of Tuesday 13 June 1832, news arrived in Sevenoaks that the Reform Act had been passed by parliament. This was marked by the town being lit up, lights shining in many house windows. This exuberant response was a public expression of the views of local people on a national political issue in this most conservative of counties. At general elections in the early nineteenth century 'by convention, one

---

1   David R. Fisher (ed.), *History of parliament – the House of Commons 1820–1832, 2, constituencies Pt 1* (Cambridge, 2009), p. 523.

Whig and one Tory were returned unopposed, one from East Kent, one from West Kent'. This made the return of two Whig candidates in 1831 and 1832 surprising and illustrates the depth of local feeling over the Reform Act.[2] Precise analysis at a local level of why and how people's opinions were formed on the question of electoral reform is difficult. What is beyond doubt is the influence and power wielded by local aristocratic landowners such as the Marquess Camden, Earl Amherst and Viscount Holmesdale, and the wealthy gentry, such as Multon Lambarde and Thomas Austen. They formed the core of the local Tory party and saw themselves the God-given natural rulers of society, talking of 'Liberty, Loyalty, and Property'. Their influence is not hard to discern in the political affairs of west Kent.[3]

From 1832 west Kent had two members of parliament. Elections that decade were fought on partisan lines between Tories and Whigs, organised in their local Associations. Most electors had two votes. A few Sevenoaks electors (five out of 62 in 1835, for example) split their votes between candidates from both parties, some voting out of deference or for specific local reasons, others failing to vote at all.[4] In some ways west Kent seemed politically non-partisan, at least before the Tories assumed their now familiar hegemony in 1841, 1857 being an exceptional year. And later in the century, although elections were normally hard-fought contests, it seems to have been common for the politically minded to attend meetings of both the Conservative and Liberal parties in Sevenoaks.

Throughout the long nineteenth century Britain's domestic history was marked by major national political issues – the slave trade and slavery; Roman Catholic emancipation; parliamentary reform; the Corn Laws; temperance; and free trade – although opinions often cut across party lines and reflected deeper prevailing ideas, beliefs and values. In common with parish pump issues, national political matters were shot through by religious and moral considerations and questions of cost, whether it was the relief of the poor, improved working conditions and labour relations, the position of women and children, foreign policy, education, housing or social welfare.

The slave trade and slavery
One of the great moral political questions of the years 1770 to 1840 was the slave trade and slavery in Britain's overseas colonies. By 1760 British ships dominated the transatlantic slave trade and the slave economies of the Caribbean provided

---

2   Brian Atkinson, 'Conservative and Liberal: national politics in Kent from the late 1820s to 1914', in Frederick Lansberry (ed.), *Government and politics in Kent, 1640–1914* (Woodbridge, 2001), p. 141.

3   Good examples are conveyed in the reports of the 'Grand Review' given by Camden at Wilderness for the Duke of Wellington, *Morning Post*, 2 July 1832, p. 3; and the language used to describe the 'assemblage of the Nobility, gentry and yeomanry' at Morant's Court for the meeting of the Holmesdale Agricultural Association, *MJ*, 27 Oct. 1835, p. 4.

4   *The poll for the knights of the shire, to represent the western division of the county of Kent in parliament* (London, 1835), pp. 142–6.

a steady flow of goods and wealth into Britain, principally sugar, coffee, molasses and rum. It was difficult for almost anyone in British domestic commercial life, and consumers, not to be touched directly or indirectly by this brutal exploitation of black people. Families that had grown rich on slavery bought or owned estates in west Kent – people whom Cobbett later derisively referred to as 'West Indians, nabobs'.[5] Opposition to the slave trade was increasingly seen by Quakers and evangelicals as primarily a moral and political question.[6]

Supporters of the 'West Indian lobby' often argued that the Bible justified the slave trade and slavery, and their opponents quoted scripture to refute this. In May 1787 an extra-parliamentary campaign was launched from London by the Committee for Effecting the Abolition of the Slave Trade, founded and led by Christians. Kent, with its long coastline, naval dockyards and proximity to London (a large slave trading port) was not promising ground in which to plant similar organisations, and Thomas Clarkson, effectively the agent of the Committee, returned from his one-month tour of the county disappointed at the poor response.[7] However, a significant meeting place for those engaged in planning anti-slave-trade strategy was the village of Teston, above the Medway, where the Rev. James Ramsay was the incumbent. He owed his position to Elizabeth Bouverie of Teston House, which she shared with her friends the Middletons, who were also actively opposed to the slave trade. A few miles west, at Holwood, Keston, prime minister William Pitt met Grenville and Wilberforce and they decided to introduce a bill into parliament to end the slave trade. In the Sevenoaks area the London Committee had the support of Peter Nouaille, the silk manufacturer at Greatness, who gave five guineas to Committee funds in 1787.[8] In its campaign the Committee used a wide range of methods to promote their cause – pamphlets and books, meetings, petitions, local societies with subscribers and iconic medallions. The Committee argued that the nation would never truly prosper if it continued to thwart God's rules for humanity. After a 20-year campaign, the British slave trade was banned in 1807.

Slavery continued in the British colonies, and it was not until after the end of the war with France that campaigning for emancipation began. Petitions were sent to parliament from Tonbridge, Dartford and Sevenoaks in 1824, again from Tonbridge in 1826, and from Westerham, and from churches in Tunbridge Wells and Sevenoaks, in 1830. An Anti-Slavery Society was formed in Tunbridge Wells in 1831.[9] George Thompson (1807–78), on behalf of the newly formed Anti-Slavery

5   William Cobbett, *Rural rides* ([1830] London, 1973) vol. 1, p. 45.

6   Christopher Leslie Brown, *Moral capital: foundations of British abolitionism* (Chapel Hill, NC, 2012).

7   See David Killingray, 'Kent and the abolition of the slave trade: a county study, 1760s–1807', *Archæologia Cantiana*, CXXVII (2007), pp. 107–25; and a local study by Toby Ovenden, 'The Cobbs of Margate: evangelicalism and anti-slavery in the Isle of Thanet, 1787–1834', *Archæologia Cantiana*, CXXXIII (2013), pp. 1–32.

8   Society (Committee) for Effecting the Abolition of the Slave Trade, *List of the Society, for the purpose of effecting the abolition of the slave trade* (London, 1787).

9   *SEG*, 29 Nov. 1831, p. 4.

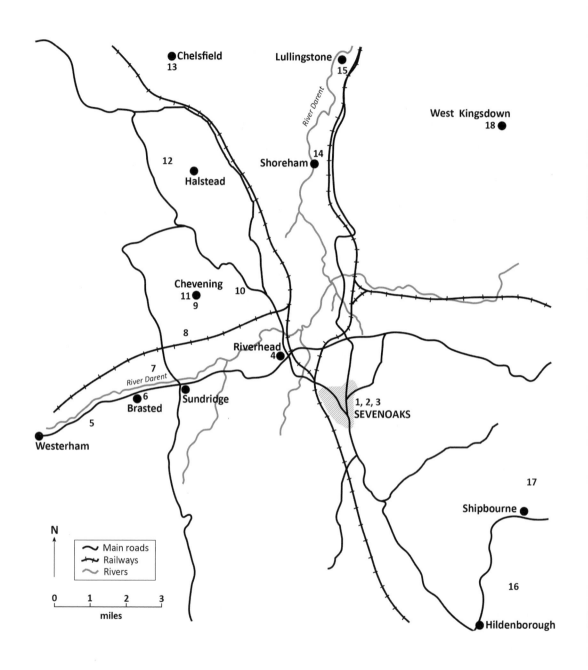

Map 13 Sevenoaks: beneficiaries from the slave trade and slavery, 1770–1840.

English/British ships dominated the trans-Atlantic slave trade from the 1660s to Britain's abolition of the trade in 1807. When slavery in the British colonies was abolished in the 1830s the vast sum of £20 million was raised by the Treasury to 'compensate' British slave owners for 'loss of property'. London's economy was closely involved with the slave trade and the exploitation of colonial slave labour. West Kent, adjacent to the capital, offered a pleasant environment in which to live for those who benefitted from this brutal business. People living in the Sevenoaks area who can be identified as direct and indirect beneficiaries of the slave trade and slavery, are shown on the map, while their involvement with slavery is indicated on the accompanying table as follows: P plantation owners; T trade interests; A agents for the West Indian colonies; C those receiving compensation (C* indicates those failing in such claims).

	Colony/interests
Sevenoaks	
1 Ann Aislabie (d.1843, widow of Benj. Aislabie)	P Dominica
2 Martin Blake	C* St Vincent
3 Mary Philippa Whitton	C St Kitts
Riverhead	
4 Rev John Thomas Wilgress (1775–1850), vicar of Riverhead 1831–50	C Antigua
Westerham	
5 John Henry Barrow, Hall Park (Valence)	P Barbados
Brasted	
6 John Pollard Mayers (1777–1853) (m. Ann Barrows of Valence,1800)	A Barbados
Sundridge	
7 William Manning MP (1763–1835) Coombe Bank	P St Kitts, Nevis
8 William Grassett (1775–1841), Ovenden House (m. Elizabeth Barrow of Valence, 1818)	P Barbados
Chevening	
9 Philip Henry Stanhope, Earl Stanhope, Chevening House	T
10 John Fry (1774–1847), Morants Court	P Jamaica
11 John Sargent, George Edward Arnold, (1748–1805)	T
12 John Atkins (1760–1838), Halsted Place	T
Chelsfield	
13 Rev. John Edward Tarleton (Rector)	C St Lucia, Grenada
Shoreham	
14 Sir John Humphrey Mildmay (1794–1853), (m. to a Baring – bankers)	C British Guiana
Lullingstone	
15 Rev. Edward Owen (b.1808), curate 1834–5	C Jamaica
Hildenborough	
16 George Athill (1806–57), Coldharbour ('a free man of colour'; farmer)	C* Antigua
Shipbourne	
17 John Simpson, Fairlawn	C Jamaica
West Kingsdown	
18 Duncan Campbell (1726–1823); (bought estate W. Kingsdown 1784)	P Jamaica

Source: Nicholas Draper, *The price of emancipation. Slave-ownership, compensation and British society at the end of slavery* (Cambridge, 2010), UCL Slave Compensation records.

Figure 4.1 William Wells Brown (1814–84). Brown was born a slave in Kentucky and 'kept functionally illiterate' until his escape at age 19. Brown became an active abolitionist and his *Narrative of William W. Brown. A Fugitive Slave* (1847) became a best-seller on both sides of the Atlantic. From 1849 to 1855 Brown lived in Europe, mainly in London, speaking against American slavery. In the autumn of 1853, he toured Kent and spoke in the old assembly room, Sevenoaks. *Source*: Drawing by Richard Woodman, 1855. National Portrait Gallery, Smithsonian Institution, NPG.2016.148. CC0

Agency Committee, toured Kent and Sussex in late 1831, his circuit including Tunbridge Wells, Tonbridge and Sevenoaks.[10] The result was several anti-slavery societies, including one in Tonbridge, although it is not known if Thompson lectured in Sevenoaks.[11] He probably did, as in mid-1832 a Sevenoaks Anti-Slavery Society had been established that sent ten pounds to the Agency Committee.[12]

Further petitions to end 'negro slavery' followed as emancipation became a major issue in 1833, when slaves in the British Empire were notionally set free.[13] At an emancipation meeting in London, in April 1833, 360 men signed a petition on the 'question of Negro Slavery'. Twenty-nine were from Kent, four from Sevenoaks – the Rev. Thomas Shirley, minister of the London Road Baptist church; Thomas Southern, a trustee of the Baptist church; George Pickance; and Henry Webb – and two from Westerham – Henry Warters and John Gibbard.[14] Emancipation took five years and a petition from Westerham urged the 'abolition of negro apprenticeship', which occurred in 1838.[15] By 1853 William Wells Brown, 'a fugitive slave', was lecturing in Sevenoaks about American slavery, including 'his own bondage, trials and escape' from captivity.[16]

Roman Catholic emancipation

Under the Test and Corporation Acts of 1662 both dissenting Protestants and Roman Catholics lacked full civil rights and were denied access to public office – a clear diminution of their choices that many felt was unfair and campaigned to remove. Catholics continued to be popularly viewed as subjects of the pope, a foreign monarch, their compromised loyalty posing a potential risk. This had become more important since the Irish Act of Union in 1800 and the formation of the Catholic Association by the Irish MP Daniel O'Connell in 1823. Catholic emancipation was largely dictated by events in Ireland. Although the number of recusants in Kent was relatively small in 1800, there was fierce opposition within the county to any question of reform. A petition from Sevenoaks to the House of Lords in 1827 urging against granting Catholics political and civil rights was supported by local ultra-Tories such as the fourth Earl Stanhope and J.C. Herries.[17] A wider hostility was vividly demonstrated in early October 1828 by a large anti-papist gathering

---

10   Manchester University Library REAS/2/1, Letters of George Thomson to his wife Anne, Autumn 1831.

11   *Brighton Gazette*, 14 Nov. 1831, p. 3.

12   *Northampton Mercury*, 4 Aug. 1832, p. 1.

13   KG, 20 April 1833, p. 3; 3 May 1833, p. 3.

14   School of Oriental and African Studies Archives, University of London, Wesleyan Methodist Missionary Society, Box 662, FBM 44, fiche 1966, 22 April 1833.

15   *Southern Reporter and Cork Commercial Courier*, 7 April 1838, p. 1.

16   MJ, 25 Oct. 1853, p. 5. David Killingray, 'Black people in Sevenoaks since 1600: history and research methods', *The Local Historian*, 51/4 (2021), pp. 297–308.

17   *Morning Chronicle* (henceforth MC), 17 Feb. 1827, p. 1.

on Penenden Heath, outside Maidstone, which denounced Catholic demands.[18] The Catholic Relief Act eventually became law in 1829. Dissenters were also involved in a long-drawn-out political campaign for full civil rights, 'Congregations of Protestant Dissenters' in Sevenoaks twice petitioning parliament in 1827.[19] Partial relief came in 1828, and a further petition, 'from Protestant Dissenters in the town praying for redress of grievances', was sent in 1834.[20]

The Relief Act allowed Catholics to hold public office, but suspicion of their activities remained politically live. Later the Maynooth question, relating to the payment by the government of an annual grant to a Roman Catholic seminary in Ireland, exacerbated anti-Catholic feeling that rumbled on throughout the 1840s and beyond, the *Maidstone Journal* referring to 'a strong anti-Popery sentiment' in the county.[21] The restoration of the Roman Catholic ecclesiastical hierarchy in 1850 caused further offence, as it was widely seen (by Protestants) as an assault on a Protestant state aligned to ideas of British liberty and democracy. At a meeting in Sevenoaks, J.C. Herries denounced this 'insolent and insidious' action, which displayed 'the aggression of the Church of Rome'.[22] The Church of England clergy were seen as the front line against the Church of Rome and Thomas Curteis supported establishing a Sevenoaks branch of the Society for the English Church Missions to the Roman Catholics.[23] In 1870, Protestants of all persuasions opposed the pronouncement by Pope Pius IX of papal infallibility. The Irish famine of the 1840s and resulting migration to Britain increased the number of Roman Catholics and the demand for schools, raising the contentious issue of public financial aid to these institutions, a subject that provoked anxiety among local Protestants over the Catholic school in Hartslands.[24] A Catholic church was built in Sevenoaks in the 1880s. By 1901 William Cunningham, the local Catholic priest, felt secure enough to join with his fellow Catholic clergy to publicly protest the declaration made by Edward VII at the opening of parliament, in accordance with the 1689 Bill of Rights, which denounced various central Catholic doctrines as superstitious.[25]

---

18 Kathryn Beresford, 'The "Men of Kent" and the Penenden Heath meeting 1828', *Archæologia Cantiana*, CXXV (2005), pp. 151–71.

19 *London Evening Standard*, 13 June 1827, p. 2.

20 *London Courier and Evening Gazette*, 1 March 1834, p. 3.

21 See *SEG*, 10 Feb. 1857, p. 8. *MJ*, 22 April 1845, p. 3.

22 *The Spectator*, 30 Nov. 1850, pp. 1131–2. He lifted the indignant phrases from a speech by Lord John Russell.

23 *SEG*, 3 Dec. 1850, p. 3. Curteis' sermon was published but no copy has been found. *MJ*, 22 Aug. 1854, p. 5.

24 Southwark Diocesan Archives, William Cunningham, 'Short Account of the Previous History of the Mission to Sevenoaks'.

25 Christopher Bell, 'The speech from the throne, 1901', *English Catholic History Association Newsletter*, 2/18 (March 2003), pp. 12–13.

The Corn Laws

The Corn Laws, first introduced in 1815, were a controversial protectionist measure. As Britain's population grew and the country relied more on imported foods, a duty was put on wheat imports, with the support of landowners, farmers and the Conservative party. Opposition came mainly from northern industrial centres and, after 1838, from the Anti-Corn Law League (ACLL), led by Richard Cobden. The Corn Laws were eventually repealed by Robert Peel's Conservative administration with the support of the Whig opposition in 1846.

There is little obvious evidence of sustained opposition to the Corn Laws in the Sevenoaks district. The area, dominated by agriculture but with relatively few farmers who grew corn, nevertheless appears to have been overwhelmingly protectionist.[26] Substantial support came from local Conservatives and large landowners, and those in related industries such as malting and brewing. Farmers faced a dilemma: how to safeguard their own economic wellbeing without curbing labourers' wages and presiding over policies that further increased agrarian hardship by pushing up the price of bread. Leading protectionists in the area included the fourth Lord Stanhope; Swing victim William Tonge, a wealthy farmer at Morant's Court; and James Selby.[27]

ACLL agents visited Sevenoaks in mid-1845, handing out 'several printed, inflammatory speeches on the corn laws, lately made by Mr. Cobden! They also applied to Mr John Sutton for the use of his assembly room to lecture in, but he with becoming and Tory spirit refused to encourage such customers.'[28] The agents then said they would speak outdoors, at which 'an express was sent off by the beadle ... to Col. Austen [a local JP] to desire his attendance to save the "Constitution of Sevenoaks"'.[29] Fortunately Austen either could not be found or wisely allowed the rule of law to take its course. A counter to the ACLL was the West Kent Agricultural Protection Society, formed in 1844 and chaired by Austen.[30] Repeal stimulated a demand for wider protectionism, the prominent voice in west Kent being that of Stanhope.

Demands for parliamentary reform

Parliamentary reform demanded an extension of the franchise, which challenged existing structures of power and authority, both nationally and locally.[31] This was not about democracy but about representation. A widely used vent for popular

---

26   *Kentish Mercury*, 2 March 1839, p. 3, for a petition from Sevenoaks farmers against the repeal of the Corn Laws.

27   Dennis Clarke and Anthony Stoyel, *Otford in Kent: a history* (Otford, 1975), pp. 192, 199, 202.

28   Probably John Sutton (1801–75), a woolstapler, who lived in the High Street.

29   *SEG*, 24 June 1845, p. 5. Austen presumably did not wish to inflame the situation by reading the Riot Act.

30   *SEG*, 28 Jan. 1845, pp. 4–5.

31   Further demands by reformers included parliamentary representation for large towns without MPs. There were no 'rotten boroughs' in west Kent.

At a General Meeting of the London Corresponding Society (LCS), held April 14, 1794, at Chalk Farm, Kentish Town,

Resolved unanimously,
That this Society have beheld with considerable pleasure the confident respect which the House of Lords displayed for their own Constitutional Rules and Orders, on the fourth of the present month, upon the motion of Earl Stanhope, concerning the interference of Ministers in the Internal Government of France; and that it is the firm conviction of this Society, that this circumstance, when properly detailed, will have a considerable effect in convincing the country at large, of the true dignity and utility of that branch of His Majesty's Parliament.

Figure 4.2 The third Earl Stanhope congratulated by the radical London Corresponding Society, 1794. The LCS was a radical organisation, formed in 1792 to press for universal male suffrage and annual parliaments. Although it and similar organisations took care to operate within the law, they were expressly prohibited by special legislation in 1799.
Source: Kent History and Library Centre, U1590/C78.

expression was petitioning parliament, 'a key component of the shifting ecosystem of popular participation and representation during the long nineteenth-century'.[32] Unsurprisingly, the issue ignited political passions throughout the long nineteenth century. During the 1790s the British authorities believed that social discontent resulted from war with France and was fostered by republican ideas from the newly independent United States and from revolutionaries across the Channel. They reacted with a series of coercive acts labelling radical ideas and actions as treason. The Society for Constitutional Reform, established in 1780, the Revolution Society and the London Corresponding Society were all seen as suspect. Radical ideas had little purchase in west Kent. Probably the most prominent radical voice in west Kent was the third Earl Stanhope (see Plate 3). His 'seat' at Chevening was listed (not by name) as one of the places to which the London Corresponding Society had sent letters, along with Sevenoaks and Tunbridge Wells.[33] As a wealthy aristocrat, often regarded as eccentric, and related by marriage to the prime minister, his personal position was reasonably secure, unlike men and women of little privilege who found themselves dragged before the courts charged with sedition or treason. Less secure

32   Richard Huzzey and Henry Miller, 'Petitions, parliament and political culture: petitioning the House of Commons, 1780–1918', *Past & Present*, 248 (Aug. 2020), pp. 123–64 (p. 124).

33   UKPP, House of Lords, *The Report from the Committee of Secrecy ... relative to the proceedings of different persons ... engaged in a treasonable conspiracy*, Sessional Paper, 002, 27 May 1799.

was Shoreham farmer Robert Colgate, a member of Bessels Green Baptist chapel, who had advanced republican ideas. He thought it wiser to leave the country in 1798 to breathe the freer air (for a white man) of the United States.

Local reactionaries in west Kent, notably the Lords Camden, Earl Stanhope (the fourth earl who had ideas and attitudes very different from his radically minded father), and Amherst, plus local gentry such as Percival Hart Dyke at Lullingstone and Charles Francis Farnaby, who had lands at Dunton Green, argued that extending the franchise would threaten the social and political order. This reactionary view was also promoted publicly by the painter Samuel Palmer.[34] They opposed even the mild parliamentary reforms eventually enacted in the 1832 Reform Act. Their joint efforts to prevent reform ran counter to widespread local political ambitions, and even Mrs Allnutt, whose interest in politics was minimal (given how infrequently it merits entries in her diary), wrote in October 1831 that she had 'heard that the Reform Bill was lost in the Lords by a majority of 42'.[35]

Demands for parliamentary reform came from radicals, many Whigs and discontented Tory 'Ultras'. Extra-parliamentary pressure came from political unions, the first formed in Birmingham in January 1830, with others established in towns across the country.[36] Besides demands to clear out 'Old Corruption', political unions had a range of ambitions, often shaped by local interests, embracing electoral reform, repeal of the Corn Laws, an extension of free trade and an end to vested monopolies. Fortified by the Reform Act, discussions took place in Sevenoaks to form a local political union, as recorded by William Knight in his diary: 'Lent the schoolroom to some of the working class for the purpose of forming a Political Union'.[37] In June 1832, a large meeting to assess 'public opinion' on reform was called in Sevenoaks to match a demonstration held in London, which may indicate contact between radicals in the town and in the capital. When the result of the vote for reform reached the town, according to William Knight, many houses and shops were illuminated, some with illustrations of Grey and Lord John Russell in the windows.[38] Some members of the Sevenoaks Political Union (SPU), 'which had been formed in the neighbourhood', addressed the multitude, and by 'their advice the people that were assembled on the occasion conducted themselves with the greatest order'.[39]

---

34 Samuel Palmer, *An address to the electors of West Kent* (1832).

35 Sevenoaks Library B ALL, Mrs Allnutt's Diary, 9 Oct. 1831. After this defeat prime minister Lord Grey brought forward a new Reform Bill that became law in March 1832.

36 See Nancy LoPatin, *Political unions, popular politics and the Great Reform Act* (Basingstoke, 1999).

37 Private archives, Knight, *Diaries*, vol. 1, 28 Aug. 1832.

38 Private archives, Knight, *Diaries*, vol. 1, 13 June 1832. See also *SEG*, 21 Aug. 1832, p. 3.

39 *SEG*, 21 Aug. 1832, p. 3. The predominantly well-educated middle-class leaders of most political unions were keen to promote them as upholding law and order and, as the toasts to Grey and Russell indicated, loyal supporters of government.

The SPU were wise to do this. In 1820, at a time when most radicals supported Queen Caroline (the estranged wife of George IV, who had tried to be crowned next to him at Westminster Abbey but was refused admission), a local mob had attacked Austen's Kippington House because he supported the king. And in September 1831 George Kelson's house in the centre of Sevenoaks had been attacked and seriously damaged because he had failed to illuminate his property to mark the coronation of William IV, the mob then repeating the abuse at Austen's house at Kippington.[40] Subsequently a 'public committee' in the town awarded Richard Parrish, secretary of the SPU, £5 for helping to keep the peace of the town. In the first week of July the 'triumph of Reform' was celebrated by a joint demonstration of people from Sevenoaks, Tonbridge and Tunbridge Wells (see Plate 4).[41]

At the subsequent parliamentary elections in December 1832, the two reformist Whig candidates Thomas Law Hodges and Thomas Rider were returned for west Kent.[42] By 1834 the Sevenoaks Political Union had petitioned parliament and established a committee presided over by Joseph Bradly, then a miller at Otford.[43] A gathering of the various political unions, held near Wrotham in 1833 and reportedly attended by 3,000 people, resolved to form a West Kent Political Union (WKPU). A petition was sent to the House of Commons seeking an end to 'injurious taxes' and the system of tithes and asking for short parliaments, an extended franchise, the end of the poor law settlement system and the reform of the House of Lords, that 'house of incurables' with its mix of 'priest and legislator'.[44] Little more is currently known of the Sevenoaks Political Union, which seems to have had a short life. It was still alive in December 1834, a report describing the 'posting of bills' to announce a meeting, which was 'well and respectably attended' at the time of the abrupt dismissal of Melbourne's cautiously reformist cabinet by the reactionary king William IV. Various resolutions were passed demanding reform of the House of Lords, an extension of the franchise 'at least to all householders', 'reform of the established church' and reduced taxation.[45] All this indicates the social class and religious beliefs of the audience, which was made up of taxpayers of one kind or another and a sizeable presence of nonconformists.

---

40 *MJ*, 13 Dec. 1831, p. 2, which reports the trial of four Sevenoaks labourers guilty of leading the violence. As there was no evidence that they intended to demolish the house, a capital offence, the sentences were imprisonment for 15 months with hard labour; *KWP*, 13 Jan. 1832, p. 3.

41 *SEG*, 17 July 1832, p. 3.

42 *SEG*, 25 Dec. 1832, p. 4.

43 *Cobbett's Weekly Political Register*, 16 March 1833, p. 4; *SEG*, 16 Dec. 1834, p. 4.

44 *SEG*, 23 July 1833, p. 4. 'Grand Meeting of the West Kent Political Union at Wrotham', 'Neighbouring Conservatives and a gentleman attempted to prevent the meeting taking place'. The long-held idea of a regional union was largely due to Major Charles Wayth (1769–1852) of Bearsted; see *SEG*, 17 July 1832, p. 1, and an obituary, *ibid.*, 22 June 1852, p. 4. The secretary of the WKPU was a Sevenoaks shoemaker, James W. Parrish, who had been a witness for the defence in the Riverhead tithe dispute.

45 *SEG*, 16 Dec. 1834, p. 4.

These developments concerned and amazed Robert Herries, as revealed in the letters he wrote to his cousin during the Reform crisis of 1831–2 and which serve as a commentary from the Sevenoaks right wing on those events as they unfolded. During the 1831 general election, which was won decisively by the Whig reformers, he took 'the gloomiest view of our prospects' and predicated the possible 'complete overthrow of everything'.[46]

There is little evidence that reform-minded men in Sevenoaks turned towards Chartism, despite the appeal of the Charter of 1838, with its 'six points' that proposed, among other things, adult male suffrage. One exception may have been Joseph Bradly, who in 1850 organised a petition to parliament for a reduction in taxes and for 'the benefit of household suffrage, vote by ballot, triennial parliaments, and equal electoral districts'.[47] Reform associations were established in Sevenoaks, Wrotham, Tonbridge and Westerham in 1837.[48] The Tonbridge Patriotic Reform Association adopted the Charter in January 1839 at a packed meeting of agricultural workers and tradesmen, with strong support coming from Mr Whiting, editor of the *South Eastern Gazette*, and sent off 407 signatures to London.[49] By late 1841 a branch of the National Chartist Association had been founded in Tonbridge.[50] If Tonbridge had a radical voice, Sevenoaks was largely passive and able only to raise one or two subscribers to Chartist causes.[51] Chartist meetings were held in Tunbridge Wells and members contributed to both the Chartist National Defence Fund and its Co-operative Land Society scheme. The Land Scheme, which had subscribers in Tunbridge Wells and Dartford, was a humiliating failure; at its peak in 1847–8 it had attracted 70,000 subscribers, but only 234 were settled on land.[52]

Despite the failure to halt reform in 1831–2, the political strength of Toryism in Sevenoaks – it boasted a flourishing Conservative Association in 1834 – was never under serious challenge in the longer term. Conservative-paid lawyers scrutinised voters' lists and challenged claims to the franchise, as, for example, in 1838, when Thomas Southern and 11 'other trustees of the Baptist Chapel claimed to be on the registry and were opposed' by Conservative agent George Calverley Cole (1797–1871).[53] As all were dissenters, and liable to vote Liberal, considerable electoral

46 Private archives at St Julian's, Sevenoaks, Herries Papers. Robert Herries to John Charles Herries, dd. St Julian's, 8 April 1831; dd. Lynmouth, 9 Dec. 1831.

47 *SEG*, 9 April 1850, p. 6.

48 *Morning Advertiser*, 14 Nov. 1837, p. 2.

49 *SEG*, 22 Jan. 1839, 3. See also John Rule and Roger Wells, *Crime, protest and popular politics in southern England, 1740–1850* (London, 1997), p. 131.

50 *Northern Star* (henceforth *NS*), 11 Sept. 1841, p. 3; 18 Dec. 1841, p. 5; 5 Feb. 1842, p. 6.

51 *NS*, 9 April 1842, p. 4.

52 *NS*, 2 July 1842, p. 15; 1 Oct. 1842, p. 14; 6 June 1846, p. 14.

53 *MC*, 19 Sept. 1838, pp. 3–4.

significance rested on their inclusion or exclusion from the voters' list. The trustees failed in their claim.

A Liberal response to an electorate determined by property came through the National Freehold Land Society (NFLS), founded in 1849 by Richard Cobden and John Bright, which bought land in so-called 'gentle rising towns' such as Sevenoaks, which might produce a new Liberal electorate. At a crowded meeting of 'tradesmen and working men', the scheme was launched in the town.[54] The Society bought land in St John's, northern Sevenoaks, and laid it out in plots for sale 'to men of small means to acquire freehold property and thus the vote'. A map and a prospectus were duly drawn up, and new roads cut in the wedge of land. But there were few prospective buyers and by 1853 the NFLS had run its course.[55]

In the lead-up to the Reform Act of 1867, local pressure to encourage a change in the franchise was brought to bear in the form of meetings held in Tonbridge to speak on behalf of those 'non-electors who are unrepresented in Parliament'.[56] At most parliamentary elections, political parties, individuals and local interest groups produced their own political posters and propaganda. For example, at the 1868 election in Sevenoaks an anonymous Wesleyan produced a poster urging his fellow-believers to vote for the Conservative cause in this time of 'Political crisis' where 'the bulwarks of our common Protestantism are assailed' by Liberals seeking to disestablish the Irish church. Religion and politics then were as interwoven as they were for many electors later in the century.[57]

General elections were popularly followed political entertainment for much of the nineteenth century. The various rituals performed by the candidates and their agents at elections involved those entitled to vote and those who were disenfranchised, the latter assuming 'that it was their birthright to participate in the election in other ways'.[58] This is visible in conflicting accounts of the hustings on the Vine in 1868. A contemporary press report declared that

> The proceedings, with few exceptions, was very quiet and orderly, except at one
> period, when an attempt was made to drag a carriage filled with blue, or Liberal
> electors, immediately in front of the hustings. The attempt was, however, prevented
> by the police and the proceedings went on without interruption.[59]

---

54   *SEG*, 11 March 1851, p. 5.

55   Sevenoaks Library D876A, 1852. See also *Kentish Mercury*, 22 March 1851, p. 3; see also M. Chase, 'Out of radicalism: the mid-Victorian freehold land movement', *English Historical Review*, 106 (1991), pp. 319–45.

56   Tonbridge Public Library, Local history collection, Yellow Box No. 1, poster dated 7 April 1866.

57   Sevenoaks Library D200, Methodist Church. 'A few Words from an Old Wesleyan to his Brother Wesleyans, on the coming Election', November 1868.

58   Frank O'Gorman, 'Campaign rituals and ceremonies: the social meaning of elections in England, 1780–1860', *Past & Present*, 135 (May 1992), pp. 79–115 (pp. 81, 92).

59   *Standard*, 21 Nov. 1868, p. 2.

In contrast, noted military historian Sir John Fortescue (1859–1933), recording his childhood memory, wrote that

> When we reached the ground the fun had already begun, which is to say that the hustings were already thronged and that a huge mob was gathered below them and was shouting themselves hoarse … Then the proceedings became lively. The crowd began to rock and sway in an ominous fashion and the yells turned to the smothered growls of hounds worrying a fox. Presently the police rose to their feet, and falling in marched across the ground 30 or 40 strong in columns of four.[60]

One suspects the former account to be more accurate than the latter.

Secret voting was introduced by the Ballot Act of 1872, but even afterwards parliamentary elections often remained noisy affairs, the 1880 general election in Tonbridge developing into a serious riot.[61] Demands to extend the franchise to working-class men in the counties had not disappeared, however, and Charles Bassett records how he, his father (both men were active members of the Kent & Sussex Labourers' Union) and two brothers were part of a 5,000-strong Kent contingent, many carrying hop poles, who marched in support of 'Mr Gladstone's … County Franchise Bill' from Victoria Embankment to Hyde Park in 1884.[62]

Attempts to extend the franchise to women were unsuccessfully made in parliament and elsewhere from the 1860s onward. In west Kent the earliest known advocates were in Tunbridge Wells.[63] A majority of Liberals and Conservatives opposed this enhancement of choice, believing it to be a dangerous measure. Ironically, women were enlisted for party political purposes, most notably by the Primrose League founded by the Tory Lord Randolph Churchill in 1883. The objectives of the League, as enunciated by a speaker when the Sevenoaks habitation (the name given to local branches) was inaugurated in 1885 at Lord Amherst's Montreal House, were 'to extend and maintain this great Empire, to preserve liberty, and to maintain the religion and constitution of this country'.[64] It had sections for women, who played an active part in national elections by canvassing, committee work and general organisation. Membership locally and nationally grew at a rapid pace: the Sevenoaks habitation had 374 members in 1887, 689 by 1890 and 761 by 1897. Other habitations were founded at Ide Hill, Tonbridge, Chevening and

---

60   Sir John Fortescue, 'The Old Hustings. A memory of 1868', *The Times*, 27 May 1929.

61   Anthony Wilson (ed.), *Tonbridge through ten centuries* (Tonbridge, 2015), pp. 127–8. The Tonbridge Local Board laid the blame on the county police for using 'outrageous and uncalled for violence'; see *KSC*, 25 June 1880, p. 8.

62   Charles Bassett, *A life in Seal* (Seal, 1991), pp. 11–12; *Kent Times* (henceforth *KT*), 11 June 1887, p. 3.

63   See Elizabeth Crawford, *The women's suffrage movement: a reference guide, 1866–1928* (London, 2001), pp. 191–3, 635–6.

64   *MP*, 3 Nov. 1885, p. 2; see also *SC*, 6 Nov. 1885, p. 5; *KSC*, 25 Sept. 1885, p. 3.

Seal.[65] At its national conference in November 1887, the Primrose League supported the parliamentary franchise being extended to women householders. This did not accord with the gendered view expressed by an MP speaking at a League meeting in Seal in 1902, where he distinguished between women, with a 'more poetic idea of politics', and the enfranchised 'man[,] with his rough and ready matter-of-fact politics'.[66] For a growing number of women, parliamentary suffrage was a right denied by a male-dominated society.

A more forceful response came from the National Union of Women's Suffrage Societies (NUWSS), founded in 1897 and led by Millicent Fawcett. This believed in the 'vindication of moral forces' and campaigned by 'lawful and constitutional methods'.[67] Local branches were established in west Kent; that in Sevenoaks, begun in 1908, was run by a committee composed of determined and often well-heeled women, including Mrs Reinhold Rynd, Lilian Thompson and the renowned Canadian painter Sophie Pemberton of Wickhurst Manor, Weald.[68] Ellen Hickmott was a prominent member of the Sevenoaks branch of the NUWSS, which by 1913 had over 100 members.[69] Lilian Thompson, a noted advocate of women's rights, regularly regaled the local press with well-argued letters from the vicarage at Kippington, one strongly stating her view 'that the enfranchisement of women is one of the distinguishing marks of Christianity'.[70] Suffragist public meetings in Sevenoaks, such as that addressed by Mrs Fawcett in 1908, were often greeted with riotous behaviour. Young men suspected of being troublesome were turned away by the police from that meeting, but older, more respectably dressed men interrupted speakers by blowing whistles, ringing bells and stamping their feet, along with jeers and general noise.[71] The NUWSS was often tarred with the same brush by ignorant and hostile electors as the militant Women's Social and Political Union (WSPU), the suffragettes, a breakaway body dating from 1903, whose behaviour attracted the headlines but whose influence has been often exaggerated. Indeed, the violent actions of the WSPU helped boost the membership of the rival NUWSS. Several women in Sevenoaks chose not to join suffrage organisations, preferring

---

65 *SC*, 1 April 1887, p. 5, 8 Aug. 1890, p. 8, 24 June 1898, p. 5; Myriam Boussabha-Bravard (ed.), *Suffrage outside suffragism: women's votes in Britain, 1880–1914* (Basingstoke, 2007), ch. 8.

66 *SC*, 2 May 1902, p. 8.

67 *SC*, 12 Nov. 1909, p. 5; 8 March 1912, p. 7.

68 Sophie Pemberton (1869–1959) is referred to in the local press as 'Mrs Beanlands', the wife of Canon Arthur Beanlands, an active supporter of the NUWSS; at one of its meetings in the Club Hall, Sevenoaks, over the platform there was 'a beautiful motto designed by Mrs Beanlands, "Be just and fear not"', *SC*, 7 Feb. 1913, p. 8.

69 *Women's Franchise*, 10 Sept. 1908, p. 113.

70 *SC*, 12 June 1908, p. 5.

71 *SC*, 29 May 1908, p. 5; *Women's Signal*, 8 Oct. 1908, p. 163.

to work for that cause through the Liberal party.[72] Sevenoaks also had a branch of the Conservative and Unionist Women's Franchise League and its Tory rival the Women's National Anti-Suffrage League, which led to lively local public debates.[73]

Temperance

The temperance movement was unusual in that, fundamentally, it sought to restrict choice, not augment it, although its adherents believed that restriction was essential – for good health and social reasons – to remove the risks posed by the demon drink. It grew into a powerful political force, particularly from the 1830s, when various temperance bodies were formed.[74] For many Christians, particularly dissenters, this was an intensely moral cause. Excessive consumption of spirits and beer, they argued, risked compromising individual dignity and respectability, robbed women and children of vital earnings and undermined home and family. Many of the cases brought before west Kent magistrates in the nineteenth century were for drunkenness and related misbehaviour. The problem was amplified by navvies building the railways in the 1860s, and thereafter by weekend excursionists to Sevenoaks. Licensing was a local responsibility, but the Beerhouse Act of 1830, passed to increase competition and lower prices, resulted in large numbers of local beerhouses being opened; for example, the tiny hamlet of Underriver, just to the south of Sevenoaks, had two by 1832.

Local Bands of Hope (an organisation founded in 1832) existed in Sevenoaks and surrounding villages such as Leigh. A Sevenoaks Temperance Association was founded in 1852 and a West Kent Temperance Union inaugurated six years later.[75] These temperance bodies, along with a variety of local denominational societies, had regular programmes of lectures, galas, flower shows, missions and church services, all designed 'to win people to sobriety and rational amusements' and rescue them from the excesses of alcohol, 'impoverishment, disease, curtailment of industry, crime, and irreligion'.[76] These activities were duplicated by the Church of England Temperance Society, the Salvation Army, Father Lazzari at the Roman Catholic church in Sevenoaks and various Blue and White Ribbon organisations, which sought to enlist children and young people to the temperance cause. One argument against temperance, and the more severe total abstinence, was the questionable quality of the water supply in mid-nineteenth-century Sevenoaks. But another counter against drink was the creation of coffee shops and temperance

---

72 *Women's Franchise*, 29 April 1909, p. 542, letter from Helen Lely to editor, from Waverly, Vine Court Yard [Road], Sevenoaks.

73 *SC*, 20 Nov. 1908, p. 5. See also *SC*, 5 Jan. 1912, p. 5, and 8 March 1912, p. 7.

74 Brian Harrison, *Drink and the Victorians: the temperance question in England 1815–1872* (Keele, 1994), ch. 8.

75 *SEG*, 4 Dec. 1860, p. 5; *MJ*, 24 July 1865, p. 6.

76 *KG*, 8 Feb. 1870, p. 6; see also *MJ*, 31 Jan. 1870, p. 4.

hotels; that opened in Lime Tree Walk, Sevenoaks, in the 1880s was largely a result of the efforts of two local 'Bible women' and the local Lay Association.[77] A 'coffee tavern' opened in Seal in 1881 and soon established itself as a major meeting place in the village.[78] Women were among the most resolute and numerous campaigners for temperance, those involved in charitable social work being all too aware of the ravages that alcohol inflicted on families. Prominent in the public campaign against drink in Sevenoaks was Lilian Thompson, who determinedly supported the Temperance War Pledge in late 1914.[79]

Although Sevenoaks had two breweries in the town centre by mid-century, local consumption of spirits and beer steadily declined after the 1860s as working men spent less of their wages on drink. By then the local water supply was better. More tea was being consumed and working-class diets were slowly improving. The Liberals embraced temperance in 1891, but the Conservatives emphasised restraint only and thus were more likely to be supported by brewers and publicans.

Inns, public houses and beer retailers in west Kent

By 1906 there were 29 pubs in Sevenoaks serving a population of 8,103, or 279 per pub. The broad trend is that the ratio of pubs to population declined during the nineteenth century. The high demand in Tonbridge probably came from working-class railway labourers. The relatively few pubs in Cranbrook in 1824 might have been a hangover from its active dissenting past.

	1824			1882		
	Pubs	Population	Per pub	Pubs	Population	Per pub
Cranbrook	6	3,683	614	10	4,216	422
Sevenoaks	8	3,942	492	20	8,305	415
Tonbridge	8	2,633	329	36	9,256	257
Tun' Wells	13	4,773	368	54	20,443	379
Westerham	5	1,742	348	7	2,301	328

Sources: *Pigot's directory of Kent*, 1824; *Kelly's directory*, 1882.

---

77 *SC*, 23 Nov. 1883, p. 8.

78 *SC*, 4 Nov. 1881, p. 5.

79 *SC*, 4 Sept. 1914, p. 2; 11 Sept. 1914, p. 4; 25 Dec. 1914, p. 3.

Public houses in the Sevenoaks district 1906: report of Sevenoaks Brewster Session

The villages around Sevenoaks show marked discrepancies in pubs per head, Riverhead apparently being an especially thirsty place.

	Pubs	Population	Per pub
Brasted	7	1,304	186
Chevening	5	1,074	214
Halstead	2	573	297
Kemsing	3	644	214
Otford	9	1,698	198
Riverhead	7	802	114
Seal	10	1,688	168
Sevenoaks	29	8,103	279
Sevenoaks Weald	5	833	166
Shoreham	9	1,515	168
Sundridge	7	1,724	246
Westerham	9	2,915	322

Source: SC, 16 February 1906, p. 8.

Tariff reform

Since the 1850s free trade had been the dominant commercial policy of successive British governments, supported in Sevenoaks by men such as John Bligh, who firmly described himself as the 'free trade' grocer. Free trade, however – so it was feared at a public meeting in Sevenoaks in 1850 – threatened 'Agricultural and Commercial Interests'.[80] From the 1880s alarms were raised about the country's vulnerability to foreign competition and there were demands, mainly from Conservatives, for 'fair trade'. Protectionism raised several questions: would agricultural and manufactured imports merit tariffs, how would the electorate react to higher prices on foodstuffs, should there be a system of imperial preference, and what of foreign retaliatory responses? For the Tariff Reform League, formed in 1903, which enjoyed the support of many landowners, a major consideration was 'Empire Unity'. Both Conservative and Liberal parties were split over tariff reform.

The Sevenoaks Tariff Reform League had its origins in 1904 and came to effective life the following year.[81] An international recession in 1908–9 helped support the

80   *MJ*, 25 Jan. 1850, p. 1.
81   *SC*, 1 Dec. 1905, p. 8.

GOOD ADVICE.

JOHN BULL.—" You will be glad to know that the Old Age Pensions have commenced."

BRITISH WORKMAN.—" Yes. That's all very fine, guv'ncr; but I've no work, and I can't live on air for the next 30 years in order to get five bob a week at 70."

JOHN BULL.—" Well, if it's work you want, you must try Tariff Reform."

Figure 4.3 'Good Advice' cartoon, taken from the *Sevenoaks Chronicle*, 1 January 1909, p. 4. In 1895 Joseph Chamberlain, the pro-tariff Liberal, suggested that old age pensions could be paid for 'by an import duty on wheat'. Fourteen years later at a time of severe recession when working-class voices lamented unemployment in west Kent, Old Age Pensions were introduced. The handful of local recipients collected their weekly payments from the Post Office. © The British Library Board. All rights reserved. With thanks to The British Newspaper Archive (www.britishnewspaperarchive.co.uk).

---

protectionist cause, and by early 1909 the League in the district could muster nearly 530 members. Five hundred people attended a tariff reform meeting in the Club House in December 1909, and many heard speakers condemn free trade in Sevenoaks market square in January and December 1910.[82] The numerous meetings, some with acclaimed 'working man speakers', and head counts of members were of little avail, but they demonstrated the strength of feeling among Conservatives in a

---

82   *SC*, 14 Jan. 1910, p. 8; 2 Dec. 1910, p. 5. The January meeting demanded 'British work for British people'.

small market town in west Kent, a county where tariff reform had good purchase. This was manifest on 'Hop Saturday' in May 1908, when hop growers and pickers, badly hit by competition from abroad, converged on central London to demand a tariff on foreign-grown hops. As one of the banners unfurled in Trafalgar Square proclaimed: 'And shall hops picked by Chinamen make England's hop trade die, here's 50,000 Kentish men will know the reason why.'[83] In 1914 Britain entered the Great War ostensibly as a free-trade nation.

War

Attitudes to war in the period varied greatly, much depending on the moral positions individuals took, which were in turn underpinned by their broader ideas, beliefs and values. The wars with France to destroy the power of Napoleon enjoyed popular support, as did the Crimean War to arrest Russia's perceived assertive policies. However, imperial wars that engaged British forces for a large part of the nineteenth century, whether in China, India or parts of Africa, divided opinion, partly because the risks involved did not, to many, appear worth the putative gains that may have resulted. The strength of what can be described as a 'peace party' in Sevenoaks cannot easily be determined, as the decision to protest wars was more likely to be an individual matter of moral and Christian conscience; Albert Bath, for example, was a long-term member of the International Arbitration and Peace Society and sat on its Council in 1888. When a local man, Charles Ogle, was murdered by Ottoman irregulars in the Greek–Ottoman war of 1878, Sevenoaks' passions were raised. One possible gauge of 'patriotic' feeling in west Kent is the increased involvement of men in the local militia, the Volunteer movement and rifle clubs. By 1898 a Drill Hall was opened in central Sevenoaks, and four years later the local Volunteers numbered 180 men, some of them on active service in the South African war of 1899–1902.[84]

That conflict also provides a well-documented instance of local opposition, however. It was generally a 'popular' war, although enthusiasm for it declined as the campaigns dragged on, casualties increased and British excesses were publicised in the press. Arthur and Ellen Hickmott, as socialists and pacifists, were labelled 'pro-Boer' for their opposition to the war, as were Lilian and Percy Thompson at Kippington.[85] A meeting at St John's to protest the war was invaded by working-class roughs, and Arthur Hickmott entered into robust correspondence in the pages

---

83 *The Times*, 18 May 1908, p. 8; *KSC*, 22 May 1908, pp. 8–9. The rhyme and rhythm of the sentiments come from Robert Hawker's patriotic Cornish song of 1824; the reference to 'Chinamen' probably reflects the recent political furore over Chinese mine labour in South Africa.

84 *SC*, 11 April 1902, p. 5; *SC*, 12 April 1901, p. 5.

85 Lilian Thompson, *Sidney Gilchrist Thomas – an invention and its consequences* (London, 1940), p. 299.

of the local press to defend his views.[86] Another opponent of the war in South Africa, the artist Alfred Emslie (1848–1918), who lived at Otford, was burned in effigy by some of the villagers.[87]

Letter, Mrs Hickmott to Mrs Unwin, 1902

Ellen Hickmott wrote to fellow radical Jane Cobden Unwin (often known as Mrs Fisher Unwin) on the efforts that she and her husband Arthur had made to oppose the war in South Africa and the disruption of a meeting at St John's:

> [At the] evening meeting Friday [against the South African war] those wretches rather spoiled it all. We were not far from the door and several times I really thought they would have burst in. I was not afraid for myself but I knew that if they got in they would never have permitted us to hear a word our speakers were saying. I am convinced that this systematic mobbing and rioting at all or nearly all peace meetings is a part of the regular plan of campaign and is all arranged by some of the influential people the same probably that have bought and coerced the Press and Pulpit.

Source: West Sussex Record Office. Cobden Unwin papers, GB 3 DM 851. 569–570G. Ellen Hickmott to Jane Cobden Unwin, dd. St John's Hill, Sevenoaks, 12 March 1902.

The Hickmotts' anti-war position continued to attract hostility, their premises on St John's Hill being mobbed by several hundred people on two nights in July 1901 because Arthur was thought to be complicit in an earlier visit to the town by hundreds of members of the National Democratic League (NDL), a Liberal–Labour body founded in October 1900.[88] Fred Hooker's home in Argyle Road was similarly assailed by a large crowd opposed to his supposed 'pro-Boer' views. The violence did not end there, for an NDL meeting on the Vine was interrupted 'by a group of well-known local residents'; a struggle ensued and League members were jeered by a crowd as they walked to the railway station, where, as they awaited their train, they were pelted with mud and stones.[89] Political discourse in nineteenth-century

---

86   *SC*, 28 Oct. 1899, p. 5 and subsequent correspondence, 'Mr. Hickmott and the War'.
87   Clarke and Stoyel, *Otford*, p. 232.
88   *SC*, 19 July 1901, p. 5.
89   *KSC*, 19 July 1901, p. 4.

Britain could be rude, vulgar and at times violent, often far removed from the image presented by John Dunlop of Sevenoaks in his general history as a 'pleasant town'.[90]

This chapter, and chapters 2 and 3, have set out west Kent's broader political context, both national and local, as its power structures changed dramatically during the nineteenth century. It was within those frameworks that anyone – especially the lower social echelons – who sought significantly to improve their economic, social and cultural circumstances beyond the bare necessities, had to operate. But how, precisely, were they able to reduce the risks they ran and enhance the choices they could make? The next few chapters assess the challenges, opportunities, fortunes and misfortunes of the ordinary people of Sevenoaks as they lived, married, had children and grew older in a century in which the economic, social, cultural and political order was steadily changing.

---

90 John Dunlop, *The pleasant town of Sevenoaks: a history* (Sevenoaks, 1964).

Chapter 5

'The necessities of life': housing and fuel

Personal and family wellbeing, comfort and happiness are universal desires. For much of the period under discussion they could not be taken for granted by the poor, who constituted most people in west Kent. Several everyday risk factors – low wages, lack of regular work and bouts of unemployment – made it difficult for the poor to afford what the novelist George Eliot called the 'primitive wants': adequate food, clothing, housing and fuel.[1] Their absence led to hunger, cold, poor sanitation and disease. Such risks continued to plague the poor well into the twentieth century; for example, in the winter of 1908 the Rev. Walter Raikes said 'there were between 20 and 30 at Ide Hill who were practically starving because they were out of employment there being such a lack of work in the stone quarries'.[2] The more prosperous generally considered themselves immune from such misfortunes, but could still suffer occasional crises, including financial catastrophes such as bank failures.[3] All children, of whatever social station, were susceptible to tuberculosis and other lethal diseases such as diphtheria (a major outbreak occurred in Hartslands in 1902), measles, influenza and many others.

Housing

Houses do not become homes until the investment in bricks and mortar is complemented by a similar investment in human capital, or the emotional, moral and often spiritual inputs that allowed families to be brought up safely, privately and in accord with accepted sets of values, such as respectability. Privacy, an important element of respectability, was quite a new idea, emanating from the later eighteenth century, such that 'Home was a private space, guarded watchfully

---

1   George Eliot, *Silas Marner* ([1861] London, 1985), p. 5.

2   *SC*, 20 Nov. 1908, p. 8.

3   It is significant that Swing's demands included 'lower cottage rentals and cheaper food'; Roger Wells, 'The moral economy of the English countryside', in Adrian Randall and Andrew Charlesworth (eds), *The moral economy and popular protest: crowds, conflicts and authority* (Basingstoke, 2000), p. 250.

from contamination by the life of the world.'[4] This was seen most obviously in the radically different vernacular architecture of that period, some of which is still visible in west Kent and elsewhere. The farmhouse at Elses Farm, Sevenoaks Weald, for example, was built in 1812 to replace a medieval structure. Its construction and layout are entirely familiar two centuries later, with kitchen and living space on the ground floor and bedrooms on the first, and it was occupied by a single, private, family with a few servants.[5]

The private, respectable nineteenth-century home was the optimum space for raising families, so either having an inadequate house or losing a house for some reason were deemed especially serious. That ideal also centred on a husband and wife living harmoniously together, so separation was always grave and subject to severe social disapproval. The only place it was officially (and forcibly) sanctioned was in the workhouse, and that only as part of a regime that encouraged its residents to depart elsewhere as quickly as possible.

As ever, income determined housing quality. In 1810 author George Cooke called Sevenoaks 'remarkable for the many good houses throughout it, and the respectability of its inhabitants'.[6] Looking at the properties occupied by the upper social echelons, his comment was accurate enough. To take a single example, in 1817 or 1818 cousins John Charles and Robert Herries commissioned architect John Buonarotti Papworth (1775–1847) to build St Julian's, just below Knole Park. The Jacobean-style, two-storey country house was set in 15 acres and completed in 1821 at a cost of £3,000. The design included, in addition to 14 bedrooms, 'a thatched dairy, stable block, laundry, ice-house, an oast house, a summer house and a walled kitchen garden'.[7]

Accommodating the poor

Cooke completely ignored the dwellings endured by the poor. A very different picture was painted in 1832 by William Knight. He saw how they lived in 'houses with no backdoors, one room below with a little closet, and one above with a sort of landing place at the top of the stairs; the chamber just large enough to hold a bed and a couple of chairs'.[8]

In 1826 another artist, Samuel Palmer, endured poor accommodation himself after he moved to a run-down cottage in Shoreham. It was 'so dilapidated and

4   Judith Flanders, *The Victorian house: domestic life from childbed to deathbed* (London, 2003), p. xlvii.

5   KHLC U1109/T34.

6   George Cooke, *Topographical and statistical description of the county of Kent* (London, 1810), p. 322.

7   Private archives at St Julian's, Sevenoaks, Herries Papers. Robert Herries to Charles James Herries, 6 July 1832; Margaret Bates and David Killingray, 'The Herries family and the building of St Julian's, Underriver, 1819–1837', *Archaeologia Cantiana*, CXXIII (2003), pp. 273–90; Herries papers, Robert Herries to John Charles Herries, dd. Lynmouth, 9 Dec. 1831; dd. King Street, Tuesday, 1837; dd. St Julian's, early 1837.

8   Esmond Knight, *Seeking the bubble* (London, 1943), p. 5.

vermin-infested that he dubbed it Rat Alley'.[9] He, however, had an element of choice in his embrace of this aspect of his bohemian lifestyle, unlike the 'very many of the labouring people [who] are unable to choose their habitations'.[10] Even respectable people could suffer from substandard housing, for when Mr and Mrs Foreman entertained visiting Methodist preachers in Shoreham in the first half of the nineteenth century, 'if there was much rain, the room had to be vacated, as the water would flow in over the floor'.[11]

Proper privacy and respectability required a home good enough to preclude excessive privation and hardship; bad accommodation dramatically increased the risk factors for its inhabitants. In 1841 Edward Tufnell, the Assistant Poor Law Commissioner responsible for Kent, described in Tunbridge Wells 'a very old building of wood, quite out of repair, not weather proof in any part'. It had two rooms on each floor, the front room ten foot square, the rear smaller. It had been occupied for twenty years by a man, his wife and their six children, the eldest then aged 14. The rent had been reduced to £7 from £9 a year due to the 'man's inability to pay so much'.[12] The cottage had cost just £30 to construct and could have injured them or left them destitute had it fallen or burned down, while the constant dampness must have been particularly unhealthy. The rest of this section will seek to answer William Knight's rhetorical question 'What are the places that the labourer who can save 2s 6d or 2s 5d out of his weekly pay of 12s or 14s is able to hire?'[13]

As was often the case, many of the lower or artisanal classes in nineteenth-century Sevenoaks were spatially segregated from the rest of the town. They lived in alleyways in the centre of the town or in the new working-class estate at Hartslands. The middle classes of Sevenoaks were content to remain in their pleasant hilltop locale, while the growing working-class element was slowly but surely relegated 'outside', down to the St John's Hill district to the north. The development was close, in yardage, to the existing centre. But it contained literally, symbolically and spatially, more than one 'home of wretchedness', as Catherine Martin described one she visited.[14] And even those Hartslands dwellings that were spick and span, as many surely were, remained a million miles away, socially, from many members of respectable middle-class society. As Lilian Thompson wrote about Sevenoaks at the end of the nineteenth century, 'Well-to-do people, while anxious to avail themselves

---

9   *Oxford dictionary of national biography* (henceforth *ODNB*), 'Samuel Palmer', https://www. oxforddnb.com/.

10 Private archives, Knight, *Diaries*, vol. 1, 15 April 1832.

11 William Franks, 'An old local preacher's reminiscences', *Methodist Recorder* (Winter 1905), p. 79. A copy is held at KHLC M2/1/6/8.

12 E.C. Tufnell, *On the dwelling and general economy of the labouring classes in Kent and Sussex* (London, 1841), p. 5. See also his *ODNB* entry.

13 Private archives, Knight, *Diaries*, vol. 1, 15 April 1832.

14 Benjamin Field, *Sincere devotion: exemplified in the life of Mrs. C.E. Martin, of Sevenoaks* (London, 1862), p. 107.

of the services of their poorer neighbours, are apt to feel they should be housed out of sight.'[15]

Housebuilding in the nineteenth century was invariably a hazardous endeavour. Developers faced a series of risks that could compromise cashflow and/or turn profit to loss, often in a very short time, and lead to bankruptcy. Financial competence did not always come easily to men more skilled with bricks and mortar. Factors included construction risk (completing the build); finance risk (access to sufficient loan capital at viable interest rates); tenant risk (ensuring the house was let, at an adequate rent, as soon as possible after completion); and sale risk (subsequently selling it, normally to an investor at auction). But from the 1870s rudimentary (by today's standards) planning and building controls were introduced. They imposed a low level of regulatory risk on the developers but at the same time slightly reduced the occupational risks to the tenants.

Hartslands seems to have been constructed in the standard way for mid-nineteenth-century English towns, by 'small speculators of limited resources'.[16] Development arose from strong occupier demand in Sevenoaks, for 'Speculation in the building of cottages, by tradesmen and other capitalists, is going on to a considerable extent, and is very successful.'[17] The initial developer of Hartslands, Daniel Grover, started from humble beginnings, being poor enough in 1830 to be allocated to a charitable employment scheme.[18] But he subsequently prospered to the extent that his personal estate was valued at about £800 when he died in 1880.[19] He was also financially astute enough to drip-feed small groups of freehold plots onto the market, since it was never in his commercial interest to over-supply it at any point.

Other developers, such as Thomas Gibbon and Thomas Bartholomew, were active in Hartslands in the 1840s and 1870s respectively, erecting at mid-century a few cottages costing £60 or so each to construct (see Plate 5).[20] On completion, they usually (but not always) had little trouble finding tenants because 'The present demand for cottages in this locality (being near to the railway station), is greatly beyond the supply.'[21]

This was underlined by the 'snapshot' census returns, for rarely were properties in Hartslands vacant on the decennial census nights – in 1871 only one out of 155 properties, for example – although few censuses took place during economic

15   Thompson, *Sidney Gilchrist Thomas*, p. 315.

16   Asa Briggs, *Victorian cities* (London, 1963), p. 19.

17   UKPP, Commons, *Report ... Inquiring into the Administration and Practical Operation of the Poor Laws* (1834), No. 44, 875a.

18   KHLC P330/8/5, 16 Nov. 1830.

19   Wills & Administrations 1858–, 'Grover, Daniel', 1880, p. 452.

20   *SEG*, 18 July 1848, p. 1; *MJ*, 9 Sept. 1872, p. 7; John Burnett, *A social history of housing* (London, 1986), p. 21.

21   *MJ*, 16 April 1866, p. 1.

downturns, when vacancy rates were probably far higher.[22] Since this implied rising rents, developers normally found it straightforward to sell properties to investors, although the yields at which they did so could vary substantially.

Hartslands: typical weekly rents, 1846–1902

1846	4s
1850	2s 6d
1860s	3s
1882	3s 6d
1886	6s
1889	5s
1902	7s

Sources: various Kent newspaper advertisements, 1846–1902.

Average farm cottage rents, England, late eighteenth to mid-nineteenth centuries

	1797		1850	
	yearly	*weekly*	*yearly*	*weekly*
Cheap	£1 10s	7d	£3	1s 2d
Average	£2	9d	£4	1s 7d
Expensive	£3	1s 2d	£5	1s 11d

Sources: Frederick Eden, *The state of the poor*, 3 vols (London, 1797; facsimile edition 1966), vol. 3, appendix 12; James Caird, *English agriculture in 1850 and 1851* (London, 1852; facsimile edition 1968), pp. 474–5. See also John Burnett, *A social history of housing* (London, 1986), pp. 38–41.

Development and finance

Most houses across the Sevenoaks area were let rather than owned outright since mass owner-occupation was a phenomenon of the twentieth century; only 4 per cent of Hartslands residents owned their homes before 1913. A rare exception was chimney sweep Alfred Budgen, who by 1909 had invested in a row of six cottages

---

22   Census Return for 1871: Sevenoaks (Hartslands).

in Bethel Road, one of which he lived in himself.[23] The money may have come from an inheritance. Houses were sold at auctions that were advertised in the local press, which indicate rental levels in Hartslands and elsewhere.

Wealthier residents of the town could save to buy their own places, a process made easier by the rise of building societies, 'a major source of finance for new building'[24] in the second half of the nineteenth century. They existed to share the cost risks inherent in housing development and/or ownership. Unlike the 'permanent' societies of the twentieth century, many, including the Sevenoaks Benefit Building Society (SBBS), were 'terminating' institutions, dissolved at the end of a pre-determined period. The SBBS was founded in March 1868 for a set term of 14 years, with the object of raising 'by monthly subscriptions a fund to make allowances to members ... to erect or purchase one or more houses'.[25] Members paid entrance fees of 2s 6d and subscriptions of 10s a month (£84 over the full term) for shares that had a redemption value of £120 – or an uplift of almost 50 per cent on the total subscription cost. Multiple shares, or alternatively half or quarter shares, were also available for those with more or less to invest.[26] Its trustees and directors (including Daniel Grover) mainly comprised the Sevenoaks elite and, somewhat unusually for local financial institutions in the nineteenth century, the Society appears to have been well managed, since it was fully solvent and held £5,000 in cash when it was dissolved in 1882. Borrowers included Methodist preacher William Franks and Sundridge stone digger and carrier Henry Quittenden, each of whom had been loaned around £200.

How well did investments such as these perform? Across the UK investors were attracted to working-class cottage property because it provided relatively safe long-term income (so good for the elderly and for widows), offering yields of at least 6 to 7 per cent – far above government gilts, consols or bonds – although rents had to be collected, repairs made and vacant cottages relet.[27] Investors, many of whom were from outside west Kent, sought sound long-term investments. London solicitor J. O'Brien, for example, bought three Hartslands cottages in 1882 for £340, giving an annual return of about 8 per cent.[28]

Sevenoaks was a popular location with middle-class occupiers, too, for in 1878 'The demand for building land in this district has become so great that another estate is now passing into the hands of the builders, and Old Vine Court may be numbered among the things of the past.'[29] The Lambarde family's substantial house

---

23 TNA IR 58/85843/46–47, Hartslands.

24 Burnett, *Housing*, p. 24.

25 TNA FS 6/84/80 KENT – Rule Book (1868).

26 *Ibid.*

27 Burnett, *Housing*, p. 152.

28 *SEG*, 15 May 1882, p. 5.

29 *KT*, 9 March 1878, p. 6. Vine Court Lodge was separate from and not part of the Vine Court estate.

Figure 5.1 Vine Court Lodge, Sevenoaks, under construction, 1903. Most building work was labour intensive, much of the work involving shovels and wheelbarrows. Craftsmen were better dressed, their aprons and bowler hats denoting skill and status. Most of the men in the photograph are labourers wearing cloth caps.
Source: Sevenoaks Society, D0713.

stood on 18 acres of open country between Hartslands and the town centre. After the estate was sold and the house demolished, the area was gradually filled in with the kind of large, elegant middle-class villas – costing up to £1,000 to construct – that most Hartslands residents entered only through the tradesmen's entrances, or as domestic servants.[30] The broad trend was that Sevenoaks was becoming 'more built up and suburbanised' during this period.[31]

However, it appears the town then became over-supplied with such property, for later that year another Sevenoaks auction performed spectacularly badly, when 'Of the ten town lots only one was sold, and of the fifteen lots of building land, four had been sold privately, and no bid at all was made for those offered publicly.'[32] Another prime development that failed to attract the anticipated interest was the St Botolph's Estate, directly south of Vine Court and just a short walk from the new Sevenoaks main-line station. Weak demand was but one of several drawbacks, however, for

---

30   Burnett, *Housing*, p. 199.

31   Thompson, *Sidney Gilchrist Thomas*, p. 307.

32   *SEG*, 22 June 1878, p. 3.

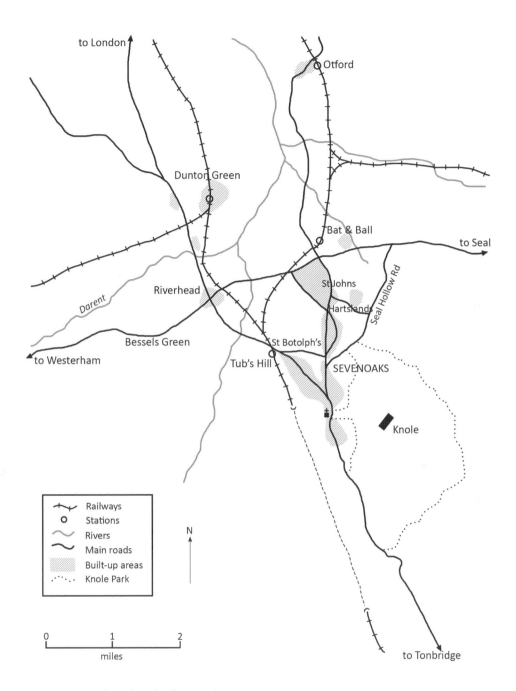

Map 14 Sevenoaks: urban development by *c.*1890.

buyers by the early 1870s wanted freehold, rather than leasehold, plots.[33] Perhaps its developers should have concentrated instead on profitable cottages for the 'labourers and mechanics [who] have two, three, and four miles to walk to their work; from Seal, Riverhead, Chipstead, the Weald, and Ide Hill'. The correspondent, 'A Friend of Honest Labour', went on to urge that

> some land should be set aside for cottages, and these gentlemen would confer a great benefit on the working class and the public generally if they would from this new purchase of 'Vine Court' parcel out a portion of the land upon which cottages could be built.[34]

His advice was rejected.

Even if working-class tenants were queuing to rent the space, so that an income stream was assured, developers could still be tempted to enhance profits by cutting corners with build quality. This immediately led to construction risk. In 1843 'a house in a forward state of erection, at Hartslands, belonging to Mr Gibbon, being just ready to receive the roof, fell with a tremendous crash'. No lives were lost, but the report blamed the 'catastrophe' not on 'jerry-building' (a term that dates from the 1830s), but on building on sandy soil in heavy rain.[35] But significant and potentially deadly risks such as this were slowly mitigated by regulation over the next few decades. Thus, when Thomas Bartholomew proposed to build cottages in Hartslands in 1872, his plans had to be 'accepted and passed' by the new Sevenoaks Local Board before he could start work.[36] This gave tenants and owners a legal space to object to actions of builders that hitherto posed risks to their health long after completion. However, the new regulations were limited and effective only if other vital structural requirements were adequate. In 1875 Hartslands resident John Tomline complained to the Board, on behalf of eleven families, 'that the drainage at the backs of their houses, within a few feet of the doors, was very bad, and that the effluvium was not only offensive, but dangerous to health'.[37] A few months earlier the Medical Officer for Sevenoaks, reporting to the Board, blamed those inadequate facilities squarely on there being: 'no public drainage whatever each builder left to his own device has either constructed a cesspool within a few yards of the dwelling to become a nuisance to its inmates or corrupted the sulliage further off, to become a nuisance to others'.[38]

---

33 David Killingray, 'A London city church estate in Kent: St Botolph's, Sevenoaks, 1646–2002', *Archæologia Cantiana*, CXXIV (2004), pp. 291–307.

34 *SEG*, 22 July 1876, p. 3.

35 *MJ*, 7 Nov. 1843, p. 3; Burnett, *Housing*, p. 21.

36 *MJ*, 9 Sept. 1872, p. 7.

37 *SEG*, 6 Nov. 1875, p. 3.

38 KHLC UD/Se/Am/1/1, 7 Aug. 1875.

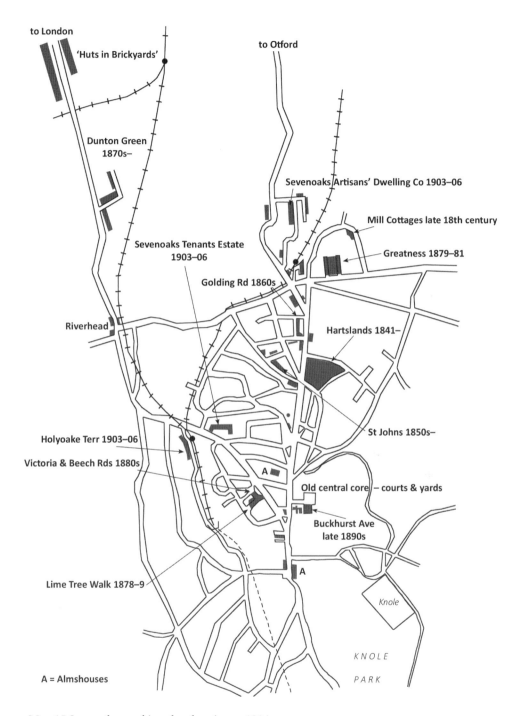

Map 15 Sevenoaks: working-class housing to 1914.

As soon as the properties were completed and occupied, as Tomline quickly discovered, the tenants began to share the risks, and they had to pay rent to the landlord while waiting, hopefully, for repairs to be carried out. The main risk of failing to pay the rent, for whatever reason, was summary eviction. But tenants, no matter how aged or infirm, could be forced out for other reasons. Mrs Sarah Tasker, aged 75 and blind, lived in an almshouse at Penshurst until it was 'forcibly entered by the Rev. W. Green, 40-year-old rector of the parish, who broke open the back door with an axe, and had all the doors of the house carried away'. The subsequent court case revealed that Mrs Tasker's son had taken up residence there without permission; the press report suggested that, having lost her residence for good, his mother would be better off in the workhouse.[39] Proceedings were taken against the prosperous Rev. William Green who left assets under £6,000 in 1877; Mrs Tasker, a pauper, died in the Tonbridge workhouse c.1861.[40]

The late nineteenth century and beyond

Besides Hartslands, and a few streets with two-up two-down terraces, very few new working-class homes were being built in the later part of the century. Even fewer boasted any architectural or environmental distinction. The exception was Lime Tree Walk, designed by renowned architect Thomas Graham Jackson. He objected to the trend towards the gentrification of Sevenoaks, such that 'the poor people were being pushed clean away from the town', down to Hartslands or beyond, and he rejected the social engineering that implied the 'mischievous sorting out of classes into distinct districts for rich and poor'.[41] His enterprising solution was to buy a field in the town centre, where he built 24 new cottages. As he proudly wrote, 'A great number of families were eventually well and cheaply housed on a beautiful site commanding lovely views equal to any enjoyed by their well-to-do neighbours.'[42] But the scheme also had architectural merit, the cottages being considered 'especially successful, exploiting the slight slope to add variety to an already varied array of gables, dormers and oriel windows'.[43] At the start of the twentieth century more of what is now termed social housing had been built by the Sevenoaks Artisans Dwelling Company, the Sevenoaks Tenants Estate and the Tenants Association (some people in neighbouring well-heeled Kippington complained at having clerks and artisans located so close by), but this comprised little more than 100 dwellings in total.[44] Few working-class Sevenoaks families lived in houses as good as those

39 *SEG*, 29 Jan. 1856, p. 5.
40 Grave of Green in Penshurst churchyard, National Probate Administration (Index of Wills and Administration), 6 Nov. 1877.
41 Basil Jackson, *Recollections of Thomas Graham Jackson, 1835–1924* (Oxford, 1950), p. 130.
42 *Ibid.*
43 John Newman, *Buildings of England – Kent: Weald and the west* (New Haven, CT, 2012), p. 528.
44 Killingray and Purves, *Dictionary*, pp. 177–8, 41.

Figure 5.2 Model working-class housing, Lime Tree Walk, in the centre of Sevenoaks, built 1878–82. This drawing by architect Thomas Jackson, *c*.1890, shows the development of 24 cottages, the Temperance Hotel (centre right) and the view to the skyline of Knole Park.
Source: Sevenoaks Society, folder 3.

in Lime Tree Walk, whose occupants were less likely to suffer the residential risks faced by their counterparts elsewhere in the town. One might reasonably ask how they managed to secure such fine accommodation, but there is no evidence extant about how Jackson chose his occupiers.

It is instructive to compare the residents of two very different developments, over time, using the 1881 and 1911 censuses. In 1881 the population of Lime Tree Walk was 182, giving an average of 7.3 people in each of its 25 households. This was half as many again as Redman's Place, the alley at the centre of the town that was renowned for its poor housing (17 households totalling 82 people, or 4.82 per dwelling) and the median for Hartslands that year of 4.46. By 1911, however, the average Lime Tree Walk household numbered just 4.75 – a remarkable drop on 30

99

years earlier – while Redman's Place had, conversely, become slightly more crowded, with an average occupancy of 5.2 people per dwelling.[45]

We have no idea of the length of leases, nor for how long dwellings were occupied, but since the average age of the heads of families was 43.2 in Lime Tree Walk and just 37.6 in Redman's Place in 1881, it may be that they were able to remain longer in the former. By 1911, however, the equivalent figures had risen substantially to 53 in Lime Tree Walk and 43 for their counterparts at Redman's Place.[46] This enhanced life expectancy, even in the working-class areas of the town, indicates almost certainly the significant impact of better nutrition and sanitation.

Those three decades saw a significant shift in the occupations of heads of households and, probably, class allegiances too. In 1881 there was no substantive difference between the two streets, almost all heads of households being either skilled artisans (carpenters, bricklayers and laundrywomen) or unskilled workers (labourers, porters and painters). By 1911, however, Lime Tree Walk had changed greatly to become much more middle class, with a dairy foreman and a wine merchant both in occupation. Redman's Place, by contrast, was becoming resolutely more working class and/or less skilled, with households headed by a boot repairer, a charlady and a milkman.[47]

Housing the poor, before council houses were constructed after the Great War, demanded a comprehensive solution, over and above the piecemeal initiatives above. This was a major preoccupation from the 1840s, after 'the whole sordid story' of the many urban slums had been exposed in parliamentary papers and – more positively – in George Godwin's new *The Builder* magazine, by highlighting new and better construction methods; both ensured that 'the problems of the poor were brought constantly before the eyes of an often unwilling public'.[48] Thomas Graham Jackson was in the tradition of a number of prosperous individuals who stimulated the charitable idea of housing the poor in that period, but their benevolent paternalism worked in a very particular way. Key to it was their willingness to assume the considerable risks inherent in being landlords to the poor, especially given the latter's frequent inability, or disinclination, to pay the rent on time. The investment returns that resulted were generally far lower than those from other assets, such as bonds or equities. Such 'Five Per cent Philanthropists', as they were later called, subsidised their tenants by, effectively, willingly accepting the transfer of their housing risk onto themselves. This is a fundamental point, for we would argue that any significant social progress or improvement always involves the transfer of risk from one party, less able to bear it, to another more capable

---

45 Census Return for 1881: Sevenoaks and Hartslands; Census Return for 1911: Sevenoaks.

46 Census Returns for 1881 and 1911: Sevenoaks.

47 Census Returns for 1881 and 1911: Sevenoaks.

48 Quoted by John Nelson Tarn, *Five per cent philanthropy: an account of housing in urban areas, 1840–1914* (Cambridge, 1973), pp. 3–4.

Figure 5.3 Redman's Place. Photographed here on Victory Day 1945, Redman's Place was one of the narrow alley ways east of Sevenoaks High Street. It is not known when the houses were built, certainly badly and some originally with a weatherboard construction, later faced by brickwork. They are shown on a map of 1867. There were outside privies and water was drawn from a well and pump in the yard, the former noted as polluted in 1888.
Source: Sevenoaks Society.

of doing so. That process may take place willingly, or it may occur only under compulsion, perhaps through national or local taxation systems. The wealthy or the independent may be perfectly capable of bearing many of those risks, should they so desire. But when those risks are not transferred, meaningful social changes in the lives of the mass of the poor are rendered impossible. Jackson's willingness to assume the risks inherent in building Lime Tree Walk could never benefit more than 200 people at any one time. Welcome though that was, it still left many more of the poor in Sevenoaks mired in housing squalor, where their lives were nastier and generally much shorter than those of their better-off counterparts. Only when national and/or local government was itself prepared to assume housing risk, from the early twentieth century, by constructing dwellings for the lower orders, did they stand a reasonable chance of living in decent homes.

Paying the rent

Actions for eviction, even against tenants who did not pay the rent, were not bound to succeed and the landlord's legal position did not improve significantly as the nineteenth century progressed. Even after the Small Tenements Recovery Act of 1838 established a less cumbersome process of eviction for such tenants, it could still take many weeks to remove non-payers who were alive to the strategies available to them; the legal emphasis therefore focused more on 'security of tenure than speed of repossession' and landlords often fumed in impotent rage.[49] This may be seen in the paucity of actions for eviction in the pages of the local press. Even when they did take place the court often sided with the tenant, albeit sometimes on technicalities. In 1898 George Everest was sued for possession of a cottage in Sevenoaks (possibly Weald) by his landlord. Everest told the court he was unable to find alternative accommodation; he had offered to lease another but its occupants were in the same position. Asked by the magistrate whether there was 'any difficulty in getting cottages in the Sevenoaks district' he said that there was, but added that he 'was agreeable to pay the rent if time was given him to find another cottage', and he was given another month to pay.[50] This, importantly, reveals not only the sympathy of the magistracy toward the tenant but also the long-term disequilibrium of cottage demand over supply, which was as pronounced at the end of the nineteenth century as it had been when Grover developed Hartslands sixty years earlier. Some tenants received sympathetic treatment from property owners. For example, in May 1892 William Goodman, a 70-year-old chemist who had traded in the town for thirty years, received help and offers of assistance, only being evicted, surrounded by his meagre goods in the London Road, when he was unable to pay his rent. The poor man was helped by local private charity, but, ill in mind, he was removed to the Barming asylum, where he died that September.[51]

Tenants might find themselves unable to occupy a property if it was in very poor repair. In 1870 master bootmaker Frederick Luckhurst suffered that occupational risk when he was sued by Daniel Grover junior for a quarter's unpaid rent, £9. His defence was that 'after heavy rains the rain poured through the roof into three of the bedrooms, and ran through to a sitting-room below, damaging the furniture, and a lodger was compelled to leave through it'. The magistrate sympathised and Grover had to settle for just £5.[52] Another occupational risk was overcrowding, often necessitated by poverty, which even by the early twentieth century 'remained the most critical and most persistent aspect of the housing problem in the UK'.[53]

49   F.M.L. Thompson (ed.), *The Cambridge social history of Britain, 1750–1950*, vol. 2, *people and their environment* (Cambridge, 1990), p. 228.

50   *MJ*, 27 Oct. 1898, p. 7.

51   *SC*, 27 May 1892, p. 5, and 9 Sept. 1892, p. 4.

52   *SEG*, 6 June 1870, p. 5.

53   Burnett, *Housing*, p. 145.

Hartslands was not immune. One cottage was occupied by a family of 11 in 1841 and the problem remained over sixty years later, for in 1904 the sanitary inspector found a shoemaker, his wife and nine children living in a single small cottage.[54]

Dealing with the risks of fire

A further important risk was fire. The Sevenoaks Fire Engine Association had been established in 1826, funded by subscription. In 1843 the great and the good in the town subscribed from £2 to 2s and its treasurer, William Morphew, was well aware of the dangers of fire, having received a letter threatening arson against his own property during the Swing disturbances.[55] A strong element of *bourgeois oblige* permeated the published list; respectable middle-class residents were expected to support many worthy local causes, and such lists helped others to keep track of who was funding what. Moreover, many residents would also have been quite happy to bask in the public eye, as such displays of generosity allowed them to demonstrate simultaneously their wealth, social status, civic responsibility and charitable concern. But, despite that layer of additional meaning, many middle-class people in the area, as also others lower down the social scale, understood the hazard of fire, so invested hard cash to try to lessen the possible impact.

Middle-class residents could also embrace more practical assistance. In 1842 a fire broke out at the premises of William Ring, a baker and confectioner in Sevenoaks. Causing over £1,000 of damage, it consumed much of his house and several outbuildings, and his family and servants only just got out alive. Two fire engines attended but what was most impressive was how – if the newspaper reports are to be believed – the 'assembled multitude' of Sevenoaks, numbering from 'eight hundred to a thousand' turned out to check 'the progress of the flames and supplying water'. Here was co-operative risk mitigation seen at its most urgent, although no doubt some did display a measure of self-interest as they sought to prevent the conflagration spreading to nearby properties.[56]

The Association later publicly thanked residents for 'the judicious activity displayed by all parties' and urged 'the town to adopt some plan by which an ample supply of water may be obtained at any moment'.[57] Here, albeit after the event, was risk being assessed, total disaster averted by co-operative, town-wide effort and a proposal put forward to minimise future losses. Despite this severe setback, Ring re-established his business and was trading in the town by 1848.[58] But villagers far distant from a fire engine could only watch blazes helplessly, as at

---

54 Census Return for 1841: Sevenoaks (Hartslands); *SEG*, 5 Feb. 1904, p. 6.

55 *SA*, 1 Feb. 1843, p. 141; *MJ*, 21 Sept. 1830, p. 3.

56 *SEG*, 19 July 1842, p. 3.

57 *SA*, 1 Aug. 1842, p. 117.

58 Sevenoaks Library D176, manuscript notebook at (12 High Street), Isaac Loveland, 'Some names of tradesmen who resided in Sevenoaks about 1848 and later on'.

Figure 5.4 'The Ready'. This horse-drawn fire engine was deployed by the Sevenoaks Fire Engine Association, on behalf of the Local Board, from 1882 until at least 1902. In 1880 the Association advised 'hanging blankets, rick-cloths … well saturated with water … nearest the fire' and urged anyone inside a burning building, if unable to escape, to 'not precipitate themselves from the window whilst the smallest chance of assistance is left'.
Sources: Sevenoaks Library, no. 1019 and B167, *Rules and Regulations of the Sevenoaks Fire Brigade* (1880), pp. 10–11.

Ide Hill in 1905, when 'By the time the fire brigade arrived [the thatched cottages] were cinders.'[59]

The most obvious and effective way of mitigating the financial costs of fire was through insurance. Tenants, whose possessions were highly likely to perish in a conflagration, normally assumed the risk themselves, although the poor would have found premiums hard, if not quite impossible, to afford. There is no evidence of Hartslands residents, for example, insuring their goods in the period. Insurance was, in theory, available to all who could afford it unless, like Thompson in 1830, the size and frequency of their claims made insurers decline cover. And often claimants were not covered for the full extent of the loss – Ring was insured for only £1,000,

---

59   KHLC WU13/Z1, vol. 2.

for example.[60] However, the policies taken out in west Kent indicate that both the wealthy and artisans were alert to the dangers of fire and acted accordingly. So from 1803–05 Earl Camden insured his property at Seal with the Kent Fire & Life Office for £8,000 and John Atherfold, a butcher in the same village, insured three houses (one of which he occupied himself) with the same office for £250.[61]

Moreover, buying fire insurance reflected, in microcosm, an important contemporary trend in west Kent. Housing its population was a necessity but it was associated with several risk factors, from ensuring adequate construction quality to preventing cottages being overcrowded to putting fires out quickly. Linking them all was institutional oversight and official regulation by a series of increasingly influential statutory and non-statutory authorities for much of the latter nineteenth century. Extinguishing fires provides an excellent example. Self-help – only – before 1826 was superseded by the voluntary Association that managed, just, to douse Ring's flames. But the risk and costs of conflagrations were so severe that voluntary effort was administered by the Local Board from 1871 and taken over fully by the new Urban District Council in 1894.[62] More broadly, the huge expansion of government and quasi-governmental institutions in this period was underpinned by 'the principles of state responsibility' and are explained, in great part, by the overriding imperative to manage risk.[63]

Fuel

Fuel was essential for west Kent residents for lighting, heating and cooking. Its price rose during the especially harsh winters of the 1830s and 1840s, leading to increased distress among the poor, such as Tufnell's labourer family, whose 'consumption of coal is very uncertain … none is used until the evening'.[64] Their plight was in stark contrast to the situation at St Julian's, where in 1831 Robert Herries noted that 'fuel is cheap, and we must keep good fires'.[65] Although the rooms of even respectable members of the middle classes 'were much colder than we now expect', the main fuel risks were borne by the lower social orders, for the middle classes of Sevenoaks never did without an indoor fire or had to eat their food raw.[66] By contrast, many poor people in and around Sevenoaks would have risked going both hungry and cold for much of the nineteenth century. But, unlike accommodation and food, which could, to an extent, be improved by government legislation in general and an improved regulatory regime (i.e., one effectively enforced) in particular, the

---

60   *SEG*, 19 July 1842, p. 3.

61   KHLC U2593/B81.

62   Killingray and Purves, *Dictionary*, p. 57.

63   Burnett, *Plenty and want*, p. 188.

64   Tufnell, *Dwelling*, p. 5.

65   Private archives, Herries Papers, Robert Herries to Charles James Herries, 9 Dec. 1831.

66   Flanders, *Victorian house*, p. 73.

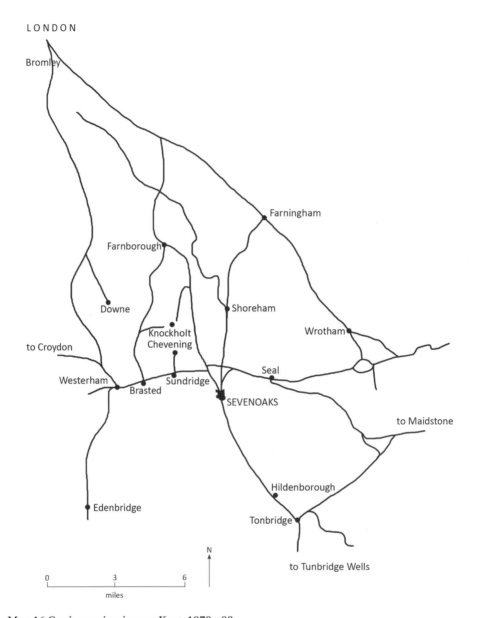

LONDON

Bromley

Farningham

Farnborough

Downe

Shoreham

Knockholt
Chevening

Wrotham

to Croydon

Seal

Westerham

Sundridge

Brasted

SEVENOAKS

to Maidstone

Hildenborough

Edenbridge

Tonbridge

N

0   3   6

miles

to Tunbridge Wells

Map 16 Carrier services in west Kent, 1870s–80s.
Nineteenth-century Britain was a horse-drawn society, with 3½ million horses in the 1890s.
Carriers with horse-drawn light carts and vans operated across the country, increasing in number
as the railway system expanded. They provided a delivery and collection service linking towns and
railways stations to villages. Carrier services from Tonbridge to London came through Sevenoaks
and provided an additional service. Smithies and wheelwrights were an essential support system for
this business; in Kent in the 1890s there were over 350 wheelwrights and more than 600 smithies.
Sources: Kelly's directory of Kent (1882) and Alan Everitt's, *Landscape and Community in
England* (London, 1985), pp. 304–5; the *Bromley directory* for 1876, and W.T. Pikes, *District
Blue Book. Weald of Kent and Romney Marsh directory 1884–85* (Hastings, 1885).

provision of fuel more resembled clothing, in that charity was often essential, although gathering wood 'was perceived as a customary right'.[67] So in autumn 1830 the poor of Sevenoaks were allowed to gather from Knole Park 'a seasonable supply of fuel at a time when it is so much needed' and the very important Sevenoaks Coal Charity supplied fuel to the town's poor until 1908.[68]

The railway reduced the price of coal after 1862. In 1905 Hills Bros, coal merchants at Tubs Hill station, claimed their customers had been 'personally managed for nearly 40 years'.[69] The presence of such fuel suppliers suggests that Sevenoaks houses were much warmer than they had been a hundred years earlier. Before the railways, coal deliveries came from the wharves at Tonbridge or Dartford. In 1912 William Knight's son Charles recalled how, in his youth, 'coal was brought from Tonbridge station to this town by wagon'.[70] The poor benefited especially from the prospect of cheaper freight rates. In 1841 one resident of Tonbridge (which gained its main-line connection to London and the coast the following year) thought coal prices would fall by two thirds, which would make a big difference. 'An addition of 10s or 20s to the price of coal may perhaps be unworthy of notice at Oxenhoath or Kippington [richer districts]; but what do the poor of Sevenoaks, Westerham, Edenbridge and twenty other places say?'[71]

A satisfactory method of lighting the streets of the town was slow in coming and could only be implemented by local government. Before 1839 Sevenoaks High Street and a few other roads in the town were lit by the 'small, dim, dusky light, that suddenly flashes up, and as quickly sinks again'.[72] That fuel, Corozo oil, was replaced by town gas; one contemporary press report praised it, insisting that 'The new gas has succeeded beyond the most sanguine expectations, and burns with a brilliancy that is not surpassed by any other company in Kent.'[73] After 1913 electricity, from a generating plant at Sundridge, was being distributed to a growing number of homes for lighting and heating.

For the wealthier middle classes their experience of the later nineteenth century was, as usual, a story not of reducing risk but of moving towards greater choice and convenience in the types of fuel available. In 1842 Sevenoaks ironmonger John Shewen was selling American Reflecting Ovens.[74] By 1884 the Sevenoaks Gas Company was offering to supply 'coke of the best quality', that was good for both

---

67   Clive Emsley, *Crime and society in England, 1750–1900* (London, 2010), p. 152.

68   *MJ*, 19 Oct. 1830, p. 4; Sevenoaks Library D462, Sevenoaks Coal Charity (1865).

69   *Salmon's directory of Sevenoaks*, 1905, advertisement at front – no pagination.

70   *SC*, 27 Dec. 1912, p. 8.

71   *SEG*, 9 Feb. 1841, p. 3.

72   *SA*, Aug. 1840, p. 18.

73   *Kentish Courier*, 23 Feb. 1839, p. 2.

74   *SA*, 1 April 1842, p. 101. Reflector ovens baked by capturing radiant heat from an open fire and reflecting it towards the food. The method avoided food being flavoured by the smoke.

Figure 5.5 Sevenoaks Housing Association, *c*.1908. This gathering of middle-aged Liberals and socialists represented the 'Progressive' element in Sevenoaks, eager to promote social welfare and improved working and living conditions for working-class people, children and the elderly poor, and the parliamentary votes for women. Seated second left in the front row is Arthur Hickmott, elected to the Urban District Council for the Independent Labour Party. For more than two decades he remained a persistent critical voice and public social conscience in predominantly Tory Sevenoaks.
Source: Author's collection.

heating and cooking.[75] Two years later it rented gas cooking ranges at 2s a quarter.[76] For those unable to afford to buy new stoves, they could at least get hold of cheap winter fuel through the Coal Charity. Operating by 1851, regular deliveries of three quarters of a ton (about 760kg) began late each year and carried on for about ten weeks. In the early 1870s, some 100 families in St John's and a similar number in the rest of the town benefited.[77] To qualify they had to have lived in the parish for six months, have a total family income of under 15s a week and not be guilty of

75   *SC*, 22 Feb. 1884, p. 4.
76   *SC*, 14 May 1886, p. 5.
77   *MJ*, 23 Dec. 1851, p. 3; *SEG*, 31 Dec. 1872, p. 5; 4 Nov. 1873, p. 5.

'gross immorality and misconduct'.[78] The coal was sold at half price in 1885, a policy that was considered 'very effective' since '[i]t does not wound the feelings or tend to pauperise those whom it is designed to assist'.[79] The cost was subsidised, as usual, by donations from the town's elite, which, in the winter of 1864–5, amounted to almost £50. Sums ranged from £10 from the owner of Knole to ten people who contributed 1s.[80] The press was also quite sure that the wealthier residents of the town had an undoubted moral obligation to contribute to relieve the suffering of the poor – and unequivocally encouraged them to do so: 'As winter has now set in with some severity we would urge upon the more wealthy among us, of whom there are several, who have not already contributed, that they should do so at once.'[81] Finally, fuel could be stolen; coal was a more lucrative target than wood, although it was more difficult to conceal in quantity and normally took longer to dispose of by burning. Such a theft took place in 1889, when John Kingswood and William Redsella, carman (or carrier), employed by George Humphrey, were fined £3 for having stolen 46lb (21kg) of coal worth 4s.[82]

Securing reliable accommodation at reasonable cost and ensuring the necessary fuel to heat the place and to cook food were major concerns for people living in nineteenth-century west Kent. Many of the houses inhabited by poorer people in Sevenoaks and the surrounding villages were of poor quality, damp and cold, with leaky roofs and lacking a reliable supply of clean water and adequate drainage for 'nuisance' waste. Occupation depended on rent being paid regularly, a constant challenge to those reliant on irregular work, such as farm and general labourers. Housing tied to employment might offer a degree of security of occupancy, but it increased the power of employers over those they employed. We now turn to examine two other vital necessities of life: food and clothing.

---

78   Sevenoaks Library D462.
79   *SC*, 25 Dec. 1885, p. 4.
80   Sevenoaks Library D462.
81   *SEG*, 30 Dec. 1873, p. 5.
82   *SC*, 13 Dec. 1889, p. 5.

Chapter 6

'The necessities of life': food and clothing

Clothing

Clothing was a bare necessity, essentially to protect and make presentable; suitable clothes for work were vital. For the poor 'a choice was always necessary; there was never enough money to pay for clothes *and* food *and* fuel *and* rent'. In those circumstances clothing often assumed a higher priority, because wearers' 'identity was forged, as well as expressed, through what they wore'.[1] Dressing to even minimal standards was costly and Curteis' labourer, 'G.B.', spent £2 10s a year on shoes for his family and a further £2 on clothing them.[2] Knitting was one solution, for woollen items at least, and Sevenoaks retailer James Payne was advertising his 'good stock' of knitting needles in 1837.[3] But some poor people did overspend on inappropriate clothing. William Cobbett was fiercely critical, on utilitarian grounds, of those labouring women and girls whose 'dress of their choice is showy and flimsy … today, they are ladies and tomorrow as ragged as sheep with the scab'.[4]

Clothing was the most visible outward manifestation of class, since '[i]t was obvious who they [the poor] were by the clothes they wore'.[5] For middle-class inhabitants of the Sevenoaks area, clothing partly revolved around achieving and maintaining appropriate and acceptable displays of respectable status. Headgear was an immediate signifier, as shown in nineteenth-century photographs: lower-class men wore cloth caps, while the middle classes and wealthy were crowned by top hats and 'stove pipes'.[6] The class distinctions surrounding clothing were encapsulated in newspaper correspondence in 1879. 'A Sevenoaks Ratepayer' bemoaned the fact that he could not get a seat on the new 'handsome benches' around the Vine at cricket matches as they were occupied by those 'whose dress

---

1   Vivienne Richmond, *Clothing the poor in nineteenth century England* (Cambridge, 2013), pp. 3, 296.

2   Curteis, *Peel*, p. 46.

3   *MJ*, 7 March 1837, p. 1.

4   William Cobbett, *Cottage economy* ([1822] Oxford, 1979), p. 117.

5   Simon Fowler, *Workhouse: the people; the places; the life behind doors* (Kew, 2008), p. 23.

6   Anckorn, *A Sevenoaks Camera*, A.

and manners show they are non-ratepayers', and asked if they could be reserved for local taxpayers (see Plate 6). 'JBS' sarcastically responded by suggesting that 'an officer be appointed with discerning powers ... whose duty it shall be to drive away' all such inferior beings.[7]

Catherine Martin provides a good example of an ultra-respectable middle-class Sevenoaks woman who, perhaps unconsciously, noted such distinctions in working-class apparel, even though it was irrelevant to her missionary outreach. So, when paying visits to local cottages in the early 1840s, she remarked upon the man 'smoking his pipe in his dirt and dishabille' and the old woman who was 'dressed in the costume of 1800'.[8] Jane Edwards, too, remembered from her youth (in the early nineteenth century) a Miss Paine who 'dressed quite in the old style, she wore handsome dresses with elbow sleeves and ruffles'.[9]

Clothing the poor

One of the prime functions of the Poor Law Amendment Act of 1834 was to reduce the annual poor rates. It did so by forbidding 'outdoor' (home-based) relief and replacing it with 'indoor relief' in the workhouse. Samuel Bligh of the Sevenoaks Guardians informed the Poor Law Commissioners in 1834 that 'since this arrangement, our Pension List has been considerably reduced'.[10] One of the Act's less well-known consequences was how it made the overall standards of dress of the very poorest even worse. In 1837 the Sevenoaks workhouse sought to ensure the adequacy of its inmates' dress by returning to one supplier items of apparel that were not of the quality of the samples sent earlier and demanding their replacement. The extensive range included 48 men's and 36 boy's suits and 36 women's and 48 girl's flannel petticoats as well as shoes for the women and boots for the men and boys.[11]

Before 1834 outdoor relief money was often given for clothes, although that was, in theory, abolished by the new legislation. Its self-help replacement was the clothing, shoe and blanket society/club movement, often run by churches. Their prevalence might indicate that they were trusted more than retailers' similar organisations, for the latter could easily cease trading – for whatever reason – with the local poor their helpless unsecured creditors. Churches were, by contrast, permanent fixtures, providing another example of how risk was mitigated by trusted local institutions.

The poor who benefited (such as the 75 young members of the Dunton Green Sunday School clothing club in 1881) paid from 1d to 6d a week, and better-off residents, too, often subscribed.[12] Their contributions topped up weekly deposits

---

7   *KSC*, 4 July 1879, p. 8; 11 July 1879, p. 8.

8   Field, *Sincere devotion*, pp. 101, 111.

9   Jane Edwards, *Her recollections of old Sevenoaks* ([1863] Sevenoaks, 1985), p. 11.

10   TNA MH 12/5315, 4 Oct. 1834.

11   KHLC G/Se/ACb1, 54, 6 May 1837. Richmond, *Clothing*, pp. 190–1.

12   *SC*, 5 Aug. 1881, p. 5.

to fund a bonus paid on each share at the end of the year, with fines levied for late payments or failure to pay. In 1881 Sevenoaks draper Isaac Corke offered 'special advantages to clothing clubs'.[13] The societies 'fostered self-respect and a degree of self-reliance'.[14] Middle-class subscribers were not acting entirely philanthropically, as they also aimed to reduce the poor rates. More interesting is what clothes the poor wore, whether personally bought new through societies (which implied a degree of choice) or donated by charity (which did not). At Otford in 1827, for example, the Charman Bequest gave 7s to Mr and Mrs Taylor, which they spent on hose (stockings, socks or breeches) and calico (a cheap, coarse cotton cloth).[15] Clothing clubs operated widely throughout west Kent during our period, including the Trinity Provident and Clothing Club in Tunbridge Wells.[16]

Shoes, especially working boots, were absolute necessities, so boot clubs existed for both adults (as at Farningham in 1852) and children (such as that run by Fordcombe Sunday School in the late nineteenth century).[17] Boots were the staple footwear sold in vast quantities to people of all classes by the later nineteenth century. In 1890 the Sevenoaks Clothing Company's High Street shop was advertising women's strong boots for the fields at prices ranging from 4s 6d to 5s 3d a pair.[18]

Aristocratic and gentle ladies played a major part in the organisation of local clothing clubs and blanket societies across west Kent. The clothing club in Plaxtol was reported as offering 'creature comforts ... liberally supplied by ladies of the parish ... [to] their poor sisters'.[19] In the village of Seal the clothing club ran from at least 1868 to 1892.[20] It sought to promote 'frugality and self-help' among the poor and needy by providing warm clothing for winter.[21] Members paid a monthly subscription and annually received a clothes parcel. This charitable work in Seal was promoted by the indefatigable Ladies Pratt, the Hon. Misses Boscawen and Mrs Alexander. They also created a Needlewomen's Society, which flourished during the late 1860s–70s, its purpose being to cause 'a weekly supply of materials to be distributed to the working members [poor married women], to be made up into articles of clothing', which they could buy 'at the cost price of the materials'.[22] Clearly, 'clothing societies helped with the provision of a basic, utilitarian

---

13   *SC*, 11 Nov. 1881, p. 4.

14   Richmond, *Clothing*, p. 194.

15   KHLC P279/25/1, 'An account of Clothing given to the Poor from money received by will of John Charman'.

16   *MJ*, 17 Nov. 1863, p. 5.

17   KHLC P145/25/30; P287B/25/1.

18   *SC*, 25 July 1890, p. 6.

19   *MJ*, 3 Dec. 1866, p. 6.

20   *MJ*, 29 Nov. 1892, p. 7.

21   *MJ*, 2 Dec. 1872, p. 7.

22   *MT*, 26 Dec. 1868, p. 6; *MT*, 28 Jan. 1871, p. 8.

wardrobe', provided some employment for women and, possibly, as its founders hoped, strengthened working-class households.[23]

At the end of the nineteenth century voluntary clothing provision expanded further. It became, on the one hand, more formal and institutionalised on a national level, with the foundation of Needlework Guilds, and, on the other, still more localised and informal, with the emergence of charity jumble sales. The guilds were started in 1882 by Lady Wolverton. Aristocratic patronage not only lent them prestige but also contributed to their success. However, although 'they aimed to supplement, not supplant' clothing societies, it did not turn out quite like that in west Kent.

The guilds differed from the societies in three key ways: first through their county-wide structures; secondly in how they supplied clothing through intermediaries, especially church ministers, rather than directly to individual and institutional recipients; and thirdly in how members, primarily ladies with time to spare, agreed to provide two items a year, either bought or made, increasingly on the new sewing machines then becoming available.[24] The sewing machine was a double-edged sword, however, for although it promised a 'less arduous future for milliners and dressmakers' and could be both useful and a potent status symbol in middle-class homes, within factories and in the homes of domestic workers it could easily 'be an instrument of exploitation'.[25] But by 1860 the 'Boudoir Sewing Machine' was one of a number of patent devices being advertised (mainly to the middle classes) across west Kent at prices ranging from £10 to £20.[26]

The evidence suggests that formal guild activity took off slowly in west Kent. It began as late as 1893, but by 1899 it had distributed the grand total of 6,787 garments (an increase of 400 on the year before) to 89 separate parishes and benevolent institutions.[27] The Sevenoaks group delivered 817 items, or just under 12 per cent of the total. In 1901 recipients were chiefly members of the armed forces, although 'the poor labourers and their wives and children have not been forgotten'.[28]

The driving force behind the Sevenoaks Guild were the three Ladies Pratt, Eleanor, Clara and Frances, the latter 'unceasing in good works', as her obituary put it when she died aged 81.[29] Those good works included clothing the poor of west Kent from at least 1868 to 1912; 'they also did a lot of work for the church and every Monday [the] three of them took clubs at the [Seal] village hall'.[30] Their approach also highlights how this charitable endeavour was organised locally and

23 Richmond, *Clothing*, p. 210; *MJ*, 23 Dec. 1871, p. 3.

24 Richmond, *Clothing*, pp. 225–6.

25 Asa Briggs, *Victorian things* (London, 1988), pp. 284, 285.

26 *SEG*, 21 Feb. 1860, pp. 7–8.

27 *SC*, 11 May 1900, p. 5.

28 *SC*, 29 March 1901, p. 5.

29 *SC*, 6 April 1917, p. 7.

30 Seal Public Library, Jim Johnson, 'A lifetime in Seal', typescript memoir, n.d. but late nineteenth century.

Figure 6.1 Fashionable ladies conversing in Sevenoaks High Street. This drawing by William Knight dates from the second quarter of the nineteenth century. Note the badly dressed poor man and child on the left, who may play no part in the middle-class conversation taking place in the middle of the street.
Source: Sevenoaks Society, C0023/D.

how it changed during that period. For in Seal, rather than supplement the existing clothing societies, the Ladies Pratt saw that the stronger institutional structure of the Kent Guild offered a better way to clothe the poor than the Seal Clothing Club ever could.

Another popular method of clothing the poor, jumble sales, appears to have been ineffective in the Sevenoaks area. Only a single sale was mentioned in the *Chronicle* before 1900, although a significant number in 1910 coincided with outreach by the London City Mission to local fruit pickers: 'Several jumble sales have been held … The proceeds … have been spent in purchasing bread etc for free distribution to every picker.'[31]

Within the context of the makeshift economy, the poor had several sources of cheap clothing that became increasingly institutionalised and more widely available by 1900. And they ran less risk of being cold or appearing disreputable, at least to other members of their own class. Once properly clad they might have considered acquiring other necessities, or even a few luxuries, including more or better-quality garments. One important way respectable members of the working class sought to

31   *SC*, 20 May 1898, p. 8; 29 July 1910, p. 5.

distinguish themselves from those poorer than themselves was by owning 'Sunday Best' suits, although in so doing they could inadvertently become targets of middle-class censure or ridicule. In 1899 George Pannifer, a horse dealer from Edenbridge, was sued for non-payment of a debt. In court the judge said he was an example of how a defendant might dress 'especially for my instructions'. Amidst laughter, Pettifer indignantly replied that he was not then wearing his Sunday Best, as he had on the previous occasion: 'I have my working clothes on today, as I have just come here after clearing the stables out.'[32]

Shopping for clothes – an example of greater choice

Shops in Sevenoaks and other west Kent towns provided for men and women of means 'a quiet abundance' of choice if they wished to buy clothes and keep up with the latest fashions.[33] By 1843 Sevenoaks boasted a wide variety of tailors, drapers, habit-makers, milliners, dressmakers, hatters and hosiers. Arthur Fenner, for example, offered a wide range of fabrics and products, including broad cloths from 6s 6d a yard, summer frocks from 18s and beaver hats from 5s.[34] Choice was the developing theme of the nineteenth century; in 1843 many shops were described along those lines, being 'well stocked with the best description of goods, which secure the patronage of members of the gentry and wealthy'.[35] The well-to-do wanted good shoes of differing kinds, so shoemakers supplied a variety of styles and quality. By 1882 there were no fewer than 30 traders selling clothing and footwear.[36] Fenner seems to have supplied the upper end of the market, but another Sevenoaks draper had a rather less affluent clientele. On a single day in March 1831 Messrs Prickett's sales included calico for Mrs Janner (1s 1d), gloves for Miss Moon (1s 8d) and socks for Mr Boaks (1s 5d).[37]

The most important macroeconomic shift in the clothing industry during our period resulted from the railways. To emphasise the point made earlier, before they arrived most products consumed in Sevenoaks were made within the immediate west Kent area, so the 1841 census shows eight 'shoemakers' living in Hartslands. They would have made shoes and boots themselves with leather sourced from local tanneries such as those at Riverhead or Underriver.[38] By 1912, however, footwear would have originated in specialist industrial centres (such as Northampton) and arrived by train for sale in the town. So it is significant that the Beehive Boot and Shoe Stores of Sevenoaks High Street that year retailed 'K Make' boots and

---

32 *MJ*, 18 May 1899, p. 6.
33 *SA*, 1 Sept. 1840, p. 23.
34 *SA*, 1 April 1843, p. 149.
35 *Ibid.*
36 *Kelly's directory of Kent* (1882), pp. 495–8.
37 KHLC U1000/29/B1, 23 March 1831.
38 Census return for 1841: Hartslands; Killingray and Purves, *Dictionary*, pp. 190, 203.

Figure 6.2 The children of James and Daisy Bolton. They are pictured at the family home, Bradbourne Road, St John's, Sevenoaks, *c.*1912. Daisy is posed with Alice aged nine, William seven, and Olive five. The children are dressed, probably in their best clothes, for this posed photograph. The small front garden is well-maintained, the tree pruned, outward signs of respectability in a street which contained other owner-occupied houses. On the house wall is a board describing Jim Bolton's skilled occupation: 'Sign writer, Marbler and Grainer'. He was an aspiring member of the growing class of skilled men in Sevenoaks who had a reliable source of income, were proudly independent, intent on respectability, moderate in lifestyle, and able to buy their own homes, and to maintain their families.
Source: Census Return, 1911: Sevenoaks. Photograph: author's collection.

shoes but also specialised in 'repairs'.[39] Such work was probably contracted out to someone like Frederick Terry, of Hartslands, who was described in the 1911 census as a boot *repairer*.[40] Sevenoaks had in the previous seventy years moved decisively from an almost entirely self-contained artisanal centre, where consumer goods were locally manufactured, to one where they were instead made in northern or Midland factories, sold in Sevenoaks shops and then serviced or repaired by that same artisanal class of west Kent workers.

Food, glorious food

In an agrarian economy such as that of west Kent food for consumption had to be grown locally, so bad weather was always a risk. The vicar of Tudeley described the great storm that took place in August 1763 as being so severe that the district's corn was 'shattered upon the ground … we hear children crying aloud for bread'.[41] But, even when crops did grow, access to even the barest necessities of life was constrained by consumers' incomes. The story of food consumption in west Kent was, broadly, in line with what happened across southern England. The low wages, just a few shillings a week, received by agricultural labourers in the early part of the period, combined with higher food prices to create a vicious circle of epic proportions.[42] Although wages in Meopham, for example, were raised from 1s 8d to 2s a day in 1795, the price of bread rose 167 per cent in Kent between 1793 and 1812 and the hunger caused by the ongoing depression of the later 1820s was a major cause of the violent protests in west Kent during the early 1830s.[43] It did not end then, for the entire 'first half of the nineteenth century was miserably hungry for many labourers', whose 'usual diet' at Meopham in 1795 had been 'bread, cheese, butter, pudding and sometimes beef or mutton'.[44] It had worsened considerably a few decades later.

Even the benefits of self-provisioning were restricted. A family of five owning a pig for their own consumption had a protein source providing 'less than an ounce of meat a week per person', and growing vegetables on an allotment or in the garden would have 'added variety to diets but most gardens were small' (as in poorer districts such as Hartslands) so, again, 'the benefits were limited'.[45] Having said that, a vestry meeting in Ightham in September 1830 resolved to build eight new cottages

---

39   *SC*, 2 Aug. 1912, p. 1.

40   Census return for 1911: Hartslands.

41   John Hedges, *A description of the storm that happened in west Kent in the month of August 1763* (London, 1763), p. 4.

42   Burnett, *Plenty and want*, p. 22.

43   Frederick Eden, *The state of the poor* (London, 1797), vol. 2, p. 290.

44   Burnett, *Plenty and want*, p. 35; Eden, *State of the poor*, p. 290.

45   Emma Griffin, 'Diets, hunger and living standards during the industrial revolution', *Past & Present*, 239 (2018), pp. 71–111 (p. 89); Rebecca Earle, 'The political economy of nutrition in the later eighteenth century', *Past & Present*, 242 (2019), pp. 79–114.

'for the use of the paupers of this parish', each with up to a quarter of an acre of parish land allotted to it, which would undoubtedly have enabled their residents to grow more food for the table and improve their diets.[46]

Food was important to the lower classes in another way, for many earned their livings from producing it, although precisely how changed greatly over the second half of the nineteenth century. In 1841 46 per cent of male Hartslands heads of household were agricultural labourers, so their wages came directly from primary (food) production. By 1901 that had fallen to under 10 per cent, with just four individuals so described.[47] The remainder were employed no longer as primary producers but had instead moved further up the supply chain, and were, for example, bakers or grocers. The additional value many added to the process and the enhanced wages that resulted go some way to explaining the better standards of living many Hartslands residents enjoyed by the 1890s. They had a wider choice of occupation as well. Eighteen per cent of Hartslands men and 28 per cent of its women had non-manual jobs (a very rare phenomenon sixty years earlier; they included schoolmaster, clerk, stationer's assistant and nurse). Even manual workers could enter the burgeoning steam laundry businesses that had sprung up in the 1890s; no fewer than 55 women were employed there in 1901.[48]

Improving nutrition?

By 1914 several additional and significant macroeconomic factors, in particular higher wages and falling food prices, had transformed the position of many working people. Common labourers earned wages 30 per cent higher in 1885 than they were in 1857 (from about 15s to 20s a week) and agricultural workers did even better (up from 8s to 13s a week; in Kent they averaged about 10s a week in 1850).[49] And the combination of free trade leading to the arrival of more foreign food (wheat imports rose from 8.6m hundredweight in 1840 to over 64m hundredweight in 1883), more intensive farming methods and more efficient, cheaper distribution caused food prices to fall dramatically over that period. That of wheat, for example, decreased from 66s 4d per hundredweight in 1840 to just 41s 7d in 1883.[50] The result was that everyone except the very poorest was eating more, better-quality food than had their grandparents. For the upper and middle classes, who were well represented in late Victorian Sevenoaks, this implied a much greater and conspicuous choice of food and beverages to consume, both inside and, increasingly, outside the home. The Sevenoaks Coffee House was in existence as early as 1800, but by 1891 The

---

46   KHLC P202/8/2.

47   Census Return for 1841: Sevenoaks (Hartslands); Census Return for 1901: Sevenoaks.

48   Census Return for 1901: Sevenoaks.

49   Leone Levi, *Wages & earnings of the working classes, report to Sir Arthur Bass* (1885), p. 30, see Burnett, *Plenty and want*, p. 94; MC, 6 March 1850, p. 5.

50   Levi, *Wages*, p. 89.

International Tea Company and a mineral water supplier were trading in the town centre; in that year, too, opened the temperance Lime Tree Buffet, the first restaurant, or 'refreshment room', distinct from a hotel, to serve the town.[51]

'Necessity determined food consumption.'[52] The very poorest lived and were fed in the workhouse. In 1813, the *Articles for maintaining and employing the poor of Wrotham* set out the *Quantity and quality of victuals to be served to the poor.* It included their diet and what it cost. As an example, on Sundays, Tuesdays and Thursdays men received bread and gruel for breakfast, beef, suet pudding and vegetables for dinner and bread, cheese and butter for supper. Children ate smaller portions of the same. Men received a pint of beer every day at dinner, women three quarters of a pint. The sick were 'dieted as directed by the surgeon'. The budget per pauper each week was 5s 6d during the summer and 5s in winter.[53]

Diets at the Union workhouse, Sundridge, 1889

The food and conditions provided at the New Poor Law Union workhouse at Sundridge in its early days were very basic. As the causes of poverty were better understood, so the diet and clothing provided improved. In 1889 the contracts for tenders for food included bread, flour, meat, 'American corned meat (in 14lb tins)', 'new milk', porter, beer, grocer's and chesesemonger's goods, cod liver oil and coal. Ten years later the workhouse inmates numbered 194 and included a constant flow of paupers and tramps. Food was the major item of expenditure, totalling £1,530 for the year.

Sources: SC, 8 September 1889, p. 6; and 16 September 1899, p. 5.

The quality of the food workhouse inmates ate presented another risk factor. In 1841 Poor Law inspectors, following a visit to the Sevenoaks workhouse, reported that the 'meat puddings are an indigestible form of food, and that it would be better, and we think cheaper, to have baked or at any rate boiled meat' instead.[54] Those inside endured a meagre, monotonous, penny-pinching diet, which was another

---

51 British Library Cup.21.g.36/47, General Reference Collection, advertisement, 'An assembly and ball, at the Coffee House, Sevenoaks; Tuesday, October 28, 1800', etc.; *Kelly's directory of Kent, Surrey and Sussex*, 1891, pp. 560–3.

52 Rachel Rich, *Bourgeois consumption: food, space and identity in London and Paris* (Manchester, 2011), p. 12.

53 KHLC P406/18/7, 19 April 1813.

54 UKPP, Lords, *Appendices B–F to the eighth report of the Poor Law Commissioners*, No. 399 (1842), No. 25, p. 116.

reason why the poor so feared and hated the institutions they called 'bastilles'. In a good example of how almost any form of choice was denied, at Sevenoaks a visiting solicitor was not even allowed to give an inmate an apple.[55]

Even those poor who were not held within the workhouse had to subsist on a monotonous dietary regime. The weekly diet of the eight members of the Tunbridge Wells family described by Tufnell in 1841 comprised seven gallons of flour, three gallons of potatoes, three pounds of salt butter, two pounds of cheese, two ounces of tea, one pound of sugar and some milk. They never ate meat, although their allotment of one twentieth of an acre supplied 'a considerable quantity of potatoes and other vegetables'. Their food bill totalled 'over 17s a week, leaving them barely able to pay the rent or afford shoes and clothing'.[56]

By mid-century, however, many residents of west Kent enjoyed better diets, including the generic Kentish labourer who 'is a stronger and heartier man than the other [his counterpart in Dorset] because his wages suffice to procure him a more nutritious diet'.[57] The middle classes of west Kent were largely untroubled by such concerns, for one important way in which they differed from the lower orders was their 'ability to make choices about what to eat'; thus, they never risked going hungry.[58]

The Sevenoaks workhouse, 1841

'On 22 April last, there were 57 men in 31 beds, and 40 women in 20 beds, in the Sevenoaks Workhouse. On the 25 December last five women were confined in two beds, in the same room, and three women were actually delivered in the same bed at the same time. Proper attention was not paid to them, and one woman died in her accouchement ... no inquest was held, and little notice was taken of her death.'

Source: *The Times*, 10 November 1841, p. 4.

Not every food retailer thrived in a competitive marketplace. Sevenoaks baker and grocer Stephen Jessup owned a shop in the early 1830s and his account books reveal his trade with the town's mainly middle-class residents. So 'Covell, Sevenoaks', who might have been local pork butcher John Covell, bought no fewer than 70 loaves in May 1833. Jessup also sold a wide range of other goods, including sack (wine), sugar, raisins, butter, soap and cheese, to customers such as John Colands,

55 G.R. Whythen Baxter, *The book of the Bastiles* (London, 1841), p. 163.
56 Tufnall, *Dwelling*, p. 5.
57 *MC*, 6 March 1850, p. 5.
58 Rich, *Bourgeois*, p. 12.

Figure 6.3 Bligh advertising, 28 June 1852. Sevenoaks boasted plenty of food shops even in the 'hungry forties'; in 1848 Sevenoaks High Street alone contained eight grocers, four butchers; two bakers, a greengrocer; a fishmonger and a bun shop. Retailing was competitive, prompting advertisements such as this hand bill from John Bligh, 'Grocer', with a shop in Market Place. He stressed his free trade ideas here too.
Source: Sevenoaks Library, D176, Loveland ms, 3, 30 High Street.

who lived at Borough Green, over seven miles away by road.[59] Another (unnamed) Sevenoaks grocer generated much of his custom from the leading Methodist families in Sevenoaks, but unlike Jessup, who could supply wholesale, this was a much smaller-scale retail business. In August 1837 the largest single sale was 2s 8½d for coffee, candles and butter and many were for small single purchases, such as 1½d on salt.[60] Such establishments appealed to Hartslands residents, especially because no evidence exists of any shops trading there before 1855, when there were two grocers, a baker and a butcher (and three beershops).[61] Before then its residents must have shopped in the centre of the town or at the few shops on St John's Hill.

A prime focus of the makeshift economy was putting food on the table. Opportunities included, first, charitable donations to the poor from the wealthy of Sevenoaks, especially at Christmas time. At Knole House in 1862 'seven prime beasts [were] fatted on the estate … 602 families, comprising 2,118 persons, were the recipients'.[62] Secondly, if food was still in short supply it could simply be stolen. This was a much rarer phenomenon than the theft of fuel or even clothing, but at Bat and Ball, Sevenoaks, in 1854, 'some thieves entered the house of Mr. Bunn, shopkeeper … they ransacked the place, and stole a quantity of tea, tobacco, bread, cheese'.[63]

Diets, especially in the poorer villages, could remain meagre even at the end of the nineteenth century. Gilbert Gasson 'was brought up on goat's milk, cod liver oil and honey', and ate bread made 'in the big oven shared with two neighbours' and rabbit pie. Branded Scotch Porridge Oats were 'too dear', however, so the family made do with bread and skimmed milk. At the village school the children were fed on boiled bones from local farms made into soup that included vegetables sourced from the vicarage; those 'who had come furthest were served first'.[64] But in other parts of Britain at that time 'large sections of the working class were making impressive strides towards comfort and prosperity' and were able to afford more food, including bacon and eggs for breakfast, potatoes and beef for lunch and an evening meal of bread and butter, vegetables and fish.[65] One Hartslands trader who benefited from this trend from 1891 was 'Tea Dealer, Grocer and Provision Merchant' Frank Rowley. His extensive press advertising offered 'the best quality goods at moderate prices' and his shop was, that Christmas, described as having 'a good show of all kinds of groceries and

---

59   KHLC Q/C/i/114/1–4. Covell was trading from 22 High Street, Sevenoaks, in 1848 – Loveland ms, p. 2.

60   KHLC U1000/29/B2, 19 Aug. 1837.

61   *Post Office directory of Essex, Herts, Kent …* (London, 1855), Part 1, pp. 485–8.

62   *SEG*, 30 Dec. 1862, p. 5.

63   *SEG*, 21 Feb. 1854, p. 5.

64   KHLC WU13/Z1, vol. 1.

65   Burnett, *Plenty and want*, p. 178.

wines and his windows are tastefully decorated'.[66] Lower-class residents by then enjoyed disposable incomes far beyond those of their predecessors in the 1840s. They also bought a much wider choice of products.

The later nineteenth-century economic improvements were reflected in more specialist production, wider distribution and better marketing. The tithe award maps of the late 1830s for Sevenoaks and Tonbridge show that Elses Farm, in Sevenoaks Weald, was then roughly half pasture and half arable.[67] But after Albert Killick became its tenant around 1887 he concentrated on dairy produce; the renowned war poet Edward Thomas and his wife Helen lived at the farm from 1904 to 1906, with Helen remembering that about 50 cows 'were turned out into the meadow in front of the house' and how 'all day the farm boys washed milk cans and churns'.[68] By 1889 Killick had also opened a shop in Sevenoaks, Elses Farm Dairy, from where he sold farm products directly to consumers.[69] There, the 'shop front below the windows was covered in ceramic tiles decorated with cows and rural scenes' in order to make its products more attractive.[70] The main-line railway south of Sevenoaks bisected the farm, where a goods siding was built so that Killick could supply milk not just to Sevenoaks but also to London and elsewhere in the south-east.[71] When Elses Farm was sold in 1919, only 20 acres of the 110 being farmed were arable and that was for cattle feed.[72]

The adulteration of food

In west Kent, as more food became available during the nineteenth century, *quality* became an increasing concern. Inadvertent contamination was always a concern, since even well into the twentieth century in Sevenoaks 'food was largely displayed without the benefit of covering. Meat was usually hung on display racks outside the shop, uncovered', so prey to dust and flies.[73] In addition, food was deliberately and regularly adulterated by dishonest producers and retailers. In 1820 a leading contemporary campaigner against the practice wrote 'of all the frauds practised by mercenary dealers, there is none more reprehensible and at the same time more prevalent, than the sophistication of the various articles of food'.[74] He then proved

---

66   SC, 18 Dec. 1891, p. 8; 24 Dec. 1891, p. 5.

67   Tithe and apportionment surveys: Sevenoaks (1839); Tonbridge (1838), www.kentarchaeology.org. uk. Elses Farm stretched over both parishes, with a very small part in Leigh too.

68   Helen Thomas, *Under storm's wing* (Manchester, 1988), p. 103.

69   SC, 7 June 1889, p. 4; *Kelly's directory for Kent* (1891), p. 562.

70   Ron Terry, *Old corners of Sevenoaks: the yards, courts and passages of historic Sevenoaks* (Sevenoaks, 2000), pp. 29–30.

71   Roy Brigden, *Victorian farms* (Marlborough, 1986), p. 224.

72   Sevenoaks Weald Historical Society Nizels Estate, 1919 sale particulars.

73   Anckorn, *A Sevenoaks Camera*, A.

74   Friedrich Accum, *A treatise on adulterations of food and culinary poisons* (London, 1820), p. 1.

that almost every commercially sold edible product 'was more or less heavily adulterated'. This posed very serious potential health risks. Bread made with alum had an improved taste but was harmful to children's health, as was milk diluted with water.[75] A Tonbridge baker called Featherstone was fined 10s in 1874 for selling bread laced with alum.[76] Another routinely adulterated staple was tea, both green and black varieties, of which 'large quantities were manufactured from English hedgerows', including ash and elder leaves.[77] Both tea varieties were on sale at the Ives' shop in Sevenoaks in 1843 and cost up to 8s a pound. It is more likely than not that they had been adulterated, either by the retailers themselves or with their direct knowledge.[78]

Far worse was the use of known toxic ingredients: lead in cayenne pepper caused paralysis and children were poisoned by mineral dyes in sugared sweets.[79] And the advertised pickles of 'Draper, Grocer, Cheesemonger & Co' John Bowers, of Chipstead, would then almost certainly have been contaminated by copper sulphate, another extremely poisonous compound.[80] The issue of food quality generally clearly concerned Sevenoaks residents, since in 1856 a 'lecturer on chemistry, gave an interesting lecture … on "Popular errors and medical fallacies respecting the drinks we use"'.[81]

Efforts to promote voluntary reform failed and only with the Sale of Food and Drugs Act 1875 could consumer confidence in food purity increase, although even then adulteration was a 'difficult offence to police'.[82] This re-emphasises another overarching theme of this book, which is that the serious risks affecting west Kent residents, in many different areas of life, were mitigated or removed only by legislation and tougher regulatory action by statutory authorities at national and local level. Surprisingly, since the problem was widespread elsewhere, there is no evidence that any Sevenoaks retailers were prosecuted for adulteration before the 1880s. This probably indicated that the relevant authorities, such as the police, were reluctant or unable to enforce the law – or so it appeared to one magistrate, Major James German, who believed that 'scarcely nothing had been done with regard to the inspection of milk for the past ten years'.[83]

---

75 Burnett, *Plenty and want*, pp. 74–5, 88–9.

76 *The Times*, 22 Jan. 1874, p. 6.

77 Burnett, *Plenty and want*, p. 75.

78 *SA*, 1 April 1843, p. 93.

79 Burnett, *Plenty and want*, p. 89. The main cause of these poisonous adulterations was ferocious price competition from other retailers, p. 83.

80 *SA*, 1 Feb. 1842, p. 149.

81 *SEG*, 4 March 1856, p. 5.

82 Burnett, *Plenty and want*, p. 230; Emsley, *Crime and society*, p. 165.

83 *SC*, 5 Dec. 1884, p. 5.

Conclusion

The better-off inhabitants of west Kent rarely needed to worry about life's necessities. It was not so for the poor. The four primitive wants simply had to be obtained somehow, but very low wages meant that, when they could not be bought, the various strategies within the makeshift economy were employed. Failing that, privation or the workhouse were the only possible options. Middle-class residents of the Victorian town slowly came to understand that poverty was less the result of moral failure (although some was, for the demon drink had to be paid for somehow) and more a consequence of economic factors. They were, however, generally most intolerant of lower-class residents caught thieving, even if it was done directly to acquire or pay for those necessities. But many recognised their own responsibilities in that quarter, so the subscription lists for charitable or voluntary endeavours to provide coal for the poor or fire prevention for the town were generally long. Being seen to be contributing also bolstered both their respectability and standing and, conversely, called public attention to those who were absent from those lists and who, in the minds of right-thinking locals, should not have been.

The last two chapters have shown how the poor – most people – struggled to overcome the main risks of life by obtaining regular quantities of the bare necessities. For most people in west Kent that could only be achieved from the fruits of their labour, the subject of the next chapter.

Chapter 7

Work

West Kent industries to 1914

Agriculture was the major industry and employer in the Sevenoaks area for much of the period. It was generally prosperous throughout, although from the 1870s it was harder to make money from farming owing to declining rents and falling prices, which reduced the incomes of farmers and landowners. The region's non-agricultural employees had other opportunities for work, including quarrying ragstone, clay and lime for building and gravel for roads. In the late eighteenth and nineteenth centuries the River Darent and its tributaries were a key power source for pockets of rural industry based on water mills. Shoreham mill, originally a fulling mill, was converted to papermaking in the late seventeenth century and bought by William Willmott in 1737. Hs family owned and operated it for the next 190 years. Latterly the mill produced high-quality hand-made paper from rag brought from London, which was used for government ledgers.[1]

At Sundridge, Shoreham and Eynsford, papermaking mills employed a proto-industrial proletariat of skilled men. Those mills depended on rag from London, the supply of which improved with the advent of the railways. From the 1770s to 1828 the Greatness water mill produced silk and in 1816 employed a labour force of over 100 people, predominantly women and children. The Nouaille family, its owners, were in some ways model employers: although the children worked long hours, they were provided with schooling, clothing and medical care.[2] There were several windmills in the area, in Weald and near the centre of Sevenoaks, each employing a very small labour force. Water and windmills used the skills of 'engineers' to set and trim grinding stones, and further skilled roles were required with the advent of

---

1   The Wilmott's paper mill at Shoreham employed 58 workers in 1851 and 70 in 1879; see Malcolm White and Joy Saynor, *Shoreham: a village in Kent* (Shoreham, 1989), pp. 149–50; Rod Shelton, *Darent. The history and stories of a river and its communities* (Otford, 2015).

2   UKPP, Commons, *Report ... Select Committee on the State of the Children Employed in the Manufactories of the United Kingdom*, No. 397 (1816), pp. 80–3.

iron machinery and steam power.[3] By the mid-nineteenth century steam was making inroads into local industry, farming included. It was used at the brick and tile works at Dunton Green, which was opened by William Thompson in 1862; for the quarrying of ragstone, sand and gravel; and in the construction of the rail tunnels under the North Downs and the sandstone ridge on which Sevenoaks is situated.

The old Wealden industries of textiles, ironmaking and glassmaking had largely ceased by the second decade of the nineteenth century. Others closed in the face of lethal competition from newer industrial centres; the Greatness silk mills, for example, closed in 1827 as silk production was concentrated in east London and Coventry. A similar fate awaited other local manufacturing concerns, which suffered from rival competitors and new sources of supply of materials, often from overseas. These changes also had a significant impact on patterns of employment in west Kent between c.1800 and 1910. Many industrial processes were agrarian-related, such as corn milling, brewing, tanning, lime burning below the North Downs and even the making of cricket bats and balls.[4] To operate effectively, many required consistent supplies of motive power, which was not straightforward to achieve before the Industrial Revolution. Another significant industry was timber sawing for local building, furniture making, hop poles and chestnut fencing or paling, as well as for fuel. Although much sawing was done manually in saw pits, increasingly water and steam power was used.

The Industrial Revolution created new sources of motive power that drove new industrial technologies. Nationally, iron and steelmaking and railways were two of the best known. They resulted in vastly improved outputs and underpinned the almost unshakeable Victorian confidence in invention, science and technology, summed up in the evocative word 'progress'. New machines and methods influenced agriculture, and the coming of the railway had a profound influence on local economies, not least the increased supply of coal for gasworks, brickmaking and other industries. New ideas of mechanisation spread to west Kent, helped by its proximity to London, and drew on existing local skills and innovators, people such as millwrights, clockmakers and smiths, who experimented to improve or adapt older methods of production. George Meredith, born in Shoreham, trained as a clockmaker but his abiding passion was the utilisation of compressed air for industrial purposes.[5]

New technologies and mass production brought advantages but steadily undermined local skill sets, such as those of the fellmongers and glovers and lath-

---

3   For more see Alan Stoyel, *Memories of Kentish watermills. The rivers Cray and Darent* (Ashbourne, 2008).

4   William Pett of Sevenoaks was the first recorded bat maker. His craftsmanship was praised in a letter from Mrs Rishton to Fanny Burney in 1773; she advised asking 'for the very best sort, which cost 4s or 4s 6d each'; *The Times*, 14 Aug. 1931, p. 13.

5   White and Saynor, *Shoreham*, p. 119.

cleavers who worked in Sevenoaks in 1784, listed in a directory published that year.[6] As older craft skills slowly declined, new forms of employment were created. In 1851 jobs performed by Hartslands residents included poulterer and cordwainer; by 1911 those had gone, superseded by roles such as engine driver and telephone engineer. This change usefully illustrates the extent to which new labour skills were being continuously required and developed throughout the long nineteenth century.

Sevenoaks, local occupations 1784

Henry Arnold	Salesman
Francis Austen	Attorney
Thomas Baker	Surgeon
John Baker	Inn-keeper
Anthony Barton	Currier
Phillip Breadley	Wine merchant
John Chappell	Distiller
Thomas Clou	Bookseller
Thomas Covell	Stone-mason
Robert Crossley	Wheelwright
Henry Gage	Patten-maker
Robert Gates	Cooper
Joseph Gatward	Watch-maker
William George	Mercer and draper
John Harvey	Plumber and glazier
John Holmden	Miller
Nicholas Lock	Ironmonger
Peter Nouaille	Silk throwster
John Osborn	Carpenter
Thomas Pett	Turner
Richard Ring	Brazier
Thomas Stoneham	Brewer
Sarah Streatfeild	Milliner
Henry Sutton	Fellmonger and glover
Thomas Turner	Gingerbread-baker
Thomas Wood	Lath-cleaver

Source: Bailey's British directory, 1784, pp. 899–901.

---

6   Bailey's British directory (1784).

By the early twentieth century local corn milling and brewing were increasingly subject to take-over, closure or relocation. Local industries that did survive, such as brewing and papermaking, primarily served niche markets, being carried on, in part, by small-scale artisanal proprietors. Other craft industries and retail services, such as shoemakers, tailors and blacksmiths, were similarly challenged by industrial mass production. One industry that did survive and thrive was brick and tile manufacturing. It used local sources of clay to meet the growing demand as housebuilding increased in the area. But the employment it generated was never guaranteed, being subject to contraction in bad winter weather. At such times brickmakers and builders were likely to be laid off.

By the early twentieth century Sevenoaks' economic focus had undergone a major structural switch, from small-scale manufacturing to services. Perhaps the most important of the latter were the several laundry businesses based in Hartslands, which offered generally unskilled, low-paid jobs to local women. In a neat historical reversal, the dirty old gasworks was taken over by the 'new' businesses, which were much more salubrious neighbours for the increasing number of neat middle-class villas that had sprung up on the nearby green fields since the 1840s. The growth of laundry work helps to explain the modest growth in the percentage of Hartslands working wives, which rose from 7.4 per cent in 1851 to 9.7 per cent in 1901. It must also have contributed to the growth in the female percentage of its total working population between 1851 and 1901, from 16 per cent to 22.5 per cent.[7]

Sevenoaks and the wider world

Even before the railway arrived at Tonbridge in 1842, local farms and other businesses sold a wide range of agricultural goods to customers outside west Kent, particularly in London. Locally grown hops were regularly sent to the market at Southwark.[8] In 1811 James Cramps, an Otford miller, told a House of Commons select committee that he sent wagonloads of flour to the capital 'very frequently'.[9] Local people also travelled to the metropolis for medical and legal appointments and properties for sale were advertised in the London press.

After the 1860s, when Sevenoaks was linked into the national rail network, the mobility of both labour and goods was increased such that west Kent was tied yet more closely to London. The growing pull of the city helped change Sevenoaks from a small, autonomous market town with an overwhelmingly agrarian economy and society to one based far more on services and commuting to London. Those developments helped reshape local people's sense of identity, while simultaneously expanding their knowledge of the nation and wider world.

---

7   Census Returns for 1851 and 1901: Sevenoaks (Hartslands).

8   Celia Cordle, *Out of the hay and into the hops. Hop cultivation in Wealden Kent and hop marketing in Southwark, 1744–2000* (Hatfield, 2011).

9   UKPP, Commons, *Reports from Committees – Session 1 November–24 July 1810–1811*, vol. 2, p. 9.

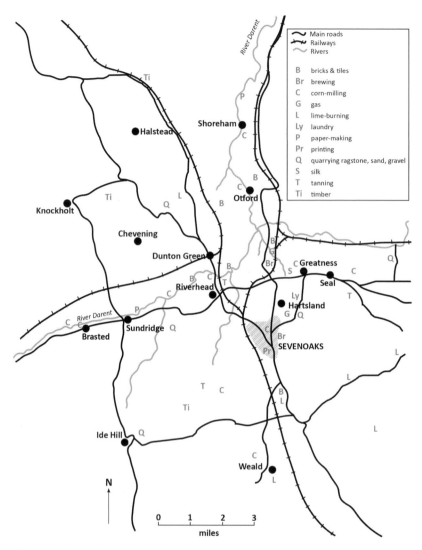

Map 17 Sevenoaks: industries and manufacturing, 1770–1912.

For much of this period the major industry in Sevenoaks was agriculture, including hops, corn, and from the 1840s soft fruit grown on the North Downs. Several industries were closely related to agriculture, e.g. corn milling, brewing, tanning and leather work, and lime burning. The river Darent was a major source of water power for manufacturing silk at Greatness and paper-making at Sundridge and Shoreham (the latter with supplementary steam engines post-1860). Small scale proto-industrial occupations – blacksmiths, wheelwrights and agricultural engineering – also existed. The data for this map is derived from local directories, Ordnance Survey maps, newspapers, and local knowledge.

Kelly's directory of Kent (1882) lists the following smiths (s), wheelwrights (w), and agricultural engineers (ae) in Sevenoaks and the surrounding villages: Sevenoaks 2s 1w; Riverhead 1s 1w; Brasted 2s; Sundridge 1s; Dunton Green 1s 3w; Chevening 1w; Seal 1s 1w 1ae; Kemsing 2s 1w; Underriver 1s; Weald 2s 1w; Ide Hill 1s 1w 1ae; Brasted Chart 1s; Knockholt 1s; Halstead 1s; Otford 1s 3w; Shoreham 1s 1w.

Movement in the long nineteenth century

How people moved about also changed dramatically over the period, although for much of the time the only option available to many was travel on foot, which involved negotiating the often-complained-about 'vast puddles [which] lay for weeks' in the roads.[10] Before the advent of modern systems of public transport, most people walked to work and to visit friends, often over long distances. For many, as noted, walking was the only option and it was certainly the cheapest way of getting from one place to another, well into the twentieth century. In the 1970s Mrs Norah Everest recalled how, early in the century as a young child, in company with her mother and siblings, she regularly walked the four miles from Ide Hill to Sevenoaks and back to do the weekly shopping.[11] Horses were used in agriculture and for commercial delivery. A 'steam-coach' travelled the 21 miles from Deptford to Sevenoaks in under two hours in 1841.[12] Members of the gentry and some farmers enjoyed sufficient income to afford the luxury of a horse-drawn carriage, and invariably ownership of one or more horses.

By 1790 a system of turnpike roads, regularly improved and extended, connected Sevenoaks with London and neighbouring towns. Other roads were maintained by the parish authorities. This was a relatively expensive process, particularly in the Wealden area of west Kent, on heavy clays where roads became 'deep and miry'.[13] Few surfaces were metalled, so constant maintenance and repair was required. The steep North Downs scarp made horse-drawn transport using the turnpikes costly and effortful, and by the 1840s the old route through Knockholt had been abandoned for a new road with a gradual gradient cut into the side of Polhill.

Proximity to London greatly influenced Sevenoaks: a daily service of carriers and stagecoaches moved goods and passengers to and from the metropolis and other local towns and villages. Poorer people could make a living from carrying; so, for example, Mr Smith, from Chevening, was conveying 'small parcels' to and from Sevenoaks via his donkey and 'light cart' in 1842.[14] The railway arrived in Tonbridge in 1842 and Sevenoaks in the 1860s. Closely associated with the railway was the electric telegraph, an essential tool for the safe and efficient working of a communications system that daily moved an increasing volume of freight and passengers. The expansion and increased speed of postal deliveries, after the reforms of 1840, was also allied to the railway system.

Risks attached to work

A steady job with an adequate regular wage helped mitigate some risks of life. Only a small percentage of people, those with well-paid, secure jobs and/or substantial

---

10 *SA*, Jan. 1841, p. 44.

11 A personal memory related to David Killingray.

12 *The Times*, 14 Sept. 1841, p. 6.

13 Hasted, *History and topographical survey*, vol. 3 p. 180.

14 *SEG*, 22 March 1842, p. 3.

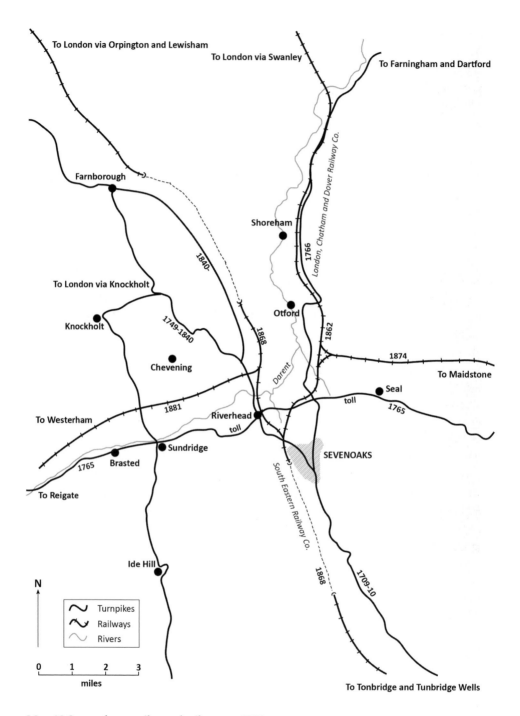

To London via Orpington and Lewisham

To London via Swanley

To Farningham and Dartford

London, Chattham and Dover Railway Co.

Farnborough

Shoreham

1840

1766

To London via Knockholt

1749-1840

1868

Knockholt

Otford

Chevening

Darent

1862

1874

To Maidstone

Seal

toll

1765

1881

Riverhead

To Westerham

toll

SEVENOAKS

Sundridge

Brasted

1765

South Eastern Railway Co.

To Reigate

Ide Hill

1868

1709-10

N

Turnpikes
Railways
Rivers

0   1   2   3
miles

To Tonbridge and Tunbridge Wells

Map 18 Sevenoaks turnpikes and railways to 1881.

Figure 7.1 Gilbert (1893–1986) and Jessie Gasson. The Glassons were typical west Kent residents, except that Gilbert was one of very few local working-class people to record his memories of growing up in the area in the late nineteenth century. Born at Ide Hill in 1893, he married Jessie Pratt in Sevenoaks in 1913 and worked at various jobs, including stone breaking and carting in the quarries at Knole Park and St Julian's.
Sources: Kent History and Library Centre, WU13/Z1; www.familysearch.org, accessed 13 March 2018.

incomes from land or investments, were effectively immune from all the financial risks of life. According to the 1851 census for Sevenoaks, for example, besides the wealthiest landowners, only 76 people (or 1.6 per cent of the total population of 4,878) were described as annuitants, fundholders, retired or living off their property investments.[15] For the remainder, which included most artisanal and even middle-class residents of west Kent as well as those lower down the social scale, savings normally stretched to cover only short-term emergencies, such as brief periods of unemployment. That meant that any sustained improvements in living standards ultimately depended on the efforts and good fortunes of the main breadwinner: 'work was inevitably central to working-class experience'.[16]

Much ink has been spilled on the so-called 'standard of living debate' – did real wages and working conditions improve so that the lower orders were better off as the nineteenth century progressed, or was Karl Marx right to stress their ongoing 'immiseration' over the period?[17] Tentatively, one may conclude that, nationwide, standards of living 'probably rose in the thirty years after 1820 and certainly rose in the second half of the nineteenth century'.[18]

But many aspects of work came replete with their own sets of risks, some entirely random and beyond human prevention, but which had potentially devastating consequences. So, as late as 1889, Gilbert Gasson recalled how, in a terrible thunderstorm, the building housing the family laundry business blew down. Although they retrieved the clothes, 'their living was gone', so his grandfather was asked 'if he could find them a house, and perhaps a job'.[19] He did obtain a cottage for them, but it was four miles away in Sevenoaks Weald, so the episode must have proved enormously disruptive to the family's economic and social relationships. Unforeseen misfortunes could touch people of all social classes, although the poor and vulnerable invariably suffered more.

Time

It is important here to contextualise growing public awareness of time in this period, especially in terms of how it impacted upon people's employment. Prior to the eighteenth century, most people experienced the passage of time through seasonal weather patterns, the church calendar, church bells and sundials.[20] Some institutions

---

15 Census Return for 1851: Sevenoaks.

16 John Rule, 'Against innovation? Custom and resistance in the workplace, 1700–1850', in Tim Harris (ed.), *Popular culture in England, c. 1500–1850* (Basingstoke, 1995), p. 168.

17 David Conway, *Farewell to Marx. An outline and appraisal of his theories* (Harmondsworth, 1987), pp. 130–3, 161; Gareth Stedman Jones, *Karl Marx. Greatness and illusion* (London, 2016), pp. 179, 414–18.

18 Hoppen, *Mid-Victorian generation*, p. 87.

19 KHLC WU13/Z1, vol. 1.

20 Mark Hailwood, 'Time and work in rural England, 1500–1700', *Past & Present*, 248 (2020), pp. 87–121.

relied on specific time: mail and passenger carriers with advertised arrivals and departures, shops' opening and closing hours; and bells that called children to school. Later, 'industrial time' was intrinsic to the mechanical work regimes of the factory system, 'as new labour habits were formed and a new time-discipline was imposed'; for example, the Greatness silk mill operated from 6 a.m. to 6 p.m.[21] A similar discipline with regard to time was also central to the complex domestic organisation of large houses with numerous servants.

The coming of the railway introduced 'railway time', applied to west Kent as soon as the line from London to Ashford was completed. The ability to tell the time enabled status and display. By mid-century many middle-class people owned pocket watches and a clock, and watch clubs enabled the less affluent to own them through 'collective hire purchase' agreements. Bensons Watches of Ludgate Hill, for example, advertised in the *South Eastern Gazette* in the 1860s its willingness to supply such clubs.[22] The wealthier could afford their own timepieces, such as the eight-day turret clock made in 1824 by watchmaker Whitehead of Sevenoaks for St Julian's at a cost of £40.[23] Public clocks became important civic status symbols. It is significant that the *Sevenoaks Chronicle* urged that the £200 cash balance assumed to be left over after the Sevenoaks Savings Bank was taken over in 1888 should be spent on a new timepiece for the town.[24]

Changing patterns of work

The southern Swing rioters and the Luddite machine breakers of the northern industrial cities highlighted working-class resistance to changing employment patterns, but broader macroeconomic upheavals were unstoppable and were seen clearly across Kent. The diminished profitability of cereal farming, for example, 'led to a marked contraction of the county's arable area and an exodus of agricultural labour from the land' in the second half of the nineteenth century.[25] In Hartslands in 1841 60 per cent of male householders had unskilled jobs, over three quarters of whom were agricultural labourers. Of the skilled 27 per cent, a quarter were shoemakers or repairers, while the remaining 12 per cent worked in white-collar occupations.[26] But, although employment in farming declined rapidly in the later

21   See E.P. Thompson, 'Time, work-discipline and industrial capitalism', *Past & Present*, 38 (1967), pp. 56–97; also in E.P. Thompson, *Customs in common: studies in traditional popular culture* (London, 1993), p. 394, ideas critically assessed by later historians; UKPP, Commons, *Report ... on the State of the Children*, p. 80.

22   *SEG*, 30 Oct. 1860, p. 7.

23   Private archives at St Julian's, Sevenoaks, Herries papers. Robert Herries to John Charles Herries, 11 Dec. 1824.

24   *SC*, 20 April 1888, p. 4; KHLC C/E/S/330 2/4, 4 Oct. 1888.

25   Tom Richardson, 'Labour', in Alan Armstrong (ed.), *The economy of Kent, 1640–1914* (Woodbridge, 1995), p. 258.

26   Census Return for 1841: Sevenoaks (Hartslands).

nineteenth century, mainly due to mechanisation, those broad proportions had not altered greatly by 1901. Fifty-five per cent of male Hartslands householders remained unskilled, although many farming jobs had evolved into gardening or horticulture for private or commercial employers, and labourers (mostly termed 'general', rather than 'agricultural') were clearly still required. Twenty-seven per cent may be identified as skilled, although many were builders and carpenters benefiting from the contemporary construction boom; shoemaking comprised just 5 per cent of that total. Eighteen per cent were then in other low-skilled employment, a third of those being in domestic service of some description.[27]

Hartslands male occupations, 1841–1901 (%)

	1841	1901
Manual – unskilled	60	55
Artisanal	27	27
Non-manual	12	18

The expanding rail network enabled west Kent residents actively to seek employment opportunities elsewhere, if perhaps they were dissatisfied with their current job. It was significant that, in 1870, a 22-year-old 'thoroughly experienced' 'young ladies' maid', then working at the Ide Hill vicarage, decided to advertise her services not in a west Kent newspaper but in the *London Evening Standard*. This indicates that she was not averse to moving to the capital for the right employer, although she did 'not object to the country'.[28] London became accessible to Sevenoaks residents in ways inconceivable even a few years earlier. Trains allowed them to consult lawyers and doctors in the City; London-published newspapers could be bought in Sevenoaks; the latest fashionable clothing could be delivered to households; pamphlets, books and radical ideas moved down the conduits of commerce and communication; and orchestras and choirs in the town could more easily draw on the services of London-based professional musicians and singers.

Commuting to London every day for work even became feasible for some after 1868, but it was still time consuming and difficult, even more so from the farther-flung villages of west Kent. Gilbert Gasson records how Mr Lock of Ide Hill, 'a clerk

---

27   Census Return for 1901: Sevenoaks.
28   *London Evening Standard*, 28 Oct. 1870, p. 8.

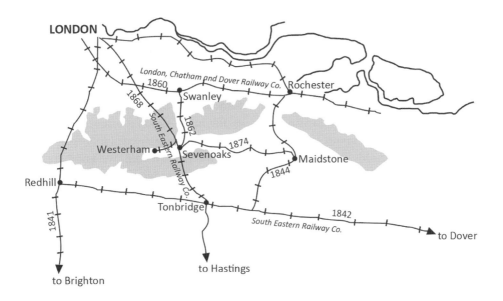

Map 19 The railway network of west Kent 1836–81.
Source: adapted from Terence Lawson and David Killingray (eds), *An historical atlas of Kent* (Chichester, 2004), p. 125.

in a City bank', was obliged to walk 'daily to Sevenoaks station' in all weathers before he could board his train.[29]

By the 1880s bicycles were becoming popular and people of the middling sort could hire a horse, and a trap if needed, from specialist businesses within the town. The upshot was that, while walking remained the normal mode of transport for many, both people and goods could move around the district, the region and the nation far more quickly and conveniently than ever before. This had the most profound economic and social consequences for west Kent.

Few Hartslands residents were employed on the railway from the 1860s, or at the gasworks, which had moved a short distance away, although some generic 'carpenters' or 'bricklayers' probably did work there. James German provided an upper-class view of Hartslands in 1877–8. In a letter to the archbishop of Canterbury, arguing for St John's to become a separate ecclesiastical parish, he described the area as 'a poor neighbourhood'.[30] A year later a printed appeal letter, which German seems to have had a hand in writing, said of St John's that

29   KHLC WU13/Z1, vol. 1.

30   LPL 163.231, Tait papers, St John's, German to Tait, 18 April 1877.

a very large proportion of the population therefore is composed of journeymen and day-labourers, whose business is to supply the wealthier classes with the requirements of their everyday life. From this quarter of the town daily emerge the Masons, Bricklayers, Carpenters, and Painters; Men-Servants and Maid-Servants; Laundresses and Charwomen; Nurses and Needle-women; and all the mixed multitude who form the rearguard of the wealthy. Here do they live; here are their children trained; and here if at all must they go to Church.[31]

Wage levels were often very low and working hours very long. We know a great deal about the early career of Charles Bassett. He began work on a construction site near Sevenoaks in 1873, aged 12, and earned 6s for a 65-hour week – or just over a penny an hour. Three years later he worked on the Wildernesse estate of Sir Charles Mills, at 8s a week, but soon resigned to become a hod carrier on a Sevenoaks building site. There he earned the handsome weekly wage of one pound, approximately 4½d per hour. Bassett's quadrupling of his weekly wage between the ages of 11 and 16 was not, however, typical and indicated how upwardly mobile he was, even as an adolescent. By 1882, aged 21, he was a carpenter on a London site earning 8d an hour, or £2 4s a week, but that obliged him to work six 11-hour days each week, with no time off even for Good Friday and bank holidays.[32]

By 1901 more than 5 per cent of the people who lived in Hartslands were employers and almost 12 per cent were self-employed. Another surprise, in a relatively poor, artisanal district, is that not all could be described as wage-slaves, either. Although few managers or employers of labour lived in Hartslands until the twentieth century, a small number of men and women had saved up or enjoyed inheritances such that they were able to derive retirement incomes from pensions or annuities. A few men were ex-military and Chelsea Pensioners. This broad group generally averaged just over one per cent of the total population, a figure skewed somewhat in 1851 and 1881 for reasons unclear.[33]

Many employers required staff to wear uniforms. They included the nascent emergency services, such as the police and fire brigades, as well as rail staff and postmen. Uniforms represented rank, deference, discipline and order. This was most marked on the railways, with its ultra-strict codes of discipline. Many managers insisted upon 'near-military control' and, revealingly, its total labour force was often called the 'railway army'.[34] Such codes often included 'an elaborate system of fines and punishments', hierarchical career structures, weighty rule books and 'endless

---

31 *Ibid.*, p. 218, St John's printed appeal letter dd. November 1878.

32 Bassett, *Seal*, pp. 4, 5, 6, 9.

33 Census Return for 1851: Sevenoaks; Census Return for 1891: Sevenoaks; Census Return for 1901: Sevenoaks.

34 George Revill, 'Liberalism and paternalism: politics and corporate culture in "Railway Derby", 1865–75', *Social History*, 23 (1999), pp. 196–214 (p. 208).

exhortations to comply … for the sake of safety and efficient operation'.[35] Uniforms thus underlined hierarchy and status. They also symbolised and defined the restricted access ordinary workers, even volunteers, had to the debates taking place in the local 'public square'. This was obvious at the 1889 Sevenoaks Volunteer Fire Brigade annual dinner, which the firemen attended 'dressed in their uniforms'.[36] However, they sat in resplendent silence throughout, since only their captain, W.H. Stepney, and the Brigade's middle-class subscribers were permitted to air their views on the pressing issues of the day. Strict dress codes, if not actual uniforms, also prevailed in many other working environments, such as schools, banks, offices and shops.

The risks of withdrawing one's labour

West Kent employees operated within a changing framework of employment law and labour relations during the nineteenth century. In the late eighteenth century many workers, especially those uniting to defend against the imposition of lower wages, were viewed by parliament as potential political conspirators. In 1795, six agricultural labourers were charged with 'tumultuously assembling in Eatonbridge [Edenbridge], for the purpose of stirring up the minds of the poor to have their wages raised; and the price of wheat lowered and for divers other dangerous purposes'.[37] For this act of 'conspiracy' and 'riot' the men were each fined 1s and discharged.[38] The Combination Acts of 1799–1800 were passed in a frenzy over possible revolution, driven externally from France and internally by Tom-Paine-inspired agitators of the lower orders. They sought to prevent any 'dangerous combination' of workers, for example by journeymen papermakers in Kent, including along the Darent Valley, who in 1796 were prepared to strike for higher wages.[39]

By 1824 the right to join a trade union had become enshrined in law, although the Original Society of Paper Makers had been operating since 1800 and was very active in the Cray and Darent valleys by 1820.[40] Giving evidence to a select committee in 1825, St Paul's Cray papermaker Thomas Gardner must have surprised his interviewers by his candid disclosures: that the Union already had 1,000 members in Kent and the same number again in the rest of England; that it collected subscriptions of 5s or so a month from members, who could afford them as those skilled artisans earned good wages; and that the cash was used to support

35 Mike Richardson and Peter Nicholls, *A business and labour history of Britain: case studies of Britain in the nineteenth and twentieth centuries* (Basingstoke, 2011), pp. 24, 20, 21.

36 *SEG*, 12 Jan. 1889, p. 4.

37 *MJ*, 17 Feb. 1795, p. 4.

38 *MJ*, 24 March 1795, p. 4.

39 *KG*, 4 March 1796, p. 4. See also Alfred Shorter, *Paper-making in the British Isles: an historical and geographical study* (Newton Abbot, 1971).

40 Paul Hastings, 'Radical movements and workers' protests to c.1850', in Frederick Lansberry, *Government and politics in Kent, 1640–1914* (Woodbridge, 2001), p. 99.

unemployed members and to relieve the wives and children of strikers, to the tune of 4s and 2s a week, respectively. The strength of the Paper Makers Society, coupled with the strong bargaining position of the skilled west Kent workforce, made strikes uncommon, as 'everything [had] been peaceably arranged between the masters and men', often to the latter's advantage.[41]

Rarely were employees able to dictate terms and conditions of work. Labour relations operated within the confines of the Master and Servant Acts, of 1823 and 1867, that sought 'the better regulations of servants, labourers and work people'.[42] This legislation was heavily biased towards employers as it was primarily designed to discipline employees and repress combinations of workers. It required obedience from 'servants' to their employers, with breach of contract by employees punishable in the criminal court, whereas employers were subject merely to civil law penalties. For example, William Shepherd, a Sundridge labourer, received 14 days' hard labour in Maidstone gaol in 1861 for 'neglect of duty';[43] eleven years later William Bowen of Halstead prosecuted a labourer 'absenting himself' from his master's service, who was fined 10s.[44]

Unions could be regarded as illegal because they could act 'in restraint of trade'. Master and Servant legislation was used against workers organising for better conditions until well after the Trade Union Act of 1871, which 'gave legal recognition to Trade Unions and enabled them to protect their funds by registering under the Friendly Societies Act' – although they were still liable to criminal prosecution.[45] But, even then, union efforts could be thwarted by a judiciary generally hostile to their ambitions. In 1901 the infamous Taff Vale judgment in the House of Lords struck at the heart of union activity, as it decreed that they were liable for damages for loss of profits to employers from any industrial action that was instigated by its officials. It was not reversed until the Liberal government passed the Trades Disputes Act of 1906.

Work for most working-class people throughout the nineteenth century involved hard labour and long hours; it was, as E.P. Thompson said, 'neither poverty nor disease but work itself which casts the blackest shadow over the years of the Industrial Revolution'.[46] In 1872 Sevenoaks carpenters and joiners were requesting a reduction to 'fifty-eight working hours per week; work to cease on Saturday at four o'clock', but failed to secure it.[47] Arthur Hickmott, the sole socialist councillor

---

41   UKPP, Commons, *Minutes of Evidence Taken before Select Committee on Combination Laws*, No. 417 (1825), pp. 26–9. See also D.C. Coleman, *The British paper industry 1495–1860: a study in industrial growth* (Oxford, 1958), pp. 267–8.

42   Master and Servant Act 1823.

43   *MJ*, 29 Jan. 1861, p. 5.

44   Percival Bowen, *Diary*, 26 June and 30 Aug. 1872, William Bowen archives; *MJ*, 2 Sept. 1872, p. 6.

45   Henry Pelling, *A history of British trade unionism* (Harmondsworth, 1969), p. 72.

46   E.P. Thompson, *The making of the English working class* (London, 1964), pp. 487–8.

47   *SEG*, 17 Sept. 1872, p. 5.

in Sevenoaks, championed what would now be called workers' rights. At a meeting of the town's Urban District Council in 1898 he moved that the 'non-permanent hands employed by the Council shall cease work on Saturdays at 1 o'clock, as is the case with labourers in the building trade', as the council was, he said 'guilty of "sweating"'.[48] His motion was roundly defeated.

The living conditions of railway navvies in the 1860s

The German economist Karl Marx, living in exile in London, was an assiduous collator of the evils of industrial capitalism. In his classic work *Das Kapital* (1867) he described the living conditions of the 'nomadic' navvies, whom he called 'the light infantry of capitalism', building the railway to Sevenoaks through the North Downs and on to Tonbridge.

> ... Nomadic labour is used for various building and draining works, for brick making, lime-burning, railway-making, etc. A flying column of pestilence, it carries smallpox, typhus, cholera and scarlet fever into the places in whose neighbourhood it pitches its camp ... huts built in several places along the line of works by the contractor ... for their special occupation [but] possessed no ventilation, nor drainage, and ... were necessarily overcrowded ... these poor people were compelled to endure all the horrors of suffocation to avoid the pestiferous smells arising from the filthy, stagnant water, and privies close under their windows.

Source: English translation of Karl Marx, *Capital* ([1887] London, 1990), vol. 1, pp. 818–19.

Some west Kent employers were more enlightened. From 1881 Henry Owen was advertising his 'Sevenoaks Steam Joinery' and he appears to have been a popular employer. When he stood for the Local Board in 1882 many working men asked ratepayers to vote for him because 'he had been the greatest employer of labour for the last five years'; he paid 'good pay for an honest day's work' and 'he is the chief supporter of the Mechanics and Labourers in Sevenoaks'.[49] However, he expanded, or over-expanded, and eventually went bankrupt in 1889 to the tune of over £17,500.[50]

---

48 *SC*, 22 April 1898, p. 8. 'Sweating' refers to exploiting workers with long, arduous, low-paid toil.
49 *SC*, 31 March 1882, p. 4.
50 *Commercial Gazette*, 17 April 1889, supplement, p. 154.

White-collar workers, although better paid, often worked long, tedious hours. Richard Perry, born in 1841, was appointed Master of Sundridge National School in 1873 on an initial salary of £55 a year, plus most of the 'school pence' (fees). His contract with the rector of Sundridge stipulated that, in addition to instructing the pupils, he was also to teach a night school three times a week, take pupils away on 'Gala Days' such as school treats, oversee choir practice once a week and take a Sunday school class. He was also required to manage the school building, including supervising its cleaning, and had to share the unfurnished house provided for him with an assistant whenever necessary.[51]

For many middle-class people work involved business and entrepreneurship. Unfortunately, few west Kent business records are extant for the nineteenth century, but one rare survival is for the Wheatsheaf Timber Yard, Halstead.[52] It was run for many decades by the Bowen family, from the 1870s legally in the name of William (1838–99), but effectively by his brother Percival (1861–1919). Percival was an active Wesleyan, and he combined the timber business with farming. In 1883 he advertised that he could 'deliver first class potatoes to your address for ready cash'.[53] His business expanded in the late nineteenth century in response to the coming of the railway to Chelsfield and the demand for building materials. The archive indicates the extent of Bowen's other activities. Sales invoices show he erected a timber-framed chapel, with fittings, in Kemsing in 1885 and supplied fencing to Multon Lambarde's seat at Sevenoaks Common and to property developers the St Botolph's Estate Company in 1881 and 1888, respectively. A large collection of business cards shows that he was visited by a variety of company salesmen, chiefly from the south-east and central London, such as coachbuilders Muskett Bros from Bromley. Many of his suppliers were from Sevenoaks, including ironmonger William Franks, leather merchant James Outram and Horncastle's the outfitters. It emphasises the importance of the town as a business location – and the diversity and strength of its economy – at the beginning of the twentieth century.

An Employment Society established in Sevenoaks in 1843, which sought 'to provide permanent employment for labouring men when ordinary sources fail', did not long survive.[54] Employees working in industries in long-term decline could, potentially, avoid unemployment by changing occupation. That was, however, easier said than done for working-class people in the nineteenth century, since many skilled trades required new entrants to serve apprenticeships of five years or more. Even unskilled workers, with no such obligation, found it relatively difficult, for few who lived at Hartslands changed jobs, and those who did mainly went into similar employment. So skilled tradesmen, including bricklayer Robert Chatfield and shoemaker John Heaver, carried on those

---

51 KHLC P357/25/12.

52 William Bowen archives.

53 SC, 5 Oct. 1883, p. 4.

54 SA, 1 Aug. 1843, p. 167; 1 Sept. 1843, p. 171.

trades from at least 1841 to 1871. But less skilled agricultural labourers Richard Frederick and Samuel Wheeler became, respectively, a general labourer (the census term) and gardener, it being as easy to wield a spade on a road or in a flowerbed as in digging farm ditches.[55] In crisis, men could also send their children and wives out to work, if they had not done so already. This often took place under gang masters who paid children just 4d to 6d a day, or about 2s for a 55-hour week, as was reported to the Eynsford Agricultural Association in 1864, when labourers' wages locally were 9s a week.[56]

'Striking work'

Labourers seriously dissatisfied with their pay and conditions could 'strike work' to improve them. But withdrawing labour was fraught with risk: loss of income, an employer's lockout and even legal action, the most famous example being the transportation to Australia of the Dorset 'Tolpuddle Martyrs' in 1834. Despite those real obstacles, and the fact that west Kent was never a hotbed of industrial militancy, it is possible to identify both a steady undercurrent of trade union membership and a series of strikes (or attempts to strike) during the nineteenth century – even if very few achieved their aims entirely. One example was the strongly unionised Darent Valley papermakers, who on a different occasion in the 1820s struck because of 'an overabundance of apprentices' (which threatened wage levels) so that 'the men have made the regulation [to limit their number] and required the masters to agree to it'.[57] But the papermakers were a rare instance of a strong union and most other workers, even skilled ones, found it far harder to force the pace. One example was the insipid responses of the carpenters and joiners of Sevenoaks, who met in 1872 'to consider the present low standard of wages … and to adopt means for obtaining increased wages'. Two weeks later, when 'nothing definite had arrived', the nascent industrial unrest fizzled out.[58]

The Swing riots provide the best example of working-class dissatisfaction with their terms of employment in nineteenth-century west Kent, but it would be wrong to call this movement industrial action – although its participants certainly sought to scare their employers into paying higher wages – for rioters never went on strike. Although many were close to starvation, they could not risk losing even the very low wages they were offered.[59] That did not prevent local farmers trying hard to prevent any recurrence of those disturbances. Many were active in the various agricultural associations that sprang up in west Kent after 1830. Initially they functioned mainly as pressure groups

---

55 Census Returns for 1841, 1851, 1861, 1871: Sevenoaks.

56 *The Times*, 3 Nov. 1864, p. 9.

57 UKPP, Commons, *Minutes of Evidence*, p. 28.

58 *SEG*, 17 Sept. 1872, 5; 1 Oct. 1872, p. 5.

59 Griffin shows that the single strike in Kent in 1830 took place in Maidstone: *Rural war*, p. 331. However, see John Lowerson, 'Anti-Poor Law movements and rural trade unionism in the south east, 1835', in Adrian Charlesworth (ed.), *An atlas of rural protest in Britain, 1548–1900* (London, 1983), pp. 55–8, and Hastings, 'Radical movements', pp. 98–9.

Figure 7.2 National Fire Brigades Union procession, Tonbridge, 1909. The NFBU was established in 1895. The local brigade's 'success in national and international pumping and hose running competitions led to the selection of Tonbridge as the venue for a major international display in 1909 … The teams from all visiting brigades camped on the sports ground and a group of Belgian fireman were guests of honour. It is said that this display is the most photographed event in Tonbridge's history'.
Source: Tonbridge Historical Society, 23A.006.

serving the farmers' broader economic interests. The Kent Agricultural Association, for example, was formed 'expressly for the purpose of … [counteracting] … those delusive theorists who … are desirous of effecting the abolition of the corn laws'.[60]

Somewhat chastened by Swing, however, the Holmesdale Agricultural Association claimed in its foundation document of 1832 that it sought the 'Promotion and Encouragement of Servants and Agricultural Labourers', in part achieved by a well-publicised annual ploughing contest.[61] Its annual dinner in 1834 revealed its double-sided agenda. Samuel Love, whose Shoreham farm had been attacked in 1830, may have urged the adoption of better agricultural techniques, which would 'necessarily require more labour', perhaps by bringing more land into cultivation. But he thought the Association had another, very different, employment-related function. It should seek 'the reformation of the bad' and to set a 'meritorious example to the good, which must always render the labouring classes better members of society'.[62] 'Meritorious' implied reduced wage demands, no strikes and no recurrence of Swing.

---

60 *Bells Weekly Messenger*, 4 Dec. 1825, p. 8.

61 Sevenoaks Library B546; see also KHLC U840/E50.

62 *MJ*, 14 Oct. 1834, p. 4.

Other strikes did take place in that period, however. In 1834, after a builders' trade union was established in Tunbridge Wells, 'a spirit of discontent has manifested itself in the mechanics', after three plasterers walked out as a result of the employment of a non-union bricklayer, emphasising union solidarity.[63] In Sevenoaks in 1861 building workers petitioned to work only until 4 p.m., instead of 5.30 p.m., on Saturdays. A mass meeting agreed that, if the employers' response was unfavourable 'they should discontinue working on Saturday, the 13th'. The *South Eastern Gazette* was aghast, saying that 'This decision is in fact a "strike" which we hope will yet be averted, as the evils resulting from it are so wide spread and disastrous.'[64] The fact that the regional press never referred to any dispute (so it may never have happened) and that, more than a decade later, the workers had still not achieved their ambition of ceasing work on Saturdays at 4 p.m., indicates that this attempt to improve working conditions also failed.

The local press rarely reported industrial unrest, but were ready to report successful activity by the authorities to prevent strikes or other disruptions to normal working patterns. In 1859 a group of railway navvies at the St Mary Cray works sought to use a mid-Lent celebration to assemble to deal with the 'settlement of a dispute of long standing'. The *South Eastern Gazette* was pleased to inform its readers that 'a strong body of police' was on hand to prevent any breach of the peace and that 'everything passed off without any disturbance'.[65]

Organising west Kent farm labourers

Agricultural labourers were difficult to organise. Poorly paid, working on scattered farms, often living in tied cottages, they were invariably subject to farmers who had the power to lock out or blacklist them (see Plate 7). It is therefore not surprising that in 'low wage areas' such as the Weald earnings rose only very slowly over decades; at Brenchley they increased from 12s a week in the 1830s to about 14s a week in the 1870s, 'a mere 17 percent in forty years'.[66] By 1899 agrarian wage levels in the Weald had struggled up to 18s a week, when railway navvies were being paid twice as much. Thousands of young men and women sought alternative employment, which often involved migration.[67] An attempt to create a Kent Agricultural Labourers' Protection Society in 1866 was short-lived.[68]

By the early 1870s changed circumstances made it easier to organise farm workers: recent legislation gave trade unions greater legitimacy and growing industrial trade unions set an example to rural workers, while the railways, the penny post and a

63   *MJ*, 4 March 1834, p. 4.
64   *SEG*, 9 July 1861, p. 5.
65   *SEG*, 12 April 1859, p. 5.
66   Richardson, 'Labour', pp. 258–9.
67   *Ibid.*
68   The Society had 300 members in ten branches in the Maidstone area; it was dissolved in November 1867.

burgeoning press all aided regional and national organisation. A measure of success
came with the 'Revolt of the Field' in Kent in the 1870s. There were two competing
unions in west Kent: the Kent Agricultural Labourers' Union, later the Kent &
Sussex Labourers' Union (KSLU), created by Maidstone journalist Alfred Simmons
in May 1872, and the National Agricultural Labourers' Union (NALU), founded by
Joseph Arch three months earlier.[69] The two unions engaged in turf wars to recruit
members, offering a number of benefits, such as housing schemes and strike pay.[70]
The NALU in west Kent held a gala day in Sevenoaks in late July 1873, when the
town was filled with local labourers, many wearing union initials, representing
the 1,400 claimed members in the district.[71] Six months later Arch was again in
Sevenoaks and spoke at the local NALU branch meeting, which was chaired by
Andrew Swanzy and attended by James German.[72]

Simmons' tactics of high-profile mass demonstrations antagonised west Kent
farmers and, in 1873, those at Swanley and Farningham tried to cow the Union
through wage reductions and dismissals, when many labourers in 'low-paid' counties
such as Kent were still being paid about 12s a week.[73] From 1872 to 1894 KSLU
branches operated in the Sevenoaks area, along the Darent Valley and in the villages
of the Downs and the Weald.[74] In 1874 Simmons requested a daily labourer's wage
of 3s, plus 4d per hour overtime. Many Kent farmers then locked their men out, but
the KSLU's ability to provide opportunities for members to emigrate, especially to
New Zealand in early 1879, forced the farmers to back down for fear of seeing their
workforce literally disappearing over the horizon. It was a remarkable and unusual
victory for the agricultural labourers of west Kent and the rest of the county.[75] J.
Bonwick, the KSLU's district secretary, said of the Sevenoaks Weald branch, with its
claimed 65 members, that it 'offered greater benefits than any other society'.[76]

Union membership rested heavily on the state of the rural economy. When work
was plentiful in the early 1870s and in 1890–2, unions thrived; when it was scarce,

69 See Rollo Arnold, 'The "Revolt of the Field" in Kent, 1872–79', *Past & Present*, 64 (August 1974),
    pp. 71–95; in April 1873 the KSLU claimed 117 branches with 8,000 paying members, in April
    1875 over 10,000, and in October 1878 some 15,000 members; Felicity Carlton, '"A substantial
    and sterling friend to the labouring man": the Kent & Sussex Labourers' Union, 1872–95', MPhil
    thesis (University of Sussex, 1977).
70 *KT*, 21 Sept. 1880, p. 6, reporting a large KSLU meeting at Weald.
71 *Gravesend Reporter*, 2 Aug. 1873, p. 5.
72 *Dover Express*, 16 Jan. 1874, p. 4; *KSC*, 16 Jan. 1874, p. 3.
73 Gordon Mingay, *Rural life in Victorian England* (London, 1976), p. 79.
74 See the text and series of maps by Felicity Carlton in Adrian Charlesworth (ed.), *An atlas of rural
    protest in Britain, 1548–1900* (London, 1983), pp. 173–7; Jean Fox, David Williams and Peter
    Mountfield, *Seal. The history of a parish* (Chichester, 2007), pp. 124, 126.
75 Arnold, '"Revolt"', pp. 71, 80, 82.
76 *SC*, 26 Sept. 1884, p. 8.

they shrank.[77] NALU membership peaked in 1874, that of the KSLU in 1879. Rural unionism had a limited impact, enlisting nationally only 100,000 members from a total farm labour force of more than one million. By 1895 the KSLU had folded and three years later the NALU also dissolved. The lessons of the 1870s were not lost on agricultural labourers, however. They had been given a taste of power and this gave them a new self-confidence as wage earners that helped them escape from the stereotypical image of the inarticulate, dull-minded, clod-hopper 'hodge' favoured by *Punch* cartoonists.

In 1913 a revived but different National Union of Agricultural Labourers (NUAL) enrolled members in Sevenoaks, Swanley, Horton Kirby and other villages along the valleys of the Darent and the Cray.[78] In June 1914 nearly 500 agricultural labourers in the Swanley and Crockenhill district, members of the NUAL, went on strike 'for higher wages [a minimum of 24s per week], shorter hours, and recognition of their Union'. The strike was timed to hit farmers when labour was in high demand for picking soft fruit. Farmers responded by evicting workers from tied cottages and employing blackleg labour. The *Daily Citizen*, a Labour Party paper, stated: 'We protest against such infamy being permitted in a civilised land. We warn these landlords and farmers that by their ignorant, reckless despotism they are bringing on themselves the deluge.'[79]

Given the high value of the crops and the difficulties of finding alternative supplies of labour at short notice, fruit and hop pickers could find themselves in a strong negotiating position against their employers, with short-term strikes a very viable option. In 1872 stoppages took place at hop fields at both Chartwell and Ightham, where 'strikes have been common'.[80] In 1891 fruit pickers in Sevenoaks 'struck work' after 'some grievance'. Their employer, Charles Walton, who had already by custom deducted 5s from their first week's pay packets as security, in case they did not complete their picking contract, declined to pay them. Four of the men sued Walton for non-payment of wages, but lost.[81]

Cricket-ball making was a skilled craft job, mainly for men, based in the upper Medway and Eden valleys. In 1899 a total of £200 per week was paid in wages to the men, and a few women, working in small local factories.[82] The Amalgamated Society of Cricket Ball Makers, founded in 1892 with branches in Tonbridge and some neighbouring villages, agitated for 'better terms with employers' in 1898,

---

77 J.P.D. Dunbabin, *Rural discontent in nineteenth century Britain* (London, 1974), pp. 80–1, for figures of union membership.

78 *SC*, 11 July 1913, p. 8. That year a branch of the National Farmers Union was formed in Sevenoaks, with 20 members.

79 *Daily Citizen* (Manchester), 18 July 1914, p. 4.

80 *MJ*, 16 Sept. 1872, p. 5.

81 *SC*, 31 July 1891, p. 5.

82 *Sussex Agricultural Express*, 11 March 1899, p. 5.

when men were finding it difficult to live on an average wage of 25s a week.[83] In May 1907 (the start of the cricket season!) some 200 cricket-ball makers waged a successful strike, demanding a uniform rate of wages and a fixed minimum income.[84]

The building trades

The most militant workers in west Kent throughout the nineteenth century were employed in building-related trades. As early as the 1870s skilled workers were flexing their muscles. Charles Bassett was employed as a 'hawk boy', delivering plaster to skilled workers. But because many of these boys were learning the trade themselves, without serving apprenticeships, 'this the skilled plasterers objected to, hence the discontinuance of the Hawk Boys'.[85] Skilled employees such as plasterers successfully resisted the employment of unqualified labourers who had not completed an apprenticeship.[86] In the 1890s labour disputes of many types abounded across Britain, following the rise of the 'New Unionism', a 'broader movement advocating more positively aggressive … policies [that] sought to appeal in *class* terms to all grades of labour' and which represented a 'qualitative transformation of the British Labour Movement'.[87] A Carpenters and Joiners Union pamphlet reveals that there was a branch of the Eight Hours Movement operating in Sevenoaks in 1891. In 1895 the town's building trades operatives struck for an extra 1s 2d per hour and 'after a stoppage of three months obtained the concessions demanded'; 50 builders' labourers received wage increases.[88] However, an attempt the previous year by the Sevenoaks branch of the Amalgamated Society of House Decorators and Painters (ASHDP) to obtain a halfpenny an hour wage increase failed, although the Union's branches in Eastbourne and Hastings did obtain that raise through a 'mutual arrangement with the employers'.[89] Building workers went on strike in early 1914, delaying work on the new Sevenoaks swimming baths.[90]

Neither of those actions was reported in the *Sevenoaks Chronicle*. One that did reach the local press (although not the *Chronicle*) was in July 1900, when yet another dispute in the Sevenoaks building industry, 'which had begun to assume a

---

83 *MJ*, 28 April 1898, p. 8.

84 *The Sportsman*, 3 May 1907, p. 6.

85 Bassett, *Seal*, p. 4.

86 *Ibid.*

87 Keith Burgess, *The challenge of labour – shaping British history 1850–1930* (London, 1980), p. 65; Eric Hobsbawm, 'The new unionism in perspective', in Eric Hobsbawm (ed.), *Worlds of labour: further studies in the history of labour* (London, 1984), p. 156.

88 *Eight Hours Movement 1891* (London, 1892), p. 35; UKPP, Commons, *Board of Trade – Strikes and Lock-outs (Labour Department)*, No. C8231 (1896), p. 17; UKPP, Commons, *Wages and Hours of Labour (Board of Trade, Labour department)* … *wages and hours of labour in the UK, 1895*, No. C8374 (1896), p. 26.

89 UKPP, Commons, *Board of Trade*, p. 328.

90 SC, 30 Jan. 1914, p. 8.

SEVENOAKS
FROM PARISH CHURCH TOWER

Plate 1 A view of Sevenoaks, c.1900. A postcard view looking north from the top of the 30-metre-high St Nicholas church tower, clearly shows the North Downs in the distance.
Source: Author's collection.

Plate 2 Edward Kraftmeier, 1858–1916. Sevenoaks had several wealthy benefactors in the late nineteenth century. They included the German-born, naturalised citizen, Edward Kraftmeier who made a fortune manufacturing explosives. Despite his generosity to the town, and his work in support of the Great War, his German origins attracted hostility. Kraftmeier changed his name to 'Kay' in 1915.
Source: Courtesy of Dieter Friedrich, a descendant of the German family, with special thanks.

Democratic Leveling:—Alliance a la Françoise;— or—The Union of the Coronet & Clyster-pipe.

Plate 3 Charles, third Earl Stanhope (1753–1816). Stanhope, who lived at Chevening and had pronounced radical political ideas, is shown in this cartoon by James Gillray. Stanhope, on the left, attends the marriage of his daughter Lucy to Thomas Taylor, a surgeon of Sevenoaks. As a freakish apothecary assembled from medical equipment, Taylor symbolises the worst 'levelling' tendencies of revolutionary reform.

Source: 'Democratic levelling; - alliance a la françoise [sic]; – or – the union of the coronet and clyster-pipe' by James Gillray, published by Hannah Humphrey, hand-coloured etching, published 4 March 1796. NPG D12560 © National Portrait Gallery, London.

Plate 4 A view of the 1832 election in Tonbridge. It looks north up the High Street with the Chequers Inn sign on the left.

Source: Lithograph by Joseph Josiah Dodd and Charles Tattershall Dodd, *c.*1832. Yale Center for British Art, Paul Mellon Collection, B1977.14.20189.

Plate 5 A street in Hartslands, Sevenoaks. No early images are known to have survived. This modern photograph shows that most houses were built of local brick. A number also show external weatherboarding typical of the area.
Source: Author's photograph.

Plate 6 Philip John Ouless (1817–85), the Jersey-born painter and photographer, painted this view of the Vine Cricket Club in the mid-1850s. Cricket was primarily a game for 'gentlemen', although at village level squire, parson, farmers and labourers formed teams together. The Vine Cricket Club made few concessions to such democratic selection. The painting shows the well-dressed social elites separate from the working classes, who are merely on-lookers. It emphasises how important clothing was in signifying contemporary class distinctions.
Source: Sevenoaks Vine Cricket Club.

Plate 7 Solomon Brigden (1758–1826). Brigden was a farm labourer on the Knole Estate in 1783. His portrait, along with many other of his co-workers, was painted at the behest of the third Duke of Dorset. These are probably the only images we have of working-class west Kent residents of that time. Brigden, noted as a 'carter', appears to have been a man of some ambition. By the 1820s he had eiither inherited or saved money sufficient to buy some land. His improved status meant he left a will.
Source: Knole House estate.

Plate 8 Emily Jackson, (1840–1916). She was the sister of the architect Thomas Jackson and made for herself a career in social service to the community. In 1872 she founded in Sevenoaks the Children's Hospital for the Treatment of Hip Disease.
Source: Sevenoaks Museum.

Plate 9 Sevenoaks, 1905. This painting of the road junction in central Sevenoaks, by Charles Essenhigh Corke, looks north down the London road. The shape of the town centre today is little changed from then. The great difference is the volume of traffic. The lone motor vehicle and sheep being driven down the centre of the road indicates one established pattern of town life soon to be superseded by another. *Source*: Elizabeth Hope, *English Homes and Villages (Kent and Sussex)* (Sevenoaks, 1909), p. 192.

serious aspect', was 'satisfactorily settled' when it was agreed that 'all carpenters, joiners and labourers working within three miles of the Vine will receive an advance in wages of 1s 2d an hour'.[91] The tone of relief is palpable and raises the question of how the west Kent elite regarded the risk factors inherent within employee relations in general – and strikes in particular.

The 1911 rail strike in west Kent

West Kent (although not Maidstone) remained very quiet during one of the most significant disputes of the early twentieth century, the national railway strike of 1911. In Tunbridge Wells the strike had 'hardly ... any further effect on the public inconvenience', and in Tonbridge 'a number of meetings were held to discuss the situation, but no definite decision was arrived at, and fortunately a settlement was arrived at before any serious steps were taken'. Much more dramatically, 'the tunnels between Sevenoaks and Hildenborough and Sevenoaks and Knockholt were guarded at either end by military, and 20 special constables were sworn in for service if necessary', but as it turned out Sevenoaks too 'was not greatly affected by the strike'.

Source: *SEG*, 22 August 1911, p. 5.

A socialist method of advancing class solidarity was to encourage the formation of a local Trade Council. In 1896 the Sevenoaks branch of the ASHDP, which had 4,000 members nationally, called a meeting at the Greyhound Inn, St John's Hill. This was chaired by Arthur Hickmott and speakers included Councillor Fred Hooker, who with Hickmott provided a radical voice on the SUDC. The unanimous resolution of the meeting was to 'call upon the wage earners of Sevenoaks, to enrol themselves in the ranks of the Trade Unions, and to organise a Trades Council'.[92]

Middle-class responses

Some of the upper social echelons actively tried to improve employee relations, by implication recognising the risks involved should they sour. The Shoreham branch of the Girls Friendly Society was formed in 1881 for 'the benefit of the girls of the working classes', wherever they were employed, seeking to 'promote a feeling of unity between employers and employed'.[93] Middle-class Sevenoaks opinion about working-class industrial action was summed up in an editorial in the conservative

---

91 *KSC*, 20 July 1900, p. 3.
92 *SC*, 9 Oct. 1896, p. 4.
93 *SC*, 30 June 1882, p. 8.

Chronicle after the Taff Vale strike ended in 1901. It was far less interested in the employment rights and wrongs of the dispute than in the significant macroeconomic risks it and other disputes posed to the nation. Calling such stoppages 'a national peril', it warned of lost markets, which would gleefully be seized by America and Germany, and called for the Board of Trade to be given 'the power to intervene authoritatively' to prevent future occurrences.[94]

Later in the nineteenth century west Kent farmers were still trying to reduce their business risks by minimising costs, especially wages, when farm prices were falling. In 1890, one farmer complained that his 'wages bill was too heavy now that there was all this clamour about eight hours a day', but by this time such views were likely to be sharply criticised.[95] The previous year, a Kemsing correspondent had drawn attention to how one farmer complained about his wage bill while paying his workers just 14s a week, suggesting that *he* should try to 'live and keep out of debt on that fair week's pay'.[96]

Perhaps the worst middle-class nightmare was for different groups of workers to combine to alter the political as well as economic structures of the nation. Although some suggested links between the papermakers and Swing are fairly tenuous, there is no doubt that the former could be as hostile to new technology as the latter.[97] So in 1830 Sir Edward Knatchbull presented a petition to parliament 'from the journeymen papermakers of Kent against the new machinery' and, two years later, at a Whig political dinner in Maidstone, one speaker complained bitterly about the 'poverty and misery occasioned by the use of machinery in making paper', which led to 'many papermakers being thrown out of employment'.[98] Although there is no evidence of any direct link between the industrial workers of the Darent Valley and the farm workers of west Kent, as they drank in the same pubs and attended the same churches – to give just two examples of many possible meeting places – many indirect contacts must have taken place between them. One anonymous papermaker did try to raise agricultural wages at Shoreham during the 'Revolt of the Field'. He wrote to local farmers demanding 18s a week on their behalf, plus 4d an hour overtime and reduced hours on Saturdays. The *South Eastern Gazette* called it 'a remarkable document', but 'deficient as it was not from the farm workers themselves', and hoped those seeking 'the maintenance of that good feeling which should exist between master and man, will be preferred to those of outsiders whose only desire appears to be to set class against class'.[99]

Domestic service formed a vital part of the workforce, especially for women, and their wages surely played a part in raising the standard of living of working-class families of the period. In Sevenoaks in 1851, 299 people were employed in service,

---

94   *SC*, 7 Sept. 1900, p. 4.
95   *SC*, 23 May 1890, p. 4.
96   *SC*, 3 May 1889, p. 5.
97   Carl Griffin, 'The violent Captain Swing?' *Past & Present*, 209 (2010), pp. 149–80 (p. 163).
98   *MJ*, 4 May 1830, p. 2; *SEG*, 11 Dec. 1832, p. 3.
99   *SEG*, 17 Aug. 1872, p. 2.

or 6 per cent of the total population, the great majority (204, or 68 per cent) being called either 'general servant' or a maid of some description in that year's census. Knole House employed 24, or 8 per cent of that total. In 1881, in a single, admittedly prosperous, street in Sevenoaks – South Park – 21 out of the 54 residents (or 39 per cent) of the eight dwellings were live-in domestic staff. All were female, ranging in income and status from 17-year-old Mary Garwood, an under-housemaid, to 31-year-old governess Ellen Evans, who taught three girls aged 4 to 15.[100]

Population of Sevenoaks in domestic service, 1851

Domestic service was the largest single occupation of female employees in the nineteenth century.

General servant	124
Maid	80
Cook	18
Groom	15
Housekeeper	14
Footman	10
Nurse	10
Bailliff, gamekeeper	8
Coachman	6
Governess	2

Source: Census Return for 1851: Sevenoaks.

Conclusion

A steady, secure wage was the most effective way most working-class people in west Kent could overcome the major risks they faced and obtain the bare necessities they needed. For local farm labourers that became almost impossible on at least two occasions. In 1830, many across west Kent felt they had no viable option for redress other than arson and riot – the risk factors they faced were so severe they believed they had no other realistic choices left. Their palpable desperation and misery led some, at least, of the more thoughtful middle-class commentators to realise that repetitions simply had to be avoided – especially if they had themselves felt the hot breath of Swing on their necks, as had several in the Sevenoaks area.

By the time of the 'Revolt of the Field' in the 1870s, however, the position had become markedly different. A more lenient legal environment, within which

---

100 Census Return for 1851: Sevenoaks; Census Return for 1881: Sevenoaks.

industrial action was possible, and the attractive potential choices offered by emigration, meant that Unions blessed with deep pockets, strong leaders and effective tactics could defeat employers in ways hitherto considered impossible. Although west Kent saw few other major industrial disputes during the long nineteenth century, its workers always knew that, should they prove able to organise themselves as Simmons had the KSLU, strikes might well succeed. That point was not lost on their masters.

The risks of taking industrial action were, therefore, a great deal less than they had been earlier in the century, so striking became a more realistic option and the resulting fear factor among employers may well have played a significant part in increasing working-class wages (and thus standards of living) in the later nineteenth century. It might also have persuaded them to conciliate or negotiate with, rather than confront, their employees, so strikes became a weapon of last resort. Other parts of Britain (even nearby towns such as Maidstone), however, had very different industrial relations experiences, so it would be wise not to generalise from the experience of west Kent.

If stoppages became more likely to succeed in their aims, why did so few take place in the later nineteenth century? Answering that question may require introducing an inverse variant of E.P. Thompson's 'moral economy of the poor'.[101] Thompson believed that dispossessed English working-class communities of the late eighteenth and early nineteenth centuries had a profound understanding of what constituted the rightful ordering of society. If it did not function properly, for example by failing to supply the bare necessities at acceptable prices, that provided ample moral justification for food riots and other acts of rebellion. The aggrieved felt they had no other choice but to upend society, albeit briefly, to remove those risks. One way of doing this was by transferring them to their social and economic superiors, either physically, symbolically, or both.

But once those risk factors had been overcome and those bare necessities normally achieved, then the moral economy could operate the other way round. Although work remained hard for most working-class people, obtaining sufficient food, a reasonable cottage and a warm fire went a long way towards dissuading those workers from striking, particularly if such action would result directly in hard-earned wages disappearing. That reduced risk was also combined with enhanced levels of choice. For those workers also had (slightly) more money to spend on goods in the shops and more time to enjoy it as working hours (slowly) decreased. They also knew that they were legally permitted to go on strike, if provoked, and if all else failed they could (if there were means or money to hand) choose to emigrate.

---

101 E.P. Thompson, 'The moral economy of the poor', in E.P. Thompson, *Customs in common: studies in traditional popular culture* (London, 1993).

Chapter 8
Self, family, friends, neighbours, townspeople

Because two Sevenoaks families, from very different social classes, play such key roles in this chapter it begins with their brief biographies.

The Coppers and Hows

Copper family

Carpenter Robert Copper (1813–90) and his wife Mary (1821–1909) lived at Hartslands in 1871 with their three younger sons: Henry (1846–80), a general labourer; Robert junior (1848–1914), a gas labourer; and Silas (1858–1934), a bricklayer's labourer. Their eldest son, William (1843–1916), a farm labourer, lived four doors away with his wife Sarah (1844–1914) and their four small children. The family supplemented its income with regular criminal activities, mainly poaching, but also theft and receiving. Henry suffered a serious industrial accident in 1863 while working at the railway tunnel being constructed in Sevenoaks.

Robert junior married Mary, a laundress, in 1872. Their children attended the boys' and girls' school that opened in Cobden Road, Hartslands, in October 1884. John, born in 1876 and described as 'very dull', was caned three times between 1884 and 1887. Another son, George (born in 1879) was punished for playing truant in 1888. His elder sister Rose caught ringworm in April 1887. The Poor Law Relieving Officer paid the school fees for Robert's family in 1885, 1887 and 1888. The 1901 census reveals that he was by then a disabled 'imbecile' who 'cannot Work'. Mary had gone deaf. Both regularly received poor relief between 1898 and 1904. Their daughter Maggie (born 1880) gave birth to at least three illegitimate daughters, at different Hartslands addresses, between 1899 and 1909.

Sarah left £109 in her will. William died two years later, leaving about £320. Only one other member of the entire extended Copper family is recorded as having made a will before 1918.

How family

The will of Nicholas How (1771–1855) described him as a 'carpenter and builder'. His sons, also successful artisans, included carpenter Thomas (1798–1880), builder George (1802–83) and Samuel (1807–83), another carpenter. A daughter, Jane, who died in 1833 aged 21, received a fulsome obituary in the Wesleyan-Methodist magazine. Pillars of the Sevenoaks Methodist church throughout, Nicholas, George and cousin Stephen (1811–91) served continuously as superintendents in the Sevenoaks chapel between 1836 and 1885. Thomas, George and Stephen were trustees and officers of the Sevenoaks Wesleyan Benefit Friendly Society until its demise in 1884 and the three brothers, together with Henry, George's son (1847–1930), were leading lights in the Sevenoaks Gas Company for many years. Thomas left almost £500 in his will, Stephen £1,200, Samuel over £1,900 and Henry nearly £12,000.[1]

Previous chapters have identified the everyday risk factors that could impact on the wellbeing and happiness of the poorer classes of people in west Kent in the early nineteenth century. The best way for the able-bodied to overcome those risks was reliable income from regular work. Loss of work through illness, injury, being laid off or striking could reduce entire families to penury, making the four bare necessities even harder to obtain. Many would have thought hard about how best to mitigate these circumstances. There were no statutory welfare safety nets; private charity was often for those deemed the 'deserving poor'. Self-help, in the form of friendly societies and other options, was generally too expensive for ordinary labouring men, certainly in the early part of the nineteenth century, and trade unions were largely ineffective. The co-operative movement came to the fore only towards the end of the century.

The importance of the family

The working or artisanal classes, or most of them, were therefore forced to rely on the most effective human risk mitigation system devised, the extended family network, which might also include friends and neighbours. There, many of life's snares might best be contained, shared and, ideally, overcome. This was why, 'for most working people, what mattered most was … personal relationships', an example being the Halstead parishioners who petitioned the Poor Law Commissioners on behalf of a widow and her two sons and the great 'advantage' they would gain 'by being among her connections and friends'.[2] In crisis, middle-class residents, too, found the emotional and practical support provided by their extended families similarly essential. The concentric rings of family and 'informal network communities' of

---

1   Sevenoaks and Hartslands census; *SEG*, 22 December 1863, 5; KHLC C/ES 330 2/4; TNA IR 58; https://probatesearch.service.gov.uk/#calendar; *Wesleyan Methodist Magazine*, August 1833, p. 605; KHLC M2/1/6/16; M2/1/2/1.

2   John Burnett (ed.), *Useful toil: autobiographies of working people from the 1820s to the 1920s* (Harmondsworth, 1984), p. 17; Curteis, *Peel*, pp. 42–3.

Figure 8.1 Quarrymen, Sevenoaks *c*.1900. These quarry labourers worked long hours for meagre and often irregular pay out in all weathers. As can be seen from this photograph, some of the men were well past middle age. Ill-health or injury posed a constant threat to loss of livelihood; precarious employment meant dependent families were constantly haunted by the risk of stark poverty. *Source*: Sevenoaks Library.

friends and neighbours provided the crucial human terrain on and through which many of those risks were managed, on both the tangible and emotional levels. For the poorest sections of society they were 'most important for survival in times of hardship, and for companionship'.[3]

Potentially, the family offered not only mutual affection and companionship but also, materially, increased security for women and better care for men, and vice versa. Both these factors applied equally to any children involved, either from a current relationship or any prior affiliation. The broader risk strategy of the Victorian family, especially the poorer sort, worked in three ways. First, it could when needed pool whatever financial and other resources were available, or better access the makeshift economy, for the common good of its members. This implicitly co-operative approach offered 'a network of support at times of crisis', but it could only work if those networks were based on the essential ingredient of trust.[4] If ever

3   F.M.L. Thompson, 'Town and country', in F.M.L. Thompson (ed.), *The Cambridge social history of Britain, 1750–1950*, vol. 1, *regions and communities* (Cambridge, 1993), p. 59.

4   Burnett, *Housing*, p. 151.

that trust broke down, as we shall discover, it exacerbated rather than mitigated the risk factors. Secondly, it enabled division of labour, so family members could focus their time and skills on those tasks they were best at performing. Given the prevailing nineteenth-century economic and cultural norms, the husband was almost always the main breadwinner, with the wife perhaps able to earn a second income if grandparents or other relatives could assist with childcare. If not, or if those relatives were themselves too old or infirm to contribute, the position would be reversed, so that the wife had to care for both them and the children. Thirdly, if work was unavailable, the poor had to make a living in other ways. The makeshift economy could include financial or in-kind help from family or charities; taking in lodgers; remarriage for widows and widowers; local borrowing networks (especially pawnshops and moneylenders); and various forms of begging, crime and petty dealing, including prostitution.

In December 1832 Mrs Allnutt, visiting the Nouailles at Greatness, remarked that in a single day no less than 'nine beggars came'; she does not say if, or to what extent, they were relieved.[5] If all else failed there was poor relief, or 'going on the parish'. The very poor, invariably those without means of support, might find shelter within the overcrowded workhouse on St John's Hill, which in the transitional period of 1840–1 housed 338 people.[6] For those suffering temporary loss of work or misfortune outdoor relief was still available, *de facto* if not *de jure*: this was short-term aid designed to keep people in their own homes and tide them over their present difficulties. The Sevenoaks Vestry minutes for the early nineteenth century contain the repeated phrase 'the applicant begs … ', emphasising the relationship of the supplicant poor to the parish authorities as they sought food, shoes, clothing and fuel. Also available were weekly cash payments and in some cases grants of small plots of land or assistance to emigrate.[7]

In 1799–1800, a time of severe hardship, the Sevenoaks Overseers resorted to a 'soup shop', or 'Public Kitchen', offering food at cost price, via a ticket system, to relieve 'the industrious Poor during the present high price of provisions'. Overseers argued that it was better, and presumably cheaper, 'to relieve in soup and not in 'Money except in extraordinary cases'. The daily offering of 60 gallons of soup was increased to 130 gallons over time, and poor children of the parish were provided with a daily dinner. In 1804 the Vestry planned 'to establish a manufactory' of Linen, Woollen and Linsey 'for the purpose of employing and setting to work the poor … who may be under necessity of making application for relief'.[8]

---

5   Sevenoaks Library B ALL, Mrs Allnutt's Diary, 4 Dec. 1832.

6   *The Lancet*, 22 Jan. 1842, pp. 588–90.

7   Elizabeth Melling (ed.), *Kentish sources. IV. The poor* (Maidstone, 1964), pp. 157–62 for examples from Ightham, Chevening, Seal and Malling.

8   KHLC P330/8/1, 10 Dec. 1799; 3 March 1800; Jan. 1804. However, no action appears to have been taken to establish such a 'manufactory'.

The Poor Law Amendment Act of 1834 (the 'New Poor Law'), introduced the much-hated 'indoor relief', so that 'running out of relatives was a short cut to the workhouse'.[9] However, parish 'allowances were rarely anywhere near subsistence level, obliging kin to give what material help they could', and the Poor Law Guardians also obliged families to contribute to the upkeep of members eligible for relief, although some striking examples of wealthy people who sought to avoid such responsibilities were recorded.[10]

Coping was much more difficult for those without family, so widows or unmarried women with children often found life especially hard, as they have done throughout history. Remarriage was, therefore, a most attractive option. And the only way those lower down the social scale could overcome the very real problem of penury in old age was to have children who would be able to care for them. Many parents in that position knew that, if their children moved far away in search of better lives for themselves, it would come at the price of a much riskier old age for them.

Unsurprisingly, in view of all these factors, single occupants were very scarce in Hartslands. In 1871, for example, just three out of 164 householders lived completely alone. All were women: a teacher; a woman whose income was 'derived from letting'; and Elizabeth Playfoot, a 70-year-old widow and pauper.[11] Single lodgers, who provided a welcome boost to many family incomes, were commonplace. In addition, several older single men employed housekeepers to both run the home and provide companionship: for example, 77-year-old widower John Corker of Hartslands had a 24-year-old servant, Melisa Dovey, who looked after him and his four sons in 1901. Eyebrows might have been raised, however, at how in 1881 widow Mary Ann Cass, 57, shared her house with married lodger William Coomber, aged 49 – and no one else.[12]

Yet the extended household was not the only viable family type. Much in evidence, in both working-class strongholds such as Hartslands and the more upmarket parts of Sevenoaks, were nuclear families of two generations, parents and children. Both the Coppers and Hows were nuclear families, although the family units often lived very close to each other, so Robert Copper lived a few doors away from the family of his eldest son, William, in Hartslands in 1871 and brothers Samuel and Stephen How's houses were right next door to each other at Lock's Yard a decade later.[13]

Normally, nuclear families were formed by younger married couples with children, whose surviving parents were still capable of supporting themselves elsewhere. But

9   Frank Prochaska, 'Philanthropy', in F.M.L. Thompson, *The Cambridge social history of Britain 1750–1850. Vol. 3, social agencies and institutions* (Cambridge, 1990), pp. 357–93 (p. 363).

10 Steven King, *Poverty and welfare in England 1750–1950: a regional perspective* (Manchester, 2000), pp. 172, 20; Lynn Hollen Lees, *The solidarities of strangers: the English poor laws and the people, 1700–1948* (Cambridge, 1998), pp. 169–70; Tufnell, *Dwelling*, p. 19.

11 Census Return for 1871: Sevenoaks (Hartslands).

12 Census Return for 1901: Sevenoaks (Hartslands); Census Return for 1881: Sevenoaks (Hartslands).

13 Census Return for 1871: Sevenoaks (Hartslands); http://theweald.org/P2.asp?PId=Se.LockY, accessed 7 June 2017.

those families tended to be riskier since they generally lacked immediate access to the potential financial and other support available from other family members in the event of a temporary crisis. With extended families, by contrast, if a male breadwinner suffered unemployment, illness or a serious accident, relatives – especially those living fairly close at hand – could clear rent arrears, pay doctors' fees or offer childcare, if the wife suddenly had to go out to work. But some longer-term risks could not, normally, be assuaged by the help of relatives or friends, no matter how close by or committed to the family. These included bad housing, inadequate sanitation and being a victim of crime. And many risk factors, such as unemployment or disease, also had significant mental and emotional consequences, in addition to the physical, financial and physiological. In 1901, for example, Robert and Mary Copper were, as noted, severely disabled; she was 'deaf', he an 'imbecile' who 'cannot work', possibly because of an industrial accident.[14]

Finding a partner

Given its potential capacity to reduce the very real risks of contemporary existence, being part of a successful, functional family was therefore a highly attractive proposition. In Victorian England it invariably meant marriage, which also conferred respectability on both parties, so good matches were sought. Great must have been the consternation, therefore, when it was discovered that all 112 marriages contracted at the new church at Halstead after 1881 were technically invalid because the building was unconsecrated, a situation rectified only in 1919.[15] Both men and women preferred 'conjugality to independence' and 'very few working class women made the conscious decision to live on their own'.[16] Middle-class women had similar aspirations, although, by the mid-nineteenth century, the number of jobs available to them had become somewhat restricted in a masculine-orientated society dominated by manufacturing and trade. Women were obliged to resort, in the main, to dressmaking, millinery and teaching. They survived by becoming part of a family household, either by marrying and running the home or, if single, by contributing their earned or unearned income to its economy or overseeing it as its housekeeper. Their entire identity became familial, therefore, as opposed to occupational.[17]

The rest of this chapter examines the (often tortuous) process by which Victorian families in general, and those of Sevenoaks in particular, became established. It seeks to answer the key question: how effective was the local family in mitigating

---

14 Census Return for 1901: Sevenoaks (Hartslands).

15 Killingray, *Sevenoaks people and faith*, pp. 138–9.

16 Ginger Frost, *Promises broken: courtship, class and gender in Victorian England* (Charlottesville, VA, 1995), p. 72; Francoise Barret-Ducrocq, *Love in the time of Victoria: sexuality, class and gender in nineteenth-century London* (London, 1991), p. 73.

17 Leonore Davidoff and Catherine Hall, *Family fortunes: men and women of the English middle class 1780–1850* (London, 2002), pp. 312–15.

Figure 8.2 Strudwick family. Susan Ruth Strudwick (1847–1931) with (L–R) her three children, Bertie (1877–1965), Susan Ruth 'Tudie' (1880–1974) and Florence (1878–1923). Born Susan Levett, she met cabinet maker and undertaker Frederic Strudwick when she was working as a cook at Brasted Place and he came to hang the bells at the house. They married in 1875 and the 1881 census records them living at London Road, Westerham. The photograph dates from 1881.
Source: Roger Quick collection.

the risks run by its members? Doing so will involve focusing on the five stages from being unmarried towards forming and growing a relationship, potentially leading to marriage and establishing a new family, initially nuclear, later perhaps non-nuclear. Those stages were meeting; courtship; engagement; marriage; and, finally, having children. But the course of true love was not always smooth. Children could and did appear before the wedding, which could prove highly inopportune.

Bastardy carried very significant risk factors that often derailed the entire marital enterprise forever. In the later nineteenth century if a single mother was unable to look after an illegitimate child there were orphanages, including a few in Sevenoaks, such as that run by the Church of England Society for Waifs and Strays, which in 1891 was occupied by ten girls aged from 2 to 13. In 1890 Dr Thomas Barnardo wrote to the Sevenoaks Guardians offering to take boys housed by the Union to

Canada. The master declined as 'They had not got any boys to part with.'[18] Although the experiences of children in Barnado's homes were not always pleasant – one boy arrested in Tonbridge for begging in 1890 said he had been 'knocked about by the other boys', for example – their lives were generally much less risky, either at home or abroad, than were those of their predecessors.[19]

But other risks were inherent in this complex journey. Even if a marriage agreement was made the path to the altar was often strewn with difficulty, for its ritual steps – especially courtship and engagement – could prove similarly hazardous. Even before anybody eyed up a member of the opposite sex to assess if they were a suitable potential spouse, they had some awareness that marriage was predicated upon a cost–benefit analysis conducted by the couple concerned and their families. The emotional desire for marital union was tempered by the recognition that, if marriage took place at the wrong time or to the wrong person, 'there would be serious consequences in terms of socio-economic position and personal happiness'.[20] Marrying up the social scale was a good way of obviating this risk, or so it appeared, and there was a grim but realistic logic in referring to courtship as a 'Matrimonial Market'.[21] But bettering oneself by a potentially 'good' marriage, financially, was itself a hazardous strategy, for 'cross-class matings faced numerous problems'.[22] Specifically, class differences were a major cause of broken engagements, and the social stigma and emotional pain that so often resulted.

Those risks were of course framed within a context of choice of marriage partner. The nineteenth century also saw enhanced choice in the location of the marriage ceremony itself, particularly after the passage of The Dissenters' Marriage Act 1836.[23] The 1887 Matrimonial Returns revealed that 610 of the 4,934 marriage ceremonies conducted in Kent (or just over 12 per cent) that year had taken place in registry offices, but while church weddings, especially those involving the upper echelons, often generated significant press coverage, one searches in vain for any report of a civil ceremony in the *Sevenoaks Chronicle* before 1914.[24]

This exploration will be conducted partly, but not exclusively, through detailing the lives of the dysfunctional working-class Coppers of Hartlands and the respectable, churchgoing middle-class How family, who lived in the much pleasanter upper part of the town. This highly significant spatial distinction illustrates a broader socio-

---

18   *SC*, 4 July 1890, p. 5.

19   *MJ*, 25 Oct. 1890, p. 3.

20   Alan MacFarlane, *Marriage and love in England: modes of reproduction 1300–1840* (Oxford, 1987), p. 291.

21   *SC*, 23 July 1886, p. 5.

22   Frost, *Promises broken*, p. 80.

23   Rebecca Probert, 'How to get hitched, Victorian-style', *BBC History Magazine* (Christmas 2018), pp. 38–43 (p. 41).

24   *SC*, 25 Jan. 1889, p. 4.

Figure 8.3 Charles and Ann Bassett with their family, Seal, *c.*1880. Charles Bassett jnr (1861–1933) – top left – was born in Seal, his father Charles snr being a farm labourer who was determined to better his lot. Charles inherited these ambitions and the political radicalism of his father, who had taken his two sons to London in 1884 to join the mass demonstration demanding the extension of the franchise. In the early 1900s Charles jnr was publicly listed as politically 'Progressive'. By then, due to hard work and study, he had moved from being a plasterer's mate, farm worker, gardener, indoor servant, and builders' labourer, to a skilled carpenter, and then a teacher of handicrafts. From 1898 until his retirement in 1926, Charles taught at Bayham Road School, Sevenoaks, and elsewhere, a proud Member of the Royal Society of Teachers. His social mobility was also marked by his move from a rented house in Hartslands to his own house in Bradbourne Road.
Source: Author's collection.

economic divide: the two families moved in such different circles and experienced such dissimilar risk factors that they may never have met and probably had little or no understanding of how the others lived their lives.

There is an extensive literature on the Victorian family and its formation. It startled one contemporary French commentator that young people in England could 'see and associate together in perfect freedom, without being watched'.[25] Such easy formation of relationships led, at least in theory, to a wider choice of prospective marriage partners, so the path to the altar was 'a game that ... people played for themselves'.[26] However, they tended to express those choices within 'a carefully controlled context of mutual values and religious concerns'; the lower middle classes, in particular, sought and found their spouses mainly through their friendship, kinship and social networks, church being especially important.[27] Or, like Charles Bassett's parents, they met through their employment. His mother was born in Twineham, near Burgess Hill, Sussex in 1835. She was in service at Ightham and met his father when he was a labourer there. They married in 1861.[28]

Finding the right person to marry could be difficult for those of more genteel social status. William Knight spent much time visiting 'Miss Rose' in 1833, but she received a proposal from another man the following year and Knight eventually married Ann Nash at Tonbridge in 1835.[29] There is little evidence of courtship ritual in the Sevenoaks area, in the form of diaries or letters, for example, for the first half of the nineteenth century, but Andrew Reed's moralistic novel, *No Fiction* (1823), set in Sevenoaks, provides an imaginative romantic relationship.[30] Conversely, blossoming relationships could be snuffed out by family disapproval or one or the other party being under age, for under Hardwicke's Marriage Act of 1753 no marriage of a person under the age of 21 was valid without the consent of parents or guardians. Clergymen who disobeyed the law were liable to 14 years' transportation.[31] One romantic solution – at least for the wealthy – was elopement, such as that of a 17-year-old girl in Sevenoaks in 1836, when there was 'little doubt that the adventurous couple were destined for Gretna-green'.[32] Those lower down the social scale had more opportunities for casual meetings, especially in the big cities, but rural calendars too allowed for 'feast days and fairs, wakes and revels'.[33] Such encounters

---

25 Hippolyte Taine, *Notes on England* (London, 1872), p. 97.

26 MacFarlane, *Marriage and love*, p. 295.

27 Davidoff and Hall, *Family fortunes*, p. 219.

28 Bassett, *Seal*, p. 1.

29 Private archives, Knight, *Diaries*, vol. 1, 5 July 1833; 28 Feb. 1834; https://familysearch.org, accessed 7 June 2017.

30 Andrew Reed, *No fiction*, 2 vols (London, 1823), vol. 2, pp. 37, 62.

31 www.parliament.uk: the law of marriage.

32 *The Globe*, 13 July 1836, p. 3.

33 John Rule, *The labouring classes in early industrial England, 1750–1850* (Abingdon, 2013), p. 193.

might not be subtle either, since it was culturally quite acceptable for young men brazenly to accost single girls in the street. Moreover, particularly in later Victorian Britain, when 'very large numbers of the employed population increasingly enjoyed approved leisure time', they could encounter each other in parks, music halls, on a seaside excursion or, again, in church.[34] If all else failed both sexes could resort to the 'well-established spots where young people strolled in the evenings'.[35]

Those haphazard encounters might lead to courtships, which tended to be short, then to engagements, which tended to be far longer. If boy and girl got on together, the young courters might start by 'speaking', then they 'walked out together', then they were 'keeping company'; only then would they get engaged.[36] At each point risk issues became more acute. Economic factors often drove this process, especially for less affluent couples from the lower middle classes or below, who had to save or wait for inheritances before they could get married.[37] Such risks were normally managed within very traditional courtship behaviour, with a series of prescribed ritual and/ or symbolic stages well known to and accepted by both sexes. But long courtships and engagements could be risky, exposing a couple to physical and geographical separation, rival attractions, an increasing sense of incompatibility and family pressures to end the relationship. If this led to the man jilting the girl she could and often did obtain monetary compensation via a lawsuit for Breach of Promise.[38]

Sex and its consequences

Sexual activity was another high-risk activity in the nineteenth century, both physiologically and emotionally. It could result in unwanted pregnancies or disease. However, premarital sex seems to have declined within the lower middle class in the early to mid-nineteenth century, possibly as a result of a combination of 'Christian evangelism reinforced by medical campaigns against venereal disease', both of which the Hows and other Methodists would have heartily approved of.[39] There is little extant evidence that such infections were widespread in west Kent then, although the ubiquitous advertisements for cure-all proprietary medicines might indicate otherwise. Venereal disease figured prominently in several 'society' divorce cases, such as that of Lord and Lady Colin Campbell, which was generously covered in the *Sevenoaks Chronicle* in 1886. Working-class attitudes to pre-marital sex were more tolerant, but only if it was justified by a prior promise of marriage, which was again highly ritualised. So important was this promise, whether pronounced

---

34 Douglas Reid, 'Playing and praying: leisure and religion in urban Britain', in Martin Daunton (ed.), *The Cambridge urban history of Britain, vol. 3, 1840–1950* (Cambridge, 2001), p. 746.

35 Barret-Ducrocq, *Love*, pp. 75–8; Joan Perkin, *Victorian women* (New York, 1995), p. 57.

36 Barret-Ducrocq, *Love*, p. 86.

37 Frost, *Promises broken*, pp. 62–3.

38 See for example *Surrey Comet*, 30 Nov. 1898, 6, 'Haynes v. Haynes'.

39 John Gillis, *For better or worse: English marriages 1600 to the present* (Oxford, 1985), p. 238.

orally or by letter, that not only did some women regard it 'as a solemn oath' but it immediately legitimised sexual activity.[40]

Managing sexual desire underpinned what might be termed the social and emotional 'intimacy risk' run by both parties during courtship and engagement; it has been accurately described as 'tightrope walking' for both parties concerned.[41] Social class was relatively unimportant here. If the girl allowed too much or too little sexual intimacy, her man might walk away. Conversely, if he demonstrated too much or too little ardour, he risked losing a wife. Courtship was therefore a serious cultural game played according to complex sets of rules. While attractive and competent players could ascend the ladders to marriage, quite as many snakes lurked to trap the unwitting or the unwary and to return them swiftly back to square one. One who suffered in this way was Liberty Durrant, a farmer from Edenbridge, who was sued for breach of promise by Sarah Benson in 1888. Although he denied that he had attempted to seduce her, he admitted he did not see 'what difference there was between young people keeping company and becoming engaged lovers', which was an implicit admission of his own sexual misconduct. She was awarded substantial damages of £200.[42]

The family was regarded, therefore, as the 'basic unit of society' and marriage 'became increasingly the gateway to respectability and stability'; the latter minimised the economic and social risks and the former the reputational risks.[43] For the vast majority of people, even though not everyone enjoyed a happy marriage, it was seen as 'an indissoluble union which ended only when one or other partner died', and the law actively sought 'to deter cohabitation outside marriage'.[44] This meant that divorce was rare (in 1914 fewer than 1,000 a year out of a total UK population of 40 million), always carried 'a strong social stigma' and was so expensive that only the well-off could afford it.[45] But marriages could also be ended by annulment (or declared null and void by legal procedure) in cases of consanguinity, bigamy or one or both partners being underage. And, especially for the poor, discontented husbands might simply abscond, and legal separation was possible. In England and Wales 8,000 or so such orders were being made each year in the early twentieth century.[46] For those (still relatively few) people involved, the emotional risks of remaining with a partner they no longer loved or felt safe with outweighed the social and economic risks of reverting to singleness.

---

40   Barret-Ducrocq, *Love*, pp. 98, 100, 108.

41   MacFarlane, *Marriage and love*, p. 304.

42   *KSC*, 8 June 1888, p. 3; 15 June 1888, p. 6.

43   Jeffrey Weeks, *Sex, politics and society: the regulations of sexuality since 1800* (Harlow, 2012), pp. 33, 34.

44   Perkin, *Victorian women*, p. 122; Rebecca Probert, *The changing legal regulation of cohabitation: from fornicators to family, 1600–2010* (Cambridge, 2012), p. 107.

45   Perkin, *Victorian women*, p. 130; Weeks, *Sex, politics and society*, p. 34.

46   Weeks, *Sex, politics and society*, p. 82.

The working-class family

Turning to working-class family formation and relationships within the Sevenoaks area specifically, it is difficult to explore courtship and engagement rituals and progress for any individuals before the later nineteenth century, as personal evidence simply does not exist. But it is possible to draw some general conclusions, for Hartslands especially, from close scrutiny of the census returns from 1851 to 1901, supported by a variety of family history sources. Also helpful are comments and letters in relevant regional and local newspapers, local bastardy returns and correspondence with Poor Law officers about illegitimate children.

The arrival of the railway explains one of the most dramatic social shifts those returns reveal. In 1851 more than 58 per cent of Hartslands residents had been born within five miles of the town, only 7 per cent coming from over 50 miles away. But by 1901 the former figure had dropped to 46 per cent and the latter more than doubled, to 16 per cent. Improved letter communications, driven by improving literacy, also benefitted from the penny post from 1840; by 1871 over 12,000 letters a week were being delivered to addresses in Sevenoaks, together with nearly 2,000 parcels and almost 1,500 newspapers.[47] That total would have included a fair number of love letters, which illustrate another important shift – the places from where townspeople found their marriage partners. In 1851, 59 per cent came from five miles away or less – a percentage that more than halved, to 26 per cent, by 1901. And, conversely, those from 50 miles away or more rose from just 4 per cent to 30 per cent over the same period. This trend is visible in the relationship history of the Copper family. For, while both Robert senior and his brother Peter, who was born in 1816, took up with Sevenoaks girls, Elizabeth (born 1858), the partner of Silas Copper (born 1857) came from Birmingham.[48] There is no telling exactly how any of those couples first met, but the increased demand for female domestic servants within Sevenoaks from mid-century onwards certainly added to the number of marriageable young women available in the town.

Middle-class family formation

The How family, as staunch and ultra-respectable Methodists, often found their spouses through their church connections. So, for example, George How married his second wife Emily Humphreys (1818–63) in 1842. Her sister Ann-Sarah's daughter, Elizabeth (1839–1928), married William Franks (1837–1930) in 1864, making him How's nephew by marriage. Franks, who began preaching on the Sevenoaks circuit in 1858 when just 21, and How were also closely connected in the ministry and another relative, George Humphreys (1842–82), regularly attended Quarterly Circuit meetings with How until his death.

---

47   Archie Donald, *The posts of Sevenoaks in Kent* (Tenterden, 1992), p. 281.

48   Census Returns for 1851 and 1901: Sevenoaks (Hartslands); Census Return for 1891: Sevenoaks (Hartslands).

Later in the century, the process by which the respectable middle classes met potential marriage partners may be traced through how Valentine's Day was portrayed in the west Kent press. Press editorials were unsure of the day's value,[49] for example the Ladies Column of the *Sevenoaks Chronicle* which regularly, but wrongly, predicted the 'death of St Valentine', who would soon be as redundant as 'May Day dances around Maypoles'.[50]

But those romantic invitations were very popular with its readers, as many saw 14 February as an excellent opportunity to find true love. This was a major sales opportunity not lost on those local shops, such as the Sennocke Stores, which sold 'Presentation Valentines'. Not everyone succeeded, however. In 1889, a 31-year-old 'Bachelor' wrote to the *Chronicle* lamenting that he was likely to remain so in Sevenoaks for 'There's no sociability about the place', as the town lacked the requisite social functions where 'the daughters of Sevenoaks [had the] opportunity of meeting the young men who may become their husbands'.[51] His insertion was comically answered by 'One in Hopes of a Sevenoaks Bride', but who was now living in Ramsgate. The latter considered Bachelor 'quite unreasonable', insisting there was 'no paucity of merry meetings' in the town. He suggested that the fault instead lay with Bachelor, whom he advised to 'Dress becomingly and without affectation [and] make yourself agreeable'.[52]

The significance of this exchange, together with the fact the editor saw fit to print it, lies less in the emotional plight of the love-lorn bachelors than what it reveals about the town's contemporary matrimonial market. Whereas the Hows (and perhaps the Coppers) had earlier found their wives and partners through local kinship and especially social networks, the improved transport and communications opportunities swiftly created a more transient population in both the growing urban centres and in smaller market towns such as Sevenoaks. Potential partners could now be found much further afield, if those available in west Kent were not acceptable, in other words. While Robert Copper's sons and grandsons might easily have been able to accost girls their age in the streets of Hartslands or elsewhere, that was never an option for the respectable Hows, 'Bachelor' and so on. This all points to a demand for meeting opportunities that would best be satisfied through devising a more effective 'culture of encounter', as it might be termed, that would enable young middle-class men and women to meet and assess each other's suitability as potential marriage partners, as 'Bachelor' and no doubt a number of others in his position desired, while hopefully minimising the not inconsiderable social and emotional risks attached to that process.

Most residents of Victorian Sevenoaks and elsewhere considered that the risks of courtship, engagement and marriage were far outweighed by the benefits that

---

49 *SC*, 17 Feb. 1882, p. 4.
50 *SC*, 19 Feb. 1886, p. 6; 18 Feb. 1887, p. 7.
51 *SC*, 15 Feb. 1889, p. 5.
52 *SC*, 1 March 1889, p. 5.

resulted from forming a family and having children, who gave their parents emotional joy in the present and hoped-for tangible support in the future. This was certainly the case for Charles Bassett, who met his future wife Adelaide (Ada) Lock while working as a carpenter 'on the old Hip Hospital on the Vine' in Sevenoaks. They married at Seal church after a two-year courtship when he was not quite 22. The ceremony of a working-class couple – unlike many of those involving the higher social classes – received no mention in the local press. Shortly before he died in 1933, Bassett paid tribute 'to my wife and helper during the last fifty years and to her devotion in looking after the home and health and rearing of our family of eight children'. It was an object lesson in how important the family was to working-class people as they sought to minimise the risks inherent in life.[53]

The wedding of Charles and Ada Bassett, Seal, 9 October 1883

'Weddings in those days for the working classes were not the elaborate affairs they are now. No motor cars, no horses and carriages and those very limited in the country villages. We walked to the church and formed quite a procession as we all walked back with the church bells ringing a merry peal ... My father and mother were so well known and respected that almost the whole of the village turned out and lined the street from the church to my home, to cheer my wife and myself and voice their good wishes to us both for the future. By the time we reached home my black suit was white with the dust from the rice showered upon us (no confetti in those days). The people generally admitted that it was the prettiest wedding that had been held in the village. We did not have money to spend on honeymoons but came straight home to our house in Sevenoaks at night and I only had the day off for the wedding and was at work next morning.'

Source: Charles Bassett, *A life in Seal* ([1933] Seal, 1991), pp. 10–11.

The perils of illegitimacy

The respectable Victorian ideal was that all children should be born within the safe confines of marriage. However, premarital sex complicated relationships to the extent that, all too often, it became a major impediment to living happily ever after. The obvious risk was falling pregnant; recent research indicates that, for the working classes in the middle of the nineteenth century, 'over half of all first-born

---

53 Bassett, *Seal*, pp. 7, 15.

children were conceived outside marriage'.[54] It is instructive to trace what 'bastardy' then implied for both the mothers and fathers concerned in west Kent.

Local illegitimacy may usefully be studied in three ways: first through the Clergy Returns of Illegitimate Children to Parliament in the late 1830s; secondly through the few extant 'Returns in Bastardy' for Sevenoaks for the 1840s and 1850s; and finally by looking at some earlier Poor Law/settlement correspondence relating to illegitimacy. Although the local Poor Law report of 1834 put the number of illegitimate births at 'from eight to ten per annum', the local Clergy Returns show that they rose from 18 in 1834 to 28 in 1837, making the Sevenoaks area the fourth highest in Kent after Maidstone (102 and 62), Greenwich (42 and 28) and Tonbridge (28 and 39).[55] However, ten years later the Sevenoaks returns revealed that, of more than 50 cases itemised, none of the mothers and only three of the fathers in the district came from Hartslands, perhaps indicating that its morals were not quite so base as some of the town's other residents might have assumed them to be.[56]

Those returns sought to 'affiliate' the mother with the putative father. The man responsible was 'expected to reimburse the parish of any expenses for lying-in', the fees and travel costs associated 'with the process of affiliation' and either a lump sum or regular weekly amounts 'for maintenance of the child' – but only if the mother could show she had a strong case.[57] For example, in 1847 Joseph Smith, who had been born in 1829 and as a boy lived in Hartslands, was required to pay 1s 6d a week for the child of Elizabeth Spire.[58] However, sometimes those paternity claims were officially rejected, such as that of Elizabeth Hayman against George Kimble that year, although he had to pay her 2s a week for a second child.[59] Parishes took a close interest in local bastardy, as they did with every financial risk to their ratepayers, and sought to mitigate it as effectively as possible. When in 1833 Sarah Seal, a single woman from Wrotham, declared on oath that 'she is with child who is likely to be born a Bastard and which is likely to become chargeable to the said Parish', and claimed that William Botton, a local labourer, was the father, the parish Overseer acted promptly. He brought Botton before Quarter Sessions, which ordered him 'to find security to indemnify the said parish' in the child's support.[60]

---

54   Griffin, *Liberty's dawn*, p. 137.

55   UKPP, Commons, *Report ... operation of the Poor Laws*, 875a; UKPP, Lords, *Miscellaneous: Illegitimate Children: Abstract of the Returns of the Number of Illegitimate Children*, No. 113 (1839), p. 22.

56   KHLC Q/RSp/4/3.

57   Samantha Williams, 'They lived together as man and wife: plebeian cohabitation, illegitimacy and broken relationships in London, 1700–1840', in Rebecca Probert (ed.), *Cohabitation and non-marital births in England and Wales, 1600–2012* (Basingstoke, 2014), p. 69. In the early nineteenth century such payments ranged from 1s to 2s 6d a week.

58   Census Return for 1841: Sevenoaks (Hartslands); KHLC Q/RSp/4/3.

59   KHLC Q/RSp/4/3, 27 Nov. 1847.

60   KHLC P406/15/7, 4 March 1833.

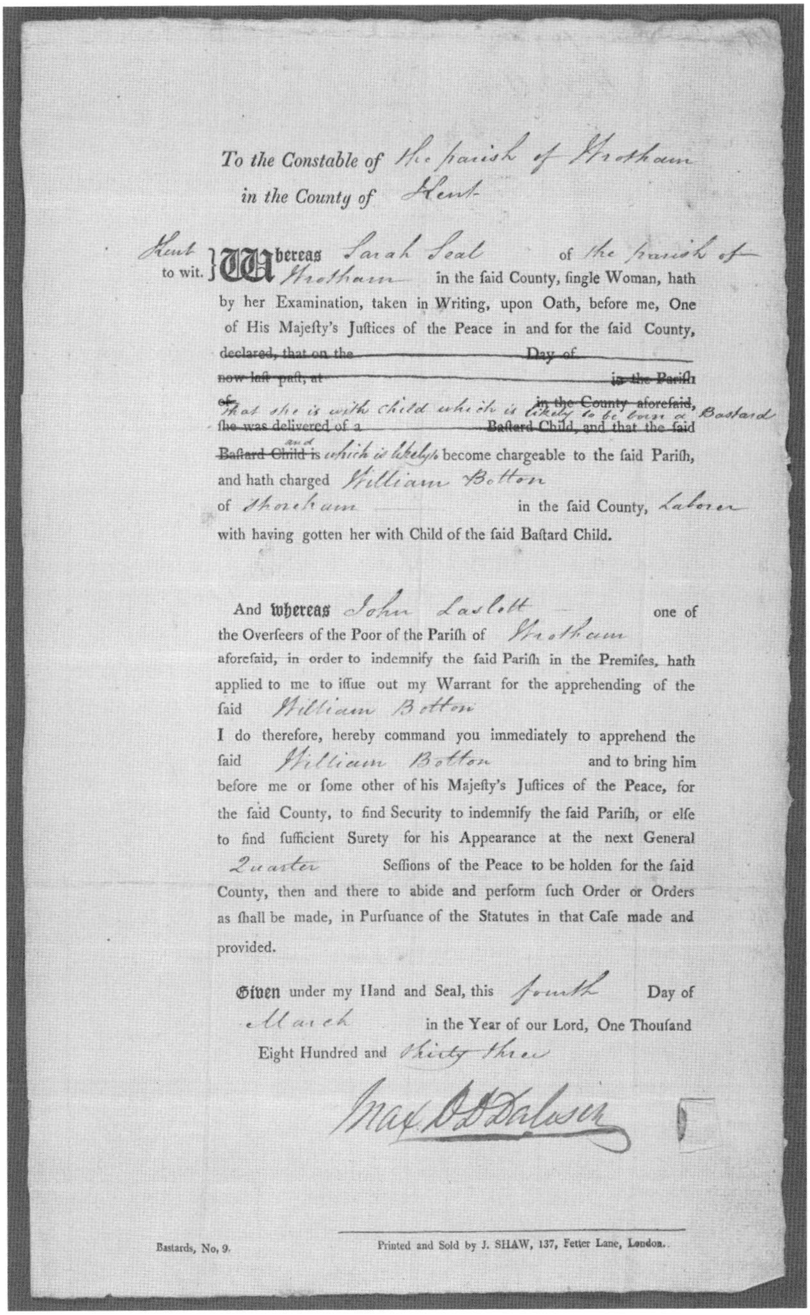

To the Constable of the parish of Wrotham
in the County of Kent

Kent } Whereas Sarah Seal of the parish of
to wit. } Wrotham in the ſaid County, ſingle Woman, hath by her Examination, taken in Writing, upon Oath, before me, One of His Majeſty's Juſtices of the Peace in and for the ſaid County, ~~declared, that on the Day of now laſt paſt, at in the Pariſh of~~ That she is with child which is likely to be born a Bastard ~~in the County aforeſaid, ſhe was delivered of a Baſtard Child, and that the ſaid Baſtard Child is~~ and which is likely to become chargeable to the ſaid Pariſh, and hath charged William Botton of Shoreham in the ſaid County, Laborer with having gotten her with Child of the ſaid Baſtard Child.

And whereas John Laslett one of the Overſeers of the Poor of the Pariſh of Wrotham aforeſaid, in order to indemnify the ſaid Pariſh in the Premiſes, hath applied to me to iſſue out my Warrant for the apprehending of the ſaid William Botton

I do therefore, hereby command you immediately to apprehend the ſaid William Botton and to bring him before me or ſome other of his Majeſty's Juſtices of the Peace, for the ſaid County, to find Security to indemnify the ſaid Pariſh, or elſe to find ſufficient Surety for his Appearance at the next General Quarter Seſſions of the Peace to be holden for the ſaid County, then and there to abide and perform ſuch Order or Orders as ſhall be made, in Purſuance of the Statutes in that Caſe made and provided.

Given under my Hand and Seal, this fourth Day of March in the Year of our Lord, One Thouſand Eight Hundred and thirty three

Bastards, No. 9. Printed and Sold by J. SHAW, 137, Fetter Lane, London.

Figure 8.4 Bastardy examination. This is the examination of Sarah Seal, with putative father William Botton clearly identified. Note the printed form, as such examinations became routinely bureaucratised in the nineteenth century.
Source: Kent History and Library Centre, P406/15/7.

Sometimes cases were more complex, and the authorities could demonstrate slightly more sensitivity, although risk mitigation was always their prime concern. In 1825 the Wrotham overseer received a letter from Sevenoaks about Jane Dunk, whose two daughters, then aged nine and eight, had been fathered by a Captain Vyvyan while he was stationed at the Sevenoaks barracks. The family initially followed him to postings elsewhere, but the relationship had ended seven years previously. Dunk returned to Sevenoaks, where 'the poor woman [deserved] some credit', the letter sympathetically believed, for having 'supported herself and two children by her own industries and a trifling occasional remittance' from Vyvyan. Since he was no longer paying that, she was 'consequently necessitated to apply for an allowance of maintenance' from Sevenoaks. But Dunk originally came from Wrotham. The settlement laws gave Sevenoaks every right to return her there, by force if necessary, so that she was a burden to its ratepayers, not theirs. Furthermore, Sevenoaks helpfully volunteered to assist Wrotham to trace the captain's whereabouts if, as was highly likely, it decided to make an order for him to support his children, saying 'if you should wish to obtain any information where the Captain is to be found, we will readily give you every information ... and we have the means of tracing him from place to place should he evade any order you may make'.[61]

The main significance of the letter, beyond showing that parishes were as keen to compel middle-class army captains as they were lower-class agricultural labourers to pay for the upkeep of their illegitimate children, lies in how it reveals each party's desperate scramble to transfer elsewhere the financial risks to the parish represented by single-parent families. They included even those headed up by women such as Dunk, who had for seven years 'supported herself and two children by her own industries' and who was likely to be able to do so again, at least in part.[62] It is noteworthy that Sevenoaks stressed both her 'industries', to suggest she should prove a minimal cash burden, and also her unfortunate 'poor woman' status, to elicit as much sympathy for her as possible. Both were designed, quite deliberately, to persuade Wrotham neither to complain about her return, nor to make that process in any way difficult.

The risk transfer strategy that each party adopted is quite apparent and is an entirely circular process – and a vicious one at that. First, Vyvyan decided that he could no longer afford the 'trifling' sums he had hitherto remitted to Dunk.[63] Secondly, she, staring at poverty and/or destitution, called on the Sevenoaks parish, where she was living, for relief. Thirdly, keen not to bear this burden, Sevenoaks used the law to remove her the few miles back to Wrotham. Fourthly, in turn, Wrotham would have been quite entitled to seek to recover the money from the captain, especially since, as an officer, he was easier to track down than were other

61   KHLC P406/15/8, 30 July 1825.
62   *Ibid.*, 30 July 1825.
63   *Ibid.*, 30 July 1825.

ranks. And, finally, should he refuse to pay, the merry-go-round would begin all over again. Those who had no choice in the matter, however, yet who bore most of the risks of the forced upheaval and its concomitant uncertainty, were Jane Dunk and her girls. The sources are silent, however, as to their fate.

Caring for the poor adequately, like housing them, required that the risks of so doing be transferred to someone, or to some institution in a position to accept them. And as the scale of the housing problems in Sevenoaks revealed the limits of Thomas Graham Jackson's worthy philanthropic endeavours at Lime Tree Walk, so the Dunk case showed that it was impossible for that family to be properly looked after if the prime imperative of the institutions responsible – in this case the local authorities of Sevenoaks and Wrotham – was instead to shift responsibility for it elsewhere.

In the absence of adequate institutional care, the stories of the Seal and Dunk families also underline how valuable a viable, ongoing adult relationship was in shielding family members from many of the risks then inherent in living in west Kent. Comparing the Hows and Coppers also indicates that social class was a major determinant of the qualities of lives they lived, the choices they had and the risk mitigation strategies they pursued or were able to pursue. But the sensible mitigation for longevity risk (bearing children as support in old age) often collided with mortality risk. For early death paid little heed to wealth or social status in Victorian Sevenoaks; there was simply no guarantee that any children would live long enough to provide that support.

Early mortality

Both the Coppers and the Hows felt the full force of young adult mortality, George How in particular. Although he and two of his brothers lived into their late 70s or early 80s, his sister Jane died, in her 21st year, of an 'extremely painful … inflammation of the brain' in 1833.[64] The following year his first wife, Harriet, died of influenza and pulmonary consumption aged 22, a few months after they were married. He remarried in 1842, as we have seen, but lost his son Frederick, in 1881, aged 26.[65]

The Coppers, too, lost several family members, for poorer Sevenoaks residents generally worked in riskier industries and were more prone to suffer serious, even life-threatening injuries, such as in 1862:

> Shocking Accident.—On Sunday an accident of a very serious nature happened
> to a lad named Copper … hearing a noise in his master's slaughterhouse, he went
> to see the cause, and… the place being dark, a hook caught in his eye and tore it
> completely from the socket.[66]

---

64   *Wesleyan Methodist Magazine*, Aug. 1833, pp. 605–7.
65   Sevenoaks Library D200; *SC*, 18 Nov. 1881, p. 4; https://www.freebmd.org.uk, accessed 7 June 2017.
66   *SEG*, 15 July 1862, p. 5.

The victim was Henry Copper, the son of Peter, and he had another serious accident the following year, when he fell 30 feet down a shaft while working on the new railway tunnel in Sevenoaks. He died two years later aged 18, those incidents almost certainly contributing to his early demise.[67] But, unlike many other local families, the Copper household was large enough to cope even with tragedies as grievous as Henry's by supporting those members most affected. This may be seen in a slightly unlikely source, perhaps – newspaper reports of the family's many convictions for poaching, for that was one of its favourite makeshift-economy solutions to the risk of going hungry, or to make some cash on the side. Poaching was a highly risky activity with potentially serious consequences. In 1818 George Gunner, of another serial Sevenoaks poaching family, received a personalised form from the Knole estate threatening an action against him for trespass if he should seek to 'Hunt, Hawk, Course, Shoot, Fish, [or] Fowl' on any of Lord Sackville's lands.[68] Knole even had printed special poaching tickets to give to those perpetrators apprehended by its gamekeepers, indicating how common it was.

For the Coppers, poaching was a joint enterprise, an activity involving all the family. William and Henry Copper and two other boys were each fined 14s, with 6s 6d costs, for taking rabbits from Earl Amherst's wood in 1864.[69] And when their cousin, 18-year-old Stephen Copper, was convicted of poaching in 1872, it is significant that, after he was fined the large sum (for poor people) of £1 with 7s costs, or three weeks' imprisonment, 'some person stepped from the back of the court and paid the money'. This was almost certainly a relative, so the extended family was thereby mitigating the criminal risk of being caught by pooling its resources to keep one of its members out of jail. The fine was, no doubt, paid out of the spoils of some previous illicit nocturnal activity.[70]

But avoiding early death and growing old also carried significant risks, even for law-abiding working-class Sevenoaks residents. Without any state support the elderly had to live off their savings in old age. For those not in that fortunate position, however, the only means of survival was to continue working, which was especially necessary for widowers with dependent children. Thus, in 1881, Thomas Wheeler, aged 75, continued working as a manual labourer to support his daughter of 25 and his 5-year-old grandson. While many in that position could carry on only if offered work less arduous, some still had to labour almost until they dropped. The most remarkable, albeit atypical, example was long-standing Hartslands resident George Goldsmith. In 1881 he was working as a gardener to support his

---

67   *SEG*, 22 Dec. 1863, p. 5.

68   Carolyn Conley, *The unwritten law: criminal justice in Victorian Kent* (Oxford, 1991), p. 199; KHLC U269/E29, printed notice 19 Dec. 1818. The fact that it was a printed form shows how prevalent poaching must have been at the time.

69   *SEG*, 2 Feb. 1864, p. 5.

70   *SEG*, 29 Oct. 1872, p. 5.

daughter and son. Twenty years later, he was still maintaining two dependents while employed as a groom – when he was 91 years old.[71]

If local smuggling enterprises could be defined as an early form of organised crime, the poaching escapades of the Copper boys and others were far less so. But even opportunistic crime was a risk to the property-owning classes of Sevenoaks, so they took decisive – or so they thought – steps to counter it. Building on the anti-Swing Association formed in the town in 1830, the Sevenoaks Prosecuting Society ran for forty years from 1836.[72] Members included Rev. Thomas Curteis and Earl Amherst and subscriptions were used to pay cash rewards for information leading to convictions, for example that offered after a burglary at Greatness Mill in 1851.[73] It is not recorded if informers ever led to any of the Coppers being apprehended, but Thomas How attended the dissolution meeting in 1876.[74] Perhaps the only time the Hows and Coppers crossed paths was related to criminal activity.

Abusive relationships

Being part of a family or household was never a panacea for avoiding risk entirely; it carried perils all its own, especially if the implicit trust that bound it together broke down. Abuse was certainly prevalent in Victorian west Kent. Female domestic servants were especially prone, and they could often find themselves in very difficult positions, since they could be at great risk of attracting unwanted sexual interest both from other servants and their employers. Should their trust be so exploited, the woman risked 'dire consequences should her liaison be discovered or a pregnancy be known'.[75] Specifically, it almost always meant instant dismissal, shame and the prospect of future unemployment, destitution and poverty. Unsurprisingly in such circumstances, many became 'obsessed with sexual propriety'.[76]

A good example, albeit one with exceptional consequences for the employer–perpetrator (who was normally rarely prosecuted), was the remarkable event that took place at the country seat of Valence, Westerham, in 1865. Hector Toler (1810–73), the 3rd Earl of Norbury, was accused by his 14-year-old servant Hannah Isaacs of having indecently assaulted her in a case brought and financed by the Society for the Protection of Women and Children. Norbury was convicted not of sexual assault (which carried a possible £20 fine) but of common assault, which carried a maximum penalty of only £5.[77] Norbury had previously offered

---

71 Census Returns for 1871; 1881; 1901: Sevenoaks (Hartslands).

72 *SEG*, 14 Sept. 1830, p. 1; KHLC U442/O67.

73 KHLC U1000/20/O48; *SEG*, 8 April 1851, p. 5.

74 *SC*, 21 Aug. 1931, p. 9.

75 Gillis, *For better*, p. 244.

76 *Ibid.*

77 *The Times*, 25 Feb. 1865, 9; 4 March 1865, 12. For a more detailed account, see *SEG*, 7 March 1865, p. 5.

to pay Isaacs' parents to drop the charges. They refused and sought the Society's assistance to initiate the prosecution. It must have considered hers a strong case and informal mediation inappropriate, since 'it is unlikely that they would have agreed to prosecute otherwise'.[78]

Norbury's reputation and respectability were ruined. His wife left him, with their children, immediately after the trial, never to return, and an obituary considered him 'a man who is not to be ranked among those whose names smell sweet'.[79] He paid a painful price for being found guilty of the assault, as sexual misdemeanour, or at least being caught, was a big risk factor in Victorian England. It carried a high cost, one not easily expunged, even for the aristocracy.

Domestic abuse, often fuelled by alcohol, was a major risk for married women and demonstrated a gross breach of marital trust. In 1877 Otford bricklayer Thomas Kimber was charged with using threatening language to his wife Harriet. She said he was a good husband and father except when he was in liquor – which was often – when he beat her.[80] Children also risked being abused, as, for example, at Riverhead, where 'William Walker, brickmaker … was charged … with having neglected to maintain his two infant children … From the neglect of the children their health was likely to become seriously endangered.' Walker received six months' hard labour and his children were sent to the workhouse.[81] In 1868 a Mr Daley was tried for felonious (i.e., sexual) assault of a 10-year-old girl, aided and abetted by her mother, and 'so strong was the feeling in Brasted that effigies of the prisoner and the mother were burnt in the village'.[82]

Girls were potentially vulnerable in other ways. In 1812 Mary Westfield of Sevenoaks petitioned for her 'pretended marriage' to Joseph Mould to be set aside 'by reason of minority'. The wedding had taken place in Yorkshire in 1808 but as she was then under 21 it required parental consent. Since Mould could not prove he had that, the marriage was voided, giving Mary 'full liberty to … solemnise marriage with any other person'.[83] One might speculate that she was initially happy to be Mould's wife, but subsequent marital problems led her to seek a way out. Nullity was the obvious and effective answer, but escaping Mould would have been almost impossible without it, since divorce was too expensive for working people. An unorthodox alternative, straight out of the *Mayor of Casterbridge*, was occasionally employed by a working-class husband: the 'sale' of his wife. An example of such a 'disgusting transaction' took place in 1828. Mr Skinner had lived with his wife in a parish-owned

---

78 Kim Stevenson, 'Fulfilling their mission: the intervention of voluntary societies in cases of sexual assault in the Victorian criminal process', *Crime, Histoire et Societé*, 8 (2004), pp. 93–110 (p. 105).

79 *MP*, 31 Dec. 1873, p. 7.

80 *SEG*, 5 Nov. 1877, p. 5.

81 *MJ*, 8 May 1871, p. 5.

82 *SEG*, 6 July 1868, p. 5.

83 LPL VH80/60/1–6.

cottage at Speldhurst. After he left her, a Mr Savage moved in, but the parish strongly disapproved. Skinner thus agreed to 'legitimise' the new relationship by selling his wife to Savage for a 'shilling and a pot of beer'. This exchange was severely frowned upon when the case came to court and all three served a month in prison.[84]

Divorce

Divorce was rare in the Sevenoaks area in the first half of the nineteenth century, since it was both expensive and, especially in cases of adultery, could drag the finances and reputations of both husband and wife through the mire. Early remarriage was not an option, either, as it was for Mary Westfield. Ironmonger Edward Eldrid and Elizabeth Hards (only daughter of the 'highly respectable' Mr Hards of Sevenoaks) were married in 1828, 'with the consent of the friends of all parties' and ten years later they were living in north London with their four small children.[85] In November 1839 he petitioned for divorce after Elizabeth and George Cross, one of the house servants, were accused of 'carnal use and knowledge of each other's bodies'; the adultery 'was also pleaded to have been committed with several individuals'.[86] The judge granted the divorce but the costs of the case exceeded £200, a huge sum. Eldrid then sued Cross for 'criminal conversation' (adultery) with his wife and won damages of £500, although it is unlikely that a mere stable groom was ever going to pay an amount as punitive as that.[87]

Although it is not known if Eldrid received his due damages, even a lower-class servant such as Cross was running a huge employment and reputational risk by treating his employer as he did. Adulterous wives such as Elizabeth faced even steeper penalties, as they could also be deprived of their children. The Infant Custody Act 1839 enabled the court to grant the mother access to her infant children and custody of those under seven (before then the father had legal custody), although even those rights were forfeit had she committed adultery.[88]

Family life was therefore never risk free, especially for vulnerable women and children, and one historian believed the crucial division in English society in 1860 was between 'the households where the children are cared for and those where they are left to shift for themselves'.[89] But the more critical distinction, certainly in terms of risk mitigation, lay between those who were members of fully functioning families (even less respectable ones, like the Coppers) and those who were not, since the former were far better able to cope. Proof of the overwhelming desire to be part of a family

---

84   *MC*, 25 July 1828, p. 4. See further E.P. Thompson, 'The Sale of Wives', in E.P. Thompson, *Customs in common: studies in traditional popular culture* (London, 1993), pp. 426–7.

85   *Leicester Chronicle* (henceforth *LC*), 7 Dec. 1839, p. 1.

86   LPL VH80/91/1–20; *The Times*, 13 Nov. 1839, p. 6.

87   *LC*, 7 Dec. 1839, p. 1; *NS*, 7 Dec. 1839, p. 7.

88   Perkin, *Victorian women*, pp. 113–18.

89   G.M. Young, *Victorian essays*, ed. W.D. Handcock ([1936] Oxford, 1962), p. 123.

in nineteenth-century Sevenoaks may be seen, at its simplest, in just how few single people, across all social classes, there were in the town. As a postscript to her tale, even the shamed Elizabeth Eldrid eventually succeeded in recreating a household for herself. In 1881 she was living in Sevenoaks with three grandchildren, Edward having died in 1858, but not having remarried. This evidence, from Eldrid and the other examples, also answers the question posed earlier about how effective the family was in mitigating risks run by its members, for being part of a family – of whatever social class – was without doubt an effective way of obtaining the primitive wants and mitigating the risk factors inherent in living in west Kent in the nineteenth century.

Conclusion

But how might that family actually function? The Hows undoubtedly received the emotional support needed when they lost close relatives. Family support was essential in coping with life's vicissitudes and its value may be seen clearly in the account of the death of Jane How in 1833. This stresses above all her piety: she 'so prayerfully riveted upon the truths of the Gospel' and was clearly much comforted by her father Nicholas at her death, after which her life was portrayed as 'truly exemplary'.[90] Even though, as with many obituaries, it contains a strong hagiographical element, one cannot doubt the strength of this family relationship and how helpful it was to its members, as they coped with both her impending demise and that of Harriet shortly thereafter. Marriage was an indispensable precondition, as far as they were concerned, to any successful and respectable family.

The Coppers' case was less clear cut. Family support, both practical and emotional, was essential when, all too often perhaps, its members suffered serious accidents at work or were fined or imprisoned for poaching. But they generally saw marriage as an optional extra. Robert Copper senior married Mary in 1842 and had three sons. One, Robert, also got married, in 1872, before having children, but they were exceptional. His uncle Peter, his brother William and most of his cousins clearly felt no need to marry before their children arrived. And his daughter Maggie, who was born in 1880, had at least three illegitimate children as she weaved her peripatetic progress around three different addresses in Hartslands between 1899 and 1909.[91]

Instead, the Coppers demonstrated that marriage was not an essential element of the family risk-management strategy, even in Victorian Sevenoaks. Were the extended family large enough, cohesive enough and resilient enough (as the Coppers' most certainly was), then its cohabitation model worked perfectly adequately. Such unorthodoxy came at a price. This was because it also implied forgoing any social standing or reputation, if not within Hartslands, then certainly in the eyes of respectable Sevenoaks society, as represented by the Hows. But one suspects the Coppers were not terribly bothered about that.

---

90 *Wesleyan Methodist Magazine*, August 1833, pp. 605–7.
91 Census Returns for 1891 and 1901: Sevenoaks (Hartslands); KHLC P330/E/1/1 and P330/E/1/2.

Chapter 9

Health, welfare and environment

Medical treatments and advances

In 1853 carpenter Isaac Jinks, from Hartslands, was employed at the Sevenoaks Almshouses when he 'fell from a scaffolding several feet from the ground and sustained much injury'.[1] He was 54 years old and was living with his wife (whom the 1851 census did not record as being in work) and two daughters, one a dressmaker, the other still at school. A son aged 22 was no longer living at home.[2] Even for a skilled artisan such as Jinks, obtaining the basic necessities of life in the face of such adversity would have required a collective family effort. Similarly, disease was another significant risk that not only could remove any family member at short notice but, if the main breadwinner died or was incapacitated for long periods, led the whole of the family to suffer the consequences. Those diseases included cholera and typhus, which might arise directly from the poor sanitation then prevailing in the town, as well as smallpox, tuberculosis, typhoid and influenza. For example, typhus was 'very prevalent in Sevenoaks' in April 1833, and cholera during the pandemic in May 1848.[3]

The poor suffered disproportionately from disease. As late as 1884 Charles Baylis, Medical Officer for Sevenoaks, reported 12 fatal cases of measles in children in the previous year. All bar one were at Hartslands or Greatness, areas mainly occupied by the poor. Whooping cough killed four in Seal the following year.[4] In 1886 Baylis bemoaned the fact that 'many lives of infants have been sacrificed by inability or unwillingness on the part of mothers to supply the natural food, combined with ignorance of the proper method of artificial feeding'.[5]

---

1   *SEG*, 5 April 1853, p. 5.

2   Census Return for 1851: Sevenoaks.

3   Private archives, Knight, *Diaries*, vol. 1, 29 April 1833; Sevenoaks Library Gordon Ward notebooks No. 14, 5 May 1848.

4   KHLC UD/SE/Acr1/1, 1884, p. 4; Fox *et al.*, *Seal*, p. 170.

5   KHLC UD/SE/Acr1/2, 1886, p. 3.

Unsurprisingly, 'sickness and death ... presented the greatest personal and financial crises to working class families'.[6]

The better-off were not immune to medical problems either. In 1832 Mrs Allnutt's woman friend Miss or Mrs Knight 'burst a blood vessel, and threw up much blood from the stomach'. 'She was bled in the afternoon which brought on fainting for two or three hours.' Unsurprisingly, six days later she was 'still weak and feeble', but the diary does not record her death, so one presumes she eventually recovered.[7]

The short-term possibility, or long-term probability, of not being able to work (for at least some time in their lives) concentrated the minds of most people in west Kent towards mitigating the risk of any injury or illness that might make them unable to draw a wage, without which they would end up hungry, cold, threadbare or homeless. In the short term the best solution was to get well as quickly as possible and return to work with minimal disruption to the family budget. To an important extent, that depended on cures being developed for those diseases, several of which were tamed, if not conquered, during the period. Some histories have focused on the parts played by 'Great Men of Medicine' in this process, Dr John Snow providing a good example. He famously chained up the handle on a public water pump in Soho in 1854, making residents use an alternative supply. The subsequent sharp drop in cholera proved that it was a 'water-borne infection that could be controlled by a pure water supply good sewerage', although Sevenoaks residents could not guarantee the quality of their water and sewage disposal until the comprehensive drainage system for the entire Darent Valley was completed in 1882.[8] Before that most inhabitants of the town took their water from springs, public pumps and wells, while for some it came from open ponds. The town pond, known as Cage Pond, was declared a 'Nuisance' in the 1830s. Some gentry houses, such as St Julian's, drew water from springs on the estate, while others had pumps within the house. In 1835 public pumps stood at Oak Lane ('much out of order'), Six Bells Lane, Tubs Hill, the Town Pump and in Riverhead opposite the George Inn.[9]

But sanitary and medical progress was normally a long, hard process. The story of medical improvement (or the diminution of health risk) in the latter part of the nineteenth century, although real enough, resulted from a combination of factors. Many were much less dramatic than Snow's discovery, but nonetheless contributed to a much lower nationwide death rate by 1900. The proof is seen in the mortality statistics for the Sevenoaks District. In 1877 the death rate was 15.2 per thousand, a figure then deemed 'striking and satisfactory' by Baylis, compared to the national average of 20.5. By 1890 it had fallen dramatically, by over 50 per cent, to just

6   Geoffrey Crossick, *An artisan elite in Victorian society: Kentish London 1840–80* (London, 1987), p. 174.

7   Sevenoaks Library B ALL, Mrs Allnutt's Diary, 11 March 1832; 17 March 1832.

8   Lane, *Social history of medicine*, p. 148.

9   KHLC P330/8/6, 24 July 1835.

9.8 per thousand, which *The Lancet* was moved to describe as 'in every way satisfactory'.[10] Since the population of Sevenoaks was well over 9,000 by 1891 this meant that on average 50 fewer people were dying in the town annually compared with 13 years previously.[11]

The key point, however, is that those improvements were as much the result of institutional as clinical factors. Specifically, the various medical breakthroughs would have had far less impact on west Kent had they not been coupled with new political institutions that could affect significant change. And, in turn, those bodies only worked if they were first permitted and then imposed by central government on a society where not all were willing to accept that change, especially if (as with installing fully functioning sanitation) they carried significant long-term cost implications.

Institutional change also prompted greater professionalisation, so that patients slowly but surely placed greater confidence in the efficacy of the cures offered. Receiving treatment became less risky than refusing it, which had not always been the case before the second half of the nineteenth century. This trend was greatly advanced by the Medical Act of 1858. It meant that healthcare, at its broadest, moved from being a mainly short-term, *informal* activity, whereby individuals often actively initiated and controlled their various treatments themselves, to a more *formal*, longer-term regime. That had two major implications. First, patients became more likely to be passive recipients of medicines and remedies, which were prescribed for and performed on them by experts claiming professional status. Secondly, it might involve the active premeditated decision, often made years beforehand, to mitigate the risks of illness or injury by insuring against them. The most obvious way to do this in Victorian west Kent was to join a medical provident and/or friendly society.

That process may be traced through several sources. An obvious choice of treatment at the beginning of the 1780s in west Kent was an (always voluntary) visit to take the by-then fashionable waters at the nearby spa town of Tunbridge Wells. It may have 'copied many of Bath's arrangements ... both for amenities and a carefully managed social calendar, but it never achieved the same kind of fashionable glamour' as its more prominent rival.[12] Visitors, both male and female in roughly equal numbers and mainly of the highest social echelons, came to take a variety of 'cures'. Some involved drinking a few pints a day of the waters of the Chalybeate spring, which contemporary physician William Nisbet believed would remedy a wide range of complaints, including liver disease, rickets, nervous disorders

---

10   KHLC UD/SE/Am/1/1; *The Lancet*, 18 Oct. 1890, p. 841.

11   Killingray and Purves, *Dictionary*, p. 134.

12   Thompson, 'Town and country', p. 20.

and 'constitutional weakness as a result of venereal disease'.[13] Or, especially having tasted those waters, they might opt to bathe in them instead. A hot bath was 7s 6d, a cold one 2s 6d and showers a relative bargain at 1s 6d each. Lord Pelham enjoyed the first in 1804 and a Mrs MacLeod took no fewer than 62 showers in 1806 at a total cost of £4 13s. Very occasionally the lower orders might benefit; for example, 'Mr Jones's servant' was bought a hot bath in 1810.[14]

A wide variety of proprietary medicines was available, many of which came with promises aplenty but dubious medical provenance. A single page in the *South Eastern Gazette* in March 1862 reveals this clearly, with a column of advertisements for pills and other patent medicines. 'The most famous of all' was Dr James's Powder, a general painkiller that claimed to be 'particularly valuable, by promoting a gentle perspiration, a single dose causing immediate relief'.[15]

For the poor in the early nineteenth century, receiving any kind of medical treatment was a bonus. Under the Old Poor Law, cash payments to paupers for medicines and treatments were permitted, unlike under the post-1834 regime. But the Sevenoaks Overseers' accounts reveal that few sums were paid for healthcare of any description, apart from to midwives, for whom the going rate was 10s a birth. While expenditure on shoes and clothing for the local poor featured regularly, such as 14s 2d for 'apparel for Elizabeth Humphrey' in 1790, in 1790 and 1791 just two individual unnamed sufferers received bottles of jaundice and ague drops, respectively, at 1s each.

By the particularly hard year of 1830, probably because the Overseers were being overwhelmed with demands for relief, the sick received cash that they could spend on medicines and/or food. A poignant but not atypical entry of October 1830 stated: 'John Inkpen's family, one daughter very ill and the family in great distress – daughter since dead – £1'.[16] The risks attached to being unemployed and hungry were, therefore, substantially exacerbated by the lack of adequate medical provision. The poor then had to rely on ancient folk or home-help medicines, treatments that were 'applied in time-honoured fashion or in accordance with the many commercially available books of herbal remedies'.[17] Examples of the latter included Alder buckthorn (*Frangula alnus*), a native tree species used as a purgative. But, by 1898, when herbal remedies were being appraised more sceptically, one commentator sarcastically remarked that, if it really worked, 'from the frequency of this plant no doctor should have been required in Kent'.[18] There was also no shortage of medical advice available in print. *Hooker's Household Almanac*,

---

13   William Nisbet, *A medical guide for the invalid to the principal watering places of Great Britain* (Edinburgh, 1804), pp. 245–55.

14   KHLC U749/E1, 1 Nov. 1804; U749/E3, 12 Dec. 1806; U749/E6, 28 June 1810.

15   *SEG*, 13 May 1862, p. 7.

16   KHLC P330/12/11, Oct. 1830.

17   Bushaway, '"Tacit, Unsuspected"', p. 202.

18   *MJ*, 2 June 1898, p. 7.

published annually in Westerham, offered 'Remedies for Various Diseases' in 1864. These included a 'plaster of burgundy pitch' for bunions and, in cases of earache, 'a bag of hops, a roasted onion … seldom fail'.[19]

Even for the middle classes, with easy access to medical attention, illness was always a worrisome risk, as nonconformist cleric Robert Barratt's diary shows. His 'out of health' son Bertie was ordered a 'nourishing diet, plenty of fresh air and Cod Liver oil'. Despite this bracing regimen he was 'unable to return to school' and it was only an anonymous donation of £10 from an (Anglican) 'churchman' that enabled the 'poor sickly boy … to spend a month by the seaside', from where he eventually returned 'much improved in health'.[20]

By the twentieth century modern medical technology was becoming available in west Kent. In 1913 an X-ray machine in operation at Sevenoaks hospital was used in treating George Meekham after he broke his leg that April, illustrating the extent to which medical care was transformed during our period.[21] In the late eighteenth century it was crude and ill-informed with a meagre scientific basis. A century later doctors were observing their patients' symptoms, treating them more successfully and even looking inside the body before performing procedures, some of which are not only recognisable today but still in common use.

Healthcare professionals and institutions

The availability of medical attention, both informal and formal, improved significantly during the nineteenth century. This is seen in how the bare numbers of healthcare professionals practising in Sevenoaks rose during the nineteenth century. The 1783 Medical Register indicates that three 'surgeons and apothecaries' were based in the town.[22] In 1797 a visiting dentist, 'Monsieur Mallan', advertised his services particularly for the gentry of Sevenoaks.[23] By 1858, following the Medical Act, the profession had split, with two dispensing chemists trading separately from two firms of surgeons (which included George Kelson, 1796–1878, and George Franks, 1798–1887).[24] In 1913 the choice of healthcare providers was much wider, reflecting both the increased population of Sevenoaks and its far larger disposable income. Three chemists (including Boots) and five surgeons were complemented by three nurses, a masseuse and three dentists, including one Fred Ayling, who specialised in artificial teeth.[25]

19 *Hooker's household almanac* (Westerham, 1864), no pagination.

20 Robert Barratt, *Daily Journal*, 9 July and 13 Aug. 1875.

21 *SC*, 25 April 1913, p. 5.

22 Joseph Johnson, *The medical register for the year 1783* (London, 1783), p. 77. Apothecaries were similar to modern GPs, and could gain additional medical qualifications, such as surgery.

23 KHLC P330/8/1, has Mallan's advertisement bound within its pages, dated 3 Dec. 1797.

24 *Melville and Co.'s directory & gazetteer of Kent* (London, 1858), pp. 406–10.

25 *Kelly's directory of Kent, Surrey, Sussex* (London, 1913), pp. 628–32.

Sevenoaks medical professionals, 1858 and 1913

Melville & Co's directory of Kent (1858)

Robert Adams	surgeon
Kelson & Franks	surgeons
William March	chemist
Edward Vincer	chemist

Kelly's directory of Kent (1913)

Fred Ayling	artificial teeth
Miss M. Bird	masseuse
Blomfield, Dick & Sichel	surgeons
Boots	chemists
Janet Bridges	nurse
Frank Burnett	surgeon
Edgar Elliott	physician and surgeon
Daniel Finlayson	chemist
Hip Hospital	
Holmesdale Cottage Hospital	
Isolation Hospital, Oak Lane	
Annie and Fanny Lake	nurses
Marriott & Mansfield	surgeons
Lucy Marshall	nurse
Thomas Parsons	chemist
Richard Roberts	dentist
William Taylor	surgeon
Louis Tomlin	dentist
George William	dentist

Eventually an accepted hierarchy of medical professionals emerged. At the top were physicians, who were university educated and were accredited as Members or Fellows of the Royal College of Physicians (MRCP; FRCP). Next were surgeons, who performed operations and set broken bones, skills usually acquired via an apprenticeship, although there was also a Royal College of Surgeons, to which Kelson and Franks belonged. Finally, apothecaries only dispensed drugs – another skill acquired through an apprenticeship, which in turn led to becoming a Licentiate of the Society of Apothecaries (LSA).

It is also reasonable to suppose that the quality of medical care provided in the town improved, too, certainly if their colleagues' opinions of their abilities is any guide. A good example is Kelson, who practiced as a surgeon in Sevenoaks from the

Figure 9.1 The old Pest Cart. Despite a plea from a local newspaper, the cart never made it to the Sevenoaks Museum and presumably rotted away where it stood.
Source: *Sevenoaks News*, October 1938, at Sevenoaks Library, C852.

1830s to the 1870s, was elected Master of the Worshipful Company of Apothecaries in 1871.[26] Better-quality care resulted from not only the efforts of dedicated individual doctors such as Kelson and John Lucas Worship (1825–92) but also the establishment of institutional healthcare, including hospitals, which in Sevenoaks was provided mainly by private charity. One example, by 1900, was Emily Jackson's expanded Hip Hospital, although three years later Lady Frances Pratt and others were complaining that it was being monopolised by patients from London (see Plate 8).[27]

Many in west Kent experienced the pain of toothache and the removal of bad and broken teeth. Although professional dentistry advanced in the late nineteenth century, with drilling, filling and false teeth for the wealthy, basic dentistry was undertaken both by medical practitioners and those (who often operated at fairs and markets) who could extract an offending molar from a desperate sufferer with strong pliers and brute strength.[28] In November 1882 Percival Bowen's diary

---

26 *SEG*, 29 June 1871, p. 5. In the transitional period after the 1858 Medical Act, apothecaries and surgeons overlapped in the profession.

27 Killingray and Purves, *Dictionary*, p. 130; *The Times*, 1 Dec. 1903, p. 15.

28 Angela Boyle *et al.*, '"To the praise of the dead, and anatomie": the analysis of post-medieval burials at St Nicholas, Sevenoaks, Kent', in M.J. Cox (ed.), *Grave concerns: death and burial in England 1700–1850* (York, 1998), pp. 91–3 and 97–9.

mentioned 'a bad attack of toothache'. The next two days were wretched: 'Tooth Ache dreadful', so much so that he needed a dentist: 'Had 1 stump and 1 tooth snapped off by Dr Worship ... Never allow Mr W to draw teeth again.'[29] Bowen could afford to pay a medical man for his unsatisfactory treatment. Options for the poor were far more limited.

The Pest House, or Fever Hospital, was located far away from the populated centre of the town, isolating those suffering from infections such as smallpox, typhus and cholera. This had its own 'Pest cart', an early type of ambulance used in the later nineteenth century to 'convey residents of Sevenoaks and district, smitten with fever, to the Pest House'.[30] It was replaced in 1902 by the Oak Lane Isolation Hospital. The small Sevenoaks and Holmesdale Cottage Hospital was opened on its present site in 1873 and funded by voluntary subscriptions. The Sevenoaks area also boasted several almshouses for the 'deserving poor' aged or infirm, 20 of the 32 homes adjoining Sevenoaks School also providing an annuity of 6s a week for their occupants.[31] In 1881 the average age of the 11 occupants of the eight almshouse cottages at Sevenoaks Weald (excluding servants and lodgers) was 78. One was blind, one deaf and another described as an 'imbecile'.[32]

Funeral rituals

This account is from the 1877 diary of Percival Bowen of Halstead:

30 October. Poor Dear Carrie Died in my arms about 9¼ O'clock, p.m. after the greatest suffering. Her last words were 'I have been praying'.

31 October. Staples to make coffin. [Bowen wrote to tell Dr Worship, the family doctor.]

2 November. To see Mr Sikes [vicar of Halstead, 1866–78] arranging the burial of poor dear Carrie's body.

3 November. 'Mr Worship came soon after. Made post-mortem evaluation and took 2 tumours etc away with him. Funeral of dear Carrie 13 followers and 6 bearers – laid her beside father [John Bowen, who died 1869].

Source: William Bowen archives.

---

29   Percival Bowen, *Diary*, 27–30 Nov. 1882, William Bowen archives.
30   Sevenoaks Library SC852, cutting from *Sevenoaks News*, Oct. 1938.
31   Killingray and Purves, *Dictionary*, p. 2; James Thorne, *Handbook to the environs of London* (London, 1876), p. 549.
32   Census Return for 1881: Sevenoaks Weald.

Despite denominational differences between 'churchmen [Anglicans] and nonconformists', they did join forces to deal with local welfare problems. For over forty years, from 1868, the charitable and ecumenical Sevenoaks Lay Association sought the 'promotion of the welfare of the working classes', offering a free service for the town's poor through its parish 'Nurses Fund' and 'Sick and Convalescent Fund', while at the same time promoting temperance.[33]

New institutions and public health improvements

Better healthcare required far more than better doctors and new hospitals, important though they were, and it is noteworthy that Isaac Jinks both eventually recovered from his fall and changed job to avoid further health risks. By 1861 he was landlord of a pub in Hartslands, being fined for using false weights in 1869.[34] Mitigating the health risks caused by serious infections also required a more comprehensive approach to public health in general; how that should best be achieved became a political issue that transfixed Sevenoaks for a decade.

After 1871 the Local Board took responsibility for sanitation and the removal of nuisances, a vital role for which the Vestry had lacked statutory powers of enforcement. Although not everybody in the town appreciated it, the only effective way to solve the public health problems of west Kent and elsewhere was to transfer those risks first from the Vestry to the Local Board and secondly from that Board to national government – at least in part, and given statutory power by the Public Health Act of 1875. The issue Sevenoaks faced from the beginning was 'the very pressing and urgent need for drainage', which was such that, as Major James German reminded the town, 'the smell was something horrible' – even during the annual flower show.[35]

It took eleven years, however, for the town to remove the serious public health risks it faced by constructing its first ever fully functioning, district-wide sewage disposal system. That lengthy, tortuous and costly saga provides an excellent case study demonstrating the many risk factors inherent in a major, relatively novel infrastructure project in a small market town and the high degree of political and other skills that were required to overcome the vociferous opposition to it. Those factors included the 'active' financial, construction, political and regulatory risks of carrying out the project. But the picture was more complex than that, for several significant 'passive' risks, too, were attached to *not* solving the drainage problem quickly. These were, first, the very real public health risks to the town and, secondly, the prospect of expensive government intervention should the town fail to fix the problem itself. Perhaps most

---

33 *SC*, 28 Oct. 1904, p. 8. See also for history, *ibid.*, 23 June 1883, p. 8. The Lay Association was not free from religious division, the high church vicar of St John's, the Rev. J.S. Bartlett, accusing local dissenters in 1891 of 'meddling' and 'muddling' and not being under clerical control; *ibid.*, 30 Jan. 1891, p. 5.

34 Census Return for 1861: Sevenoaks; *MJ*, 27 Sept. 1869, p. 7.

35 *SEG*, 3 June 1871, p. 3.

Figure 9.2 Major James German (1820–1901). German was originally from Preston, where he made his fortune as an industrialist and became mayor of the town in 1849, aged just 29. A 'staunch Liberal', on several occasions he stood unsuccessfully for parliament. He moved to Sevenoaks in 1867 where he served as a county JP for many years and was Deputy-lieutenant for Kent. He held his commission in the 3rd Royal Lancashire Militia and sat on both the Sevenoaks Local Board and the Highways Board. He was also a prominent member of St John's Church, Hartslands.
Source: Sevenoaks Library, B667.

worrying of all to the town's middle-class residents was, thirdly, the reputational and competitive risks of a possible disease outbreak, whereby Sevenoaks might lose out in the civic attractiveness stakes to rivals such as Tonbridge or Tunbridge Wells. A fourth unpleasant conceivable consequence was a fall in house prices.

But implementing the necessary sanitary improvements was not plain sailing. A combination of incompetence on the part of elected representatives, many of whom had no experience of local political administration, and a series of rearguard actions by a ratepayer interest determined to keep the costs down meant that Sevenoaks was not finally connected to the sewage outfall at Dartford until 1882. This was fully seven years after Tonbridge had solved its sanitary issues, which were even more pressing than those of Sevenoaks, since its low-lying position on the Medway made it far more prone to disease. More than 1,000 people had contracted cholera or dysentery in the 1854 outbreak in Tonbridge, for example.[36]

German was the driving force behind the Sevenoaks sewer after he was elected to the Local Board in 1873. A successful industrialist and Liberal politician, he was just the type of person Sevenoaks was keen to attract, both economically and socially, making some of the most important civic and political contributions to the town in the entire nineteenth century. He also lived just a few hundred yards from Hartslands, worshipping at St John's, so he had a strong personal interest in solving the environmental problems faced by its residents.

His strategy was instructive, since he fully understood how important it was to harness both the institutional and the professional aspects of public healthcare, creating sufficient credibility for the project such that it overcame the entrenched opposition of the ratepayer party. In essence he presented the case for (albeit expensive) action as being less risky than the false economy of inaction. The pressing need for infection control eventually trumped the issue of cost. One tactic was to obtain professional support for his plans in order to frustrate strong political opposition on the Board. Another was timing. In August 1875, when the smell was presumably at its worst, German proposed at a Local Board meeting that 'a complete system of drainage should be adopted for the town'. He did so, moreover, just a few days after Baylis, the Medical Officer for Sevenoaks, had published his report into the quality of the existing sanitary arrangements. This was also leaked to *The Lancet* in advance and highlighted fever emanating 'from the existence of cesspools and the bad construction and filthy condition of certain buildings'.[37] This grim picture stood in stark contrast to the image Sevenoaks had long sought to present, which was always to be 'as pretty and becoming as possible'.[38]

---

36 Taylor, 'Not going through the motions', pp. 123–39; M. Barker-Read, 'The public health question in the nineteenth century: public health and sanitation in a Kentish market town, Tonbridge', *Southern History*, p. 4 (1982), pp. 167–89.

37 *The Lancet*, 7 Aug. 1875, p. 218.

38 *SC*, 13 May 1881, p. 8.

However, the price of transforming the public health of the town once and for all was estimated at about £20,000. Although central government (through the Public Works Loan Commissioners) was prepared to assume the contingent risk for the project by lending the town the entire capital sum (so the state was effectively accepting the transfer to it of the capital risk), the repayments would present a heavy additional burden (or revenue risk) on ratepayers for many years.[39] That was a serious worry, especially if the proposed engineering solution failed, as sometimes proved the case with such relatively untried technology, for then ratepayers would be forced to pay twice. That choice was therefore vehemently resisted by the 'economy' party, John Bridges Nunn being an especially vocal opponent after he was elected to the Local Board in 1876. German led the opposing 'efficiency' party, which argued equally strongly for progress, such that Sevenoaks had no option but to make the investment. His battle with Nunn was both personal and highly political. However, German's combination of hard work, attention to detail, political skill (seen, for example, in how he persuaded the social elite of the town, including Board chairman Multon Lambarde, to back his comprehensive solution as opposed to Nunn's *ad-hoc* expedients) and ability to get the support of the local press eventually combined to ensure completion.

Another important factor was the advent of the Local Board, as it offered individuals such as German an institutional political process through which they could work most effectively. Despite that, it took him almost a decade to overcome all the risks involved, both passive and active. Four years later, however, its success could be measured in how 'the amount of infectious disease [in the town] is at its lowest ebb'.[40] While that might demonstrate how some public health risks were slowly but surely being overcome in the later nineteenth century, progress was not entirely smooth. Sanitary improvements demanded by the Local Board could be simply disregarded, as Robert Redman (1830–95) did with the eponymous slum alleyway he owned in the town centre. Redman's Place was a local byword for poor sanitation long after those problems had all but disappeared elsewhere, for he refused to connect its dwellings to the new system of sanitation when it was completed in 1882. The Board responded by telling him to 'put in his drain as directed'.[41] The alley was overcrowded, and its toilets were still not connected to mains water as late as 1890.[42] This sewer was still deemed substandard in 1912 and the Council considered demolishing all 16 properties a few months later, but this undoubted blemish in the centre of Sevenoaks managed to survive until 1961, when it was finally 'demolished under a slum clearance order'.[43]

---

39 *SEG*, 20 March 1876, p. 5; 13 May 1876, p. 3.

40 *The Lancet*, 24 July 1886, p. 186.

41 *SC*, 7 July 1882, p. 5.

42 *SC*, 7 Nov. 1890, p. 5.

43 *SC*, 9 Feb. 1912, p. 8; 10 May 1912, p. 5; Killingray and Purves, *Dictionary*, p. 152.

Some years earlier Baylis had been candid about other weaknesses in the system, such as the much lower standards of healthcare that prevailed in more remote villages, where

> there is no such provision [of hospitals] ... or other resource save the employment
> of disinfecting nurses. Their invaluable services are, however, often unattainable,
> from the frequent impossibility of lodging them either inside or outside the
> patients' dwelling; the latter is generally unfit and often too crowded for safety and
> treatment.[44]

Gilbert Gasson's memoirs vividly validate Baylis's concerns, providing concrete examples of the severity of the prevailing healthcare risks and the consequences of not mitigating them through proper medical care provided by effective institutions. So, in 1888, Walter Raikes, the vicar of Ide Hill, 'went among the smallpox sufferers isolated under canvas ... near the workhouse. Those who died were all buried together in a part of the churchyard.' Nor was infectious disease the only weakness in the system, since 'When anyone was ill, all the utensils were kept at the vicarage (there was no hospital, only the workhouse infirmary). Brandy was also kept at the vicarage.' That regimen certainly toughened people up. When Gasson's brother suffered a bowel inflammation in 1902 'the doctor ordered him to Holmesdale Cottage Hospital. Lady Angela Campbell sent round her horse and van to take him ... after ten days he walked home.'[45] In conclusion, sickness and injury were constant risk factors across all social classes in nineteenth-century west Kent. The problem was compounded for families when illness precluded the breadwinner from working, as the loss of income reduced the family's chances of being able to pay for the bare necessities. In that situation many turned, or tried to turn, to local financial institutions to overcome the worst of those risks. The next chapter will examine how.

---

44 *SEG*, 23 June 1879, p. 6.
45 KHLC WU13/Z1, vol. 1; vol. 4; vol. 2; vol. 1.

Chapter 10

Financial risk to pension security

Risk reduction through self-help?

Towns such as Sevenoaks, with its Local Board, Medical Officer and rudimentary health services, needed both political will and effective institutions to make the necessary improvements. Good progress had been made by 1900, although in small, isolated villages such as Ide Hill healthcare was at best patchy and at worst almost non-existent. But other strategies were available for people seeking to mitigate the health and other risks they faced. The most viable was to transfer the obligation to provide or pay for medical services elsewhere, onto other individuals or institutions better able to bear them, although that process could impact significantly on those bodies, too.

The most obvious way of paying for medical attention and funding any inability to work through accident or illness was to save in advance, a widely accepted tactic in our period. 'Slate clubs' (often run by public houses) offered a short-term way for the less-well-off to put small sums aside. In a sermon entitled 'An Exhortation to the Poor', delivered at Tonbridge parish church in 1831, incumbent Thomas Knox optimistically urged the poor to put aside whatever they could by using savings banks.[1] This was, however, a somewhat perilous strategy, exemplified by the story of the Tonbridge New Bank, which would have been well known to many of Knox's listeners. Established by two wealthy local landowners, Messrs Mercer and Barlow, in 1813, three years later both had been 'ruined by the lamentable failure' of the new venture.[2] Its victims came from every section of west Kent society. Sevenoaks aristocrat the Marquess of Camden was owed £381, but he was probably easily able to bear occasional losses of even this magnitude. However, those lower down the social scale were also badly affected, meaning that depositing their money at the bank had increased, not reduced, their financial risks; Edward Jardine, from Sevenoaks, was owed £50 on a promissory note and James Norton, a labourer from

---

1   Knox, *Poor*, p. 19.

2   Gordon Woodgate and Giles Woodgate, *A history of the Woodgates of Stonewall Park and of Summerhill* (Wisbech, 1910), p. 311.

Figure 10.1 Sevenoaks bank note, 1809. The Sevenoaks Bank was founded in 1804 by William and John George together with Valentine Hackleton (1765–1835), who came to live in Sevenoaks in 1789. Little is known of these entrepreneurs who had spare capital with which to launch a bank and print their own bank notes. Hackleton had won £10,000 on the Irish National Lottery and Jane Edwards said that 'He was of a very speculating turn … very soon the Bank was closed [in 1811], for his £10,000 had itself wings, and flown away.' This note was issued in 1809, but unfortunately the name of the payee is illegible.
Source: Author's collection.

Capel, £15.[3] Even though Norton had less far to fall than the Marquess and the bank's founders, one cannot help wondering how long it took him to have his £15, or some smaller proportion of it, returned by the receivers, and how he and his family managed in the meantime.

The lesson was that all sections of society had to cope with financial risk; the key requirement for anyone with any spare cash was to find a safe home for it. That was easier said than done in nineteenth-century west Kent. Banks (and other financial institutions) were then as now based on trust and any breach of that trust substantially exacerbated the risks run by their depositors. The Limited Liability Act of 1855 introduced a measure of stability to the banking system, but the risk of fraud always remained.

The sad story of the Sevenoaks Savings Bank, which ran from about 1817 until its ignominious closure in 1888, is a case in point. Proudly established 'for the purpose

---

3   TNA B 3/3380. Creditors meeting, 21 Sept. 1816; Depositions from creditors, June 1816 to Feb. 1817.

of affording a secure investment to the industrious and lower classes of the people', by 1860 its 1,280 personal depositors had entrusted it with a total of almost £32,000, or £25 each.[4] Thirty-nine charities had deposited just over £1,915, an average of about £49 each, and 13 friendly societies £3,488 (£268 each).[5] Later, some societies had even more at stake. The Shoreham Amicable, for example, a customer of the Savings Bank since at least 1883, had entrusted it with over £1,624 by 1888, although the interest had not yet been credited 'owing to the unsatisfactory state of affairs at the bank'.[6] That was something of an understatement. Good practice was that individual depositors' pass books be regularly 'compared with the ledger'. Another pass book inspection was also necessary before the bank could be taken over by the government-owned (and thus far less risky) Post Office Savings Bank in 1888. The process of closing the hitherto safe and secure financial institution was a formality, or so it was assumed.

Great was the consternation, however, when the audit revealed not a surplus but a 'serious deficiency' of 'nearly £2,000'.[7] The bank's trustees had, sensibly they thought, sought to eliminate its depositors' investment risk by stipulating that 'All moneys belonging to the institution shall be invested in the Bank of England.' In other words, it derisked its business model, as far as possible, by investing in gilt-edged securities.[8] But that was of no account since it had simultaneously failed to obviate the fraud risk it was exposed to through its non-existent internal audit procedures. This was despite its rules and regulations piously laying down that 'The Managers and Actuary will diligently endeavour to prevent fraud' and 'The Treasurer and Actuary … shall give good and sufficient security … for the just and faithful execution of such office, or trust.'[9]

The spotlight fell on bank actuary Henry Sutton, aged 61, whose hitherto unblemished façade of respectability came crashing down as he 'sacrificed the good character he had borne', having been caught red-handed stealing depositors' cash as it was received over the counter.[10] When produced in court, the bank ledgers revealed that the sums he was charged with stealing 'had not been entered'.[11] The bank's auditors, Booker Prideaux, could have provided another layer of security as part of the standard audit process, but they denied all culpability.[12] Sutton was sentenced to 18 months' hard labour. The judge highlighted not only the egregious breach of trust his actions represented but also how they impacted the hardest

---

4   KHLC P88/5/2 Article 1.

5   *SEG*, 7 Feb. 1860, p. 5.

6   *SC*, 1 June 1883, p. 8; 1 June 1888, p. 4.

7   *KT*, 12 May 1888, p. 3.

8   KHLC P88/5/2, Article 9.

9   KHLC P88/5/2, Articles 31 and 29.

10 *SC*, 6 July 1888, p. 5.

11 *KT*, 26 May 1888, p. 3.

12 *SEG*, 21 May 1888, p. 5.

upon the most vulnerable in the community, on those who had the most difficulty obtaining the bare necessities, but who were saving hard to do so. Holmes had, he said, defrauded 'persons in a humble position in life, who had made good use of the Bank to make an honest provision for themselves'.[13] The matter was raised in parliament (one of the rare occasions in the nineteenth century when Sevenoaks made national headlines) by opposition MP George Howell, whereupon Chancellor of the Exchequer George Goschen assured the nation 'all the circumstances of the case would be investigated and the necessary action taken'.[14] The fallout was considerable. Although not legally obliged to do so, the bank's trustees, headed by the Rev. Thomas Curteis, repaid the losses in full.[15] But the lesson was clear. Any attempt by an individual to transfer his or her personal financial risk to a supposedly secure institution could fail if it was poorly managed.

Insuring against the risks

There were other, less risky, ways to insure one's health than relying on savings banks, or so it appeared. By the second half of the nineteenth century provident and friendly societies, available to all but the poorest west Kent residents, were commonplace. Membership offered some measure of insurance against medical costs, thereby sharing the risks involved. The Holmesdale Medical Provident Society (HMPS) was founded in 1869, with a membership spread across west Kent, from Westerham to Wrotham. It aimed to 'secure, on provident principles, medical advice and medicine for the working classes and others who are unable to pay the usual professional fees'.[16] But, despite its high-minded intentions, the HMPS struggled for almost its entire 68-year life, partly because 'it was not so much known as it should be, especially among the classes whom it was intended to benefit'.[17] Its poor profile had significant financial consequences, for in 1892 (when it disbursed almost £400 in fees to its medical officers) its annual meeting discussed at length ways of reducing the deficit.[18] In 1898 better public relations was a solution advocated, although the *Sevenoaks Chronicle* had already obliged, saying 'nothing could prove a greater boon to the [working class] inhabitants of the district'.[19]

The HMPS's press reports also allow us to trace the extent to which local healthcare was impacted by the National Insurance Act of 1911, one of several major government initiatives of our period that sought to reduce the risks inherent

---

13 *SC*, 6 July 1888, p. 5.

14 *The Times*, 11 May 1888, p. 6.

15 Iain Taylor, 'The Sevenoaks banking fraud and its aftermath 1888–1891', *The Local Historian*, 51/2 (2021), pp. 100–12.

16 *SEG*, 30 June 1879, p. 5.

17 *SEG*, 10 May 1898, p. 6.

18 *SEG*, 26 April 1892, p. 6.

19 *SEG*, 10 May 1898, p. 6; *SC*, 6 May 1898, p. 4.

in the lives of middle- and working-class people. Many similar local societies throughout the country now faced rivalry from a well-funded official national organisation. This eventually 'considerably weakened' them since, under the Act, medical practitioners received 7s a year for each patient on their books, 'reasonably generous terms' that most friendly societies struggled to match.[20] By 1913 it was clear that many 'men now compulsory subscribers to National Insurance did not want to subscribe to both' (i.e., to the HMPS as well).[21] It struggled on until 1936, when 'the remaining provident members were mainly elderly people or the families of employed persons, whose numbers gradually diminished'. It was wound up and its small remaining cash balance distributed among District Nursing Associations.[22]

Risk transfer and friendly societies

One reason why few working-class people in west Kent joined the HMPS was, perhaps, because they had joined friendly (or benefit) societies instead. They were hugely popular: 'the nineteenth century witnessed the heyday of the friendly society movement' such that, in 1850, about a half of the nation's adult men were members.[23] Their advantage over their medical-provident counterparts was their greater flexibility, for the sick or injured received cash payments, not specific medical treatments, which members could spend on what they felt they most needed. Particularly if they did not trust doctors or medicines, buying more or better food (especially if the family was under-nourished) could prove a better cure than various medical interventions.

Friendly societies differed significantly from welfare provision under the New Poor Law, which was tied to parish origin. By contrast, the societies were based on the voluntarist principle of free associations. Weekly contributions of 1s a week or so paid into a common sickness fund (with perhaps a separate burial fund, too) gave an entitlement to sick pay should accident or illness prevent the breadwinner from working. Friendly societies also had an important social function, offering 'regular, ritual based sociability' in addition to their insurance provision, which again the HMPS and others could not match.[24] 'Sociability' involved monthly meetings in a local ale house, elaborate annual feasts and processions. The latter became celebrated as holidays, as for example in 1868, when the combined Foresters and Oddfellows festival drew 5,000 people to Knole Park, where they were fed, beered and subsequently entertained by the Royal Marines band, a balloon ascent and a firework display.[25]

---

20 Lane, *A social history of medicine*, p. 79.

21 *SC*, 31 Jan. 1913, p. 2.

22 *SC*, 23 July 1937, p. 8.

23 Audrey Fisk, *Mutual self-help in southern England* (Southampton, 2006), p. 1; Boyd Hilton, *A mad, bad and dangerous people? England 1783–1846* (Oxford, 2006), p. 624.

24 Simon Cordery, *British friendly societies 1750–1914* (Basingstoke, 2003), p. 1.

25 *SEG*, 27 July 1868, p. 5.

Figure 10.2 Tonbridge Girls Friendly Society. Despite, or perhaps because of, the formidable appearance of this group of 'girls', nothing else is known of the TGFS.
Source: Tonbridge Historical Society, 25.087.

The third benefit was less tangible but almost as important, for society membership also conferred respectable status within the local community. This was because members were more likely to ride out the risks of sickness or injury, so were less likely to be chargeable to the ratepayers. Their capacity to mitigate their own personal risks via the self-help available from a friendly society made them less of a financial risk to that community. The high place respectability held is very visible in society rule books. In 1767 The Sevenoaks Amicable allowed no payments to any member who failed its respectability tests, by for example appearing 'disguised in liquor at the Club'.[26] Nor could they receive benefits if they had taken part in boxing or wrestling bouts, or were suffering from the 'French Pox' (syphilis).[27]

But, even if they applauded friendly society objectives in theory, some commentators were less sure of their financial stability in practice. So, when the 50-year-old Tonbridge Benefit Society failed in December 1830 (at the height of the

---

26   KHLC U1000/27/O1, Article 7.

27   KHLC U1000/27/O1, Article 10.

Swing disturbances and quite possibly because of the cash demands then made upon it), one newspaper solemnly generalised that 'from the principles upon which these societies are generally constituted, they must all in time meet with a similar fate'.[28] If they were to remain long-term going concerns, in other words, they had to overcome the key risks attached to their own members and the competitive environment they operated within, as well as the consequent risk to the respectability and reputations – of society, managers and members – if they got it wrong. As with the Sevenoaks Savings Bank, any breach of trust, for example, could have far-reaching repercussions for often long-standing relationships not only within specific societies but also, more broadly, across the entire town.

Family support networks helped minimise risk, so it is not surprising that members sought to have their relations and friends accepted into societies. In the town, most is known about two small local societies, the Sevenoaks Amicable Society (1767–1844) and the Sevenoaks Wesleyan Benefit Society (SWBS, 1841–84). Breeches-maker Henry Sutton (1745–1807), a founder member of the former, was joined by his two sons in 1794 and 1796 and his grandson in 1821.[29] As its name implies, membership of SWBS was 'strictly confined to persons connected with the Wesleyan body', which might also have been why 'there was no procession or display' at its annual gatherings and why their monthly meetings took place 'in the vestry of the Sevenoaks Wesleyan Chapel' rather than at a local inn, which was the Amicable's venue of choice.[30]

The SWBS committee was dominated for its entire existence by class superiors the How family, all of whom were well-respected middle-class tradesmen and long-lived, staunch Methodists. For many years, Thomas, George and their cousin Stephen served as trustees and officers of the SWBS.[31] George's obituary described him as 'specially and prominently a Sunday-school pillar of more than seventy years' standing'.[32] The family boasted an impeccable pedigree of church ministry and service spanning the generations.

The Amicable had an almost entirely middle-class/professional and artisanal membership, but labourers and semi-skilled workers were well represented within the SWBS, which indicates both a significant rise in disposable incomes in west Kent by the mid-nineteenth century and a desire by those lower orders to reduce risk. Several SWBS members were from Hartslands, including bricklayer John Jeffrey (1804–78). But others, such as Frederick Fowler, lived in the Methodist enclave

---

28   *SEG*, 28 Dec. 1830, p. 4.

29   The Amicable's records are in the KHLC, U1000/27/O1 and U1000/27/O2.

30   *SEG*, 2 Aug. 1873, p. 3; 8 Aug. 1865, p. 5; Sevenoaks Library D200; KHLC U1000/27/O1, Articles and Rules of the Sevenoaks Amicable Society (London, 1767) (Article 3).

31   KHLC M2/1/6/16, P.J. Franks, manuscript lecture, 'A Survey of Sevenoaks Methodism from its Commencement in 1764' (1918), p. 3.

32   *The Watchman*, 13 Feb. 1884, p. 54.

at Lock's Yard, in the centre of Sevenoaks, and a fair smattering came from the surrounding villages.

The three benefits of society membership cohered in the extraordinary story of John Jeffrey, and studying his eventful time with the SWBS coincidentally tells us more about his detailed medical history than we know about any other contemporary working-class Sevenoaks resident. His society membership also reveals much about his respectable status and how that altered over time. He joined the SWBS in 1841, the year of its inception and 12 months after his wife had died. One assumes he took this prudent step as he was a single parent with a 3-year-old son and had a relatively dangerous job, as a bricklayer.[33] In 1851 he was living with his son, his 24-year-old servant Susannah Older and their illegitimate baby.[34] The couple married later that year, a decision at least partly motivated, one assumes, by the need to restore some respectability to their relationship, but in 1862 the SWBS found him guilty of insobriety. This was most disrespectable behaviour, especially for a Methodist, and he was debarred for six months to encourage him to 'abstain from drunkenness and attend on the Sabbath day a place of religious worship'.[35] By 1871 he had somehow recovered his standing, perhaps illustrating how, for many working-class people, respectability was sought to 'extract material and social benefits from class superiors'. If that was Jeffrey's intention, he succeeded spectacularly well.[36]

Jeffrey suffered from chronic ill health and in middle age he regularly received short-term support from the SWBS: for six weeks in 1855, for example, and nearly five weeks the following year.[37] But in 1873 he was 'permanently disabled from following his trade or any employment' and was given a lifetime pension of only 4s a week. That year he received total payments of £33 3s from the SWBS.[38] In 1874 he was suspended for eight weeks following complaints he had breached society rules, although he received pension payments of £53 the following year; he was suspended again, for another eight weeks, in 1875, for 'being in a tolerable good state of health', when his payments for the year dropped to just £21.[39] He died from bronchitis three years later, aged 73, and Susannah received a further £4 for funeral expenses.[40]

His poor health, especially after he reached his 40s, meant that the family had to devise a strategy to cope with the uncertain employment of the breadwinner and the

---

33   KHLC M2/1/2/1; monthly meeting, 2 May 1876 (Quinqennial valuation).

34   Census Return for 1851: Sevenoaks (Hartslands).

35   KHLC M2/1/2/1, monthly meetings, 2 Dec. 1862; 3 Oct. 1871.

36   Peter Bailey, '"Will the real Bill Banks please stand up?" Towards a role analysis of mid-Victorian working class respectability', *Journal of Social History*, XII/3 (Spring 1979), pp. 336–53 (p. 343).

37   KHLC M2/1/2/1, Money Paid to Members in Sickness.

38   KHLC M2/1/2/1, monthly meeting, 4 Feb. 1873.

39   KHLC M2/1/2/1, Money Paid; monthly meetings, 1 Dec. 1874; 13 Jan. 1875.

40   KHLC M2/1/2/2, Medical Certificate of the Cause of Death, 23 June 1878; 5 Feb. 1878.

financial risks that entailed. Its variant of the makeshift economy involved sending their three sons out to work (the youngest, aged ten, became a farm labourer), taking in a lodger and receiving payments from the SWBS.[41] The latter totalled more than £153 from when he first took sick leave in 1844 until 1875. For those and many other members, friendly societies offered an excellent way of overcoming the risks of getting sick and old. Jeffrey's membership of the Wesleyan proved, therefore, an excellent investment.[42]

But although Jeffrey's health-risk transfer strategies worked well for him and his family, it simultaneously imposed huge financial burdens upon the SWBS. The 1875 Friendly Society Act required societies to undertake quinquennial valuations, observing more stringent actuarial tables for sickness and mortality, but this new regulatory regime was slow to be devised and only slowly accepted by the SWBS's managers. Unsurprisingly, such valuations often revealed 'chronic and extensive insolvency', for until then directors had had little clue about the extent of the long-term liabilities they were carrying, especially as members grew older.[43] The SWBS's (single page) published profit and loss account for 1861, for example, shows a 'trading' surplus of just over £40 for the year, all of which was distributed to the membership, leaving the cash balance almost unaltered, at £431.[44] But its managers, who were proud to say 'that the society is in a good position both financially and numerically', did not recognise that, every year, sick and elderly members became ever larger insurance liabilities.[45]

Even though treasurer Stephen How proudly noted that the 1876 Quinquennial Return had been 'correctly reported', it was obvious by then that something was seriously amiss, for the cash in the general fund had dropped to £410, which was caused by 'the payments to sick members exceeding the contributions'.[46] In 1879 an enormous actuarial deficiency of £2,133 – or six times the fund's total cash holdings of £351 – was reported. The solution mooted by the actuary was draconian: 'It will be necessary to take immediate steps to place the Society on a satisfactory footing … I do not see how this can be done better than a distribution' – or effectively liquidating any remaining assets and shutting down the entire organisation.[47]

Societies in this position – that is, weakened by a preponderance of frail, older members – needed to attract in younger ones, whose contributions would adequately fund the payments made to their seniors. Such societies' money would eventually run out, therefore, 'unless there was a continuous recruitment of new members at

---

41   Census Return for 1871: Sevenoaks (Hartslands).
42   KHLC M2/1/2/1, money paid.
43   Cordery, *Friendly societies*, p. 125.
44   Sevenoaks Library D200.
45   *SEG*, 3 Aug. 1872, p. 3.
46   KHLC M2/1/2/1, monthly meeting, 28 April 1876; *SEG*, 31 July 1876, p. 5.
47   KHLC M2/1/2/1, letter from H.A. Smith, 19 July 1879.

or below the ages at entry of the initial members, so that the average age remained stable'.[48] Contemporaries were not slow to recognise the problem, the Shoreham Amicable in 1889 calling on its number to 'try and induce young members to join', for example.[49] There was also no disguising the nervousness about the issue in a press report on the SWBS's annual meeting in 1878, which insisted there was 'no reason for younger members to fear the bankruptcy of the society'.[50]

But that hopeful sentiment was badly misplaced. Even though the SWBS struggled on for another five years, its eventual demise was inevitable. This was not only because it faced internal financial pressures from elderly members but also because it had to cope with serious competition, especially from the huge national affiliated friendly societies such as the Oddfellows and the Foresters; the national membership of the latter increased fivefold, to nearly half a million, between 1845 and 1875.[51]

Affiliated societies were also better able to host large, set-piece sociability events such as that in Knole Park in 1868. Symbolically they were stronger too, for the Wesleyan chapel vestry would have found it hard to compete, as a venue, with the imposing new Oddfellows Hall that opened in Sevenoaks in 1876, at the grand cost of £1,200. The Oddfellows District body then had 1,800 members and, in the past year, from its capital stock of £20,000, had paid out to its members £1,300 as sickness benefits.[52] The affiliated bodies provided the same sociability and conferred similar respectable status as the SWBS, but offered the additional benefits, to men travelling in search of work, of portability of membership to other lodges. Most importantly, they were financially far more robust than smaller societies, as insolvency and other risks could be spread widely among many different branches throughout the country, the stronger able to bail out their weaker brethren whenever needed. They had, in sum, a clear 'competitive advantage over smaller societies'.[53]

Unsurprisingly, the numbers of Foresters (to give a single example) mushroomed across west Kent, as six courts (branches) were established between 1860 and 1865; membership of the Sevenoaks court rose almost fivefold between 1865 and 1884, from 50 to 240.[54] In the same period the membership of the SWBS almost halved, from 86 in 1866 to just 44 in 1884.[55] That was not surprising:

---

48 Lawrence Eagles, 'Friendly societies', in Derek Renn (ed.), *Life, death and money: actuaries and the creation of financial security* (Oxford, 1998), p. 48.

49 *SC*, 31 May 1889, p. 4.

50 *KSC*, 2 Aug. 1878, p. 8.

51 Cordery, *Friendly societies*, pp. 104–5.

52 *KSC*, 7 July 1876, p. 6.

53 Cordery, *Friendly societies*, p. 105.

54 Dr R. Logan, of the Foresters Heritage Trust, carried out this private research for the authors; his email dated 12 Dec. 2013.

55 *SEG*, 7 Aug. 1866, p. 5; UKPP, Commons, *Reports of the Chief Registrar of Friendly Societies*, No. 322 (1884–5), Appendix, p. 165; KHLC M2/1/2/1.

there was no good reason why young men should join the SWBS, where most of their cash would support their elders, when the affiliated societies were a much more attractive proposition.

No new members meant no new revenue. The only way the SWBS could fill its financial black hole in such circumstances was by reducing expenditure – that is, benefits – to the minimum. If they had no option but to pay out to a genuinely sick member, such as Jeffrey, they could decline to meet fewer clear-cut claims, or enforce the disciplinary rules as strictly as possible, in order to deny claimants. But this strategy ran the risk of aggrieved members taking legal action to secure their benefits, with all the publicity and concomitant damage that entailed to the society's reputation.

The most blatant example took place as early as 1860, when the SWBS expelled Frederick Fowler for 'working' while in receipt of benefits, such work amounting only to 'mending his and his children's shoes' without the directors' permission.[56] Fowler, born in 1814, was a sawyer by trade and, like Jeffrey, had joined the SWBS in 1841. In 1860 he had a wife and five children, aged from 8 to 15, three of whom were at school.[57] As the sole breadwinner his income was critical, so expulsion impacted on the wellbeing of the entire family. He did not go down without a fight. After he appealed the decision the directors thought it appropriate, in the 1861 Annual Report, to specify other offences that would incur similar penalties, which included 'working in a garden or field'.[58] They justified their decision in terms of the risks that not acting according to the strict letter of its rules would pose to the health of the Society. They would in other words 'be wanting in faithfulness to the society, whose interest they are appointed to watch over and protect from imposition of every kind'.[59] Fowler took them to arbitration but the decision remained that he 'be expelled the Society'.[60] The media, however, took a very different view of the SWBS's behaviour, since:

> This explanation was evidently found necessary from the opprobrium lately
> cast upon the society through the expulsion of a poor sick member ... Strong
> representations were made ... that their afflicted brother was not working for hire
> ... The directors, however, could not be induced to alter their decision.[61]

Those directors (who included Stephen and Thomas How) knew they were losing the battle and the potential consequences that had for their reputations. In 1863

---

56 KHLC M2/1/2/1, money paid; quarterly meeting 2 Oct. 1860.
57 Census Return for 1861: Sevenoaks (Hartslands).
58 Sevenoaks Library D200.
59 *SEG*, 6 Aug. 1861, p. 5.
60 KHLC M2/1/2/1, monthly meeting 3 Sept. 1861.
61 *SEG*, 6 Aug. 1861, p. 5.

they amended the rule Fowler had breached: 'to prevent the expulsion of members in advanced years', it was made clear that starting a fire, cooking, writing letters and 'mending his personal apparel when absolutely necessary' were no longer deemed terminal infractions.[62] But even though the amendment was carried unanimously by the SWBS's 75 members, the damage had been done.[63] It was clear that, no matter what its financial position was, local opinion-formers strongly disapproved of a long-standing SWBS member being deprived of benefits to which he was entitled by a ruse of this kind, even though he had claimed almost £300 from it between 1855 and 1860.[64] Fowler, the respectable injured party, was being unfairly treated by an institution that should have acted in a reciprocally respectable way towards him, but had not – and it should have known better.

It was also a serious breach of trust, which underpins all strong family relationships, although it is often noticed only when it is absent. Strong trust-based relationships are also an integral method of risk management, since families, friends, neighbours and entire communities generally come together to confront and mitigate the risks they collectively face only if the individuals concerned trust each other to perform their allotted tasks adequately. Diminished trust combined with heightened risk for the SWBS and its managers put it in grave danger of forfeiting its respectable status. The SWBS's subsequent generosity to Jeffrey, one might speculate, may well have been an effort to rebuild the reputation so badly tarnished with Fowler a decade earlier.

Furthermore, trust worked both ways, because respectable society members were also entitled to hold their governors, such as the Hows, to account whenever necessary. Those managers had always, in other words, to undertake their leadership responsibilities with the utmost probity and in the best interests of their members. If any in that position failed to perform their duties adequately, it represented a gross breach of the trust that was always implicit in their positions. It was entirely acceptable for individuals such as Jeffrey and Fowler to transfer (as far as possible) the risks of everyday life from themselves and their families to institutions such as the SWBS, for that was the accepted reason for joining them in the first place. Conversely, however, it was totally unacceptable for the society to seek to transfer those risks *back* to its members, unless it were fully justified by a member's highly disrespectable behaviour. Should they even attempt it, their widely recognised accountability was such that the press (and many others) would take them severely to task for any perceived shortcoming.

---

62 Sevenoaks Wesleyan Benefit Society, Annual Report 7 July 1863 (Alterations to the Rules), p. 4. This (uncatalogued) small booklet is currently held at The Drive Methodist church, Sevenoaks, in an envelope marked 'Maternal Relatives and the Drive with List', dated Nov. 2008.

63 Sevenoaks Wesleyan Benefit Society, Annual Report 7 July 1863, p. 6.

64 KHLC M2/1/2/1, money paid.

The price of failure

After Jeffrey's death the SWBS's financial problems became so acute that it had no option but to revert to the small print of its rulebook – no matter what the reputational consequences might be. In 1879 the press reported that the 'greatest draw upon the funds appeared to be the pensioners ... so that this year the income had not equalled the receipts'.[65] This was crisis point and two other pensioners and founder members of the SWBS were soon in the firing line. Richard Bowyer, a retired farmer aged 87, was so concerned about the financial health of the SWBS, and his treatment by it, that he sought to preserve his benefits by leaving, on condition he was paid £5 12s in lieu. His proposal was accepted.[66] And the only claims Josiah Brown, a former 'gas maker' aged 81, had made before 1875 were for two weeks' sick pay and his deceased wife's funeral expenses.[67] He was therefore understandably aggrieved when, in 1879, he was suspended from receiving his pension benefits for six months for having been away from home when its assessor called, after which the relationship between the SWBS and Brown (and Bowyer) spectacularly soured.[68]

The two men allegedly conspired to prefer 'malicious and false charges' against the SWBS, which perhaps resembled Brown's unflattering description of the SWBS's balance sheet for 1878 (just prior to the actuarial report) as 'villainous, deceitful and fraudulent'. They unequivocally blamed the mess on Stephen How and William Reynolds, 'both Preachers of the Gospel', their astonishment and contempt for their superiors' betrayal of Methodist financial integrity ringing out loud and clear in their accusations.[69] Brown was expelled for non-payment of his dues in 1880 but he continued to complain about the managers' behaviour.[70] Later that year the SWBS went on the attack, accusing him of 'libellous conduct' and determining that, if he continued writing 'scurrilous letters', his prosecution would be sought.[71] Brown was not cowed, however, for as late as 1883 the SWBS had to decide how to deal with further 'scurrilous and false accusations' from him.[72]

This episode was, however, but a sub-plot compared to the main drama, which was the SWBS's perilous financial condition. It was dissolved in 1884, when just 30 members witnessed it finally overwhelmed by the long-term liabilities it had incurred and which it had – in common with many other smaller Victorian friendly societies – so signally failed to mitigate.[73] The trust that had been built up over

---

65 *SEG*, 4 Aug. 1879, p. 5.
66 KHLC M2/1/2/1.
67 KHLC M2/1/2/1, money paid.
68 KHLC M2/1/2/1, monthly meetings 4 Nov. 1879.
69 KHLC M2/1/2/1, monthly meetings 2 Dec. 1879.
70 KHLC M2/1/2/1, monthly meetings 3 Feb. 1880.
71 KHLC M2/1/2/1, monthly meetings 3 Feb. 1880; 28 Aug. 1880.
72 KHLC M2/1/2/1, monthly meetings 2 Jan. 1883.
73 KHLC M2/1/2/1, AGM 30 July 1884.

many years, through repeated sociability and shared Methodist values, was swiftly destroyed by the financial collapse that resulted from the increasing morbidity of its ageing population. How and the other directors had a high social price to pay, as their financial probity was impugned in a satirical piece in the *Sevenoaks Chronicle*:

> There's the Wesleyan Benefit Society of which I am a member – what a state that has got into, there are two sets of accounts, one for the Registrar and one for the club. I suppose they call that double entry. But no accountant has yet been found who can make the two statements agree.[74]

Ridicule as pointed as this, in the local newspaper, no doubt stemmed from the accusations of Brown and Bowyer and would have damaged the reputations of the SWBS's managers (and perhaps that of its remaining members) still further.

The faulty financial principles under which so many nineteenth-century friendly societies laboured were mainly to blame for their chronic mismanagement. Contemporary warnings abounded about the dangers, such as this observation, recorded in 1883, that 'As any friendly society grew older, unless there was a constant influx of new society members, the expenses would increase.'[75] But if their managers refused to admit to the long-term risks of an ageing and increasingly infirm membership, thus preventing the adoption of effective mitigation strategies, disaster regularly ensued. Unlike the Sevenoaks Local Board and its support from central government over the town drainage issue, the SWBS was simply not strong enough to withstand its growing financial burden. Attempts to cut costs to preserve societies' financial positions led, all too often, to their suffering embarrassing defeats in the courts and/or bitter attacks in the local press. Society and managerial reputations were lost, but, more importantly, ageing members who had regularly paid their dues were left without effective sickness cover when they were most likely to need it.

It is the pain of the social separation, the antithesis of the friendly society ideal, so firmly based on mutual trust, which is most apparent. That their fellow townspeople, including the respectable Hows, with whom they had lived, socialised and worshipped for many decades, should treat Fowler, Bowyer and Brown in such a heartless way was most upsetting. When it also represented a complete betrayal of Methodist integrity, Bowyer and Brown must have found it even harder to bear.

Worse, the SWBS's efforts to struggle on without any kind of bailout compromised the all-important trust and reputation that underpinned it, which in turn caused profound damage to many close and long-standing social relationships within the local Methodist church and across the district. It also illustrates that the ties of friendship, and the family and other trust networks that bound them, were not,

---

74 *SC*, 22 Dec. 1882, p. 3.
75 *SC*, 25 May 1883, p. 6.

perhaps, quite as strong in nineteenth-century west Kent as its inhabitants might have liked to believe.

One reason the Savings Bank's trustees may have been willing to bail it out was that they faced only a one-off payment to clear its debts, not the ongoing financial black hole faced by their counterparts at the SWBS. But the inescapable truth was that, by 1888, two important, long-standing Sevenoaks financial institutions had spectacularly collapsed within the last five years. Although the bank's depositors lost nothing, as the trustees made up the deficit, and the SWBS had shrunk to the extent that relatively few of its remaining members were directly affected by its demise, both events were sharp reminders that both insuring against ill-health and saving for some future rainy day were perilous endeavours. Successful self-help had very strict limits, in other words, especially for those at the lower end of west Kent's social and economic spectrum.

Local residents with long memories might have noted that the SWBS and the Savings Bank appeared as prone to failure as the Tonbridge and Sevenoaks banks had seventy years previously. Victorians might have congratulated themselves on the 'progress' they had made in many areas, such as rising disposable incomes and better public health provision, but the dangers inherent in trusting local financial organisations remained all too apparent in the eyes of their members and depositors. Who – or, more pertinently, what – could the artisans of west Kent trust, therefore, to remove those risks satisfactorily and achieve reasonable financial security for themselves and their families?

Overcoming the risks – government intervention
Solving those problems meant acknowledging, first, that the everyday risks faced by a still vulnerable, yet increasingly long-lived, population at the end of the nineteenth century remained worryingly unmitigated; and, secondly, that existing local financial and voluntary institutions remained too poorly capitalised, too badly run and too ill-regulated to be trusted to do the job with any guarantee of success – especially in the longer term. Or, to put it another way, successfully transferring risk from individual to institution was viable in the long term only if that body was sufficiently well managed and financially strong enough to bear those risks. Clearly too many local savings banks and friendly societies were not. Realistic alternatives were large national bodies secured by legislative control, or central government with its powers of financial intervention.

Eventually, Asquith's Liberal administration after 1906 was strong enough politically and economically to create the necessary institutional mechanisms that could accept those risks and thus obviate some perils faced by the elderly and the unemployed. As chancellor, Lloyd George began that process in 1909, when he introduced 'a meagre pension for the needy over the age of 70' (5s a week) and, two years later, 'helped to insure certain classes of workers against sickness and unemployment' through national insurance.[76] However, these innovations were not universally welcomed within Sevenoaks. When the National Insurance Act was introduced in 1911, Frank Robinson, vice-chairman of the Conservative-dominated Urban District Council, dismissed 'such an absurd Act'.[77] Others followed his lead, refusing to paste bills informing local people about the provisions of the Act – even though local Liberal politician and 'benefactor to the town' Francis Swanzy personally offered to meet the cost of doing so.[78]

But those were hiccups. The old age pension represented the removal of many of the financial risks the poor had suffered for years. When they were, simultaneously, replaced by a high degree of institutional trust it was no wonder that government-funded, and thus effectively risk-free, old age pensions and national insurance – the nascent welfare state – proved so popular. This was because poor people could now rely on a financial institution (the British Treasury) which was ready, willing and able to have transferred to it some, at least, of the major financial risks that had so plagued vulnerable people across the country throughout the nineteenth century.

76   A.J.P. Taylor, *English History 1914–45* (Harmondsworth, 1970), p. 25.

77   *KSC*, 21 June 1912, p. 10.

78   Killingray and Purves, *Dictionary*, p. 195.

Chapter 11

Knowledge and education

The main theme of this book is that, as some of the major risks of life, in particular the imperative to obtain adequate food, shelter, clothing and fuel, were largely overcome during the nineteenth century, and as disposable incomes rose, even some of the people towards the bottom of the social scale could start to exercise greater choice in how they lived their lives. The Factory Acts of the 1830s and 1840s, which regulated working hours and conditions, were also important drivers of this process. To put it in the broadest terms, the working classes started to become consumers as well as producers. Choice had always been 'the essence of the aristocratic life'; from the mid-nineteenth century or so onwards, the lower social groups slowly but surely began to enjoy it, too, most obviously in their capacity to afford and shop for more and better consumer goods.[1]

That inevitably points toward one long-running historical controversy, the 'Standard of Living Debate', or the attempts to pinpoint precisely *when* the growth in Gross Domestic Product per head that stemmed from the Industrial Revolution began significantly to benefit the working classes. Historians have divided between the pessimists, who 'claim no marked improvement in standards of living until the 1840s or 1850s', which we believe to be valid for west Kent, and the optimists, who, by contrast, 'believe that living standards were rising by the 1810s or 1820s, or even earlier'.[2] But how were such enhanced levels of choice to be achieved by the poorer sections of society? One highly approved Victorian strategy, which marked the idea of 'progress', was to provide opportunities for men and women of all classes to improve their education and knowledge. In a small market town such as Sevenoaks, which lacked a coherent working-class identity, this was made possible by top-down initiatives led and funded by the social elite.

---

1   Michael Levin, *The condition of England question: Carlyle, Mill, Engels* (Basingstoke, 1998), p. 8.

2   Clark Nardinelli, 'Industrial revolution and the standard of living', in David Henderson (ed.), *The concise encyclopædia of economics* (Indianapolis, IN, 2008), available at https://www.econlib.org/library/Enc1/IndustrialRevolutionandtheStandardofLiving.html.

Educating rich and poor

In the early nineteenth century people of all social classes perceived, as most do now, that one of the best ways to succeed in life and to expand their choices was to obtain an education, or at least relevant practical knowledge. That should in turn lead to a job, or a better job, conferring a higher wage, social status and respectability. Apprenticeships were an obvious example and there was much consternation in Sevenoaks in 1864 when it was discovered that the £18 Lady Margaret Boswell had bequeathed in 1682 so that 15 local poor boys could be 'taught to handicraft trades or employments' was not being spent to that purpose.[3]

But outside that tried and trusted avenue of advance, few poor families could easily obtain the requisite education or knowledge. Children were required, whenever they could, to contribute to the family budget, which even in the later nineteenth century impacted on school attendance. In October 1888, for example, 18 boys at Cobden Road school in Hartslands had still not begun the autumn term as they were away 'hopping'.[4]

It was just as difficult for children working in factories to gain useful education. Peter Nouaille claimed to pay 'every attention' to the 'instruction' of the 6- to 8-year-olds he employed at his silk mills at Greatness, Sevenoaks in 1816.[5] But he only provided one hour a day of schooling after the children had worked ten-hour shifts. That putative hour was, however, more than many other children from the lower classes of west Kent received, although there was a school in the Sevenoaks workhouse, which became a permanent feature of the new Union Workhouse at Sundridge after 1845.

Even if there was a demand for education, few local schools existed to provide it. Partly this was because many among the ruling elite, worried about the lower orders' potential to be inflamed by radical ideas, as had looked likely during the tumultuous 1790s and the Chartist upsurge fifty years later, believed the poor 'should only receive a very basic education – religion, social obedience and a few necessary occupational skills'.[6] A small minority of poor children in west Kent in the early nineteenth century benefited from charitable endeavour but few learned much more than they picked up in Sunday school, although 112 boys and girls were receiving 'gratuitous instruction' at the Wesleyan-Methodist Sunday school in Seal in 1835.[7]

The development of English elementary education was additionally contentious when local taxes were seen to support denominational schools. Many dissenters opposed maintaining Church-run schools on the rates. This deep division over

---

3   *SEG*, 31 May 1864, p. 5.

4   KHLC C/E/S/330/2/4, 4 Oct. 1888.

5   UKPP, Commons, *Report … Children Employed*, pp. 80–1.

6   Nigel Yates, Robert Hume and Paul Hastings, *Religion and society in Kent, 1640–1914* (Woodbridge, 1994), pp. 103–4.

7   Fox *et al.*, *Seal*, p. 162.

Figure 11.1 Westerham National Girls School pupils, 1889. The twenty or so girl pupils are formally posed – 'do not move' – with their teachers. The girls are not wearing uniforms. *Source*: Roger Quick collection.

the provision of education was marked by the British and Foreign School Society, founded in 1808 and more closely associated with nonconformists and Liberals, and the National Society, established in 1811 and supported mainly by Anglicans and the Tory party. The National Society helped establish some new schools in west Kent – that founded at Westerham in 1828, for example, taught 150 girls and boys. Lady Boswell's charitable endowment also provided £12 for the education of 15 'learned and of the poorer sort' children from Sevenoaks or Tonbridge.[8] The master probably taught the boys in his own house (which severely limited the number who could benefit); in 1795 just 20 boys attended, almost all from artisan families. A new school building in London Road, which still stands, was built in 1818.[9]

The foundation document of Sevenoaks School (1432) claimed that it taught 'all poor boys whatsoever coming there for the sake of learning' without charge.[10] But in 1819 headmaster John Wilgress revealed that 'the children are generally

---

8   Killingray and Purves, *Dictionary*, p. 17.

9   *Ibid.*, p. 98.

10   William Lambarde, *Perambulation of Kent* ([1570] Bath, 1970), p. 470.

Figure 11.2 Queen Elizabeth Grammar School (Sevenoaks School), *c.*1865. The image shows a group of younger boys, aged about 10–12, in front of the main school building, School House, on the High Street. It is unusual in that it shows an informal gathering of uniformed boys (many wearing mortar boards) talking in small groups rather than the more usual highly posed images of the period.
Source: National Monuments Record site, AL0176/029/01 © Historic England Archive.

sons of tradesmen and farmers' and that he had 'never had any application' from 'poor children in the neighbourhood'.[11] By the mid-nineteenth century most places in the school were allocated to the sons of better-off local parents and boarders from families located further afield. This led local tradesmen to complain 'that the advantage of this Free School is lost to the inhabitants of the town'.[12] It remained small (just 31 pupils in 1835, for example) until the late nineteenth century, when Daniel Birkett, 'an able, energetic headmaster', added a library, playing fields and

11   UKPP, Commons, *Commissioners of Inquiries into Charities in England and Wales, First Report on the Education of the Poor*, No. 83 (1819), pp. 220–7.

12   *SEG*, 23 Feb. 1864, p. 5; 31 May 1864, p. 5.

a gymnasium, and numbers rose to over 100.[13] A prospectus published sometime during his tenure (1878–98) informed parents that boys from 9 to 19 years of age would be admitted, whereupon they would be 'prepared for the universities, for the army and civil service examinations, or for business'. Fees for day boys were £5 or £6 a term, depending on age; boarders paid 55 or 60 guineas a term.[14]

Despite the temporary exigencies of the harvest and the more permanent difficulties that resulted from the highly regimented factory system, the working hours of adults and children were progressively limited during the nineteenth century, giving more opportunities for both education and leisure. Government legislation, prodded by various pressure groups such as the Ten Hours Movement of the 1830s, drove much of this process, most notably with the various Factory Acts, which limited the length of time women and children could be forced to work. Generally, 'average full time hours worked per week fell from 65 to 56 between 1856 and 1873' and 'by the 1870s the nine hour day was being widely conceded'.[15] This was a far cry from late eighteenth-century hours of employment in Kent, when agricultural labourers worked ten-hour days in summer and 'as long as daylight will permit' in winter.[16]

Minimum school leaving age in England

1870	10
1880	10
1893	11
1899	12
1918	14

The process of securing a basic education for children was advanced by successive Education Acts. The 1870 Act, riven with sectarian dispute, stated that every child must have 'a school place available to it in a building of reasonable quality and with a certificated head teacher'. During the 1880s school attendance became compulsory for every child until the age of ten. Charles Bassett was among a fortunate few, in 1873 remaining at the National School in Seal until he was aged 11.[17] This made

---

13   UKPP, Commons, *Abstract of Answers and Returns on the State of Education in England and Wales*, vols 1, 2 and 3, No. 62 (1835); Brian Scragg, *Sevenoaks School: a history* (Bath, 1993), p. 89.

14   Sevenoaks School Foundation Bequest brochure 2015; https://en.wikipedia.org/wiki/Sevenoaks_School; TNA ED 27/1974.

15   Hoppen, *Mid-Victorian generation*, p. 82.

16   John Boys, *General view of the agriculture of the county of Kent* (London, 1805), p. 195.

17   Pamela Horn, *The Victorian and Edwardian schoolchild* (Stroud, 2010), p. 7; Bassett, *Seal*, p. 3.

a great difference to working-class children. Before then, the risks of life were such that many poor children had little effective choice as to whether they received any education at all. Afterwards, younger children had no choice – in theory – *but* to go to school. Formal education might involve attending one of the new Board schools, of which nearly 3,700 had been created across the country by 1883.[18] St John's School, near Hartslands, was proposed in 1870 to serve the north of Sevenoaks, with a catchment of 600 local 'families of the labouring population ... [who] are members of the Church of England'.[19]

The problems of creating a school system from scratch to educate the junior members of a social group hitherto largely unused to such institutions were profound and many.[20] Cobden Road School, in Hartslands, opened in 1884 with 28 boys and 26 girls.[21] One important task, before teaching could even begin on Monday mornings, was to collect pupils' school fees, which were often behind even though they were generally only 1d or 2d a week. In 1885 the 'collection of school fees continues to give great trouble; several [boys] are in arrears'; in 1889 fee notices had to be sent to six different pupils, although paying the school pence was often impossible if a child's father was unemployed, as pupil George Skinner's was in 1886.[22] The following year the Poor Law Relieving Officer paid 4s outstanding fees for two of the Copper boys, from the family we met in chapter 8.[23] New admissions were prized and noted in the school Log Book, such as the 'two girls from a private school' who arrived in 1886.[24] A Catholic school was opened in Hartslands in 1881 but it closed less than twenty years later, partly because the diocese had difficulty funding it and partly because there were very few Roman Catholic children in that part of Sevenoaks. Its roll had fallen to just seven pupils by 1900.[25]

Maintaining discipline could be a problem. Three boys at Cobden Road were punished in January 1886 'for molesting one of the girls'.[26] But numbers had risen steadily to 124 boys by 1896; the curriculum had expanded, and an 1891 Inspector's report said the exam results 'showed considerable improvement'.[27] The School Board tried to play its part, too, moderating discipline by decreeing in 1891

---

18   Hoppen, *Mid-Victorian generation*, p. 599.

19   TNA ED 103/130/34, pp. 623–37.

20   Horn, *Schoolchild*, p. 23.

21   KHLC C/E/S/330/2/4, Cobden Road Board School Log Book, 1884–1910, 20 Oct. 1884.

22   KHLC C/E/S/330/2/4, 24 April 1885; 1 March 1889; 26 Nov. 1886.

23   KHLC C/E/S/330/2/4, 21 Jan. 1887.

24   KHLC C/E/S/330/2/4, 21 May 1886.

25   Southwark Diocesan Archives, William Cunningham. See also Sevenoaks Library B1227, letter from Christopher Bell to Elizabeth Purves, 26 June 2002.

26   KHLC C/E/S/330/2/4, 13 Jan. 1886.

27   KHLC C/E/S/330/2/4, 20 Dec. 1895; 16 June 1891.

that 'no one but the head teacher may inflict corporal punishment' and visiting the school regularly to chart its progress.[28]

Comparing the census data for Hartslands from 1871 and 1891 reveals the progress that was being made in educating especially younger local children. In 1871 86 per cent of Hartslands children aged 5–10 were identified by the census enumerator as 'scholars'. By 1891 that figure had risen to 100 per cent. And, of those aged 11–16, a third of the area's boys and over two thirds of its girls were in school in 1871, figures that rose to 56 per cent and 80 per cent, respectively, twenty years later, when the legal school leaving age was still just 10.[29] Ensuring the schools were properly funded, maintaining discipline and raising attainment indicates that the teachers did a remarkable job in difficult circumstances and must have been hard working and dedicated.

Adult education and libraries

Adults, too, had greater opportunities to use their free time to expand their knowledge; Charles Bassett, for example, gained a certificate in building construction at adult evening classes held at Lady Boswell's School in 1892–3.[30] Further opportunities were provided by the Sevenoaks Literary and Scientific Institution, with evening classes offered from 1850. From inception it had 'the idea of benefitting working men' and it began with 328 members, although that number shrank steadily until 1876, when it had just 89 and became defunct, for reasons that are unclear. Subscriptions were 8s a year for subscribers and 4s for apprentices and those under 16. In 1860 its library held 2,132 volumes and ten lectures were given on subjects ranging from the 'British Navy' to the 'Present State of Europe'.[31]

Public libraries also enhanced educational opportunities for both adults and children. However, establishing such apparently innocuous institutions had the unexpected consequence, perhaps, of stoking the ancient civic and cultural rivalries between Sevenoaks and Tonbridge. It is worth tracing this process in some detail.

A 'few private and subscription libraries', such as the Institution, had existed, on and off, in Sevenoaks for many years, but it lacked the free facility that Tonbridge had enjoyed since 1882. That cost over £7,000 and was heralded by Edward Cazalet, the local Liberal candidate for Mid-Kent, as advancing the cultural merit of Tonbridge over other local towns: 'The fact [...] that Tonbridge was one of the smallest towns that had succeeded in establishing a Free Library, greatly enhanced the merit of the undertaking, and was especially creditable to the public spirit of its citizens.'[32] In 1900 it moved to its current premises, nearer the railway station, so

---

28 KHLC C/E/S/330/2/4, 8 July 1891. James German visited on 16 Oct. 1895.

29 Census Return for 1871: Sevenoaks; Census Return for 1891: Sevenoaks.

30 Bassett, *Seal*, p. 12.

31 KHLC U1000/32/O3, 1860.

32 *KSC*, 28 July 1882, p. 6.

SEVENOAKS
Literary and Scientific Institution.

Patrons.

THE MOST HONORABLE THE MARQUESS CAMDEN,
THE RIGHT HONORABLE EARL AMHERST,   THE RIGHT HONORABLE EARL STANHOPE.

Officers & Committee for the Year 1860.

President.
THE RIGHT HONORABLE LORD VISCOUNT HOLMESDALE.

Vice-Presidents.

ADAMS, R. E., Esq.	COLE, G. C., Esq.	NORTHEY, Colonel.
BADDELEY, H., Esq.	FRANKS, G., Esq.	NOUAILLE, P., Esq.
CURTEIS, Rev. T.	LAMBARDE, W., Esq.	PETLEY, C. R. C., Esq.
CROFTS, Rev. C.	MOUNTFORD, Rev. J.	ROGERS, J., Esq.

Trustees.

G. FRANKS, Esq.   C. PALMER, Esq.   Mr. B. BURTON.   Mr. J. FITNESS.

Treasurers.
MESSRS. CHARLES AND JOSEPH PALMER.

Auditors.
Mr. JOHN SHEWEN,   Mr. EDWYN EVANS CRONK.

Honorary Librarians.   Honorary Secretaries.
Mr. JENKINS, Mr. E. PALMER.   Mr. T. HANCOCK, Mr. J. SHEWEN, Jun.

Committee.

ARNOLD, Mr. W.	CORKE, Mr. S.	HOW, Mr. T.
ASHDOWN, Mr. G.	CORKE, Mr. I.	HOW, Mr. G.
BIRD, Mr. W.	DON, Mr. J.	LOVELAND, Mr. W.
BRIGGS, Mr. R. R.	ELY, Mr. G.	PAYNE, Mr. G.

At the Tenth Annual General Meeting of the Members, held on Thursday, January 26th, 1860, H. BADDELEY, Esq., in the Chair, the following REPORT of the Committee for the past year was read by the Secretary :—

Your Committee for 1859, in presenting their Tenth Annual Report, will proceed to call the attention of this meeting to the following statement of the number of members.

At the close of last year	225
Withdrawn during 1859	80
	145
Elected during 1859	37
	182

The total number of enrolled members since the commencement of the Institution, 1850, is 1065.

Figure 11.3 The Sevenoaks Literary and Scientific Institution's annual report, 1860. It is noteworthy that the patrons, presidents and vice-presidents were almost all upper-class Anglicans, including the rector, Rev. Thomas Curteis, while most of the committee were middle-class nonconformists, such as William Arnold and Thomas and George How.
Source: Sevenoaks Library, U1000/32/O3.

'convenient for those travelling from the rural parts of the district' – and further afield, too, potentially, since Sevenoaks was only ten minutes or so away by train. It was opened by Lord Avebury, the 'parliamentary champion of public libraries', and the Council re-emphasised its prestige by naming the adjoining road Avebury Avenue.[33] Its chairman also saw it as a beacon to attract users from competitor towns further afield, as he 'hoped the young people of Tonbridge and neighbourhood would make all the use of the premises that they could'.[34] This was a red rag to Sevenoaks. The deficiency in cultural status had long been felt, and keenly, by its elite, one Local Board member remarking how 'The Tonbridge Free Library was doing ten times as much good with its gross expenditure of £166 than the Sevenoaks Town Library was doing with its £60.'[35]

Benjamin Harrison of Ightham

Harrison, writing sometime before 1907, remembered being a member of the Institution in the early 1850s. He 'used to walk over every fortnight to exchange books. On leaving the Institute, I frequently went into the Black Boy Inn to hear Old George, a local character, read aloud the [Crimean] war news. The paper from which he read came to Sevenoaks by the evening coach. I happened to be in Sevenoaks on the day after the Alma battle, when Sebastopol was reported taken. Papers could not be obtained for love or money.' The Battle of the Alma took place on 20 September 1854 and was a key engagement of the Crimean War.

Source: Edward R. Harrison, Harrison of Ightham. A book about Benjamin Harrison, of Ightham, Kent, made up principally of extracts from his notebooks and correspondence (London, 1928), p. 41.

It took until 1905 and a £3,000 gift from philanthropist Andrew Carnegie before Sevenoaks had its own free public lending library. Lord Avebury presided at its official opening, too, in a clear attempt to achieve civic status on a par with Tonbridge's, calling it 'a great addition to Sevenoaks'. Henry Swaffield, who had donated the land for the building, intriguingly drew a direct parallel between the library and the town's sewage system constructed over twenty years earlier, since the large loans the town raised then 'have been attended with such excellent results'.[36]

---

33   G. Hodge, 'Tonbridge free public library, 1881–1900', *Archæologia Cantiana*, CIII (1986), pp. 53–68.
34   *SEG*, 30 Oct. 1900, p. 2.
35   *SEG*, 2 Jan. 1894, p. 5.
36   *SC*, 17 Nov. 1905, p. 8.

The new investment in the civic culture of the library, he argued, was as important as the heavier capital cost of better drainage, because both provided clear benefits to the town's image, status and civic identity as it sought to keep up with Tonbridge's unambiguous challenge. Failing to provide an adequate range of cultural choices for the town's residents and visitors (especially the well-heeled ones) carried with it the serious reputational risk, in other words, of compromising or even reversing its recent economic and social success.

Adult educational facilities such as the library and the earlier Literary Institution (founded 1849), were actively encouraged, and sometimes funded, by the authorities. They were generally top-down, paternalistic initiatives to help the working classes help themselves, thereby (in theory) reducing the risks in their lives. A fortunate by-product of that process might be that west Kent would become a happier, more quiescent society altogether. But working-class people had their own spokespeople and their own leisure agendas, which might or might not conform to the expectations of respectable society. How the young and poor sought to enjoy themselves, and with what results, will be a focus of the next chapter.

Chapter 12

Leisure

Leisure – choice, risk and containment?

Before the nineteenth century leisure was largely the privilege of the monied classes. The over-worked, ill-paid labourers, servants and artisans who constituted most of the population had limited time for leisure. As one historian succinctly put it: 'Leisure time is clearly constricted by type and hours of work.'[1] Those constrictions altered during the nineteenth century, more rapidly after 1870, due to changes in hours and types of work, rising standards of living and a growing middle class.

This profound change may also be examined using the risk/choice approach. Obviously, enhanced leisure opportunities represented a significant expansion of choice. But how those hours were spent, unconstrained by the pressures of work, also had the potential to undermine or sometimes even challenge the accepted social order; those posing the greatest risk were undoubtedly the younger members of the lower classes, especially if leisure pursuits carried some possibility of risk transfer too. November 5th celebrations were an annual headache for the authorities during much of our period; in Tunbridge Wells in 1863, for example, 'a mob insisted upon rolling tar barrels about the streets, and the efforts of the police to stop this were resisted with the utmost, all rule and authority being entirely ignored'.[2] Such episodes, although they became much less frequent, illustrate how some leisure pursuits not only provided opportunities for working-class elements to challenge civil authority but could also become the settings for highly contested and often highly symbolic processes of risk transfer – which is one of the key themes of this chapter. Disorder, for example, could not only pose tangible threats to life, limb or property but might also enable risks to be transferred symbolically, simply by those lower orders exerting their own preferences (for example, in how they spent their money or their time), in ways that incurred the disapproval of their employers or social superiors. Such choices, especially when made collectively, also had the

---

1   Gareth Stedman Jones, 'Class expression versus social control? A critique of recent trends in the social history of "leisure"', *History Workshop*, 4 (1977), p. 169.

2   *SEG*, 10 Nov. 1863, p. 5. For more, see Conley, *The unwritten law*, pp. 35–7.

potential to compromise the image and reputations of the towns where they lived, which in turn carried significant implications for their economic wellbeing and social standing.

That prospect deeply concerned the governing classes and they always sought to ensure, somehow, that the various leisure pastimes enjoyed by their social subordinates never got out of control. New institutions of civil order were introduced through the nineteenth century, demanded and welcomed by a growing property-owning electorate who had a vested interest in social and economic security. Representative authorities could respond morally and politically by endorsing (while still regulating) certain activities, such as theatres, certain entertainments and the use of public spaces. Or they might seek to suppress or to sanitise any pastime that might lead to disorder. Examples examined in more detail below include the annual Sevenoaks Fair, discontinued through legal process; bare-knuckle boxing matches, suppressed by law enforcement; the November 5th celebrations, sanitised by public opinion; and the enforcement of licensing hours for public houses.

But we should not assume the ruling classes and institutions used some form of pervasive social control to deny the working classes access to leisure pursuits that they traditionally or customarily enjoyed. 'Social control' was instead an ever-present and more multi-layered presence than that, running through society in varying forms and initiated and shaped by individuals, factions and belief systems. It was firmly based on collective ideas of respectability and the civic, economic and cultural standing of the town, which spurred official measures to manage leisure. To a large extent the poor had always organised their own limited leisure time, which included conversation, music, the pub, games of skill and chance or simply time at home with their families. That continued post-1870 as changes in working conditions gave the working classes increased opportunities for leisure, much of which they collectively organised in rival team games, such as football and cricket, conducted within agreed sets of rules. Perhaps the best term to describe the ordering of leisure in nineteenth-century west Kent is not social control but what would later be called self-regulation.

We must beware, too, of endorsing too rigid a class-based narrative here. Although different leisure activities tended to be followed by different social classes, they were also shaped by personal inclination, perceived family needs, economic circumstances, health and moral and religious beliefs. For example, a rural labourer might be temperate in mind and body, eschewing the beer shop frequented by his workmates, instead digging his vegetable plot to increase his income because he was more concerned for his family's welfare and the future of his children. Likewise, a wealthier person's priorities might be focused on literature, music or understanding the natural world; they might be opposed to the conspicuous consumption and indifferent to the condescension of their prosperous neighbours. To try to generalise about the ideas and attitudes of the elites, the middling sort and the working classes without accurate personal data would be seriously misleading.

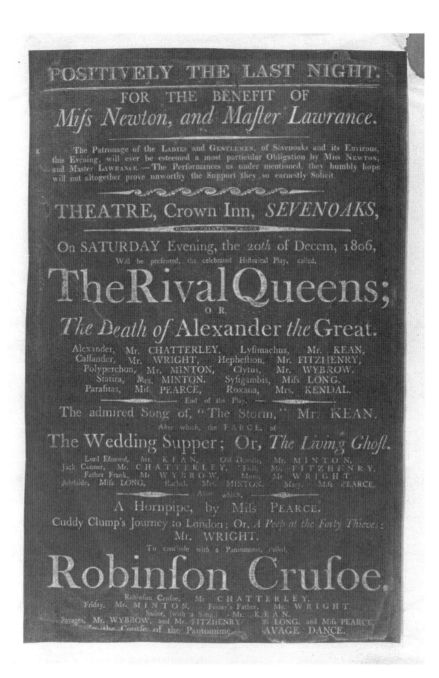

Figure 12.1 Sevenoaks playbill featuring Edmund Kean. His first outing on the Sevenoaks stage took place when he was in his late teens, 'where he played in tragedy, comedy and pantomime', with little hint of the star billing that was to come. An extant playbill from the period records the tragedy as *The Rival Queens*, the farce as *The Wedding Supper* and the pantomime as *Robinson Crusoe*. *Source*: Sevenoaks Library, SC 891.

The arts in west Kent

Although Sevenoaks was a small rural town, proximity to London via a main road and a social elite combined to promote local theatre. In the late eighteenth and early nineteenth centuries Sevenoaks was something of a theatrical hotspot, one venue being an 'old barn at the rear of Buckhurst Lodge'. In 1775 a 'company of comedians from Sevenoaks' was performing at Town [West] Malling and, the following year, productions were staged at the New Theatre, Sevenoaks, although its location is unknown. In 1779 impresario Samuel Jerrold (1749–1820) put on *The Strategem* (sic) at the same venue as a charity fundraiser after a serious fire in the town.[3] Renowned regency actor Edmund Kean (1789–1833) also performed at Sevenoaks, probably with Jerrold's company in December 1806, without incident. His next visit was very different, immediately following his triumphant first appearance on the London stage in *The Merchant of Venice* in January 1814, when:

> he found a strolling company at Sevenoaks in anything but a flourishing condition. He had known the manager and a few of the actors in his early days; and he, now the great Mr Kean, played Shylock in a barn for their benefit. The rush was very great, and a large majority were obliged to content themselves with the sound of his voice outside.[4]

In 1833 William Knight recorded that 'a company of players have engaged the room above the coffee house for a theatre'; in 1874 the Sevenoaks Amateur Dramatic Society, assisted by Lily Stone and Alice La Feuillade, 'Both of the Principal London Theatres', were staging *Old Phil's Birthday* at the Royal Crown Hotel Assembly Room, the venue that was the social centre of Sevenoaks for more than 100 years.[5]

The social world of dinners, balls, dances, card games and other private entertainments all cost money, sometimes a good deal of money. They were made possible by household servants. Private and public functions took place in the large houses and in the coffee house in Sevenoaks. At the New Concert Room in the town (location again unknown) concerts were hosted in 1790 and 1792, the latter being directed by a Mr Hindmarsh from London, showing that both musical and theatrical productions could attract London-based artists to perform before a Sevenoaks audience.[6] This was especially impressive before the railway arrived in 1862, given how difficult it was to travel before then.

---

3   Christopher Rayner, *Sevenoaks past: with the villages of Holmesdale* (Chichester, 1997), p. 89; *KG*, 18 Feb. 1775, p. 1; 10 Feb. 1776, p. 4; 13 Feb. 1779, p. 1; P.H. Highfill *et al.*, *A biographical dictionary of actors, actresses, musicians, dancers and other stage personnel in London 1660–1800*, vol. 8 (Carbonville, IL, 1982), pp. 156–7.

4   Frederick Hawkins, *The life of Edmund Kean* (London, 1869), vol. 2, p. 825.

5   Private archives, Knight, *Diaries*, vol. 1, 7–8 May 1833. Robert Herries may well have recorded the same event; private archives at St Julian's, Sevenoaks, Herries Papers. Robert Herries to John Charles Herries, 1833. Sevenoaks Library D65.

6   BL, Cup.21.g.36/47; *KG*, 19 Jan. 1790, p. 1; 25 Dec. 1792, p. 4; Edwards, *Recollections*, p. 38.

Music and choirs, based primarily on ability rather than social class, brought together members of the elite and the middling sort. A choir sang for George III at Montreal Park in 1778, and Sevenoaks Choral Society's repertoire in 1847 included works by Handel, Beethoven and – in a slightly different vein – a Mr Kemp singing 'the old arm chair'. Events such as these always took place in respectable venues, such as the Royal Crown.[7] By 1911 Sevenoaks boasted two cinemas, at Tub's Hill and the High Street, the latter supplying 'the long-felt want of a permanent and regular place of amusement in the district'.[8] The Sackvilles soon embraced the glamorous new movie business when they allowed Edison's English Company to film a short drama, 'A Daughter of Romany', in Knole Park.[9]

Those cultural activities were entirely peaceful. But artistic ability and performance could sometimes generate social class conflict in west Kent. An example was the election of a new organist at St Nicholas in April 1846, in which a local woman received more votes than an accomplished musician from a London church. Town tradesmen who supported the local and eventually successful candidate Elizabeth Morphew, daughter of William Morphew, suffered loss of business as some of their opponents withheld 'their custom'. This resulted in a letter from 'A Ratepayer', who denounced those who thought tradesmen could be treated as serfs required to vote in line with their customers. The *Maidstone Journal* described how 'the greatest excitement prevails in the town and neighbourhood as to the issue of the contest', while the *Kentish Gazette* considered that the election prompted the largest vestry meeting 'ever known in the parish, most of the nobility and gentry being present'.[10]

Leisure and the lower orders

Patrician leisure pursuits such as the theatre were unlikely to cause problems or disorder; plebeian ones far more so. They carried potential risks for broader west Kent society such that, during the nineteenth century, previous paternalist tolerance was superseded by 'a sour impatience with plebeian culture as morally offensive, socially subversive and a general impediment to progress'.[11] How and when the authorities across west Kent, with the active encouragement and connivance of polite local society, intervened successfully to enhance the general civility of the area by preventing riots and many other types of disorder (including bad moral behaviour) from taking place is a key theme of this section.

---

7   Killingray and Purves, *Dictionary*, p. 32; Sevenoaks Library D549.

8   *SC*, 18 Nov. 1910, p. 5.

9   http://m.imdb.com, accessed 14 November 2017; *The Kinematogram*, vol. 7, p. 15.

10   *MJ*, 7 April 1846, p. 3; *KG*, 28 April 1846, p. 3; Dissenters at the vestry meeting opposed payment to the church organist from the rates.

11   Peter Bailey, *Leisure and class in Victorian England: rational recreation and the contest for control, 1830–1885* (London, 1978), p. 3.

Figure 12.2 Charles Essenhigh Corke 'Sevenoaks Annual Fair', *c*.1850. The Fair is spread across the then market square and high street. In the background is Richardson's Theatre, a touring company set up by the actor John Richardson (1766–1836). By the 1830s there were several companies under that name which toured the fairs of London and the nearby towns.
Source: F. Richards, *Old Sevenoaks* (Sevenoaks, 1901), p. 16.

Fairs were a prime example of how the poor managed their own leisure, that in Tonbridge in 1843 offering a 'Ladies young or old' running race for a new straw bonnet and climbing a pole for a leg of mutton. William Richmond remembers how, in the late 1840s, the October Sevenoaks Fair 'drew together all classes in a healthy way, out of doors' as the High Street 'was entirely given up to booths, gipsy caravans and other romantic paraphernalia'. In 1842 it featured a theatre and 'wonderful performances of puppets'. Its chief attraction, however, was a menagerie, but the lioness, having recently 'produced a litter of five handsome cubs', sadly died during the event. Controlling what took place was always difficult as all the entertainers were self-employed itinerants and no-one, apparently, took any overall responsibility for it.[12]

The Fair thus implied barely constrained social liberty that could range from 'the bold musician … grinding away at his instrument with a roar that filled the

---

12 Killingray and Purves, *Sevenoaks*, pp. 53–4; Tonbridge Public Library Yellow Box No. 1; Anna Stirling, *The Richmond papers from the correspondence of George Richmond and his son William Richmond* (London, 1926), p. 109; Sevenoaks Library L668, C.J. Knight, 'Reminiscences' (manuscript, 1934), p. 12.

whole ground' to an altogether less innocent side.[13] A poem of 1783, *Se'noak Fair – An Extemporal Burlesque*, depicts young men and women 'fearless of masters' or mistresses' frown', because 'the time is their own. Blest freedom'. Eventually its author 'spied a fair maid with an innocent dimple'. After a brief encounter in Knole Park, he 'tip't her a fee and took leave of Miss Crab', which presumably meant she was a prostitute who left him with a sexually transmitted disease.[14]

Seventy years later middle-class ambitions for a 'respectable' commercial town viewed the annual fair somewhat differently. By the 1860s shopkeepers and middle-class residents had become disenchanted with its smell, noise and mess and the brief period of commercial competition it represented. New legislation, the Fairs Act 1871, gave them the opportunity they needed. Its preamble implicitly acknowledged fairs' potential for risk transfer as it asserted that many were 'unnecessary, are the cause of grievous immorality and are very injurious to the inhabitants'. In 1874 they managed to abolish it altogether, even though many poorer people demanded that it remain, not least because its stalls sold cheap clothing. Examining the names of those petitioning for the abolition or retention of the fair reveals profound social divisions in contemporary Sevenoaks. The latter group were on average forty years old, had artisanal or unskilled jobs such as carpentry or labouring and lived in working-class districts such as Hartslands and St John's. The former, on the other hand, were on average eight years older, had middle-class occupations (such as clerk) or were retailers.[15]

An altogether more spectacular entertainment was the circus, with exotic animals and performers, which made more regular appearances in Sevenoaks from the 1850s. Early shows were small, but by the 1880s 'Lord' George Sanger, rival to P.T. Barnum and 'Buffalo' Bill Cody as they sought to put on the most spectacular shows then possible, visited the town.[16] In 1888 Sanger's programme included gladiators, kangaroo and ostrich hunts, Buffalo Bill and his Cowboys and 'the best clowns that have ever appeared before the public'. Admission prices catered for every pocket, ranging from 3s to just 6d.[17] However, the formal circus performance was unlike the informal, chaotic fair in several key respects. It was organised in a defined, albeit temporary space (the Big Top) for a specific period to a set programme choreographed by the revealingly named ring*master*. This professional impresario sought to make money, something that would have been impossible had any event

---

13   J.L. Peyton, *Rambling reminiscences of a residence abroad: England, Guernsey etc.* (Staunton, VA, 1888), p. 223.

14   Julia De Vaynes, *The Kentish garland*, vol. 2 (Hereford, 1882), pp. 808–9.

15   Killingray and Purves, *Sevenoaks*, pp. 53–4; Hugh Cunningham, 'The metropolitan fairs: a case study in the social control of leisure', in A.P. Donajgrodzki (ed.), *Social control in nineteenth century Britain* (London, 1977), p. 173; TNA HO 45/9367/36927; Census Return for 1871: Sevenoaks.

16   *ODNB*, 'Sanger, George (*c.* 1825–1911)'.

17   *SC*, 17 Aug. 1888, p. 1.

got out of hand and the performers subsequently barred from the town. Its audience was seated according to ticket price, thereby emphasising established hierarchy and order. The circus therefore enhanced the choice of entertainment in Sevenoaks for residents of practically every age and social class. It did so by superficially replicating the style of the Fair, while almost entirely transferring the reputational and other risks inherent in the performance from the town to the entrepreneur. He in turn was quite happy to accept and manage them successfully in return for a satisfactory financial return. It shows, yet again, just how far the process of sanitisation had gone in west Kent by the late nineteenth century.

Holidays of a week or longer were an important extension of the leisure time (of just a few hours) that could be devoted to fairs and circuses. The rich always had the time and money to take holidays, exemplified by the lengthy aristocratic Grand Tour around Europe. Shorter breaks in England and further afield were also regular features of the lives of the upper classes. In 1860 the Marquess of Camden enjoyed a trip to France that included nights in hotels in Paris, Boulogne and Calais.[18] The working classes rarely had money or spare time for such leisurely pursuits. However, after completing a job in 1882 carpenter Charles Bassett embarked on a strenuous walking tour to Sussex to visit his mother and other relations. The first day he walked 35 miles to his uncle's house in Haywards Heath, then to Brighton, then back to Haywards Heath and on to Tunbridge Wells. He finally took a well-earned train back to Sevenoaks.[19]

By 1867 some believed that the Sevenoaks Fair had already been superseded by the cheap excursions to distant places that railway travelling had introduced. So Ightham pub landlord William Mist organised a rail excursion for 550 people to Portsmouth in July 1887 to see the Royal Navy at anchor. Such activities were always acceptable as they had undoubtedly respectable purposes and were professionally organised. Holidays for the lower classes were officially introduced by the Bank Holiday Act of 1871, which provided four official days a year with the aim of rewarding good behaviour among employees and underpinning corporate culture.[20]

Turf, pitch and ring

Before the explosion of organised sport in England after 1870, which resulted from growing working-class demand for leisure opportunities, three sports predominated. Horse racing, cricket and bare-knuckle pugilism, all popular with spectators, generated serious sums of money, including from gambling, as will become evident. Horse races were held wherever there was available land. The meetings, which were the occasion

---

18   Private archives at St Julian's, Sevenoaks, Herries papers. Robert Herries to John Charles Herries, dd. Baden Baden, 1 July 1834; KHLC U840/E42, Bundle of hotel bills, 1860.

19   Bassett, *Seal*, pp. 7–8.

20   KHLC U840/E42, 22–25 May 1860; *Kentish Mercury*, 19 Oct. 1867, p. 6; *SC*, 29 July 1887, p. 5; KHLC Q/CSu/3/9, 11 Aug. 1876.

for holidays, were watched over by the police as they sought to identify and deter thieves and pickpockets. Summer race meetings were held on Tunbridge Wells Common, including the Ladies Subscription Purse, which, in 1797, amounted to six guineas.[21] Meetings taking place in 1816 and 1821 were also enjoyed by those further down the social scale.[22] And the cricket match on the Sevenoaks Vine in 1782, between the Duke of Dorset's 11 and All England, was played for 1,000 guineas; spectators no doubt bet much on the result.[23] But cricket fixtures, like race meetings, even where large sums changed hands, were run by and for the aristocracy and gentry of the town. They were therefore always decorous enough for genteel ladies to attend, such as Elizabeth Leathes, who was 'much entertained with the sight of the company', if not the game itself, when she watched a 'great cricket match' at Sevenoaks in July 1791.[24]

Despite a game on the Vine being watched by 10,000 people in 1773, the cricket club faded in the early nineteenth century, folded in 1831 and was not reformed until 1848.[25] Sevenoaks' position as one of the most important cricket venues in the county had been eclipsed well before the (merged) Kent County Cricket Club was formed in 1870. Cricket's west Kent centre shifted decisively in 1869 to the Angel ground at Tonbridge, which was the location for the Kent county side's nursery after 1897. Kent also played at the Nevill Ground, Tunbridge Wells, from 1901, despite the pavilion being burned down by suffragettes in 1913.[26]

Pugilism was an accepted high-stakes pastime in the eighteenth century. In 1785 *The Times* reported that 'a smart battle' had been fought at Sevenoaks between a butcher from Bath and a baker from Rotherhithe for a purse of 50 guineas, won by the former after a 'severe contest of an hour and twenty minutes'.[27] But by the mid-nineteenth century pugilism was disreputable enough to be suppressed. Regulation, especially the Marquess of Queensberry's famous set of rules, published in 1867, made boxing socially acceptable again by 1900. But before then the authorities often intervened to prevent bouts taking place because they compromised reputations for respectability and could, conceivably, pose a threat to law and order. Many fights were staged covertly. One that was not was a 'Great Prize Fight', which was billed to take place at Tonbridge in 1867 between the famous, or infamous, Wormald and Baldwin. However, Kent police immediately arrested Baldwin and his trainer at Bat & Ball, Sevenoaks; both were bound over to keep the peace for £50 each.[28] Blood

---

21 Tunbridge Wells Library Local Studies 'Race Course' file, 10–11 Aug. 1797.

22 KHLC U2093/E1, 20 Aug. 1816; 28–29 Aug. 1821; *MJ*, 3 Aug. 1830, p. 1.

23 Sevenoaks Library D25, 3–4 July 1782.

24 Norfolk Record Office BOL 2/10/739.

25 Kenneth Smart, *Cricket on the vine, 1734–1984* (Sevenoaks, 1984), pp. 18, 20.

26 http://www.kentcricket.co.uk/the-club/history; http://www.espncricinfo.com, both accessed 16 May 2018; *Pall Mall Gazette*, 11 April 1913, p. 3.

27 *The Times*, 2 Sept. 1785, p. 3.

28 *MJ*, 29 April 1867, p. 7.

Figure 12.3 Arson at Nevill Ground, Tunbridge Wells, 1913. The pavilion, pictured here, was totally gutted after the incendiary attack in April 1913, just before the start of the cricket season, when 'A photograph of Mrs Pankhurst was found in close proximity'. The building was rebuilt in time for Kent's matches during Tunbridge Wells cricket week that July.
Source: Photograph by Percy Lankester on Postcard, 1913 © The March of the Women Collection / Mary Evans Picture Library.

sports such as dogfighting and cockfighting also took place, for example at the Lower Crown Inn in Sevenoaks in 1739, although a lecturer at Goudhurst in 1859 was pleased that they had by then 'fallen into disuse as national amusements'. Such illegal or disreputable activities often centred on local pubs, as they were the only covert spaces available to working-class people for such purposes.[29]

'Remember, remember' – the civic dimensions of leisure

Another public event that could and often did get seriously out of hand was the annual Gunpowder Plot celebrations.[30] Challenges to public order could be mounted from boisterous or criminal elements within the town or from neighbouring locations; both are especially important because they shed additional light on the

29   *MJ*, 15 Feb. 1859, p. 2.

30   For more, see Iain Taylor, '"The whole of the proceedings were very orderly": Gunpowder Plot celebrations, civic culture and identity in some smaller Kent towns, 1860–1890', *Urban History*, 43 (2016), pp. 517–38.

Figure 12.4 Sevenoaks 'Bonfire Boys', 1884. One solution to violent disorder on 5 November was to make a local society (often called the Bonfire Boys) responsible for it. In 1880 the Sevenoaks Society organised a 300-strong procession and a 'monster bonfire' in the town and 'the whole of the proceedings were very orderly'.
Source: Sevenoaks Society, D0596.

risk transfer process. Another hazard regularly faced by the poor, especially, if they transgressed the law, was violent (corporal) punishment of some sort by the authorities. During those celebrations, however, this risk could briefly be transferred, as the narrow, badly lit streets of west Kent provided perfect cover for those bent on fomenting disorder by attacking the forces of law and order. The police were often badly stretched on that particular night, Chief Constable Ruxton candidly admitting as late as 1880 to 'the difficulty of finding constables', for example, which further reduced the risks run by the perpetrators.[31]

31   KHLC C/PO/1/4, Kent Police Letter Book, 1 Nov. 1880.

Tunbridge Wells provides an example of what could happen. In 1870 'a riot on a small scale ensued' after the police took possession of lit tar barrels and the officers were stoned.[32] Polite west Kent society deplored such conduct and hoped for peaceful displays as a measure of civic pride. Encouraging such civility might also, they thought, improve the behaviour of the local townspeople. In 1873 the *South Eastern Gazette*'s Tonbridge reporter stated, with an element of one-upmanship, that in his town 'A large number of people were present from Tunbridge Wells, where no demonstration had been arranged.'[33] Eight years later, however, civic pride gave way to sarcastic aspersions on the respectability of some (presumably lower-class) visitors from the neighbouring town, when the Tonbridge display 'was somewhat marred by a party of Tunbridge Wells "lambs", who came over ... purposely to create a disturbance, although they were not very successful'.[34] Such behaviour also compromised the respectability of the rival town itself. Small-town civic rivalries over orderliness, market days, administrative buildings, the provision of libraries, swimming pools and public parks were part of the process of modernisation and the quest for respectability.

Elite pursuits

The possession of large estates, or social access to those who owned such, made possible field sports. Shooting and hunting on horses, often involving local farmers and usually reliant on an army of servants and paid beaters, were important in nineteenth-century Britain and continued well into the twentieth century. Shooting was a popular pursuit in which the roles of those participating and those facilitating their enjoyment were clearly segregated. Near Sevenoaks in 1806 'four gentlemen' competed in a pigeon shooting match for a silver cup, although in 1821 Robert Herries found neighbour Francis Woodgate's noisy sport at Underriver House 'quite intolerable'.[35]

Today hunting is normally associated with foxes, but stags were the more frequent prey before the nineteenth century. Its gruesome nature is indicated, admittedly in the extreme, by a hunt near Sevenoaks in 1793, when 'a hound was perceived with a human head in its mouth, which was proved once to have belonged to a boy lost from [a] workhouse'.[36] Anyone wanting to hunt foxes in the nineteenth century (and later) needed the time, the social position and the economic capacity even to be invited to do so. In west Kent many aspired to join the chase but few were chosen, a fact lamented by 'An Old Farmer' in 1867, who pointed out that

---

32 *Tonbridge Telegraph*, 12 Nov. 1870, p. 2.

33 *SEG*, 8 Nov. 1873, p. 3.

34 *SEG*, 7 Nov. 1881, p. 5.

35 Private archives at St Julian's, Sevenoaks, Herries Papers. Robert Herries to John Charles Herries, 11 Oct. 1821.

36 William Page (ed.), *The Victoria county history of the county of Kent*, vol. 1 (London, 1908), p. 485.

many 'respectable tradesmen … are particularly fond of the pastime, but from many causes are debarred from following the hounds'.[37]

Hunts were instrumental in encouraging local point-to-point race meetings, known as 'steeple-chases', such as that which took place in 1866 between Greatness and Otford, easily facilitated by the railway. It was properly organised with a grandstand that 'commanded an uninterrupted view of the entire course' and proved very successful, attracting 'heavy trains from London and the large attendance of the local population', many of whom, of every social class, would have taken the opportunity to bet on the results. Helpfully, the starting prices were printed in newspapers alongside the runners and riders, which not only acknowledged the risks involved in gambling but also conferred a measure of social respectability upon the entire enterprise.[38]

Directing leisure?

The growth of popular leisure after 1870 was accompanied by the creation of clubs with rules and subscriptions, a means of paying for facilities and managing membership. The latter can be seen in the subscriptions and donations list of Sevenoaks Town Band town for 1912: out of 300 members only three lived in Hartslands, home to nearly one tenth of the town's population. Similarly, Sevenoaks Cricket Club had just three Hartslands residents appearing on a similar list. One was Charles William French, a clerk at a local decorating firm. A long-standing club member and a good cricketer, he supported the Tariff Reform League and worked for the re-election of Sevenoaks Conservative MP Henry Forster in 1910, which may have made him socially acceptable for club membership.[39]

Civic, largely elite, control over leisure activities was possible in those areas directly subject to local administration. For example, by mid-century the potentially disruptive influence of gambling among the lower orders was perceived as a growing problem. In 1845, nearly 200 'Clergy, Magistrates and other Residents in Tunbridge Wells' demanded the race meetings in the town be discontinued because 'they foster a spirit of gambling; […] they bring together a number of disorderly characters; and […] lead to riot and drunkenness'.[40] By 1851 their campaign had succeeded. However, a rival immediately seized the opportunity to create Tonbridge Racecourse, on ground near the Castle and the River Medway 'that appears to be well adapted for the purpose … easy of access from the middle of the town'. There is also no mistaking the civic pride – and implicit one-upmanship – in the lengthy article devoted to the new sporting event and its venue.[41]

---

37 *MJ*, 25 Feb. 1867, p. 5.

38 *MJ*, 30 April 1866, p. 6.

39 Sevenoaks Library D62, Report of the Committee, 30 Sept. 1912; D25, 1909 season; Census Return for 1911: Sevenoaks; *SC*, 13 March 1908, p. 8; 14 Jan. 1910, p. 13.

40 Tunbridge Wells Library Local Studies 'Race Course' file, Aug. 1845.

41 *Tunbridge Wells Borough News*, June 2003, p. 30; *SEG*, 19 Aug. 1851, p. 5.

Figure 12.5 1st Tonbridge Girl Guides, 1915/16. The facial expressions show that guiding was a serious pastime in wartime.
Source: Tonbridge Historical Society, 25.010.

One way of overcoming the dangers of youthful high spirits, or worse, was to channel them into organised outdoor activities, symbolised in the many uniformed, quasi-military groups that were established. They were often attached to churches and/or temperance organisations. So the Band of Hope (founded in 1855) was active at Dunton Green by 1881; Lilian Gilchrist Thompson was hosting Boys Brigade (founded 1883) camps at Kippington in 1904.[42] The Boy Scouts, founded by Robert Baden-Powell, grew rapidly after he published *Scouting for Boys* in 1908. The first Scout troop in Sevenoaks started in 1909, with camps, rudimentary uniforms and a bugle band. Most of these organisations combined military discipline and obedience to authority with self-reliant healthy outdoor activities.[43]

By the 1880s, in line with the national trend, formal sports clubs of all descriptions were springing up across west Kent. A 'lawn tennis ground' was featured in a Sevenoaks property advertisement of 1884, the first evidence of the game being played in the town; its first tennis club existed by 1891. A cycling club was founded

42   *SC*, 5 Aug. 1881, p. 5; 5 Aug. 1904, p. 8.

43   Sevenoaks Library D325, 1st Sevenoaks (Hick's Own) Group Boy Scouts, the First 50 Years, 1909–1959 (1959), p. 3; *Kent Messenger and Sevenoaks Telegraph*, 20 Jan. 1912, p. 7; Sevenoaks Library D325, leaflet advertising Athletics Sports, 30 July 1913.

Figure 12.6 Holmesdale Football Club, 1898–9. The Club, formed in 1887 by Owen J. Breething (1862–1950) 'and some other gentlemen', drew members from across the district; its home ground (with a slope) was in Montreal Park, Riverhead, provided by Lord Amherst. Breething – with bowler hat – was very skilled at raising funds from members' subscriptions and concerts. Holmesdale's greatest victory was in 1898 when the team shown here defeated St George's (Ramsgate) 4–2 in the Kent League final and brought the Kent Youth Cup to Riverhead. *Source*: Author's collection.

in 1885 and based itself at the Temperance Hotel in Lime Tree Walk. Sevenoaks Town Football Club was founded in 1883 and contrived to lose 11–0 when it played (Royal) Arsenal in front of over 1,000 spectators at Knole Paddock in April 1893. Members of Sevenoaks Junior Athletics Club competed for the first time in 1885. Open spaces were used by schools for paper chases, athletics and games, the regulation of participants and spectators being crucial. A notable failure occurred at the Grammar School Sports day in 1883, when adult spectators were castigated for not exercising 'commonsense and restraint by keeping behind the ropes' cordoning off the running track, and 'the greatest difficulty was experienced in keeping the course open for the races'.[44]

Informal leisure pursuits mushroomed in our period too. Gardening was promoted as an improving diversion for the working classes that had economic value and put food on the table. By the end of the nineteenth century it had become

44   *SC*, 13 April 1883, p. 5.

an important aspect of west Kent life, sustained by local and national nurseries, seedsmen and suppliers, magazines and local competitive shows, displays and prizes.[45] Walking and rambling became more popular, helped by the Commons Preservation Society (CPS), formed in 1865, which was dedicated to saving common land from enclosure. It also sought to protect rights of way and footpaths. The CPS was active in Sevenoaks, notably during the Knole access dispute, and in maintaining public use of numerous footpaths. Another body that helped secure public access to the countryside was the National Trust, founded in 1895.[46]

Informal social networks

An interest in the natural world – in geology (especially eoliths), flora and fauna – was a passion of the shopkeeper Benjamin Harrison of Ightham and he would regularly walk into Sevenoaks to attend meetings of the Literary Institution and visit those who shared his interests: John Buckingham Bevington, de Barri Crawshay at Bradbourne, A.C. Swinton (a friend of Alfred Russell Wallace) and Sir Joseph Prestwich in Shoreham. His personal contacts also included the intellectual draper on St John's Hill, Arthur Hickmott, whom Harrison's son Edward later described as 'a young scientific pupil' of his father.

Two coronation festivals

At times local elites sought to manage and direct the leisure activities of the lower orders. Royal occasions, notably coronations, offered an opportunity to enlist working-class support for established authority. In 1838 the Sevenoaks Festival, marking Victoria's accession, was unashamedly celebrated with 'Fireworks and Fun', which included a free roast beef and plum pudding lunch, courtesy of Earl Amherst and the Countess of Plymouth and 'Limited to the inhabitants of Sevenoaks'. A total of 2,400 people sat at tables in the High Street at the ticket-only event. This was followed by a series of jokey competitions, including 'twelve men (Blindfolded) to race with wheelbarrows'. 'A Grand Rural Country Dance on the Vine' followed and, most ominously of all, as they were so often the opportunity for local disorder, there was, as darkness fell, 'A Display of Fireworks'. There had also been a 'plentiful supply of ale', and the event did not end until after midnight. Although this entertainment, with free alcohol for the inhabitants of the town,

---

45 Stephen Constantine, 'Amateur gardening and popular recreation in the 19th and 20th centuries', *Journal of Social History*, 14/3 (1981), pp. 387–406.

46 Paul Redman, *Octavia Hill, social activism, and the remaking of British society* (London, 2016), especially chapter 8.

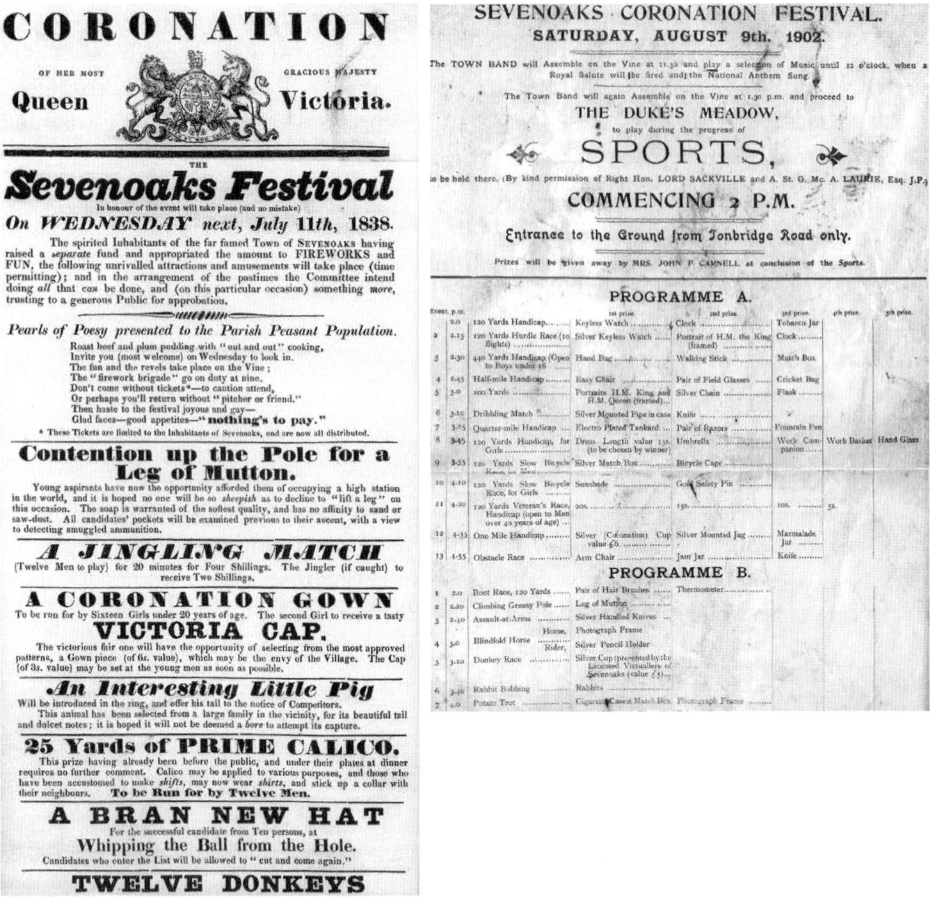

CORONATION

OF HER MOST GRACIOUS MAJESTY

Queen Victoria.

THE

Sevenoaks Festival

In honour of the event will take place (and no mistake)

On WEDNESDAY next, July 11th, 1838.

The spirited Inhabitants of the far famed Town of SEVENOAKS having raised a *separate* fund and appropriated the amount to FIREWORKS and FUN, the following unrivalled attractions and amusements will take place (time permitting); and in the arrangement of the pastimes the Committee intend doing *all* that *can* be done, and (on this particular occasion) something *more*, trusting to a generous Public for approbation.

Pearls of Poesy presented to the Parish Peasant Population.

Roast beef and plum pudding with "out and out" cooking,
Invite you (most welcome) on Wednesday to look in.
The fun and the revels take place on the Vine;
The "firework brigade" go on duty at nine.
Don't come without tickets*—to caution attend,
Or perhaps you'll return without "pitcher or friend."
Then haste to the festival joyous and gay—
Glad faces—good appetites—"**nothing's to pay.**"

* These Tickets are limited to the Inhabitants of Sevenoaks, and are now all distributed.

Contention up the Pole for a Leg of Mutton.

Young aspirants have now the opportunity afforded them of occupying a high station in the world, and it is hoped no one will be so *sheepish* as to decline to "lift a leg" on this occasion. The soap is warranted of the softest quality, and has no affinity to sand or saw-dust. All candidates' pockets will be examined previous to their ascent, with a view to detecting smuggled ammunition.

A JINGLING MATCH

(Twelve Men to play) for 20 minutes for Four Shillings. The Jingler (if caught) to receive Two Shillings.

A CORONATION GOWN

To be run for by Sixteen Girls under 20 years of age. The second Girl to receive a tasty

VICTORIA CAP.

The victorious fair one will have the opportunity of selecting from the most approved patterns, a Gown piece (of 6*s.* value), which may be the envy of the Village. The Cap (of 3*s.* value) may be set at the young men as soon as possible.

An Interesting Little Pig

Will be introduced in the ring, and offer his tail to the notice of Competitors.

This animal has been selected from a large family in the vicinity, for its beautiful tail and dulcet notes; it is hoped it will not be deemed a *bore* to attempt its capture.

25 Yards of PRIME CALICO.

This prize having already been before the public, and under their plates at dinner requires no further comment. Calico may be applied to various purposes, and those who have been accustomed to make *shifts*, may now wear *shirts*, and stick up a collar with their neighbours. **To be Run for by Twelve Men.**

A BRAN NEW HAT

For the successful candidate from Ten persons, at

Whipping the Ball from the Hole.

Candidates who enter the List will be allowed to "cut and come again."

TWELVE DONKEYS

SEVENOAKS CORONATION FESTIVAL.

SATURDAY, AUGUST 9th, 1902.

The TOWN BAND will Assemble on the Vine at 11.30 and play a selection of Music until 12 o'clock, when a Royal Salute will be fired and the National Anthem Sung.

The Town Band will again Assemble on the Vine at 1.30 p.m. and proceed to

THE DUKE'S MEADOW,

to play during the progress of

SPORTS,

to be held there. (By kind permission of Right Hon. LORD SACKVILLE and A. St. G. Mc. A. LAURIE, Esq. J.P.)

COMMENCING 2 P.M.

Entrance to the Ground from Tonbridge Road only.

Prizes will be given away by MRS. JOHN F. CARNELL at conclusion of the Sports.

PROGRAMME A.

Event	p.m.		1st prize.	2nd prize.	3rd prize.	4th prize.	5th prize.
	2.0	120 Yards Handicap	Keyless Watch	Clock	Tobacco Jar		
2	2.15	120 Yards Hurdle Race (10 flights)	Silver Keyless Watch	Portrait of H.M. the King (framed)	Clock		
3	2.30	440 Yards Handicap (Open to Boys under 16	Hand Bag	Walking Stick	Match Box		
4	2.45	Half-mile Handicap	Easy Chair	Pair of Field Glasses	Cricket Bag		
5	3.0	100 Yards	Portraits H.M. King and H.M. Queen (framed)	Silver Chain	Flask		
6	3.10	Dribbling Match	Silver Mounted Pipe in case	Knife			
7	3.25	Quarter-mile Handicap	Electro Plated Tankard	Pair of Razors	Fountain Pen		
8	3.45	120 Yards Handicap, for Girls	Dress Length value 15s. (to be chosen by winner)	Umbrella	Work Companion	Work Basket	Hand Glass
9	3.55	120 Yards Slow Bicycle Race, for Men	Silver Match Box	Bicycle Cape			
10	4.10	120 Yards Slow Bicycle Race, for Girls	Sunshade	Gold Safety Pin			
11	4.20	120 Yards Veteran's Race, Handicap (open to Men over 40 years of age)	20s.	15s.	10s.	5s.	
12	4.35	One Mile Handicap	Silver (Coronation) Cup value £6	Silver Mounted Jug	Marmalade Jar		
13	4.55	Obstacle Race	Arm Chair	Jam Jar	Knife		

PROGRAMME B.

1	2.0	Boot Race, 120 Yards	Pair of Hair Brushes	Thermometer
2	2.20	Climbing Greasy Pole	Leg of Mutton	
3	2.40	Assault-at-Arms	Silver Handled Knives	
4	3.0	Blindfold Horse: Horse,	Photograph Frame	
		Rider,	Silver Pencil Holder	
5	3.20	Donkey Race	Silver Cup (presented by the Licensed Victuallers of Sevenoaks (value £5)	
6	3.40	Rabbit Bobbing	Rabbits	
7	4.0	Potato Trot	Cigarette Case & Match Box	Photograph Frame

Figure 12.7 Sevenoaks Coronation festival programmes, 1838 and 1902. Juxtaposing the two posters is a most revealing exercise.
Source: Sevenoaks Library, Gordon Ward notebooks; B429.

presented great potential peril to order and decorum, there is no indication that any residents misbehaved. Nevertheless, it was a risky event to put on.[47]

By the end of the century social order in Sevenoaks was more safely guarded and the campaign for 'rational recreation' (defined as 'an attempt to forge more effective behavioural constraints in leisure') had been comprehensively won in most sections of society.[48] The 1897 diamond jubilee provided experience that helped inform plans

47 *MJ*, 17 July 1838, p. 3; Sevenoaks Library Gordon Ward notebooks, advertisement for Sevenoaks Festival, 11 July 1838. The programme reprinted in *SC*, 8 March 1901, p. 5.

48 Bailey, *Leisure*, pp. 6, 170.

for the coronation festivities of 1902. Both were organised by official committees, which in 1902 involved many local citizens, conscious that Sevenoaks was competing with neighbouring Tonbridge (again) to prove itself 'as a loyal, a wealthy and a patriotic community'.[49] The original celebrations were postponed because of the king's illness, which resulted in additional expenditure. Quickly reorganised, the main events took place a few months later on Duke's Meadow, part of the Knole estate. The sports included races and competitions ranging from serious events, such as the One Mile Handicap for a £6 silver Coronation Cup, to less solemn contests, such as the 120-yard boot race for a pair of hair-brushes. The event also comprised a parade through the town, an ox roast, lunch for older citizens and a children's tea. On private land with controlled access, the event was well managed to a strict timetable, without potentially dangerous elements such as the alcohol-fuelled lunch and firework display of 1838; not surprisingly, perhaps, given this extreme level of control, it was 'so successful'.[50] The accession of a new monarch began with a royal salute being fired and the singing of the National Anthem, thus imbuing the day with symbolic monarchical status and authority.[51] As a royal occasion, the expenditure was also unlikely to be opposed by most ratepayers, although any doubters were perhaps mollified by the detailed accounts published a few weeks later, revealing that the sports had cost almost £387 and had generated a small surplus of just over £2 that had been donated to the Cottage Hospital.[52]

Conclusion

By 1902 the poorer classes of west Kent certainly enjoyed significantly more leisure time than their forebears a century earlier. Much of that leisure activity was self-designed and self-regulated. Circumscription and rules existed for public games and sports organised within a system of clubs, leagues and fixtures, and were also acknowledged at informal football and cricket matches. Membership and participation invariably involved paying a regular subscription and implied acceptance of the rules and regulations, and invariably the prevailing system of management. At all levels, public spectators often proved to be the arbiters of 'fair play'. Similarly, the space where games were played was subject to a measure of control imposed by landowners and, later, rules publicly displayed at local authority recreation grounds. There were more outlets for working-class leisure, much of it within their own communities, with greater opportunities for young people to participate in activities organised by schools and social groups. Appreciation for sports and games became increasingly 'classless'. However, class divisions persisted

49   SC, 25 July 1902, p. 4.

50   SC, 15 Aug. 1902, p. 8.

51   Sevenoaks Library Gordon Ward notebooks; B429, programme for Sevenoaks Coronation Festival, 9 Aug. 1902.

52   SC, 5 Sept. 1902, p. 5.

for participants and spectators, although not as decades before, when middle-class attitudes disapprovingly viewed working-class leisure as 'half-pagan popular culture with its fairs, its sports, its drink and its picaresque hedonism'.[53]

In Sevenoaks, gaining a public recreation space at Holly Bush (as detailed in chapter 3) was a lengthy, highly contested process and one in which most of the population had little direct say. It could be argued that this decided shift from what took place in the early and mid-nineteenth century was a product of social change encouraged by ideas of order and discipline propounded by religion, the expanding education system, volunteer militias and young people's uniformed organisations. Elected institutions resulted in official acceptance of popular will, the authorities seeking civility for the town, as increasingly most people had a vested interest in behaving in a civil way while enjoying their leisure time.

Most leisure activities in Sevenoaks remained informal; most people did not participate in organised leisure pursuits. Churches and chapels, pubs, public institutions with their meetings and performances, and neighbourhoods provided places where friendships were formed. Cost was an important consideration. Informally improvised games cost little, whereas institutional leisure often involved formal clothing and curtailed freedom. Children devised their own leisure activities. Sunday schools offered certain opportunities under adult supervision, including outings, as did public and private schools, where healthy activity was by 1900 an important part of the curriculum.

By the early twentieth century many leisure activities in west Kent had been made 'safe' for players, spectators and residents by the combination of social control and self-regulation. Inter-town rivalries, such as those that had sometimes manifested themselves on Bonfire Night, still existed, but rarely did they pose a threat to public order because they were channelled into safe pursuits on sports grounds and perhaps elsewhere. Aggrieved members might leave their own clubs or leagues to form others within the existing parameters of a particular sport, but by that stage blazing tar barrels, injured policemen and clandestine bouts of pugilism featured only in the history books.

---

53 Thompson, *English working class*, p. 918.

Chapter 13

From risk to choice?

In January 1901 an editorial in the *Sevenoaks Chronicle* reviewed the past century and declared it to have been one of 'marvellous progress' and 'of extraordinary development in every direction'.[1] The writer focused on the nation's material, social and moral progress. In 1800 nine million people lived in Great Britain, by 1901 it was over 45 million; Sevenoaks' population in that time had grown from 2,400 to over 8,000. At the start of the previous century science had been in its infancy and the press fettered; now news and information were widely distributed by electric telegraph, newspapers and books were readily available, and the 'dull, guttering candle and the clumsy oil lantern' were slowly being replaced by gas and electricity. Steam power 'had revolutionised the industrial life of our country' and overcome the tyranny of distance, while huge steel ships had increased world trade. The past century was marked by the penny post and improved fiscal and penal systems. Medical and surgical progress was now allied to a knowledge of bacteriology that had defeated once fatal diseases. Of great importance was 'sanitary science' – the supply of clean water and the removal of waste by a main drainage system. This 'had resulted in the saving of thousands of lives and in tending to raise the average duration of life in every direction'. While the old century came in with 'religious bigotry rampant', it 'died with religious equality'. Of great note was the rapid growth of formal education in the last thirty years, resulting in a spectacular increase in numeracy and literacy. Enhanced choice now characterised religious worship and educational provision.

What is interesting is what was not included in the editorial but which featured in a much longer accompanying item headed '1801–1901: A Review of the Century'. This too was similarly self-congratulatory and applauded the 'progress' of the past century, providing some homely comparative examples, such as the availability of cheap foodstuffs, that would have resonated with the paper's readers. Compared with the previous century, people in Sevenoaks now had 'taken some share of [the century's] material benefits, enjoyed some proportion of its political and religious

---

1   *SC*, 4 Jan. 1901, p. 3. All the subsequent quotations on this page come from this source.

" *I wonder how it will hatch out ?* "

Figure 13.1 Cartoon, taken from the *Sevenoaks Chronicle*, 4 January 1901, p. 3. The *Chronicle* gave considerable space to the new century. This cartoon shows John Bull contemplating an egg labelled '1901'. The editorial in that issue contained the following thoughts, combining foreboding prescience with an optimistic view of the powers of science: 'One cannot help wondering how long this period of abnormal progression can last. […] Will the world witness a development of science before which even the achievements of the nineteenth century will pale? Or will the crash of nations, the jealousy of powers and the savage instincts of men bring about some tartarian catastrophy [sic] from the ruins of which the world will have to rise again and make its way painfully up the ladder of learning and along the path of science?'
Source: *Sevenoaks Chronicle*, 4 Jan. 1901, p. 5 © The British Library Board. All rights reserved. With thanks to The British Newspaper Archive (www.britishnewspaperarchive.co.uk).

freedom'. In 1801 Britain may have been involved in a lengthy war with France, but unmentioned in 1901 was the current war in South Africa, a costly conflict in terms of money and manpower. Also ignored was the changed status of women, demands for female suffrage and the fact that most working-class men still did not have the vote. Municipalisation, the growing demand for tariff reform, open spaces and leisure, the continuing growth in the role of the state at both local and national level and policing in the town were similarly overlooked. The decline in Christian belief was not referred to, although religion remained significant, not least in regard to the provision of local education. That so few young people had access to secondary education also passed the author's attention.

Whether ordinary people in Sevenoaks felt optimistic is unknown. However, in material terms, almost all were better off than their forebears in terms of work, food, clothing, health and housing. Work was relatively better paid, workers had regulated hours and more leisure time, and trade unions were legal. Safety at work had improved slightly, but seasonal unemployment remained the common lot of most agricultural labourers. In 1900 food was cheaper, more plentiful and less likely to be adulterated, while unseasonal and foreign grown fruits and vegetables were available due to canning and refrigeration. The average person had more clothes and shoes, both the results of mass production, whereas in 1800 those basic necessities had been supplied locally. It is difficult to assess health without adequate data; local medical officers of health thought the town population healthier owing to an improved diet and better living conditions. One measure was increased life expectancy, but another strong indicator was the infant mortality rate, which declined after 1899 and then fell more steeply after 1911. After 1870 houses were of better quality; separate rooms afforded more privacy and they were better heated than before. Building was also subject to regulations that had not troubled Daniel Grover when he laid out Hartslands in the early 1840s. Many homes had piped and hot water, and were supplied with gas lighting, but 62 per cent of dwellings in Sevenoaks were not connected to main drainage as late as 1912.

Working-class people owned more goods – perhaps a bicycle and a sewing machine, maybe a piano in the front room of their rented home. A local hospital catered for public health, with operations conducted under anaesthetic in an antiseptic environment, the costs possibly covered in part by a friendly society, a charitable body or the new National Insurance scheme of 1911. The cleanliness of Sevenoaks in the first decade of the twentieth century is unknown, although more roads had metalled surfaces and dust was more likely to be watered away and 'nuisances' and litter removed. Local banks were also safer places of deposit than when the Tonbridge New Bank failed in 1816 and when Henry Sutton had defrauded the customers of the Sevenoaks Savings Bank in 1888. They had been replaced by the Post Office Savings Bank, which provided a simple, risk-free deposit system for all.

Other risks, however, remained stubbornly real. The problem of penury for those living longer was reduced after limited old age pensions were introduced for those over 70 in 1909. But average life expectancy for women and men remained at about 53 and on average one in ten children in the Sevenoaks area died before their first birthday. Improved nutrition and hygiene and professional midwives helped reduce those high figures. Diseases such as smallpox, whooping cough and tuberculosis could still prove fatal, however.

Another curse was poverty, which remained widespread in Sevenoaks and the surrounding villages. The sick and elderly living on the precarious margins of need and working men on irregular wages could still face dire distress during economic downturn, such as the years 1908–9. Those were the people least likely to belong to a trade union or to receive help from any institution that sought to protect or promote their welfare. Although the author who reviewed the previous century in the *Sevenoaks Chronicle* could comment that 'never were the Poor Laws more humanely administered than they are now', for those who fell that low the Sundridge workhouse remained a threatening place of last resort.[2]

Even families with a regular income could become victims of acute poverty. For example, Henry Seal, of Redman's Place, had regular work as a carter but died suddenly in 1908 aged 41, leaving his widow 'unprovided for' with ten young children.[3] That may have been a rare case, but the Seal family joined a long list of those who faced acute distress not of their own making. Nevertheless, the systems in place by 1914 offered a glimpse of what a future welfare state might look like.

The celebratory tone of the *Chronicle* editorial was partly justified, for many risks had been overcome or reduced and choices enhanced. But it also fuelled a false sense of security; other risks lurked on the horizon. New military technologies, for example, made going to war against Germany in 1914 much riskier than war with France in 1792 had been. In the Great War not only were many more soldiers killed than ever before, by artillery, machine guns and high explosives, but civilians also died in air raids.

The arrival of the motor car – new risks and choices

Another new risk factor, which had significant local implications but was inadequately appreciated for many years, was the development of steel-framed bicycles, motorcycles and motor cars. All were faster, more convenient and private means of transport that helped to transform Britain's landscape and much else in the early twentieth century. The car also had profound implications in terms of social class, leisure, technology and government regulation, for 'Almost as soon as they appeared, motor vehicles posed problems for society.'[4] The mass appropriation of the internal combustion engine by different social classes in the early twentieth century provides an apposite conclusion for this book, for it conflated risk and choice to a remarkable and lasting degree – so much so that it looks set to have lasting consequences well into the twenty-first century.

Those new vehicles all required roads with good surfaces. Bicycles, which were widely owned by people of all social classes, may have been the principal agent for better road surfaces. They became more widespread and cheaper after 'tar-macadam' was patented in 1902. The first reported mention in Sevenoaks of this

---

2   *SC*, 4 Jan. 1901, p. 3.

3   *SC*, 3 Jan. 1908, p. 3; Census Return for 1901: Sevenoaks.

4   Keith Laybourn, *The battle for the roads of Britain: police, motorists and the law, c.1890s to 1970s* (Basingstoke, 2015), digital edition, no pagination.

improved method of metalling roads was at a meeting of the Highways Committee of the Urban District Council in October 1906 (see Plate 9).[5] Thereafter, first the main roads in 1909 and then, increasingly, side and minor roads were given new and more durable surfaces.[6] Many roads were also widened. The first motor car in Sevenoaks was owned by the Holcroft family in 1896.[7]

Cars, which were very expensive before the First World War, rapidly became the preferred mode of transport for the wealthy, although from 1905 onwards both car and motorcycle production increased rapidly.[8] Early motoring soon became identified and defined by social class, for 'the first motor car owners were plutocratic'.[9] They had to be, for new cars cost up to £1,500 (when most agricultural labourers were earning less than £1 a week) and, being open to the elements, required special clothing, which further differentiated passenger from pedestrian.[10] Those pedestrians, moreover, often had to ensure they were not knocked down by motorists emulating Mr Toad's driving in *The Wind in the Willows*, first published in 1908.

The motor car also gave birth to a new form of individualism, 'the motorist', a term which smacked of privilege, and a new high rank of domestic service employment, the 'chauffeur'. Predictably there were those who responded by stressing the risks involved in motoring, opposing the car as dangerous, while others emphasised choice, hailing it as another example of progress. There were local supporters of both internal combustion engines and of electric cars – until 1906 the latter comprised the majority of the vehicles on the roads. Electric, petrol and steam-powered cars were displayed at 'an exhibition of horseless vehicles' at Tunbridge Wells in 1895.[11] William Freeman (d. 1925) of Otford, a progressive-minded engineer who had graduated from water mills to motor cars, together with Albert Bath, strongly supported electric cars.[12] In Sevenoaks the first major car dealer and motor engineer was George Humphrey; his family company had formed as 'carriage builders' in 1790 and also operated the first motor bus service from the town to Westerham.[13] Government legislation closely followed the nascent industry

---

5   *SC*, 19 Oct. 1906, p. 5. See also Francis Pryor, *The making of the British landscape* (London, 2010), pp. 642–4.

6   Trevor Rowley, *The English landscape in the twentieth century* (London, 2006), pp. 20–7.

7   *SC*, 11 Sept. 1896, p. 5.

8   In 1904 there were still 'only about 9,000 cars in Britain': Bill Luckin, 'Drunk driving, drink driving: Britain, *c.* 1800–1920', in Tom Crook and Mike Esbester (eds), *Governing risks in modern Britain: danger, safety and road accidents, c. 1800–2000* (London, 2016), pp. 171–94 (p. 185).

9   Asa Briggs, *A social history of England* (London, 1987), p. 217.

10 Burnett, *Useful toil*, p. 29.

11 *Encyclopædia Britannica*, 'Motor Vehicles', Vol. 18, 11th edn (New York, 1911), pp. 914–30; *Illustrated London News*, 26 Oct. 1895, p. 525.

12 Clarke and Stoyel, *Otford*, pp. 230–1.

13 *SC*, 30 April 1908, p. 4. Killingray and Purves, *Dictionary*, p. 25.

and as early as 1896 Tonbridge jeweller Alfred Cornell pleaded guilty to driving his 'autocar' at speeds in excess of 2mph. He was fined 3s 6d.[14]

The Motor Car Act 1903 introduced vehicle registration, five-shilling driving licences (but not driving tests), minimal braking standards and the criminal offence of reckless driving. Notably, it raised the national speed limit for motor vehicles from 14mph to 20mph, a law that was rigorously enforced by the police in the Sevenoaks district. The local press condemned this high-handed policy, although its frequent reporting of fatal road accidents involving motor vehicles indicated that the editor recognised the need for regulation to control a new method of transport that was potentially lethal but here to stay.[15]

The risk/choice dichotomy was seen at its starkest when accidents happened, such as in 1912, when Dr Ranking of Tunbridge Wells was killed when his chauffeur tried 'to avoid a woman and [the car] dashed into a tree, where it overturned'.[16] The road safety issue was hotly debated in the new motoring magazines that appeared in this period. That year the chairman and other members of Kent County Council wrote to the *Motor Car Journal* to make 'An Official Appeal to Motorists', asking them to remind their chauffeurs that the roads would be full over the holidays and that 'special care will be necessary, not only in populous but in rural areas' of the county.[17] Editorials in the *Journal* condemned bad drivers but readers' letters revealed how some resented almost any official interference in what they considered their legitimate entitlement to unfettered motoring. One correspondent, 'JSM', complained how galling it was

> to the average motorist, who perhaps has never been in a police court before, to find that when he is hauled before a magistrate for some trifling cause or another, he is treated like a dangerous criminal, and has nothing but contumely and exaggerated statements hurled at his head.[18]

Others, however, condemned the legal system from the opposite direction, one letter in *The Times* (after a child was killed by a car in Meopham) insisting that 'Magistrates and coroners seem to think that the object of the Motor-car Acts was to legalise manslaughter.'[19] Inevitably, deaths and injuries from car accidents would 'bring the wealthiest sections of society into conflict with the majority who were not car-owners'.[20]

---

14 *KSC*, 28 Aug. 1896, p. 3.

15 See, for example, *SC*, 26 July 1912, p. 5.

16 *Motor Car Journal*, 21 Sept. 1912, p. 615.

17 *Ibid.*, 17 Aug. 1912, p. 533.

18 *Ibid.*, 12 Oct. 1912, p. 730.

19 *The Times*, 27 Aug. 1904, p. 5.

20 Sean O'Connell, *The car and British society: class, gender and motoring 1896–1939* (Manchester, 1998), p. 120. By 1914 over 132,000 private cars were licensed in Britain; that year there were 1,328 fatal car accidents, three times the number of five years earlier. Briggs, *Social history*, pp. 258–9.

Figure 13.2 Early Sevenoaks motorists. On the right is Leslie Spencer on a motorised De Dion tricycle; in 1911 he lived in Mount Harry Road, Sevenoaks. In the centre his sister and brother in law, Ethel and Clifton Hilder, in a Benz motor car. On the other De Dion is Walter Pedder Morgan, a family friend and son of Walter Robert Morgan, owner of the Nepicar Brewery and the Bull Hotel, Wrotham. The Hilders were one of the first families in Sevenoaks to buy a car. *Source*: Sevenoaks Society.

The most obvious way to deal with the risks inherent in the new motor car technology was to transfer them to an insurance company. The Locomotives on Highways Act 1896, which removed the strict rules and speed limits that had hitherto greatly restricted the use of motorised vehicles, 'prompted an immediate response from potential insurance providers ... on the emergence of a potential new risk', and the first recorded motor policy was issued by General Accident that November. By 1912, '49 companies were offering motor insurance' across Britain, but this was not a statutory requirement until 1930. Prior to that, most policies covered only liability for injury or damage to people or property, the sum insured being often capped at £100.[21]

Legal cases from the years before the First World War show how disinclined those insurance companies were to pay out. In 1908 Arthur Harling of Borough

---

21   Robert Merkin and Maggie Hemsworth, *The law of motor insurance* (London, 2015), pp. 10–11.

Green sued F.G. Garrett of London for damages of £25 after he was knocked off his bicycle and injured while riding through Ightham. Garrett, who took Harling home in his car and visited him there afterwards, was insured with the International Insurance Company but 'they denied liability and were not represented' in court. The judge believed the accident was the result not of negligence but a 'curious error of judgment' on the part of the driver and Harling was awarded £23, plus costs.[22]

Danger and accidents

The new risks posed by the car to pedestrians and other road users, the perceived social privilege inherent in exercising the choice of owning one in the first place and the ambiguous regulatory response to it all combined in what was described as 'one of the most disastrous and inexplicable motor car accidents that has yet occurred in this district', which was reported widely across both local newspapers and the national press in 1912.[23]

On a dark night that June five young men, who had been out for the evening, were walking down the main road towards Riverhead. One was Gilbert Gasson. When they were opposite the Halfway House pub, a 15-hp Fiat Landaulette (with an estimated top speed of over 30mph), driven by 29-year-old chauffeur Charles Tye, hit two of the men, leaving 18-year-old Frederick Parsons dead and another with a broken leg.[24] The subsequent lengthy coroner's inquest, which was marked by a troublesome chairman of the jury and remarks by another juror that the death was due to 'reckless driving', returned a divided verdict.[25] The jury also stated, in a rider to the coroner's statement, 'that in their opinion the rate at which some motor cars are driven through the populous urban district of Sevenoaks is a perfect disgrace to the neighbourhood and the country'.[26] The matter was then pursued by the local press and discussed in the Urban District Council, and an unsuccessful request was made to Kent County Council that the speed limit in some parts of Sevenoaks should be reduced to 10mph.[27] After the inquest, the director of public prosecutions took on the criminal case and Tye was charged with manslaughter. However, when he came to trial in September the magistrates determined that 'considering all points of evidence, it hardly justified them convicting Mr Tye of this offence and they would therefore dismiss the case'.[28]

---

22   *SC*, 10 July 1908, p. 8.
23   *Ibid.*, 5 July 1912, p. 8.
24   *Ibid.*, 5 July 1912, p. 8; 12 July 1912, p. 2.
25   *Ibid.*, 5 July 1912, p. 8; 12 July 1912, p. 2.
26   *Ibid.*, 12 July 1912, p. 2.
27   *Ibid.*, 26 July 1912, p. 5.
28   *Ibid.*, 9 Aug. 1912, p. 8; 27 Sept. 1912, p. 5.

An editorial in the *Chronicle* said the entire affair had 'from the first …
bristled with surprises'.[29] The acquittal came probably because the young men
were walking on the left-hand side of the road, which was poorly lit and had no
pavement, and not on the opposite side, which did. But the plain fact of the matter
was that an innocent group of young men had been run down by a motor car and
one had lost his life. Assessing the event on the risk/choice continuum enables us to
see just how profound a change the new motor car represented, how it impacted
upon the individuals concerned and how the political authorities responded to the
new situation.

From the individuals' perspective, Charles Tye chose to get a job as a chauffeur.
He also chose the speed at which to drive. Parsons and his friends similarly made
choices that night, most notably to walk a short distance on the 'wrong' side of
the road, but the odds were heavily stacked against the pedestrians. Those adverse
risk factors included the capacity of the driver, who had a clean licence but just six
months' experience; the roadworthiness of the car (which had already malfunctioned
that day); and the driving conditions, which were downhill on a dry road not under
repair, with minimal other traffic, but in the dark.[30] Most importantly for Parsons
and his friends, they may have not have fully appreciated how dangerous motor
cars could be, and how they posed much graver threats to life and limb than horse-
powered transport ever could.

The risks the men faced were exacerbated by a regulatory regime that had
struggled to face down the influential and politically powerful motoring lobby. Had
Tye been found guilty he would have faced a gaol sentence, which might have acted
as a deterrent to poor driving, but beyond that the authorities appeared supine in
their response. The proposed 10mph limit was rejected – on the basis, interestingly,
of risk – because government policy was only to introduce such constraints 'where
the circumstances are so exceptional as to make the ordinary precautions an
insufficient safeguard against accident'.[31] That was not the case on the Riverhead
road. The only effective remedy against those not taking those ordinary precautions
was to prosecute them for reckless driving. Other penalties were deemed worse than
useless, as, for example, 'warning boards have as much effect on the motorists as
Cabinet Ministers have on suffragettes'.[32]

But was the motor car more dangerous than horse-drawn transport? Comparing
road deaths caused by accidents involving cars in Sevenoaks from 1903 to 1912
with horse-related road fatalities over a similar ten-year period from 1890 to 1899
(before cars were commonplace in the district) shows that only one person died

29   *Ibid.*, 9 Aug. 1912, p. 5.
30   *Ibid.*, 5 July 1912, p. 8.
31   *Ibid.*, 23 Aug. 1912, p. 5.
32   *Ibid.*, 26 July 1912, p. 5.

in an accident involving horses.[33] By contrast, six people died as a direct result of collisions with cars in the Sevenoaks area, including Parsons and two small children. All except one were killed during the summer months, indicating perhaps the increased likelihood of cars skidding on dry, dusty roads.[34]

Car-related road fatalities reported in the *Chronicle*, Sevenoaks area, 1903–12

Date	Victim	Location	Circumstances
26.8.1904	Cecil Zimer (pedestrian)	Meopham	Boy hit in road by skidding car
24.8.1906	Dr Don (passenger)	Brittain's Lane	Car skidded and overturned
10.6.1910	George Hills (cyclist)	Westerham Hill	Collision at crossroads
19.8.1910	Daisy Wickens (pedestrian)	Hartslands Road	Girl aged 7 hit in road
5.7.1912	Frederick Parsons	London Road	Pedestrians hit in road
27.9.1912	T Collins (trap driver)	Tonbridge Road	Horse spooked by car

---

So car accidents were both more frequent than their equine counterparts and, when they did occur, serious injury or death was far more probable. No wonder the *Chronicle*, after Dr Don's death in 1906, drew attention to those enhanced risks and demanded that 'some amendment be made in the law to banish from the road all but thoroughly capable and experienced motor drivers'. It also bewailed the pusillanimous attitude of 'the powers that be [which] wait until calamities occur before they lift a hand to remedy the evil'.[35]

With Frederick Parsons and other road victims, however, the risks associated with faster travel were generally shifted the other way – from the owners and drivers of motor cars to pedestrians. It was the reverse of the 'progress' so beloved by the Victorians and Edwardians. It also reiterates the pattern noted in earlier chapters, whereby reducing risk or enhancing choices for some (often the rich) could impact

---

33 *Ibid.*, 26 May 1899, p. 5.

34 The number of motor vehicles in Sevenoaks is not readily available. However, the reported 700 motor cars parked at Knole in June 1913 for a Unionist garden party indicates the increasing number on local roads and also the wealth of those who supported the Conservative cause; *SC*, 27 June 1913, p. 5.

35 *SC*, 31 Aug. 1906, pp. 4, 8.

adversely on others generally less well off, such as when the Sevenoaks Fair was abolished in 1874. Similarly, cars bought out of the higher disposable incomes (of the richer few) increased the chances (for the poorer many) of being mown down in the street or knocked off their bicycles.

The Parsons incident showed all too clearly that progress could never be taken for granted, for new and often frightening dangers could hurtle around the corner at dizzying speed. Most new developments, especially major technological advances such as the motor car, might have appeared on the face of it to be merely another exciting extension of choice. But, as we have seen, it also brought risks not clearly seen nor adequately controlled. Road safety, or lack of it, in the early twentieth century also revealed how dangerous life could be if the state failed to act appropriately to contain the problem, as risk transferee of last resort.

At the start of this book we suggested that steering a way through life, and its often very real difficulties, was and is a complex and multi-influenced task – especially for the poorer members of society. That commonplace led us to try to describe that process as it played out in west Kent throughout the long nineteenth century in the form of, broadly, an often stuttering, tortuous journey towards the lessening of the risks surrounding the obtaining of life's bare necessities – or, how 'struggle and risk are constituent parts of the human soul', as Francis Fukuyama rather grandiloquently put it.[36] Then they were, over time, generally superseded by increasing choices in the consumption of material goods, educational and leisure facilities and growing political and religious pluralism. But, if this risk and choice approach works, why should it be confined merely to a small part of England in a particular century? This is not just a plea for local historians to apply it in new chronological or geographical contexts, although we do believe it could offer fruitful new avenues of study. Going further, why should it not be extended beyond historical study, so it is applied to other social science disciplines that examine current and even future events?

These lines are being written in the run-up to the major UN climate change conference in Glasgow, in November 2021. The car is not the only contributor to global warming, by any means. But we do well to remember, more than a century after Parsons lost his life in Sevenoaks, that while the internal combustion engine may have transformed many of the choices we can make it has simultaneously hastened the major environmental risks we face, by raising atmospheric temperatures and polluting the air we breathe. As ever, it is the world's poor who are most at risk from this frightening new development. Perhaps all is not lost, and a return to the electric car will be one factor enabling us to reverse this disastrous wound inflicted on the people, not just of west Kent, but of the whole world.

---

36   Francis Fukuyama, *The end of history and the last man* (London, 1992), p. 313.

Bibliography

Primary sources

British Library
Cup.21.g.36/47, General Reference Collection, advertisement, 'An assembly and
   ball, at the Coffee House, Sevenoaks; Tuesday, October 28, 1800', etc.

British Parliamentary Papers (UKPP), House of Lords
Appendices B–F to the eighth report of the Poor Law Commissioners, No. 399
   (1842)
*Miscellaneous: Illegitimate Children: Abstract of the Returns of the Number of
   Illegitimate Children*, No. 113 (1839)
*The Report from the Committee of Secrecy ... relative to the proceedings of
   different persons ... engaged in a treasonable conspiracy*, Sessional Paper, 002,
   27 May 1799

British Parliamentary Papers (UKPP), House of Commons
Reports from Committees – Session 1 November–24 July 1810–1811, vol. 2
*Report ... Select Committee on the State of the Children Employed in the
   Manufactories of the United Kingdom*, No. 397 (1816)
*Commissioners of Inquiries into Charities in England and Wales, First Report on
   the Education of the Poor*, No. 83 (1819)
Minutes of Evidence Taken before Select Committee on Combination Laws, No.
   417 (1825)
*Report from His Majesty's Commissioners for Inquiring into the Administration
   and Practical Operation of the Poor Laws*, No. 44 (1834)
Poor Law Reports 24 (1835), Appendix B, no. 2 'Report by E.C. Tufnell', p. 195
Abstract of Answers and Returns on the State of Education in England and Wales,
   vols 1, 2 and 3, No. 62 (1835)
Reports of the Chief Registrar of Friendly Societies, No. 322 (1884–5), Appendix
Board of Trade – Strikes and Lock-outs (Labour Department), No. C8231 (1896)
*Wages and Hours of Labour (Board of Trade, Labour department) ... wages and
   hours of labour in the UK, 1895*, No. C8374 (1897)
Census Returns 1841–1911

Kent Archaeological Society website – www.kentarcheaology.org.uk
Tithe and apportionment surveys: Sevenoaks (1839); Tonbridge (1838), Brasted
   (1845), Sundridge (1841).

Kent History and Library Centre (KHLC)
C/E/S/330/2/4, Cobden Road School log book, 1884–1910
C/PO/1/4, Kent Police Authority letter books, 1873–81
G/Se/ACb1, Sevenoaks Poor Law Union, Out-letter book, 1836–9
M2/1/2/1, Wesleyan Benefit Society minutes, 1859–84
M2/1/2/2, Wesleyan Benefit Society correspondence, 1864–1907
M2/1/6/8, article in *Methodist Recorder*, 1905
M2/1/6/16, Franks, ms. 'A Survey of Sevenoaks Methodism from its
   commencement in 1764' (1918)
P88/5/2, Rules and regulation of the Sevenoaks Savings Bank, 1867
P145/25/30, Farningham clothing and shoe club, accounts, 1852
P202/8/2, Ightham parish church book, 1814–57
P279/25/1, Otford parish church accounts, 'Clothing given to the Poor from money
   left by will of John Charman', 1827
P287B/25/1, Log book of Fordcombe school, 1862–97
P330/E/1/1, St John's Parish Church, Register of Baptisms, 1877–88
P330/E/1/2, St John's Parish Church, Register of Baptisms, 1888–1912
P330/8/1, Sevenoaks parish church, vestry minutes, 1796–1806
P330/8/4, Sevenoaks parish church, vestry minutes, 1826–30
P330/8/5, Sevenoaks parish church, vestry minutes, 1830–2
P330/8/6, Sevenoaks parish church, vestry minutes, 1832–59
P330/12/11, Sevenoaks Overseers' account books, 1830–2
P357/25/12, Sundridge school, terms of employment of Richard Parry, 1873
P406/15/7, Wrotham Overseers' Affiliation orders, 1689–1834
P406/15/8, Wrotham Overseers', bastardy correspondence, 1782–1833
P406/18/7, Wrotham Overseers', workhouse diet, 1813
Q/C/i/114/1–4, Kent Quarter Sessions, insolvency of Stephen Jessup, 1831–4
Q/CSu/3/9, Kent Quarter Sessions, county surveyors' papers, 1875–7
Q/RSp/4/3, Kent Quarter Sessions, Return of applications for bastardy orders, 1847
U269/E29, Sackville papers, Notices forbidding hunting, 1779–1818
U442/O67, Papers of the Association for the Detection of Incendiaries, Sevenoaks,
   1832–40
U749/E1, Rusthall manor records, Bath Book: Ladies' and gentlemen's book,
   1803–5
U749/E3, Rusthall manor records, Bath Book: Ladies' and gentlemen's book, 1806
U749/E6, Rusthall manor records, Bath Book: Ladies' and gentlemen's book, 1810
U840/E42, Pratt estate papers, hotel bills and related papers, 1860
U840/E50, Pratt estate papers, miscellaneous, 1840–1932

U840/O239–41, Pratt estate papers, John Jefferys Pratt, 1813–37

U1000/20/O48, Sevenoaks societies and organisations, official papers, undated

U1000/27/O1, Records of the Sevenoaks Amicable Society

U1000/27/O2, Records of the Sevenoaks Amicable Society

U1000/29/B1, Draper's Day Book, 1830–3

U1000/29/B2, Grocer's Day Book, 1837–8

U1000/32/O3, Annual Report and Accounts, Sevenoaks Literary and Scientific Society, 1860

U1109/T34, Nizells estate (Somerhill) title deeds, undated

U1590/C78, Stanhope papers, London Corresponding Society, 1794

U2093/E1, Farming day book of Thomas Porter of Hadlow, 1816–24

U2593/B81, Kent Fire Insurance policy register, 1846–52

UD/SE/Acr1, Sevenoaks UDC, Sanitary and Health reports, 1884–1963

UD/SE/Am/1/1, Minutes of Sevenoaks Local Board, 1871–5

WU13/Z1, Autobiographical and historical notes of Gilbert Gasson (1893–1986), 4 vols

Lambeth Palace Library

163.231, Tait papers

VG3/5a, Visitation returns. The Rev. Folliot Baugh to Archibald Tait, archbishop of Canterbury, 1876

VH80/60/1–6, VH80/91/1–20, Court of Arches

Manchester University Library

REAS/2/1, Letters of George Thomson to his wife Anne, Autumn 1831

Methodist Church, The Drive, Sevenoaks

Sevenoaks Wesleyan Benefit Society, Annual Report 7 July 1863 (Alterations to the Rules). 'Maternal Relatives and the Drive with List', dated Nov. 2008

The National Archives, Kew (TNA)

B 3/3380, Bankruptcy Commission files. Creditors meeting, 21 Sept. 1816; Depositions from creditors, June 1816 to February 1817

ED 27/1974, Secondary Education Endowments

ED 103/130/34, 623–37, Building Grant Applications

FS 6/84/80, Rule Book (1868); Deed of Dissolution, 31 Dec. 1882. Registry of Friendly Societies, Rules and Amendments etc of Building Societies

HO 11/6, 237, Transportees

HO 45/9367/36927, Census Return 1871: Sevenoaks

HO 52/8/119 ff. Home Office, counties correspondence

HO 52/8/119 ff. 259–60, ditto

HO 52/8/120 ff. 261–2, ditto

HO 52/8/168 f. 374, ditto

HO 64/1/109 ff. 313–16, Home Office, criminal (rewards and pardons)
    correspondence
IR 58/85843/46–47, Hartslands, Sevenoaks, Board of Inland Revenue, Valuation
    Office field books
MH 12/5315, Local Government Board, correspondence with Poor Law Unions, 4
    Oct.1834

Norfolk Record Office
BOL 2/10/739, Bollingbroke Collection, correspondence of Elizabeth Leathes, 1791

Private archives
Herries papers, St Julian's, Sevenoaks
William Bowen archive
William Knight, *Diaries*, vols 1 and 2

School of Oriental and African Studies Archives, University of London
Wesleyan Methodist Missionary Society, Box 662, FBM 44, fiche 1966, 22 April 1833

Seal Public Library
Jim Johnson, 'A Lifetime in Seal', typescript memoir, n.d.

Sevenoaks Library, Local Studies Collection
B ALL, copy of Mrs Allnutt's Diary for 1831 and 1832
B167, Fire Brigades of Sevenoaks 1846–1985
B429, Athletic sports in Sevenoaks, 1902–88
B546, Holmesdale Agricultural Association
B667, James German
B1227, Bethel Road and Hartslands, 1846–2005
D25, Sevenoaks cricket, 1782–1989
D62, Sevenoaks Town Band, 1875–1985
D65, Sevenoaks Amateur Theatricals, 1874–2006
D67, Sevenoaks UDC public notices, 1920–56
D176, Sevenoaks Tradesman, 1848–1982
D200, Methodist Church, Sevenoaks, 1832–2004
D325, Sevenoaks Boy Scouts, 1912–88
D462, Sevenoaks charities, 1718–1939
D549, Sevenoaks Choral Society 'Miscellaneous Concert' programme, 27 October 1847
D876A, National Freehold Land Society
D1002, St Nicholas church, Sevenoaks, 1798–1920
F443, Ratepayers, Sevenoaks
F574, J.W. Faulkner, *Answer to the reply of the Rev. Dr. Mills to the address of the
    parishioners of Brasted Kent* (1851)

Gordon Ward notebooks; 'Coronation. Sevenoaks Festival', 11 July 1838
L668, C.J. Knight, 'Reminiscences' (manuscript, 1934)
SC852, cutting from *Sevenoaks News*, Oct. 1938
SC1025, Pound Pond, Sevenoaks, 1845

Southwark Diocesan Archives
William Cunningham, 'Short Account of the Previous History of the Mission to
    Sevenoaks'

Tonbridge Public Library, Local history collection
Yellow Box No. 1, poster dated 7 April 1866

Tunbridge Wells Library Local Studies
'Race Course' file

Westerham Library
M. Fry, *Westerham Church Schools 1828–78* (undated), copy of application to the
    National Society

West Sussex Record Office
GB 3 DM 851. 569–570G, Cobden Unwin papers, 1902
Goodwood mss. Letters to the Duke of Richmond, April 1831–Dec. 1834

Contemporary publications
Anon. (John Toke), *Five letters on the state of the poor in the county of Kent*
    (London, 1770; amended 1808).
Bailey's British directory (1784).
Barrow, John Henry (ed.), *The mirror of parliament for the ... sessions of the ...*
    parliament of Great Britain and Ireland, vol. 1 (London, 1831).
Baxter, G.R. Whythen, *The book of the Bastiles* (London, 1841).
Bowen, John, *The union workhouse and board of guardian system* (London, 1842).
Boys, John, *General view of the agriculture of the county of Kent* (London, 1805).
Brown, William Wells, *Narrative of William Wells Brown, a fugitive slave* (London,
    1850)
Caird, James, *English agriculture in 1850 and 1851* (London, 1852).
Cobbett, William, *Cottage economy* ([1822] Oxford, 1979).
Cobbett, William, *Rural rides*, vol. I ([1830] London, 1973).
Cooke, George, *Topographical and statistical description of the county of Kent*
    (London, 1810).
A copy of the correspondence between the Rev. Thomas Curteis, vicar of Seven
    Oaks ... and Francis Barnett, relative to the distribution of sacramental gifts in
    the said parish (London, 1833).

Curteis, Thomas, *A letter to Robert Peel on the principle and operation of the New Poor Law* (London, 1842).

De Vaynes, Julia, *The Kentish garland*, vol. 2 (Hereford, 1882).

Eden, Frederick, *The state of the poor*, vol. 2 (London, 1797).

Edwards, Jane, *Her recollections of old Sevenoaks* ([1863] Sevenoaks, 1985).

Faulkner, J.W., *Answer to the reply of the Rev. Dr. Mills to the address of the parishioners of Brasted Kent* (1851).

Field, Benjamin, *Sincere devotion: exemplified in the life of Mrs. C.E. Martin, of Sevenoaks* (London, 1862).

Godwin, George, *Another blow for life* (London, 1864).

Hasted, Edward, *The history and topographical survey of the county of Kent*, vol. III (Canterbury, 1797–1801; Wakefield, 1972).

Hedges, John, *A description of the storm that happened in west Kent in the month of August 1763* (London, 1763).

Hickmott, Arthur, *Houses for the people* (London, 1897).

Hodgson, Robert, *The life of the Right Reverend Beilby Porteus, D.D., late bishop of London* (London, 1811).

Hooker's household almanac (Westerham, 1864).

Johnson, Joseph, *The medical register for the year 1783* (London, 1783).

Kelly's directory of Kent (1882, 1890, 1913 and 1918).

Kelly's directory of Kent, Surrey and Sussex (1891 and 1895).

Knox, Thomas, *An exhortation to the poor* (London, 1831).

Lambarde, William, *Perambulation of Kent* ([1570] Bath, 1970).

Levi, Leone, *Wages & earnings of the working classes, report to Sir Arthur Bass* (1885).

Loveland, Isaac, 'Some names of tradesmen who resided in Sevenoaks about 1848 and later on'.

Marx, Karl, *Capital*, vol. 1 ([1867] English trans. London, 1887; London, 1990).

Mayhew, Henry, *London labour and the London poor*, vol. 1 (London, 1851).

Melville and Co.'s directory & gazetteer of Kent (London, 1858).

Nisbet, William, *A medical guide for the invalid to the principal watering places of Great Britain* (Edinburgh, 1804).

Palmer, Samuel, *An address to the electors of west Kent* (1832).

Pigot's directory of Kent (1824).

The poll for the knights of the shire, to represent the western division of the county of Kent in parliament (London, 1835).

Post Office directory of Essex, Herts, Kent…, Part 1 (London, 1855).

Reed, Andrew, *No fiction*, 2 vols (London, 1823).

Salmon's directory of Sevenoaks (1899–1915).

Society (Committee) for Effecting the Abolition of the Slave Trade, *List of the Society, for the purpose of effecting the abolition of the slave trade* (London, 1787).

Taine, Hippolyte, *Notes on England* (London, 1872).

Thorne, James, *Handbook to the environs of London* (London, 1876).

Tufnell, E.C., *On the dwelling and general economy of the labouring classes in Kent and Sussex* (London, 1841).

Watson, Richard, *The life of the Rev. John Wesley, A.M.* (London, 1831).

Secondary sources

Accum, Friedrich, *A treatise on adulterations of food and culinary poisons* (London, 1820).

Anckorn, Gordon, *A Sevenoaks camera – Sevenoaks, Westerham and surrounding villages in old photographs* (Bath, 1987).

Armstrong, Ian (ed.), *The economy of Kent, 1640–1914* (Woodbridge, 1995).

Arnold, Rollo, 'The "revolt of the field" in Kent, 1872–79', *Past & Present*, 64 (1974), pp. 71–95.

Atkinson, Brian, 'Conservative and Liberal: national politics in Kent from the late 1820s to 1914', in Frederick Lansberry (ed.), *Government and politics in Kent, 1640–1914* (Woodbridge, 2001), pp. 139–64.

Bailey, Peter, *Leisure and class in Victorian England: rational recreation and the contest for control, 1830–1885* (London, 1978).

Bailey, Peter, '"Will the real Bill Banks please stand up?" Towards a role analysis of mid-Victorian working class respectability', *Journal of Social History*, XII/3 (1979), pp. 336–53.

Barker-Read, M., 'The public health question in the nineteenth century: public health and sanitation in a Kentish market town, Tonbridge', *Southern History*, 4 (1982), pp. 167–89.

Barret-Ducrocq, Francoise, *Love in the time of Victoria: sexuality, class and gender in nineteenth-century London* (London, 1991).

Barton, Sue, *Pratts Bottom. A journey through life* (Pratts Bottom, 2009).

Bassett, Charles, *A life in Seal 1933* (Seal, 1991).

Bates, Margaret and Killingray, David, 'The Herries family and the building of St Julian's, Underriver, 1819–1837', *Archaeologia Cantiana*, CXXIII (2003), pp. 273–90.

Baugh, D.A., 'The cost of poor relief in south-east England, 1790–1834', *Economic History Review*, 28 (1975), pp. 50–68.

Bell, Christopher, 'The speech from the throne, 1901', *English Catholic History Association Newsletter*, 2/18 (March 2003), pp. 12–13.

Beresford, Kathryn, 'The "Men of Kent" and the Penenden Heath meeting 1828', *Archæologia Cantiana*, CXXV (2005), pp. 151–71.

Beresford, Kathryn, '"Witnesses for the defence": the yeoman of Old England and the land question, *c*.1815–1837', in Matthew Cragoe and Paul Readman (eds), *The land question in Britain, 1750–1950* (Basingstoke, 2010), pp. 37–56.

Boussabha-Brayard, Myriam (ed.), *Suffrage outside sufffragism: women's votes in Britain 1880–1914* (Basingstoke, 2007).

Boyle, Angela *et al.* (eds), 'To the praise of the dead, and anatomie: the analysis of post-medieval burials at St Nicholas, Sevenoaks, Kent', in M.J. Cox (ed.), *Grave concerns: death and burial in England 1700–1850* (York, 1998), pp. 91–9.

Brigden, Roy, *Victorian farms* (Marlborough, 1986).

Briggs, Asa, *A social history of England* (London, 1987).

Briggs, Asa, *Victorian cities* (London, 1963).

Briggs, Asa, *Victorian things* (London, 1988).

Brown, Christopher Leslie, *Moral capital: foundations of British abolitionism* (Chapel Hill, NC, 2012).

Brundage, Anthony, *The making of the New Poor Law: the politics of inquiry, enactment and implementation, 1832–39* (London, 1978).

Burchardt, Jeremy, *The allotment movement in England, 1793–1873* (Woodbridge, 2002).

Burgess, Keith, *The challenge of labour – shaping British history 1850–1930* (London, 1980).

Burgoyne-Black, Shirley, 'Swing: the years 1830–32 as reflected in a West Kent newspaper', *Archæologia Cantiana*, CVII (1989), pp. 89–106.

Burnett, John, *Plenty and want – a social history of diet in England from 1815 to the present day* (Abingdon, 2005).

Burnett, John, *A social history of housing* (London, 1986).

Burnett, John (ed.), *Useful toil: autobiographies of working people from the 1820s to the 1920s* (Harmondsworth, 1984).

Bushaway, Bob, '"Tacit, unsuspected but still implicit faith": alternative belief in nineteenth century rural England', in Tim Harris (ed.), *Popular culture in England, c. 1500–1850* (Basingstoke, 1995), pp. 189–215.

Chadwick, Owen, *The Victorian Church – Part 2, 1860–1901* (London, 1997).

Charlesworth, Adrian (ed.), *An atlas of rural protest in Britain, 1548–1900* (London, 1983).

Chase, M., 'Out of radicalism: the mid-Victorian freehold land movement', *English Historical Review*, 106 (1991), pp. 319–45.

Checkland, S.G. and E.O.E., *The Poor Law Report of 1834* (Harmondsworth, 1974).

Clarke, Dennis and Stoyel, Anthony, *Otford in Kent. A history* (Otford, 1975).

Coleman, D.C., *The British paper industry 1495–1860: a study in industrial growth* (Oxford, 1958).

Colley, Linda, *Britons: forging the nation 1707–1837* (New Haven, CT, 1992).

Conley, Carolyn, *The unwritten law: criminal justice in Victorian Kent* (Oxford, 1991).

Constantine, Stephen, 'Amateur gardening and popular recreation in the 19th and 20th centuries', *Journal of Social History*, 14/3 (1981), pp. 387–406.

Conway, David, *Farewell to Marx. An outline and appraisal of his theories* (Harmondsworth, 1987).

Copus, Geoffrey, *Chelsfield chronicles 1450–1920* (Chelsfield, 2003).

Cordery, Simon, *British friendly societies 1750–1914* (Basingstoke, 2003).

Cordle, Celia, *Out of the hay and into the hops. Hop cultivation in Wealden Kent and hop marketing in Southwark, 1744–2000* (Hatfield, 2011).

Cragoe, Matthew and Readman, Paul (eds), *The land question in Britain, 1750–1950* (Basingstoke, 2010).

Crawford, Elizabeth, *The women's suffrage movement: a reference guide, 1866–1928* (London, 2001).

Crook, Tom and Esbester, Mike (eds), *Governing risks in modern Britain: danger, safety and accidents, c.1800–2000* (London, 2016).

Crossick, Geoffrey, *An artisan elite in Victorian society: Kentish London 1840–80* (London, 1987).

Cunningham, Hugh, 'The metropolitan fairs: a case study in the social control of leisure', in A.P. Donajgrodzki (ed.), *Social control in nineteenth century Britain* (London, 1977), pp. 163–84.

Daunton, Martin (ed.), *The Cambridge urban history of Britain, vol. 3, 1840–1950* (Cambridge, 2001).

Davidoff, Leonore and Hall, Catherine, *Family fortunes: men and women of the English middle class 1780–1850* (London, 2002).

Dodsworth, Francis, 'Risk, prevention and policy, *c.*1750–1850', in Tom Crook and Mike Esbester (eds), *Governing risks in modern Britain: danger, safety and accidents, c. 1800–2000* (London, 2016), pp. 29–53.

Donajgrodzki, A.P. (ed.), *Social control in nineteenth century Britain* (London, 1977).

Donald, Archie, *The posts of Sevenoaks in Kent* (Tenterden, 1992).

Draper, Nicholas, *The price of emancipation. Slave-ownership, compensation and British society at the end of slavery* (Cambridge, 2010).

Dunbabin, J.P.D., *Rural discontent in nineteenth century Britain* (London, 1974).

Dunlop, John, *The pleasant town of Sevenoaks: a history* (Sevenoaks, 1964).

Eagles, Lawrence, 'Friendly societies', in Derek Renn (ed.), *Life, death and money: actuaries and the creation of financial security* (Oxford, 1998), pp. 43–60.

Earle, Rebecca, 'The political economy of nutrition in the later eighteenth century', *Past & Present*, 242 (2019), pp. 79–114.

Eastwood, David, *Government and community in the English provinces 1700–1870* (Basingstoke, 1997).

Eliot, George, *Silas Marner* ([1861] London, 1985).

Emsley, Clive, *Crime and society in England, 1750–1900* (London, 2010).

Emsley, Clive and Walvin, James (eds), *Artisans, peasants & proletarians, 1760–1860* (Beckenham, 1985).

Encyclopædia Britannica, 'Motor vehicles', Vol. 18, 11th edn (New York, 1911), pp. 914–30.

Escombe, Jane, *Five years: fruits of the Parish Council Act* (London, 1901).

Fisher, David R. (ed.), *History of parliament – the House of Commons 1820–1832, 2, constituencies Pt 1* (Cambridge, 2009).

Fisk, Audrey, *Mutual self-help in southern England* (Southampton, 2006).

Flanders, Judith, *The Victorian house: domestic life from childbed to deathbed* (London, 2003).

Fowler, Simon, *Workhouse: the people; the places; the life behind doors* (Kew, 2008).

Fox, Jean, Williams, David and Mountfield, Peter, *Seal. The history of a parish* (Chichester, Phillimore, 2007).

Franks, William, 'An old local preacher's reminiscences', *Methodist Recorder* (Winter 1905).

Frost, Ginger, *Promises broken: courtship, class and gender in Victorian England* (Charlottesville, VA, 1995).

Fukuyama, Francis, *The end of history and the last man* (London, 1992).

Garraty, John Arthur and Carmes, Mark C., *American national biography*, vol. 5 *Robert Colgate* (New York, 1999).

Gillis, John, *For better or worse: English marriages 1600 to the present* (Oxford, 1985).

Griffin, Carl, 'The mystery of the fires: Captain Swing as incendiarist', *Southern History*, 32 (2010), pp. 21–40.

Griffin, Carl, *Protest, politics and work in rural England, 1700–1850* (Basingstoke, 2014).

Griffin, Carl, *Rural war: Captain Swing and the politics of protest* (Manchester, 2012).

Griffin, Carl, 'The violent Captain Swing?' *Past & Present*, 209 (2010), pp. 149–80.

Griffin, Emma, 'Diets, hunger and living standards during the Industrial Revolution', *Past & Present*, 239 (2018), pp. 71–111

Griffin, Emma, *Liberty's dawn – a people's history of the industrial revolution* (London, 2013).

Hailwood, Mark, 'Time and work in rural England, 1500–1700', *Past & Present*, 248 (2020), pp. 87–121.

Harris, Tim (ed.), *Popular culture in England, c. 1500–1850* (Basingstoke, 1995).

Harrison, Brian, *Drink and the Victorians: the temperance question in England 1815–1872* (Keele, 1994).

Harrison, Edward R., *Harrison of Ightham* (London, 1928).

Hastings, Paul, 'The Old Poor Law 1640–1834', in Nigel Yates, Robert Hume and Paul Hastings, *Religion and society in Kent, 1640–1914* (Woodbridge, 1994), pp. 112–88.

Hastings, Paul, 'Radical movements and workers' protests to c. 1850', in Frederick Lansberry, *Government and politics in Kent, 1640–1914* (Woodbridge, 2001), pp. 95–138.

Hawkins, Frederick, *The life of Edmund Kean*, vol. 2 (London, 1869).

Hay, D. *et al.*, *Albion's fatal tree: crime and society in eighteenth century England* (London, 1975).

Hay, D., 'Poaching and the Game Laws on Cannock Chase' in D. Hay *et al.*, *Albion's fatal tree: crime and society in eighteenth century England* (New York, 1975), pp. 189–253.

Henderson, David (ed.), *The concise encyclopædia of economics* (Indianapolis, IN, 2008).

Highfill, P.H. *et al.*, *A biographical dictionary of actors, actresses, musicians, dancers and other stage personnel in London 1660–1800*, vol. 8 (Carbondale, IL, 1982).

Hilton, Boyd, *The age of atonement: the influence of evangelicalism on social and economic thought 1785–1865* (Oxford, 1986).

Hilton, Boyd, *A mad, bad and dangerous people: England 1783–1846* (Oxford, 2006).

Hobsbawm, Eric, 'The new unionism in perspective', in Eric Hobsbawm (ed.), *Worlds of labour: further studies in the history of labour* (London, 1984), pp. 152–75.

Hobsbawm, Eric and Rudé, George, *Captain Swing* (London, 1970).

Hodge, G., 'Tonbridge free public library, 1881–1900', *Archæologia Cantiana*, CIII (1986), pp. 53–68.

Hollis, Patricia, *Ladies elect: women in English local government, 1865–1914* (Oxford, 1987).

Hope, Elizabeth, *English homes and villages (Kent and Sussex)* (Sevenoaks, 1909).

Hopkins, Eric, *Working class self-help in nineteenth century England* (London, 1995).

Hoppen, K. Theodore, *The mid-Victorian generation, 1846–86* (Oxford, 1998).

Horn, Pamela, *The Victorian and Edwardian schoolchild* (Stroud, 2010).

Huzzey, Richard and Miller, Henry, 'Petitions, parliament and political culture: petitioning the House of Commons, 1780–1918', *Past & Present*, 248 (2020), pp. 123–64.

Ismay, Penelope, 'Between providence and risk: oddfellows, benevolence and the social limits of actuarial science', *Past & Present*, 226 (2015), pp. 115–47.

Jackson, Basil, *Recollections of Thomas Graham Jackson, 1835–1924* (Oxford, 1950).

Jackson, Nicholas, *Recollections of the life and travels of a Victorian architect: Thomas Graham Jackson, 1835–1924* (London, 2003).

Jones, Gareth Stedman, 'Class expression versus social control? A critique of recent trends in the social history of "leisure"', *History Workshop*, 4 (1977), pp. 162–70.

Jones, Gareth Stedman, *Karl Marx. Greatness and illusion* (London, 2016).

Keith-Lucas, Bryan, *Parish affairs: the government of Kent under George III* (Maidstone, 1986).

Keith-Lucas, Bryan, *The unreformed local government system* (London, 1980).

Killingray, David, 'Black people in Sevenoaks since 1600: history and research method', *The Local Historian*, 51/4 (2021), pp. 297–308.

Killingray, David, 'Grassroots politics in west Kent since the late eighteenth century', *Archæologia Cantiana*, CIXXX (2009), pp. 33–54.

Killingray, David, 'Kent and the abolition of the slave trade: a county study, 1760s–1807', *Archæologia Cantiana*, CXXVII (2007), pp. 107–25.

Killingray, David. 'A London city church estate in Kent: St Botolph's, Sevenoaks, 1646–2002', *Archæologia Cantiana*, CXXIV (2004), pp. 291–307.

Killingray, David, 'Rights, "riot" and ritual: the Knole Park access dispute, Sevenoaks, Kent, 1883–5', *Rural History*, 5 (1994), pp. 63–79.

Killingray, David, *St Nicholas Parish Church, Sevenoaks, Kent* (Sevenoaks, 2015).

Killingray, David (ed.), *Sevenoaks people and faith. Two thousand years of religious belief and practice* (Chichester, 2004).

Killingray, David and Purves, Elizabeth (eds), *Sevenoaks: an historical dictionary* (Andover, 2012).

King, Steven, *Poverty and welfare in England 1750–1950: a regional perspective* (Manchester, 2000).

Knight, Esmond, *Seeking the bubble* (London, 1943).

Lane, Joan, *A social history of medicine: health, healing and disease in England, 1750–1950* (London, 2012).

Lansberry, Frederick (ed.), *Government and politics in Kent, 1640–1914* (Woodbridge, 2001).

Lawson, Terence and David Killingray (eds), *An historical atlas of Kent* (Chichester, 2004), pp. 122–3.

Laybourn, Keith, *The battle for the roads: police, motorists and the law, c.1890 to 1970s* (Basingstoke, 2015).

Leeds, Tessa, 'The construction of the Sevenoaks railway tunnel, 1863–68', *Archæologia Cantiana*, CXX (2000), pp. 187–204.

Lees, Lynn Hollen, *The solidarities of strangers: the English poor laws and the people, 1700–1948* (Cambridge, 1998).

Levin, Michael, *The condition of England question: Carlyle, Mill, Engels* (Basingstoke, 1998).

Light, Alison, *Common people: the history of an English family* (London, 2014).

LoPatin, Nancy, *Political unions, popular politics and the Great Reform Act* (Basingstoke, 1999).

Lowerson, John, 'Anti-Poor Law movements and rural trade unionism in the south east, 1835', in Adrian Charlesworth (ed.), *An atlas of rural protest in Britain, 1548–1900* (London, 1983), pp. 155–63.

Luckin, Bill, 'Drunk driving, drink driving: Britain c.1800–1920', in Tom Crook and Mike Esbester (eds), *Governing risks in modern Britain: danger, safety and accidents, c.1800–2000* (London, 2016) pp. 171–94.

MacFarlane, Alan, *Marriage and love in England: modes of reproduction 1300–1840* (Oxford, 1987).

Marshall, John, *The tyranny of the discrete: a discussion of the problems of local history in England* (Aldershot, 1997).

Melling, Elizabeth (ed.), *Kentish sources. IV. The poor* (Maidstone, 1964).

Merkin, Robert and Hemsworth, Maggie, *The law of motor insurance* (London, 2015).

Mingay, G.E., *Rural life in Victorian England* (London, 1976).

Moylan, Prudence Ann, *The form and reform of county government Kent 1889–1914* (Leicester, 1978).

Mudie-Smith, Richard (ed.), *The religious life of London* (London, 1904).

Nardinelli, Clark, 'Industrial revolution and the standard of living', in David Henderson (ed.), *The concise encyclopædia of economics* (Indianapolis, IN, 2008), <https://www.econlib.org/library/Enc/IndustrialRevolutionandtheStandardofLiving.html>.

Newman, John, *Buildings of England – Kent: Weald and the west* (New Haven, CT, 2012).

O'Connell, Sean, *The car and British society: class, gender and motoring 1896–1939* (Manchester, 1998).

O'Gorman, Frank, 'Campaign rituals and ceremonies: the social meaning of elections in England, 1780–1860', *Past & Present*, 135 (May 1992), pp. 79–115.

Ovenden, Toby, 'The Cobbs of Margate: evangelicalism and anti-slavery in the Isle of Thanet, 1787–1834', *Archæologia Cantiana*, CXXXIII (2013), pp. 1–32.

Page, William (ed.), *The Victoria county history of the county of Kent*, vol. 1 (London, 1908).

Pelling, Henry, *A history of British trade unionism* (Harmondsworth, 1969).

Perkin, Joan, *Victorian women* (New York, 1995).

Peyton, J.L., *Rambling reminiscences of a residence abroad: England, Guernsey etc.* (Staunton, VA, 1888).

Probert, Rebecca, *The changing legal regulation of cohabitation: from fornicators to family, 1600–2010* (Cambridge, 2012).

Probert, Rebecca (ed.), *Cohabitation and non-marital births in England and Wales, 1600–2012* (Basingstoke, 2014).

Probert, Rebecca, 'How to get hitched, Victorian-style', *BBC History Magazine* (Christmas 2018), pp. 38–43.

Prochaska, Frank, 'Philanthropy', in F.M.L. Thompson, *The Cambridge social history of Britain 1750–1850. Vol. 3, social agencies and institutions* (Cambridge, 1990), pp. 357–93.

Pryor, Francis, *The making of the British landscape* (London, 2010).

Randall, Adrian and Charlesworth, Andrew (eds), *The moral economy and popular protest: crowds, conflicts and authority* (Basingstoke, 2000).

Rayner, Christopher, *Sevenoaks past: with the villages of Holmesdale* (Chichester, 1997).

Reay, Barry, *The last rising: rural life and protest in nineteenth century England* (Oxford, 1990).

Redman, Paul, *Octavia Hill, social activism, and the remaking of British society* (London, 2016).

Reid, Douglas, 'Playing and praying leisure and religion in urban Britain', in Martin Daunton (ed.), *The Cambridge urban history of Britain, vol. 3, 1840–1950* (Cambridge, 2001), ch. 23.

Revill, George, 'Liberalism and paternalism: politics and corporate culture in "Railway Derby", 1865–75', *Social History*, 23 (1999), pp. 196–214.

Rich, Rachel, *Bourgeois consumption: food, space and identity in London and Paris* (Manchester, 2011).

Richardson, Mike and Nicholls, Peter, *A business and labour history of Britain: case studies of Britain in the nineteenth and twentieth centuries* (Basingstoke, 2011).

Richardson, Tom, 'Labour', in Alan Armstrong (ed.), *The economy of Kent, 1640–1914* (Woodbridge, 1995), pp. 235–60.

Richmond, Vivienne, *Clothing the poor in nineteenth century England* (Cambridge, 2013).

Roake, Margaret (ed.), *Worship in Kent: the census of 1851* (Maidstone, 1999).

Rowley, Trevor, *The English landscape in the twentieth century* (London, 2006).

Rule, John, 'Against innovation? Custom and resistance in the workplace, 1700–1850', in Tim Harris (ed.), *Popular culture in England, c. 1500–1850* (Basingstoke, 1995), pp. 168–88.

Rule, John, *The labouring classes in early industrial England, 1750–1850* (Abingdon, 2013).

Rule, John and Wells, Roger, *Crime, protest and popular politics in southern England, 1740–1850* (London, 1997).

Scragg, Brian, *Sevenoaks School: a history* (Bath, 1993).

Shelton, Rod, *Darent. The history and stories of a river and its communities* (Otford, 2015).

Shorter, Alfred, *Paper-making in the British Isles: an historical and geographical study* (Newton Abbot, 1971).

Skinner, Quentin, *Visions of politics*, vol. 1, *Regarding method* (Cambridge, 2002).

Smart, Kenneth, *Cricket on the vine, 1734–1984* (Sevenoaks, 1984).

Snell, Keith, *Parish and belonging: community, identity and welfare in England and Wales, 1700–1950* (Cambridge, 2006).

Standen, H.W., *Kippington in Kent: its history and its churches* (Sevenoaks, 1958).

Stevenson, Kim, 'Fulfilling their mission: the intervention of voluntary societies in cases of sexual assault in the Victorian criminal process', *Crime, Histoire et Societé*, 8 (2004), pp. 93–110.

Stirling, Anna, *The Richmond papers from the correspondence of George Richmond and his son William Richmond* (London, 1926).

Stoyel, Alan, *Memories of Kentish watermills. The rivers Cray and Darent* (Ashbourne, 2008).

Tarn, John Nelson, *Five per cent philanthropy: an account of housing in urban areas, 1840–1914* (Cambridge, 1973).

Taylor, A.J.P., *English history 1914–45* (Harmondsworth, 1970).

Taylor, Iain, 'Not going through the motions: Sevenoaks, sewage and selfless ambition, 1871–82', *International Journal of Regional and Local History*, 9/2 (2014), pp. 123–39.

Taylor, Iain, 'One for the (farm) workers? Perpetrator risk and victim risk transfer during the "Sevenoaks Fires" of 1830', *Rural History*, 28 (October 2017), pp. 137–60.

Taylor, Iain, 'Pressure groups, contested land-spaces and the politics of ridicule in Sevenoaks, Kent, 1881–85', *Journal of Victorian Culture*, 21 (2016), pp. 322–45.

Taylor, Iain, 'The Sevenoaks banking fraud and its aftermath 1888–1891', *The Local Historian*, 51/2 (2021), pp. 100–12.

Taylor, Iain, '"The whole of the proceedings were very orderly": Gunpowder Plot celebrations, civic culture and identity in some smaller Kent towns, 1860–1890', *Urban History*, 43 (2016), pp. 517–38.

Terry, Ron, *Old corners of Sevenoaks: the yards, courts and passages of historic Sevenoaks* (Sevenoaks, 2000).

Thomas, Helen, *Under storm's wing* (Manchester, 1988).

Thompson, E.P., *Customs in common: studies in traditional popular culture* (London, 1993).

Thompson, E.P., *The making of the English working class* (London, 1964).

Thompson, E.P. 'The moral economy of the poor', in E.P. Thompson, *Customs in common: studies in traditional popular culture* (London, 1993), pp. 185–258.

Thompson, E.P. 'The Sale of Wives', in E.P. Thompson, *Customs in common: studies in traditional popular culture* (London, 1993), pp. 404–67.

Thompson, E.P., 'Time, work-discipline and industrial capitalism', *Past & Present*, 38 (1967), pp. 56–97.

Thompson, F.M.L. (ed.), *The Cambridge social history of Britain, 1750–1950*, vol. 1, *regions and communities* (Cambridge, 1990).

Thompson, F.M.L. (ed.), *The Cambridge social history of Britain, 1750–1950*, vol. 2, *people and their environment* (Cambridge, 1990).

Thompson, F.M.L., 'Town and country', in F.M.L. Thompson (ed.), *The Cambridge social history of Britain, 1750–1950*, vol. 1, *regions and communities* (Cambridge, 1993), pp. 1–86.

Thompson, Lilian, *Sidney Gilchrist Thomas – an invention and its consequences* (London, 1940).

Tomkins, Alannah and King, Steven (eds), *The poor in England 1700–1850: an economy of makeshifts* (Oxford, 2010).

Vincent, John, *Pollbooks: how the Victorians voted* (London, 1967).

Walvin, James (ed.), *Artisans, peasants & proletarians, 1760–1860* (London, 1985).

Webb, Sidney and Beatrice, *English local government from the Revolution to the Municipal Corporations Act, vol. 1, parish and county* (London, 1906).

Weeks, Jeffrey, *Sex, politics and society: the regulations of sexuality since 1800* (Harlow, 2012).

Wells, Roger, 'The moral economy of the English countryside', in Adrian Randall and Andrew Charlesworth (eds), *The moral economy and popular protest: crowds, conflicts and authority* (Basingstoke, 2000), pp. 209–72.

Wells, Roger, 'Rural rebels in southern England in the 1830s', in Clive Emsley and James Walvin (eds), *Artisans, peasants & proletarians, 1760–1860* (Beckenham, 1985), pp. 124–65.

White, Malcolm and Saynor, Joy, *Shoreham. A village in Kent* (Shoreham, 1989).

Williams, Samantha, 'They lived together as man and wife: plebeian cohabitation, illegitimacy and broken relationships in London, 1700–1840', in Rebecca Probert (ed.), *Cohabitation and non-marital births in England and Wales, 1600–2012* (Basingstoke, 2014), pp. 65–79.

Wilson, Anthony (ed.), *Tonbridge through ten centuries* (Tonbridge, 2015).

Wilson, Julian, *Revolutionary Tunbridge Wells. The remarkable role of Tunbridge Wells and the development of revolutionary politics in Britain 1884–1919* (Tunbridge Wells, 2018).

Winslow, Carl, 'Sussex smugglers', in Douglas Hay *et al.*, *Albion's fatal tree: crime and society in eighteenth century England* (New York, 1975), pp. 119–66.

Woodgate, Gordon and Woodgate, Giles, *A history of the Woodgates of Stonewall Park and Summerskill* (Wisbech, 1910).

Yates, Nigel, Hume, Robert and Hastings, Paul, *Religion and society in Kent, 1640–1914* (Woodbridge, 1994).

Young, G.M., *Victorian essays*, ed. W.D. Handcock ([1936] Oxford, 1962).

Theses

Carlton, Felicity, '"A substantial and sterling friend to the labouring man": the Kent & Sussex Labourers' Union, 1872–95', MPhil thesis (University of Sussex, 1977).

Thorne, Sarah, 'Protestant ethics and the spirit of imperialism: British Congregationalists and the London Missionary Society 1795–1925', PhD thesis (University of Michigan, 1990).

Online sources

https://www.oxforddnb.com/
https://en.wikipedia.org/wiki/Sevenoaks_School
www.familysearch.org.
www.rac.co.uk/forum/showthread.php?7350-Motor-Act-1903

Index

Entries in italics are map references